CHANCES
FOR PEACE

Canadian Soldiers in the Balkans, 1992-1995

ABOUT THE AUTHORS

Sean Maloney is from Kingston, Ontario, teaches in the War Studies Programme at the Royal Military College of Canada and is a Research Fellow at the School for Policy Studies at Queen's University. The author of several works, including *War Without Battles: Canada's NATO Brigade in Germany 1951-1992* and *Canada and UN Peacekeeping: Cold War by Other Means 1945-1970*, Dr. Maloney served as the historian for Canada's forces in NATO and has BA and MA degrees from the University of New Brunswick and a PhD in History from Temple University. He is currently working on histories of Canadian involvement with the Kosovo Verification Mission and the NATO-led Kosovo Force.

John Llambias was born in Ontario and grew up in New Brunswick, where his father taught Political Science at the University of New Brunswick and his mother worked as a translator. He graduated from Fredericton High School in 1985 and enrolled at UNB graduating with a Bachelor's Degree in History and Education. He worked in the Fredericton area teaching various subjects from grades 1 to 12 and served in the Militia from 1987 to 1996, rising from the rank of Private to Lieutenant. He has also worked as a timber cruiser, cook, aerial navigator and jackeroo on a sheep station in Australia.

Sean M. Maloney & John Llambias

CHANCES FOR PEACE

Canadian Soldiers in the Balkans, 1992-1995

AN ORAL HISTORY

Vanwell Publishing Limited

St. Catharines, Ontario

Vanwell Publishing acknowledges the financial support of the Government of Canada through the Book Publishing Industry Development Program for our publishing activities.

Cover Design by Renée Giguère
Cover Painting: Firefight in the Medak Pocket, by Katherine Taylor

Vanwell Publishing Limited
1 Northrup Crescent
P.O. Box 2131
St. Catharines, Ontario L2R 7S2
sales@vanwell.com
tel: 905-937-3100
fax: 905-937-1760
Printed in Canada

National Library of Canada Cataloguing in Publication

Maloney, Sean M. (Sean Michael), 1967-
     Chances for peace : Canadian soldiers in the Balkans, 1992-1995 / Sean M. Maloney, John Llambias.

Includes index.
ISBN 1-55125-053-5

     1. Soldiers–Canada–Interviews. 2. Yugoslav War, 1991-1995. 3. Canada–Armed forces–Croatia. 4. Canada–Armed Forces–Bosnia and Hercegovina. 5. United Nations–Peacekeeping forces–Croatia. 6. United Nations–Peacekeeping forces–Bosnia and Hercegovina. I. Llambias, John II. Title.

JZ6377.C3M35 2002   949.703   C2002-903940-1

TABLE OF CONTENTS

PART III
CHANCES FOR PEACE: OPERATION KHARON AND THE 12E RÉGIMENT
BLINDÉ DU CANADA IN CENTRAL BOSNIA, 1994

LIST OF MAPS

FOREWORD

If Sean M. Maloney asked me to write the introduction to this book, he had unquestionably a good reason! Here is my explanation: during my time as UN Force Commander, from July 1st, 1993 to March 15th, 1994, I had a special affection for "my Canadians." Let me clarify.

Out of some forty national contingents I was commanding, only one tenth of them had the necessary operational capabilities, and they were not subject to unacceptable government-imposed work restrictions.

The Canadian contingent was one of them, which explains the high demands I put on it. Before adding to the accounts given in this book, based on my personal experience, I shall briefly talk about three UNPROFOR Canadians from my direct circle in Zagreb. Only three regrettably, because I can't name them all.

Major-General MacInnis was second in command. I think I can say that we complemented each other extremely well. Retrospectively, I should not have left him deal with the Zagreb mission's civilian management, when I assumed I had better things to do in the field. When I left he gave me, on behalf of the Canadian contingent, a kayak oar bearing the words "In memory of all the rapids we went down together, without a rudder!" Thank you, General!

Colonel Maisonneuve was Chief of Staff of Operations. I asked much of him, our personal relationship allowing me to frequently bypass the regular hierarchy. In November 1993, during the operation in Medak, I made him my personal representative in the field, as recounted in this book. In particular I remember vividly his surprise when I gave him back, without correction, the general guideline he had prepared according to my instructions for my subordinates shortly after I assumed command. We had to move fast. Why quibble about the wording of my intentions when he had grasped its spirit so well?

Major Marcotte was my Communications Officer. I had heard about his skills in his army through his aide-de-camp. He accompanied Canada's Chief of the Defence Staff when the latter paid me a visit in Zagreb. I asked for him to join me immediately, and that's what happened! I wished to give a voice to UNPROFOR, rather than the usual gobbledygook of the U.N. I wished to tell the Truth and to oppose Dishonesty, no matter the parties concerned. I wished to defend Love against Hatred. I was aware of the importance of words in wars where vicious language is often more dangerous than weaponry. We failed totally, because of the constant obstruction by the UN Chief of Civil Affairs who jealously protected his alleged prerogatives in the communications area. I absolve Major Marcotte, who suffered from this hindrance, but threw himself with all his might into an impossible mission!

I mention these three associates, less to promote individuals than to bring to light the extraordinary quality of the Canadian officers with whom I had the great pleasure of working. To this end, I would like to elaborate upon three actions led by Canadian battalions that I witnessed first-hand.

I encountered for the first time an operating Canadian battalion in Croatian Krajina, in the far south of the UN zone. It was the end of July 1993. I was getting ready to occupy some of the region's strategic areas, including the Peruca dam, assuming the political negotiations between

Serbs and Croatians that had been broken off in Geneva on July 16, 1993 would resume. Unfortunately, it did not happen. For this high-risk mission, I needed some reserves, which I did not have. I therefore asked Sector West to make available to me half of its Canadian battalion. The 550 kilometer ride along dangerous and rutted roads started on the morning of July 20th, with 150 armoured vehicles, and relevant command and support vehicles. Thirty-six hours later, with neither an incident nor an accident, the detachment was ready to carry out on the Molovaki Heights the mission I assigned it. In this book, the Mission Commander, Lieutenant-Colonel Calvin, relates that I kissed him when I visited his headquarters in the countryside. It is likely true as I wanted to express my satisfaction, without lengthy words.

During my command, I knew two Canadian battalions in Visoko, one from the Royal 22nd Regiment until November 1993, and one from the 12th Regiment blindé du Canada, with their reinforcement. Their mission, along the fighting line between the Serbs and the Bosnians, was difficult. They executed it remarkably well, as I observed during my visits.

My visit on December 23 and 24, 1993 to the Srebrenica enclave is no doubt my most enduring memory. The enclave, the first UN-declared "safe haven," was held at the time by less than 200 men from the Visoko battalion, under the command of Lieutenant-Colonel David Moore.

For a long time, we expected a Dutch battalion to take the rotation there, but we kept on waiting for its arrival. Considering the perimeter of the enclave (about 40 kilometres) which was staked out by thirteen observation posts with some ten men in each, the presence and humanitarian assistance mission of the Canadian detachment was particularly difficult. As for the besieged Bosnian population, the replenishment of the "Blue Helmets" depended on the good will of the Serbs.

I would like to pay tribute to these men who, in spite of their physical and mental exhaustion, held out until the last day, while knowing too well that they could not defend the enclave against an organized offensive from the Serbs, for lack of proper means.

I will finally mention the so-called "Medak Pocket Operation," in Croatia in September 1993. The decision was mine alone, and I personally got involved in it. In this book, Lieutenant-Colonel Calvin gives a detailed account of the operation, which he led. It was the most important force operation the U.N. conducted in former Yugoslavia.

To carry out the attack, I reinforced the Calvin battalion with two French armored infantry companies, and an engineering platoon. One of them was under the command of my son, who had come at full speed from the Bihac pocket in Bosnia. I went to Calvin's command post on the first day of the action, and again later during the operation.

I am proud of the effective partnership and brotherhood in arms the Canadians and the French established at that time. I am also proud of what we achieved. While we could not prevent the slaughter of Serbs by the Croatians, including elderly people and children, we drove back to its start line a well-equipped Croatian battalion of some thousand men. Together, the Canadians and the French succeeded in breaking the Croatian lines, and with their weapons loaded and ready, firing when necessary. They circled and disarmed an eighteen soldier commando from the Croatian Special Forces who had penetrated by night into their location. They did everything I expected from them and showed what real soldiers can do, even when the indefensible political mistake was made of forcing them to wear blue helmets and to paint their vehicles white, in a theatre of operations where it was no longer realistic to pretend to maintain peace, but where indeed it was crucial to curtail the war.

Concerning the use of force by the UN, I am not convinced that the lessons drawn from Medak in particular and from the former Yugoslavia in general were understood in New York. I am even sure that the opposite was true.

For the last eight years, I have said and written that because of marginalization the UN will die, if it does not exercise at least its minimum rights.

A fighting strength, wearing khaki, could be limited at first to a brigade of well-equipped, trained, and motivated professionals. Where massacres are being planned, it could be deployed within a few days, as in Vukovar before November 1991, in Kigali in April 1994, in Srebrenica in July 1995, in Sierra Leone, in Timor, in Sudan...the list of disasters carried out by perverse minor tyrants is endless. Five hundred men would have sufficed to avoid or limit these atrocities. NATO, which is restricted by the zero casualty dogma, cannot put together such a force. And if it could, in which capacity would it proclaim itself police of the world? Only the UN can legitimize the use of force if necessary, under Chapter VII of its Charter.

The issue is apparently political. Do we want the UN to fully apply the requirements of its Charter or are we trying to confine it to a humanitarian role, its Secretary-General being content enough to be a well-appointed ambassador-at-large?

The White House has already answered clearly. If miraculously the political hurdle were to be removed, Canada will have proved over and over again, particularly in the former Yugoslavia, that it would be a privileged sponsor of the development of such a fighting force along with a few other countries.

General Jean Cot

General Cot held several high responsibility positions during a career spanning more than forty years. He assumed the command of the First Army (1ère Armée) on April 1st, 1990. He was UNPROFOR Commander in July 1993. Mr. Boutros-Ghali recalled General Cot to France in March 1994: he resigned in June.

He was named Grand Officier de la Légion d'Honneur with five citations, was awarded the Commander's Cross of the Merit of the Federal Republic of Germany and the Legion of Merit (United States).

PREFACE

I would like to know what the average Canadian knows or remembers about Canada's involvement in the Balkans since the 1990s. Probably uppermost in their minds are "incidents" such as the misbehaviour of some soldiers at the Bakovici hospital, or media reports of minor disciplinary transgressions by soldiers under enormous pressure. Some Canadians may actually think the Canadian military involvement in the United Nations Protection Force (UNPROFOR) from 1992 to 1995 was a failure. This book will likely change this perception. Incredible events are described in vivid detail by the authors; events that typify the operational capability and resourcefulness of Canadian soldiers' involvement in the Balkan Wars of the 1990s.

Peacekeeping in the early 1990s brought to the fore the failure of old precepts about peace support operations. The old model was the interposition of forces between two belligerents who agreed to the deployment of the UN within a usually well-defined situation. Suddenly Canadian soldiers were thrust into chaos of the first order in Somalia, Rwanda, and the Balkans, with numerous belligerents hacking each other to pieces, rehashing centuries-old enmities, and forming non-traditional alliances for mutual advantage only to have them break up and fight among themselves.

On top of this near-incomprehensible situation, UN forces were provided difficult mandates (if any) and constrictive rules of engagement which limited action. The forces were then left to their own devices with little direction from strategic headquarters in New York. We had to come up with solutions that worked in the environments our people worked in day after day and it was a difficult task. These operations were attempts to discover new ways of dealing with an old type of conflict in an increasingly lethal environment against the insane backdrop of the post-Cold War order.

But what of the specific context within which the events of this book took place? As a former Chief of Operations in the Zagreb headquarters of UNPROFOR from March 1993 to March 1994, I had the privileged vantage point to observe, feel and sometimes direct and participate personally in the work of my compatriots. The pride I felt and the bursts of elation I could barely contain while witnessing Canadian soldiers' dedication and performance were enormous.

Canadians were never above any task in the former Yugoslav Republics. Some of the more well-known operations are described in this book by the soldiers themselves. But do many people know, for example, that Canadian troops were the ones who initially set up the first-ever UN preventative deployment in the Former Yugoslav Republic of Macedonia (FYROM)? That Canadians stopped a larger conflict from erupting in the Krajinas and attempted to stop ethnic cleansing by using force in 1993? That Canadians showed the way to peace for the Bosnian Government forces and their Bosnian Croat antagonists in the face of incredible odds and Serb provocation? That for a time they deterred Bosnian Serb attacks against Srebrenica and evacuated significant numbers of non-combatants from Gorazde?

Canadian soldiers performed the hardest tasks in Croatia, Bosnia and later in Kosovo. A former UNPROFOR Force Commander of mine, French General Jean Cot, used to ask Canadians "Why are you here?" He greatly admired the "can-do" attitude of Canadian soldiers and loved to visit Jim Calvin's battalion to talk to privates and corporals, especially when he needed to "recharge his batteries" after dealing with the frustrations of command in the Balkans.

This book was made possible by the hard work of Sean Maloney, who has developed an impressive expertise in telling the story of Canadian soldiers in the Balkans, from the more obscure such as Canadian involvement in the European community Monitoring Mission to the main battle group operations described in this book, and, when he completes them, work on the IFOR, SFOR and KFOR operations. His co-author, John Llambias, is to be equally commended for his dedication to this project.

More than 10,000 Canadian soldiers served in UNPROFOR. For them, UNPROFOR was not a failure. It came down to containing the violence, saving lives, providing hope, and showing people of other countries that there exists something other than strife and conflict: a state called "peace." This book begins to tell these soldiers' stories of frustration, but also their stories of gallantry under impossible conditions. They truly have followed in the footsteps of their wartime predecessors; they now live with the memories of these operations, and their story must be told.

Major-General J. O. Michel Maisonneuve, OMM, MSC, CD

Major-General Maisonneuve, COO of UNPROFOR March 1993-94, drafted the withdrawal agreement signed by the Croatian and Serb forces for the Medak Pocket. He returned to the Balkans in Kosovo before the NATO air campaign as a member of the Organization for Security and Co-operation in Europe's Kosovo Verification Mission, for which he was awarded the Meritorious Service Cross.

ACKNOWLEDGEMENTS

Chances for Peace owes several debts of gratitude, primarily to the men who consented to be interviewed and featured in these pages. Events in the former Yugoslavia placed significant strain on our people serving in these areas. Recounting traumatic or even exciting incidents can sometimes trigger buried emotions or stimulate perhaps unhealthy re-examinations of one's behaviour under operational stress. In other cases, finally being able to explain to an impartial and trusted observer what occurred and why is a very liberating experience. It took courage to talk to us, open up, and reveal the inner man. In doing so they all demonstrated that there is no such thing as the so-called "post-heroic" age. We thank you deeply for that.

There were other people interviewed who, because of space and time requirements, could not be included in the final project.. We would like to thank them equally. Canada should have a military oral history program someday and they will have served as the basis, and hopefully the stimulus, for such an important project.

There were numerous people who supported us throughout the writing of the book. They transcribed, listened to us vent our frustrations, provided references, and unflaggingly knew this project was worthwhile, and necessary: Fritz and Jan Heinzen, Kevin Maloney, Judith Maloney, Al Maloney, Andy Maloney, Mike Maloney, Debbie Stapleford, John Claus, Deryk Byess, Mike and Bev Hennessey, Maj Mike Boire, Lt Brian Clancy, Max and Pat Rudneu, Nick Sherwin, Capt Andrew Godefroy, Maj John Grodzinski, Capt Helga Grodzinski, David Rosenberg, Matt Larson, Glen Barney, Rob Silliman, David McDermott, Scott Staten, Mike and Kathy Applin, Julie Berebitski, John McNay, Jenny Coleman, MGen Michel Maisonneuve, and General Jean Cot.

I would especially like to thank Simon Kooter, who believed in this project enough to offer to fund it himself, Bob Kennedy for his restrained edit, to Chris Johnson for his excellent vehicle drawings, to Mike Bechthold for creating the maps, and to Katherine Tayler for graciously allowing us the use of the cover painting.

- Sean Maloney

This book would not have been possible without the tireless love, support, example and encouragement of my parents, Pat and Wendy Beggs, and my sister and brother-in-law, Mary Lou and Tom Batty. A teacher's contribution to one's life is immeasurable and it is difficult to include everyone when making a list of individuals to thank. This list is by no means complete, but I would like to thank Yvonne Vaughn, Bill Morrisson, Jim Harvey, Ed Bujold, Cindy Urquart, and Professors Francis Coughlan, Marc Milner, Shirley Dale Easely, and Robert Coburn. Their wisdom, faith and patience gave me the tools to complete this project. If I have left anyone out I apologise. I would also like to thank the people who sat down with Sean and me and opened up themselves and their lives to us so completely. Thank you for your trust and strength.

- John Llambias

INTRODUCTION AND DEDICATIONS

I first started to follow Canada's involvement in the former Yugoslavia on 3 July 1992. At that time I was conducting research in Washington D.C., taking the metro to the U.S. National Archives. The main headline on the front page of that morning's *Washington Post* shouted out: "Canadians push through to Sarajevo: UN peacekeeper's threat of force breaches Serb roadblock." A photo of a TOW anti-tank vehicle painted white and emblazoned with the black UN insignia accompanied the article. I was shocked. What was a peacekeeping unit wearing blue helmets doing with armoured TOW launchers and forcing roadblocks? My understanding of peacekeeping operations came from my uncle, Warrant Officer Mike Maloney, who had served with 8th Canadian Hussars (Princess Louise's) in the United Nations Emergency Force in the Sinai and in Gaza during the late 1950s and into the 1960s and then UNEF II in the 1970s. In those operations lightly armed Canadian troops in jeeps patrolled a buffer zone separating two belligerents who had agreed to the UN's presence and were dedicated to maintaining a relatively peaceful coexistence. This operation near Sarajevo, however, was definitely something new. Ominous and horrifying reports of something called "ethnic cleansing" seeped out in the media throughout that summer.

In the fall of 1992, I was fortunate enough to be asked to write a history of the Canadian Army's NATO forces. I arrived at HQ, 4 Canadian Mechanized Brigade in Germany, where I eventually worked with a number of people who had returned from operations in the Balkans. One of these people was Captain Dave Holt. Dave really got me interested in Yugoslavia. He had participated in Operation BOLSTER, the Canadian contribution to the European Community Monitoring Mission (ECMM), a non-UN neutral monitoring group. Dave was working on a personal memoir describing his harrowing involvement and he took the time to give his perspective on things. I also worked with Warrant Officer Wayne Ivey. Wayne participated in Operation HARMONY, the deployment of a Canadian battalion group to Sector West in Croatia as part of the United Nations Protection Force (UNPROFOR). As an intelligence NCO, Wayne had a unique perspective on the situation that he shared with me on innumerable occasions. I made a special effort to interview other officers and men from the brigade who had just returned from the first UNPROFOR deployment.

As the 4 Brigade project progressed, it became apparent that the last chapter would have to deal with Op HARMONY since the Canadian forces for UNPROFOR were drawn from and supported by 4 Canadian Mechanized Brigade. This allowed me to develop information on the first Op HARMONY rotation, an event that was included in my book *War Without Battles: Canada's NATO Brigade In Germany, 1951-1993*. I attempted to fly into Sarajevo for a research trip but my boss dissuaded me. It would be difficult, he said, to complete the 4 Brigade history from a hospital bed or a grave (I eventually made the trip in 1995, before the fall of Srebrenica, and left just in time to see my former neighbour from Germany, Pat Rechner, handcuffed to a pole by the Bosnian Serbs for the benefit of the CNN audience weeks later).

Be that as it may, I retained my interest in our involvement in the Balkans and I was struck at the time by the lack of in-depth media coverage of Canadian operations. CNN sat in Sarajevo and once the Canadians left to go back to Sector West, they vanished from TV reality. Only occasionally did the world television media mention events involving Canadian troops and there was little in-depth print analysis of what they did and why they did it. It was gratifying to see the release and success of General Mackenzie's memoir, yet it did not answer all of the questions that I wanted answered since it covered a discrete period. Certainly there was more to our involvement than the operations in Sarajevo, valorous though these operations were.

In May 1994 I was visiting New Brunswick when I bumped into an old friend and colleague of mine, John Llambias. Our units, worked closely together on many summer exercises in Gagetown and we also were history classmates from the University of New Brunswick. We both felt that the perspectives of those who served in Yugoslavia should be preserved. We determined that we should take on this project in our spare time and the result is this book.

Its production, so close to the events, necessitates a number of caveats. This cannot be a detailed history of the entirety of the Canadian Army's participation in the former Yugoslavia. We have selected what we believe to be a cross section of Canadian experiences in this conflict. It is logistically impossible to include such a complete cross section from each unit rotation, since the book would be gigantic. There have been eleven battalions and regiments rotate through the former republic of Yugoslavia, as well as ECMM and UNMO observers, RCMP officers, not to mention logistics personnel. The people we have selected are therefore representatives of the Canadian experience and it would do the reader well to remember that for every story told here there are at least four hundred more.

A note on pseudonyms: we originally put this project together in 1994. In the time that has passed since, many of our interviewees have moved on with their lives and some have entered new professions. The effects of the various boards of inquiry in the 1990s, and the belief among those in the ranks that they collectively amount to scapegoating exercises by the politically motivated, prompted several of our people to request that their identities be concealed. These men wish to be left alone. We respect this and have therefore altered the names of some of the participants in the Medak Pocket operation. Despite their anonymity, their experiences remain a legitimate representative sample of the Canadian historical fabric.

The aim of this book, then, is to record history from the perspective of Canadian soldiers involved in operations in the republics of the former Yugoslavia. The aim is not to provide an exposé or a voyeuristic forum, though the more politically minded may choose to interpret this work in this fashion. Members of the media may take discrete events out of context and magnify their significance or implications. Regiments may be upset over errors that were committed or omitted in-theatre. Be that as it may, Canadians should know what peacekeeping in the 1990s entailed, warts and all, and, just as importantly, how it affects their soldiers. Canadians have every right to be proud of their army's achievements in this hideous conflict and they should be given an opportunity to see their representatives in action, be it presence operations in Croatia, humanitarian relief in Bosnia, providing impartial observers in both areas, or in the Machiavellian intrigue of the UN and EC headquarters. Without our presence there it would have been worse for countless people and our Canadian soldiers deserve recognition.

I would like to dedicate this book to my brothers, Kevin and Andy, who both served in their own ways during those uncertain years.

- **Sean M. Maloney**

When I was a small boy I can remember my parents taking my sister Mary Lou and me to Armed Forces Day at CFB Gagetown, New Brunswick. It was a beautiful, hot, sunny summer day, the sort that one likes to remember from one's childhood. I remember playing on the tanks, riding in the APCs, firing the FN rifle and the machine gun and having ice cream with my family. I had always played with toy soldiers and thought this was great fun.

At the end of the day there was a parade. I was quite disappointed as I really would have preferred to ride in the APCs all day, but all good things must come to an end and sometimes in life we just have to accept things we don't necessarily like, so I sat patiently next to Mary Lou in the bleachers and watched the soldiers standing around for a long time. Eventually came the march past. At last some action, I thought.

I can remember the Pipes and Drums of 2nd Battalion, The Royal Canadian Regiment marching by. These men in skirts caught my attention and I think I laughed. I can remember my father putting his arm around me and saying seriously, "These are the men who stopped the Nazis. These are the men who saved us."

My father had been a small boy in Gibraltar when the Second World War broke out and he was evacuated along with his brother Johnny, my grandmother Emily, her sister Ada and her children. The trip lasted several anxious weeks in a crowded ship across U-boat filled waters, but they eventually made it to London, England. There they lived through the Blitz. Years later my father confided in me that it left him with nightmares.

I loved my father, and admired him, as most little boys do. My father taught me right from wrong, to have confidence and a sense of humour, and he admired these men. I knew also that my grandfather, Robbie Robinson, the tall man with the British accent whose laugh filled the house when he and my grandmother came every summer to visit, had also been a soldier. I remember listening tirelessly to his stories of China, Egypt, Burma, and India, most of which ended with a beer. Like most little boys, I admired my grandfather too.

My father became a teacher, not a military man, but his admiration for soldiers was something he never lost or forgot. It was something I never forgot either. Years later I joined the Militia and learned firsthand what truly wonderful people soldiers really are. They are truly the salt of the earth. I will never forget singing *Barrett's Privateers* in the back of the track as we rolled across the training area in the summer dust of Gagetown with the men of my regiment, 1st Battalion, the Royal New Brunswick Regiment, my friends. I will never forget the warmth of the welcome I received from the band when I, as a reservist, played my bagpipes for the first time with 2 RCR, the same band I saw as a young boy. I will never forget Sean Culligan showing up on my doorstep the day my father died, or the flowers from the boys half a world away on call-out with UNFICYP in Cyprus.

This book is dedicated to the man I admire most, my father Doctor Henry Llambias, Professor of Political Science at the University of New Brunswick, and the men he admired most: Soldiers, regular or reserve, everywhere. There are truly no people more giving, more enduring, or more worthy of admiration.

- **John Llambias**

When you kill one man,
they send you to the electric chair.

When you kill twelve,
they send you to an institution.

When you kill two hundred thousand,
they send you to Geneva.

– attributed to Bosnian President Alija Izetbegovic

CHAPTER ONE

THE CANADIAN ARMY IN THE BALKANS 1992-1995: AN OVERVIEW

"You have to take chances for peace, just as you must take chances in war."

-John Foster Dulles, *Time*, 16 January 1956

"The grim fact is that we prepare for war like precocious giants and for peace like retarded pygmies."

-Lester B. Pearson, speech in Toronto, 14 March 1955

The conflict in the Balkans is a complex mechanism of events, people, and places over time. It is important, therefore, to provide the reader with a clear and concise synopsis of the larger context in which the people in this book were operating. Their actions were either directly or indirectly the result of this larger context. The aim of this section is to answer the following questions: Why was the United Nations in the Balkans? Why was the Canadian Army in the Balkans? Where did the Canadian Army operate and what was it supposed to do? Finally, how was the Canadian Army organized and equipped in the Balkans to carry out its tasks?

WHY WAS THE UNITED NATIONS IN THE BALKANS?

In very basic terms, the present conflict in the Balkans started in 1991.[1] Communism had collapsed in Eastern Europe and the Yugoslavian regions of Slovenia and Croatia wanted closer economic ties with Western Europe. The Serb-dominated federal government did not want its more technologically advanced regions leaving the federation, so it attempted throughout 1991 to use the federal army, the JNA, to rein Slovenia in. This failed and Slovenia achieved independence. Croatia then declared independence, the JNA once again attempted to impose federal will, and protracted fighting started in Croatia in the summer and fall of 1991.

The Belgrade government, led by Slobodan Milosevic, decided that if overwhelming force could not be used to keep Croatia in line, it could prop up the ethnic Serb minority in the Kraijina and Slavonia regions of Croatia and thus maintain a foothold in the breakaway state *(see Figure 1)*. The Serbs in eastern Slavonia tried to purge the Croats in that area, particularly the Croat-held city of Vukovar, while the Croats simultaneously tried to purge the Krajinas of its Serb minority. A variety of factors, including international pressure, weather, logistics, and problems with command and control contributed to the stabilization of lines between the Serb and Croat forces

Figure 1: Overall Situation in the Balkans: April - May 1992

fighting in Croatia late in 1991. It took another four months of negotiation during the intermittent fighting to establish a UN peacekeeping force there in March 1992.

The Belgrade government needed corridors through Bosnia-Herzegovina (hereafter Bosnia) to support military operations in Slavonia and the Krajinas. The Bosnian Muslim/Croat enclave of Bihac, which is physically right behind the Krajinas, resisted these efforts and military forces from Serbia proper were brought in to lay siege to it. In addition, the Croatians sought to expand into southern Bosnia and link up with the Bosnian-Croat minority there to outflank the Serb Krajinas in the south. At the same time, Bosnian Serbs resented the Muslim-dominated Bosnian Presidency led by Iliya Itzebegovich and took up arms against it, a rebellion which in turn was also supported by Belgrade. In effect, a three-way war erupted in Bosnia while the situation in Croatia was stabilizing (see Figure 2).

The United Nations deployed peacekeeping forces to the Balkans because other crisis resolution mechanisms and international organizations failed to contain the violence in the region. It was the result of a process that started with the Conference of Security and Co-operation in Europe (CSCE), proceeded to the European Community (EC) and then to the Western European Union (WEU).

The CSCE, now called the OSCE, is a consultative body consisting of all European nations, Russia, the United States, and Canada. It was created to reduce Warsaw Pact - NATO tension in Europe and to act as an umbrella for the Conventional Forces in Europe Treaty, that is, to supervise disarmament. It possesses no military forces of its own, nor are any military forces dedicated to it for use. It has a Conflict Prevention Centre, which is supposed to be used to mediate between member countries involved in disputes. It was unable to mediate since the Yugoslav situation was initially a civil war and the warring factions were not represented in the conference. There was a distinct lack of will to achieve peace among the belligerent factions anyway, particularly in 1991.[2]

The European Community was originally designed to break down the economic barriers between European states and to provide for economic co-ordination in the creation of a common market. Stagnant during the Cold War, the EC now has emerged as the primary forum of Western European states on defence matters as well. Since action by the North Atlantic Treaty Organization is limited to the NATO area (that is, the sovereign territory of the organization members and the sea around them), the European countries needed a mechanism to co-ordinate military operations outside of the NATO area. The Western European Union (WEU) is, in effect, the military arm of the EC. It possesses those forces assigned to it on an ad hoc basis, unlike NATO forces, which are dedicated in peacetime to NATO commands. The WEU is a relatively untried organization but it did contribute naval assets to the enforcement of UN sanctions in the region.[3]

After it was clear by September 1991 that the CSCE was incapable of mediating the Balkan conflict, the EC was asked to try. The EC operated two missions at the same time. It deployed the European Community Monitor Mission (ECMM) to Slovenia in September 1991 when that country left the Yugoslav federation. When Croatia and Bosnia also left the federation, the ECMM expanded its monitoring activities to those countries as well. Despite valiant efforts at mediation and peacekeeping, the ECMM also was unable to contain the level of violence in the region, mostly because of their lack of communications equipment, the small number of observers, and the lack of a legal mandate or recognition from all factions.[4]

While the ECMM was being formed, the European nations continually discussed the deployment of an armed peacekeeping force drawn from the European nations and operating under the auspices of the WEU. Throughout the fall of 1991, the European nations, mediating with the Croatian separatists and the Serbian-dominated Yugoslav federation, tried desperately to come to some accommodation on how big a WEU peacekeeping force should be and who would be in it. The EC was unable to develop a consensus on these issues while the Croatian and Bosnian conflicts escalated.[5]

As the Balkan situation deteriorated, there was widespread concern in Western European capitals that the instability in the region would spread north into Eastern Europe and southeast into the southern Balkans. In 1991-1992, the Russians still maintained a significant presence in

Figure 2: The Overall Situation in Bosnia-Hercegovina, 1992-93

Germany, Poland, and Czechoslovakia. In August 1991 an extremist coup was put down in Moscow and Eastern Europe had severe economic problems. Would tension spread north into the former Warsaw Pact countries? Would the Russians crack down at home and return to a Cold War situation? The implications, so soon after the Berlin Wall collapsed, were frightening. In a more limited fashion, Hungary put its forces on alert after JNA aircraft raided refugee facilities across the border.[6]

In the south, the tension between Eastern Orthodox Greece and Muslim Turkey was at its normally high level. The possibility that the Former Yugoslav Republic of Macedonia might declare independence fuelled Greek nationalist fires. Other factors that contributed to the instability included the widespread concern that the western militaries had drawn down too far to effectively deal with a regional war in northern Europe.[7] When all these factors were considered, it was imperative in 1991-1992 that conflict in the Balkans should not be allowed to spread and create a much larger one in Eastern Europe and the Mediterranean.

The only international organization with a long-standing history of peacekeeping operations was the United Nations. The UN has not, had not, and does not now possess its own dedicated peacekeeping forces. Such missions have always been rather ad hoc affairs and the UN has always had systemic problems in conducting peacekeeping operations.[8] Nevertheless, it was the only body capable of dealing with the situation as it existed in 1991-1992 and there were enough national forces with peacekeeping experience available to mount such an operation in the former Yugoslavia.

By the end of November 1991, the Croats and the Serbs were prepared to accept a UN peacekeeping mission in Croatia for different reasons. In addition to logistic and weather problems, both sides needed a UN presence to stabilize the situation. The Croats, fearing a mass intervention by the JNA into Croatia, and the Serbs, wanting to retain their foothold in Croatia as well as to protect the Serb minorities there, agreed to the creation of UN Protected Areas (UNPAs) in Slavonia and the Krajinas. After four months of negotiation and manoeuvring, the United Nations Protection Force (UNPROFOR) took shape and deployed *(see Figure 3)*.[9]

The overall UN strategy, as it developed over time and in the face of great ambiguity, had two general components. The explicit component asserted that violence between the belligerents in-theatre must be reduced to the lowest levels possible and that violence must be contained within the territorial boundaries of Croatia and Bosnia. UN forces would monitor and mediate disagreements in-theatre and provide relief to the civilian population. The implicit component suggests that, since violence between the belligerents cannot be totally stopped, UN force must be applied selectively to keep it down to an acceptable level, thus preventing escalation and spillover out of the region. If one belligerent faction can no longer move in a particular direction, it might look elsewhere to expand, perhaps an area out of the region or an adjacent territory not at war. No one side should be allowed to achieve a decisive goal in-theatre. If this situation is imminent, then UN force should be selectively applied to maintain the status quo. This tacit policy was apparent during the two major UN operations examined herein.

WHY WAS THE CANADIAN ARMY PART OF UNPROFOR IN THE BALKANS?

Traditional Canadian strategic policy rests on the principle of Forward Security. In the past, Canada fulfilled this in two ways. First, Canada stationed forces in Europe during the First, Second, and Cold Wars. Second, Canada has participated in several peacekeeping operations in the

Third World since 1948. The primary purpose behind these peacekeeping operations was to ensure that smaller conflicts outside of the NATO area did not grow into a superpower crisis resulting in thermonuclear exchange. Canada's contribution to peacekeeping operations in the Balkans fits neatly into this scheme, given the nature of the geopolitical problem facing Europe in 1991-1992.[10]

There is much more to Canada's UNPROFOR commitment than this strategic tradition. Canada's credibility as a member of the international security community has been suspect since the 1970s. Despite a well-executed peace restoration operation during the Cyprus crisis in

Figure 3: UNPROFOR I
UN Protected Areas, 1992

1974, Canada's ability to meet its NATO commitments was seriously eroded between 1970 and 1984. Attempts at rebuilding military capability, initiated in 1985, were shelved in 1989. Canada produced a minimal contribution to the Gulf War in 1990-1991 and it had to demonstrate that it was still a player after that.

The complete withdrawal of Canadian forces from Europe and the lack of provision for a credible Canadian contribution to the ACE Rapid Reaction Corps seriously reduced political influence in the councils of the new Europe.[11] Morale in the Canadian Army was low, the raison d'être for its existence was gone. Some policymakers felt that the survival of the army itself was at stake and, since the army had no opportunity to perform, it was time to find one.

The first Canadian contribution to UNPROFOR in early 1992, an 850-man mechanized battalion and a 250-man combat engineer regiment, can be viewed in the light of traditional strategy. The remnants of 4 Canadian Mechanized Brigade in Germany were available, the men had been on peacekeeping operations in the past, and there was a paucity of well-trained units available to the UN. The second contribution, the provision of a 1200-man light armoured regiment in late 1992 for UNPROFOR in Bosnia, and the deployment of a 300-man logistics unit, could also be seen in this light.

However, it appears as though pronouncements by the government were not in line with the actual capabilities of the army. Canadian policymakers attempted to convince their European allies that the sum of the Canadian pieces committed to UNPROFOR were in fact equivalent to Canada's previous NATO commitment of a brigade group and that Canada should retain her previous influence in the councils of Europe. They had no success. Canada, despite its high numerical contribution to UNPROFOR, the naval interception Operation SHARP GUARD in the Adriatic, the air intercept Operation DENY FLIGHT, and the Sarajevo relief Operation AIR BRIDGE, was ultimately not a significant participant in the Balkan conflict's higher diplomacy. In the minds of the policymakers in Ottawa, Canada was trapped in the Balkans, at least from a diplomatic and political standpoint. The disconnect between the broad political considerations and the operational requirements of the forces deployed is not a new one in Canadian military history. Despite the lack of co-ordination between the foreign policy and defence communities, despite the serious cuts imposed on the army, Canada's soldiers still emerged as arguably the most effective peacekeeping troops in the Balkans.

WHERE DID THE CANADIAN ARMY OPERATE AND WHAT WAS IT SUPPOSED TO DO?

The Canadian Army participated in four peacekeeping operations in the Balkans prior to the advent of the NATO Implementation Force (IFOR) in 1996 and Stabilization Force (SFOR) the following year.[12]

OPERATION BOLSTER

Operation BOLSTER was Canada's contribution to the European Community Monitor Mission (ECMM). Canada provided 15 military monitors on a rotational basis from September 1991 to August 1994. As noted earlier, the ECMM was the first peacekeeping organization in the Balkans. It consisted of officers and diplomats from the twelve European Community countries plus Canada, Sweden, the Czech Republic, Slovakia, and Poland. Canada was invited to participate since it is a member of CSCE and because the roles envisioned for the ECMM were similar to those performed by Canadian UN Military Observers since the late 1940s. The mission's legal mandate was derived from the Brioni Agreement of July 1991, whereby representatives of all the republics of the former Yugoslavia agreed to allow the CSCE and the EC to monitor the situation as it developed.[13]

The ECMM's role evolved over the course of the conflict. Formed in July 1991, the ECMM monitored the withdrawal of the JNA from Slovenia and provided military and political information directly to the European Community for use in its deliberations. Once the fighting in Croatia broke out, the ECMM teams wound up brokering local ceasefire agreements and monitoring the JNA's withdrawal from the interior of Croatia. The aim here was to stabilize the ceasefire line between the Croats and the Serbs in the Krajinas and in Slavonia through local agreements. Operating in teams of three or four, the EC monitors established a series of reporting centres in Croatia and in Bosnia. Again, as in Slovenia, situational information flowed to the European Community while the monitors were conducting negotiations. The ECMM handed over their sections of the ceasefire line to UNPROFOR in 1992; EC monitors and their organization remained in place to supplement the UN Military Observers and UNPROFOR.[14] Though the ECMM duplicated the functions of the UN organizations, its information flowed to diplomatic talks in Geneva, to the EC, and to the UN. Its role was, in effect, to provide "a good second opinion."[15] Canada's contribution to the ECMM had its own special intricacies and is the subject of a separate study.[16]

UNITED NATIONS MILITARY OBSERVERS

The provision of Canadian Army officers to the UN as UNMOs does not carry a codename. Historically, the first UN operations were not intervention operations; they were observation and monitoring missions not unlike the ECMM.[17] UNMOs in the Balkans carried on this tradition. Thirty-two nations contributed UNMOs and they operated in every region. UNMOs were supposed to report directly to the UN Secretary General in New York through the Chief Military Observer and were not under national command in-theatre. UNMOs deployed in late 1991 to act as a transition between the ECMM and UNPROFOR in the United Nations Protected Areas in Croatia. Their mission was to verify that the UNPAs were in fact demilitarized and, later, to act as intermediaries in the resolution of local situations that developed on the ceasefire line and elsewhere. As with the ECMM, the role of the UNMOs evolved. They acted as information gatherers for UN HQ in New York and were extensively involved in sorting out local problems between the UNPROFOR units and the belligerent forces in the UNPAs. Information collected by the UNMOs flowed to the various UNPROFOR headquarters in-theatre as well as to New York.[18]

OPERATION HARMONY: UNITED NATIONS PROTECTION FORCE I

Operation HARMONY was Canada's contribution to UNPROFOR I in Croatia. The force was the direct result of the Vance Plan (not to be confused with the Vance-Owen Plan, which involves Bosnia), the original peacekeeping forces concept for Croatia in 1991. UN Security Council Resolution 721 (27 November 1991) affirmed the plan as a basis for action. This was re-confirmed with Resolution 740 (7 February 1992) and, exactly two weeks later, Resolution 743 formally established UNPROFOR.[19]

In its original incarnation, the force was established to operate in Croatia, using Sarajevo in Bosnia as a headquarters and airhead. At this point, Bosnia was not yet at war. The Vance Plan created four United Nations Protected Areas: Sectors North, South (the Krajinas), East, and West (Slavonia). The UN's mandate in the UNPAs was multifaceted. The UNPROFOR was to ensure that the UNPAs were de-militarized and to monitor the ceasefire line. Local belligerent forces were to be disbanded and regular forces withdrawn from the region. The UN force was then to ensure the security of people living in the UNPA, to ensure that humanitarian relief was not interfered with, and to assist the locals in returning to a pre-war standard of living.[20]

UNPROFOR I originally consisted of twelve battalion-sized infantry units drawn from twelve different countries, an engineer regiment, a signals battalion, a medical battalion, and a movement control organization, in addition to UNMOs and headquarters personnel (a total of 12, 000 men and women).[21] Each Sector was divided into three battalion areas of responsibility (AORs), all under the command of a Sector HQ (led by a brigadier-general) consisting of a multinational staff drawn from the participating countries in the Sector.

The original mandate evolved from the date of its inception. Once Bosnia spiralled into chaos, UNPROFOR HQ had to evacuate Sarajevo, thus losing access to the airport, the force's airhead. The UN expanded the mandate to permit the deployment of the Canadian battalion in Sector West to Sarajevo so that the airport could remain under UN control.[22] It also expanded UNPROFOR operating areas into the so-called "Pink Zones" and "reverse Pink Zones." These were areas adjacent to the UNPAs which were captured either by the JNA or the Croatian military, areas that were predominantly Serb in ethnicity. These areas had been seized after the UNPA boundaries were drawn but before the ceasefire took effect.[23]

The primary belligerents that Canadian soldiers encountered in Croatia included:

1. **Croats:** The Croatian Army (the HV); the Croatian Union National Guard; and the Croatian Territorial Army.
2. **Krajinan Serbs:** The Army of the Republic of Serb Krajinas (the ARSK) Armed Forces; the Serbian Volunteer Guard; and the Serbian Guard.
3. **Units of the Jugoslav National Army** (the JNA) supporting the Krajinan Serbs.[24]

Both the HV and the ARSK had mercenary contingents, either on an individual basis in the case of ethnic Croats and Serbs returning from other countries, or, in the case of the HV, an "international brigade." Organized crime should not be discounted as a force in both the Croatian and Bosnian theatres.

Operation HARMONY consisted of the following unit rotations:

Mar 92–Oct 92:	1er Bataillon, Royal 22e Régiment (with a company drawn from 3rd Battalion, The Royal Canadian Regiment), and 4 Combat Engineer Regiment.
Oct 92–Mar 93:	3rd Battalion, Princess Patricia's Canadian Light Infantry and 1 Combat Engineer Regiment.
Mar 93–Oct 93:	2nd Battalion, Princess Patricia's Canadian Light Infantry
Oct 93–Mar 94:	1er Bataillon, Royal 22e Régiment (with 1e Troope, 56e Escadron de Genie)

Mar 94–Oct 94: 1st Battalion, Princess Patricia's Canadian Light Infantry
Oct 94–Mar 95: 1st Battalion, The Royal Canadian Regiment
Mar–Sept 95: 2e Bataillon, Royal 22e Régiment

OPERATION CAVALIER: UNITED NATIONS PROTECTION FORCE II

Operation CAVALIER was Canada's contribution to UNPROFOR II in Bosnia. This force's mandate developed in a flurry of Security Council resolutions. After the Sarajevo Airport was secured and re-opened, the UN encouraged humanitarian relief organizations to use it. Continued belligerent interference with humanitarian relief flights into Sarajevo stimulated discussions between the UN and the belligerent forces over the monitoring of heavy weapons in the

Figure 4: The Situation in Bosnia-Hercegovina, 1993

region around Sarajevo (Resolution 764). All sides frequently ambushed ground convoys delivering humanitarian relief provided by non-governmental organizations (NGOs) and the UN High Commissioner for Refugees (UNHCR). Additionally, the UN's knowledge of human rights abuses in Bosnia expanded exponentially and it demanded that humanitarian organizations be given immediate and unimpeded access to areas where these were occurring (Resolutions 770 and 771). Eventually in September 1992, Security Council Resolution 776 authorized the expansion of UNPROFOR's mandate to include protection of humanitarian relief convoys in Bosnia. The force established a separate Bosnia-Herzegovina Command.[25]

In August 1992, Canada announced that it would provide a 1,200-man unit to conduct convoy escort operations. This unit, based on 2nd Battalion, The Royal Canadian Regiment, arrived in-theatre in November 1992 and was designated CANBAT 2. Its deployment from Sector West in Croatia to its operating areas in Bosnia was blocked for four months as the UN negotiated with the belligerents. In April 1993, the UN declared the town of Srebrenica a Safe Area and a company group from CANBAT 2 deployed from the battalion's base in Visoko. This deployment was essentially a test case for the concept and, the following month, Resolution 824 authorized the creation of six UN Safe Areas: Sarajevo, Tuzla, Zepa, Gorazde, Bihac, and Srebrenica. Not long afterward, UNPROFOR's mandate was expanded to include the use of force to deter attacks against the Safe Areas and protect the humanitarian relief convoys *(see Figure 4).*[26]

Another expansion took place in December 1992 when the UN Security Council authorized UNPROFOR to deploy forces to the Former Yugoslav Republic of Macedonia in what was termed a "preventative deployment." In January 1993, CANBAT 2 deployed a company group from Bosnia to Skopje and the Macedonian border regions. The aim of the mission was to deter adjacent nations (Serbia, Bulgaria and Albania) from interfering with Macedonian affairs and therefore prevent a spill-over effect from Bosnia into Macedonia. Eventually UNPROFOR established a separate command for its forces in Macedonia (UNPREDEP) after CANBAT 2's company group returned to Bosnia *(see Figure 5).*

Another flurry of UN and NATO diplomatic activity in February and March 1994 produced further changes in UNPROFOR's mandate. UN and NATO threats to use air strikes against Serb forces surrounding Sarajevo resulted in the creation of the Sarajevo Exclusion Zone (SEZ). Theoretically, the Serbs were supposed to withdraw heavy weapons from the zone (or place them under UNPROFOR observation at one of seven sites) and permit UNMOs uninhibited movement to verify that this was carried out. The reality of the situation was that the Serbs still kept heavy weapons in the Sarajevo Exclusion Zone, either right on the edge of the zone or just outside of it, prompting a number of showdowns with UNPROFOR, one of which involved Canadian forces in Visoko.

While this was going on, the Bosnian Croats and the Bosnian Muslims signed a ceasefire agreement. This agreement served as the basis for the disengagement of Muslim and Croat forces fighting in pockets throughout central Bosnia. Operation KHARON, the Kiseljak Pocket disengagement, was conducted within the context of this agreement. Thus, UNPROFOR found itself monitoring Bosnian ceasefire lines, in addition to its other activities.

UNPROFOR II itself quickly expanded to include 19,000 UN military personnel with contingents drawn from Canada, France, Britain, Spain, Russia, the Netherlands, Malaysia, Turkey, and Pakistan (as well as a Nordic Battalion) for a total of 14 battalions. In addition to the UN Safe Areas, UNPROFOR BH Command established two sectors, Sector South West and Sector North East, in March 1994.[27]

The primary belligerents in Bosnia included, once again leaving out non-indigenous, specialist or criminal groups:

1. **The Bosnian Territorial Defence Force** (a.k.a. the BiH Army, the BiH Armija)
2. **The Bosnian Croat Army** (the HVO); the HV from Croatia proper also provided support to the HVO in some areas
3. **The Bosnian Serb Army** (the BSA)
4. **The Jugoslav National Army** (the JNA) supporting the BSA and conducting its own operations

The belligerents also had mercenaries. The BiH Army had a number of contingents consisting of Mujaheddin from Lebanon, Iran, and Afghanistan. The HVO apparently had European Neo-Nazis within its ranks, while the BSA had former East Bloc nationals, including a Russian unit serving with UNPROFOR that defected.

The war in Bosnia was a three-way war (Bosnian Croats versus Bosnian Serbs versus Bosnian Muslims) until early in 1994 when the Muslims and Croats disengaged and formed the joint Bosniac command. Not all HVO enclaves entered into the joint command and some operated independently.

**Figure 5: UN Preventative
Deployment to Macedonia, 1993**

Op CAVALIER consisted of the following unit rotations:

Nov 92–May 93: 2nd Battalion, The Royal Canadian Regiment (armoured squadron from 12e Régiment blindé du Canada and an engineer troop)

May 93–Nov 93: 2e Bataillon, Royal 22e Régiment (armoured squadron from 12e Régiment blindé du Canada and 57 Escadron de génie)

Nov 93–May 94: 12e Régiment blindé du Canada (infantry company from 1er Bataillon, Royal 22e Régiment and 56 Escadron de génie)

May 94–Nov 94: The Lord Strathcona's Horse (Royal Canadians) (infantry company from 3rd Battalion, Princess Patricia's Canadian Light Infantry and an engineer squadron from 1 Combat Engineer Regiment)

Nov 94–May 95: The Royal Canadian Dragoons (infantry company from 2 Battalion, The Royal Canadian Regiment and an engineer squadron from 2 Combat Engineer Regiment)

May 95–Oct 95: 3e Bataillon, Royal 22e Régiment (armoured squadron from 12e Régiment blindé du Canada and an engineer squadron from 5e Régiment de génie de combat)

UNCIVPOL

Though the Canadian Army did not contribute to it, the United Nations Civilian Police organization also conducted peacekeeping activities. Canadian members of UNCIVPOL were drawn from the Royal Canadian Mounted Police. Their role was to watch the belligerent police forces for human rights violations and to ensure they acted as police forces and not paramilitary units.

HOW WAS THE CANADIAN ARMY ORGANIZED IN THE BALKANS TO CARRY OUT ITS TASKS?

Canada provided three primary units as part of the Canadian Contingent, UNPROFOR: Canadian Battalion One or CANBAT 1; Canadian Battalion Two or CANBAT 2; and the Canadian Logistics Battalion or CANLOGBAT. These are generic terms and the Canadian Army's contribution to UNPROFOR consists of much more than two infantry battalions and a logistics unit. Before exploring the specifics of the Canadian Army's contribution, we have included the following section for those interested in learning about the army's structure and equipment.

BASIC ORGANIZATION

The basic unit in the combat arms of the Canadian Army is either the Armoured Regiment or the Infantry Battalion.[28] An armoured regiment is commanded by a lieutenant-colonel (the Commanding Officer or CO) and generally consists of three tank squadrons and a reconnaissance (or recce, pronounced "recky") squadron.[29] Each Squadron, commanded by a major (the OC or Officer Commanding of a Squadron, also called a Squadron Commander), is generally broken down into Troops, each in turn commanded by a lieutenant, the Troop Leader. Tank and recce squadrons are organized differently. A tank squadron has four troops of four Leopard tanks per troop (plus a Squadron HQ with three more) while a recce squadron has three troops of seven recce vehicles each (Canada did not deploy tanks to the Balkans until the Operation KINETIC deployment in

Kosovo in 1999). Each recce Troop has three two-vehicle Patrols, in addition to the Troop Leader's vehicle. Canadian armoured squadrons deployed as part of UNPROFOR consisted of three Troops of seven vehicles each plus a Squadron HQ. The primary vehicle used by Canadian armoured units in the Balkans was the Cougar armoured car, a six-wheeled vehicle armed with a 76mm gun. The Cougars were tank-training vehicles delivered in 1979 and subsequently pressed into service because Canada lacked a proper armoured car.

An infantry battalion is also commanded by a lieutenant-colonel (also called the CO) and has a more varied organization. An infantry battalion could have three or four Rifle Companies and a Combat Support Company. Each subunit is commanded by a major, known as the Company Commanders or the Company OCs (Officer Commanding).

A rifle company generally consists of three Platoons, each led by a Platoon Leader, who is a lieutenant or a second lieutenant. Each platoon consists of three Sections of 10 men each led by a Section Leader, usually a sergeant. An armoured personnel carrier or APC transports each section.[30] This is either a tracked troop transporter called the M-113A2, which is equipped with a .50 calibre heavy machine gun (and called simply a "track" by the soldiers), or a wheeled turreted vehicle called a Grizzly, which uses the same hull as the Cougar but is equipped with two machine guns. As with the Cougar, the Grizzly was acquired as a training surrogate, not as an operational APC.

In an infantry battalion, Combat Support Company consists of Mortar Platoon, Anti-armour Platoon, Recce Platoon (possibly with a Sniper Section) and a Pioneer Platoon. The mortar platoon travels in M-113A2 APCs and has 81mm mortars, while the anti-armour platoon is equipped with the TOW Under Armour anti-tank missile system. The TUA consists of a turret mounted on an M-113A2. Acquired in 1989, it has Tube-launched, Optically-tracked, Wire-guided (TOW) missiles and a thermal imagery sight to allow it to operate at night or in bad weather. There are eight TUA vehicles in this platoon. Recce Platoon is a small unit for reconnaissance tasks and the Sniper Section's role is self-evident. The Pioneer Platoon is capable of handling small engineer tasks such as mine clearance, stream crossings, and the construction of defensive works. Not all infantry battalions have Pioneers. Note that armoured units in CANBAT II in Bosnia formed a Combat Support Squadron that included the armoured regiment's headquarters reconnaissance troop, the TOW vehicles, an engineer section, and a six-vehicle mortar platoon mounted in M-113A2 armoured personnel carriers.

Some of the weapons and vehicles mentioned in the chapters that follow require a brief explanation. The basic assault rifle in the Canadian Army is the 5.56mm C-7; there is a shorter version for armoured personnel, called the C-8. The C-6 is a 7.62mm medium machine gun, while the C-9 is a 5.56mm light machine gun. Man-portable anti-tank weapons include the 66mm M-72 (called a LAW) and the 84mm Carl Gustav (known informally as a "Carl G"). Some infantry units also carry 60mm mortars. Soft-skinned or unarmoured vehicles used by the Canadian Army include 2.5-ton trucks (the MLVW, usually called an "ML" or a "deuce" in slang), a 5/4-ton truck (the "five quad") and a jeep-like vehicle called the Iltis.

Other equipment mentioned in the book include Goggles, Image Intensification AN/PVS 5A (NOGS), which is used by one man (in some cases a vehicle driver) and Night Observation Device Long Range AN/PVS/502 (NODLR), which is a tripod-mounted device used in Observation Posts (OPs). Rifles and C-9 light machine guns can mount the KITE sight, another piece of night vision equipment. Armoured vehicle crews sometimes have laser range-finding binoculars. The Global Positioning System or GPS is a hand-held or vehicle-mounted navigation device.[31]

BISON ARMOURED PERSONNEL CARRIER (ambulance variant)

Crew: 3 (Commander, Driver, Medic)

Weight: 12 800 kilograms

Max Speed: 100 km/h

Armament: smoke grenade launchers (7.62mm machine gun when fitted)

Night Vision: Yes (commander and driver when fitted)

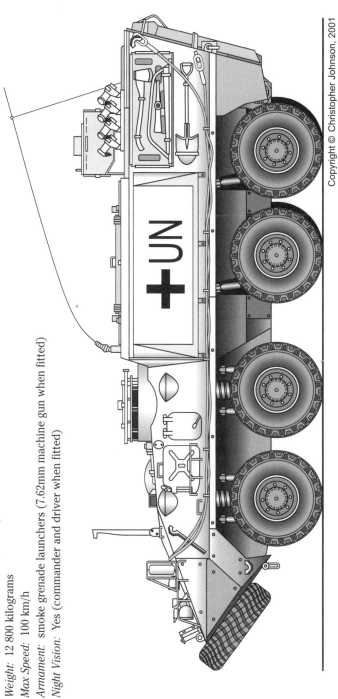

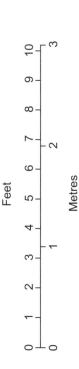

Copyright © Christopher Johnson, 2001

Feet

Metres

COUGAR ARMOURED VEHICLE GENERAL PURPOSE (AVGP)

Crew: 3 (Commander, Driver, Gunner)

Weight: 10 500 kilograms

Max Speed: 100 km/h

Armament: 76mm L23A1 , 1 x 7.62mm co-axial machine gun, smoke grenade launchers

Night Vision: Yes (gunner and driver, when fitted)

UN

Copyright © Christopher Johnson, 2001

Feet

Metres

GRIZZLY ARMOURED VEHICLE GENERAL PURPOSE (AVGP)

Crew: 3 (Commander, Gunner, Driver)

Weight: 10 500 kilograms

Max Speed: 100 km/h

Armament: 1 x 12.7mm machine gun, 1 x 7.62mm co-axial machine gun, smoke grenade launchers

Night Vision: Yes (driver when fitted)

Copyright © Christopher Johnson, 2001

Feet

Metres

17

M-113A2 TOW UNDER ARMOUR (TUA)

Crew: 4 (Commander, Gunner, Driver, Loader)

Weight: 11 253 kilograms (without turret)

Max Speed: 60 km/h

Armament: 2 x TOW missile launchers,
  1 x 7.62mm machine gun,
  smoke grenade launchers

Night Vision: Yes (TI and IR for gunner)

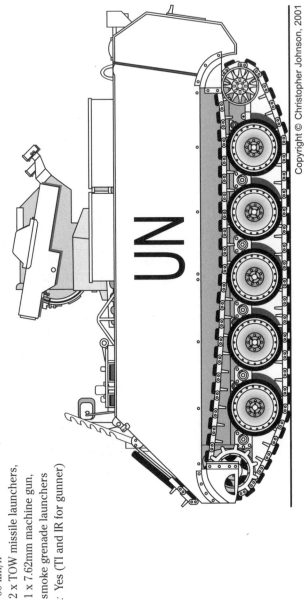

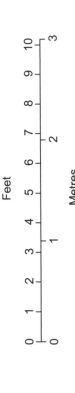

Copyright © Christopher Johnson, 2001

18

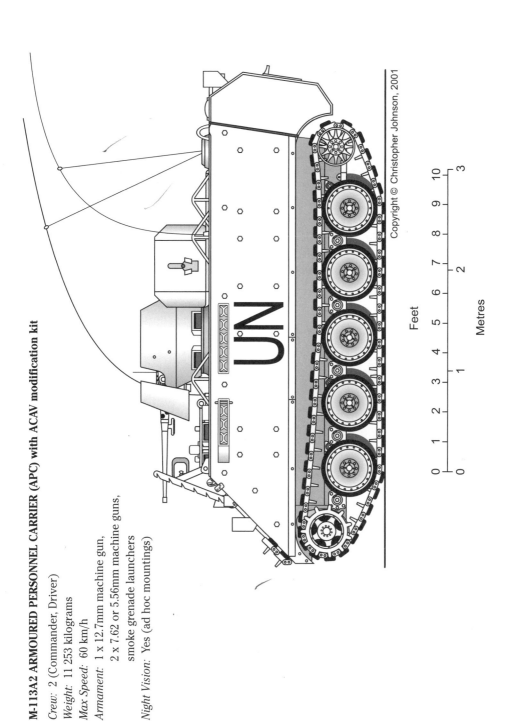

M-113A2 ARMOURED PERSONNEL CARRIER (APC) with ACAV modification kit

Crew: 2 (Commander, Driver)
Weight: 11 253 kilograms
Max Speed: 60 km/h
Armament: 1 x 12.7mm machine gun,
2 x 7.62 or 5.56mm machine guns,
smoke grenade launchers
Night Vision: Yes (ad hoc mountings)

Copyright © Christopher Johnson, 2001

BADGER ARMOURED ENGINEER VEHICLE (AEV)

Crew: 4 (Driver, Commander, Operators)

Weight: 40 800 kilograms

Max Speed: 65 km/h

Armament: 1 x 7.62mm machine gun, smoke grenade launchers

Night Vision: Yes (driver, when fitted)

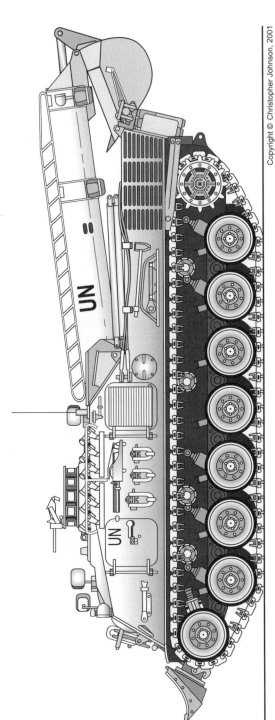

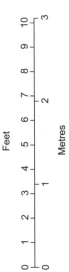

ENGINEER ORGANIZATION

Combat engineers are also organized as Regiments, Squadrons and Troops. An Armoured Engineer Squadron generally has 80 to 100 combat engineers. Its major equipment holdings include the Badger armoured engineering vehicle based on a Leopard tank chassis, the Beaver armoured bridge layer (also based on the Leopard tank chassis) and the engineer version of the M-113A2 APC or the Bison eight-wheeled APC (first delivered in 1989). A Field Squadron is mounted on trucks and possesses bulldozers, dump trucks and other construction machinery. Initially Canada deployed a full Combat Engineer Regiment consisting of an armoured engineer squadron and a field squadron to the former republic of Yugoslavia (FRY) in the first and second Op HARMONY deployment. This was later reduced to composite squadrons and in some cases, composite troops attached to the Battle or Battalion Groups. Engineering tasks range from mine clearance and mine awareness training to road construction and infrastructure repair. According to practically every Commanding Officer interviewed for this book, there are never enough engineers.[32]

LOGISTICS ORGANIZATION

The basic logistics organization in the Canadian Army is the service battalion. Normally, a Service Battalion consists of an Administration Company (personnel, pay, rations, and dental services); a Transport Company (trucks); a Supply Company and a Maintenance Company (repair). Initially, Canadian operations in the FRY were supported from 3 Canadian Support Group in Lahr through a 36-man National Support Element in Croatia. The closure of Canadian Forces Base Lahr, as well as adding the Op CAVALIER commitment and an increased ECMM contingent, produced a stand-alone in-theatre support group — the Canadian Contingent Support Group (CCSG) — which consisted of 113 people. In September 1994, in order to conform to UN unit name criteria and a greater workload, CCSG became CANLOGBAT and it increased in strength to 271 people. Initially, the National Support Element (NSE), CCSG, and the CANLOGBATs were composite units with personnel drawn from logistics units throughout Canada. In spring 1994, Canada-based service battalions became responsible for personnel rotations and command of the CANLOGBAT. The following units provided this function after 1994:[33]

Apr 94-Sept 94: 1 Service Battalion (Calgary)
Sept 94-Feb 95: 2 Service Battalion (Petawawa)
Feb 95-Aug 95: 5e Bataillon des services (Valcartier)
Aug 95-Jan-96: 1 Service Battalion (Calgary)

The NSE and CCSG operated from Camp Pollom in Daruvar, Croatia in the fall of 1992. Once CANBAT 1 moved to Sector South in the summer of 1993, CCSG moved to Sibinek and Primosten in southern Croatia.

MEDICAL ORGANIZATION

The basic Canadian medical unit is the Field Ambulance, which is the size of a battalion. None, however, were fully deployed to the former Yugoslavia, but Canada did, as part of Op CAVALIER, deploy a complete Field Surgical Team to Bosnia. An FST consists of 54 people divided into an

Evacuation Platoon, an Ambulance Platoon (which had several eight-wheeled Bison armoured ambulances with paramedics) and a Treatment Platoon (doctors and nurses). The FSTs in CANBAT 2 were all composite sub-units with personnel drawn from medical units across Canada.

TACTICAL AIR CONTROL PARTY

Rotations of CANBAT 2 also included a Tactical Air Control Party (TAC-P). The decision taken by the UN to 'sub-contract' NATO air support for UNPROFOR II meant that the ground forces had to have the capability to call in and direct NATO fighter-bombers and their munitions against belligerent targets if such action became necessary. A typical Canadian TAC-P deployed with CANBAT 2 had 8 air force officers and/or artillery Forward Observation Officers and 4 men divided into four teams. Each team was provided with an M-113A2 APC and driver from the battle group and was equipped with the LTM-91 laser designator with a 60-power scope mounted above it. Communications were comprehensive and included UHF and VHF radios, TACSAT satellite communications, and a Global Positioning System capability.[34]

SPECIAL OPERATIONS FORCES

In response to several hostage-taking incidents involving UN personnel, an ad hoc Special Operations Forces (SOF) capability was formed during an early CANBAT 2 rotation. It consisted of a group of Canadian soldiers from the battle group who had trained with allied SOF (either SEALs, SAS, or American Special Forces or Rangers) at some point in their careers. It was augmented with allied SOF. Later a more formal Canadian SOF capability was made available to CANBAT 2 for force protection operations. Their nickname was "The Wind," possibly named after W.O. Mitchell's novel, *Who Has Seen The Wind.*

ADVANCED ORGANIZATION

As noted in the introduction to this chapter, Canada deployed mixtures of these basic units to work with UNPROFOR. In a more conventional conflict, Canada would deploy a Brigade Group consisting of a brigade headquarters, an armoured regiment, two or three infantry battalions, an artillery regiment, an engineer regiment, a field ambulance and a service battalion. Canada used to possess four brigade groups but there are only three now and these are depleted after the Canadian government chose to apply the post-Cold War peace dividend to the existing small army structure. This, in addition to the United Nation's unwillingness to fund more than one Canadian battalion and a national logistic element, forced the Canadian Army's leadership to deploy smaller formations that have a greater mixture of capabilities.[35]

Mixtures less than brigade groups have a number of designations like Battalion Group, Battle Group or Regimental Group. Typically, a battalion group is an infantry battalion with extra medical, engineering and/or logistics resources. Generally Canada has deployed a battalion group to Croatia consisting of three or four infantry companies and an engineer squadron or troop.

A battle group could consist of either an armoured regiment with extra infantry resources, usually a company, or an infantry battalion with added armoured resources, usually a squadron. In UNPROFOR II deployments, Canada deployed a battle group to Bosnia; it generally consisted of two armoured squadrons and an infantry company or three infantry companies and an armoured squadron, plus a field hospital, an engineering troop and additional logistics and maintenance resources. Some Commanding Officers refer to the battle group in Bosnia as a Regimental Group to avoid the apparent contradiction between 'battle' and 'peacekeeping.' This distinction did, as we will see, become blurred at times.

In some cases, the diverse nature of operations in Bosnia required the subdivision of the Canadian battle group into smaller sub-units. For example, CANBAT 2 kept an infantry company in Srebrenica; it was augmented with other resources and was called a company group. In other cases, the armoured squadrons deploy troops on specific convoy operations outside of the primary Canadian area of operations. Engineers operate everywhere and it is not uncommon to have small engineer troops or sections involved in independent tasks.

COMMAND

National command of Canadian Army units in the former Yugoslavia was ensconced in the Commander, Canadian Contingent, UNPROFOR or CC UNPROFOR. This officer is usually either a brigadier-general or a major-general. He has a small staff and reports directly to Ottawa. He is sometimes "doublehatted" within the UNPROFOR HQ either as the second in command of UN forces or more typically as the Chief of Staff in the UN headquarters. The battalion and battle groups thus are responsible to UN command through the UN Protected Area Sector Commanders to the Force Commander and are also responsible to the Canadian Contingent Commander. The contingent commander unfortunately did not possess a national headquarters capable of effectively commanding and co-ordinating all Canadian Army activity in the former Yugoslavia in the same way as other national UNPROFOR contingents and this posed problems in protecting Canadian interests at times. The battalion and battle groups thus functioned independently and in some cases (mostly due to near instantaneous communications technology) directions came down to the commanding officers directly from Ottawa.

Notes to Chapter 1

1. Many people argue that there are a wide variety of historical reasons for the conflict. We take the short view here because the origins of the Balkan conflict are adequately explored in other works. I would recommend the reader consult the following: Lenard J. Cohen, *Broken Bonds: The Disintegration of Yugoslavia* (Boulder: Westview Press, 1992); Mihailo Crnobrnja, *The Yugoslav Drama* (Montreal: McGill-Queen's University Press, 1995) and Susan Woodward's *Balkan Tragedy: Chaos and Dissolution After the Cold War* (Washington: The Brookings Institute, 1995).

2. Michael Binyon, "Peacekeeping Body Takes Centre Stage in European Theatre," *The Times* (London), 9 Jul 92; Carl C. Krehbiel, *Confidence and Security Building Measures in Europe: The Stockholm Conference* (New York: Praeger, 1989) Ch. 1.

3. John Pinder, *European Community: The Building of a Union* (New York: Oxford University Press, 1991); the WEU naval force works alongside NATO's Standing Naval Force Atlantic in blockade operations. See "Op SHARP GUARD," in *Canadian Participation in Peacekeeping Operations and Related Missions*, August 1994 edition, produced by J3 Operations, National Defence HQ, Ottawa.

4. See Sean M. Maloney, *Operation BOLSTER: Canada and the European Community Monitor Mission in the Balkans, 1991-1994* (Toronto: Canadian Institute of Strategic Studies, 1997).

5. George Brock, "EC Pressed to send troops to Yugoslavia," *The Times* (London), 17 Sep 91; "Hurd halts EC troops plan for Yugoslavia," *The Times* (London), 20 Sep 91; Tom Walker, "Union considers peace force," *The Times* (London), 1 Oct 91.

6. George Brock, "EC ultimatum gives Serbs one week to accept peace proposal," *The Times* (London), 29 Oct 91; Michael Evans, "EC Imposes sanctions on Yugoslavia," *The Times* (London), 9 Nov 91.

7. Frederick Painton, "Attacking The Cuts", *Time*, 12 April 1993.

8. See, for examples, E.L.M. Burns, *Between Arab and Israeli* (Toronto: Clarke and Irwin, 1962) and Carl von Horn, *Soldiering For Peace* (New York: David McKay, Co., 1966).

9. James Bone, "Yugoslav presidency asks for UN troops," Anne McElvoy and Dessa Trevisan, "Serbia Changes mind on UN intervention," *The Times* (London), 11 Nov 91; United Nations Department of Public Information, "The United Nations and the Situation in the Former Yugoslavia: Reference Paper 15 March 1994," pp. 3-5.

10. Sean M. Maloney, 'Helpful Fixer or Hired Gun: Why Canada Goes Overseas," *Policy Options*, Jan-Feb 2001, pp. 59-65.

11 ACE is the serendipitous acronym of Allied Command Europe.

12. The navy participated in Op SHARP GUARD with one frigate, a support ship and two Aurora maritime patrol aircraft, while the air force provided one C-130 Hercules aircraft and an air movements unit to Op AIR BRIDGE. Sean M. Maloney, *The Hindrance of Military Operations Ashore: Canadian Participation in Operation SHARP GUARD, 1993-1995* (Halifax:Dalhousie, 1998).

13. "Op BOLSTER," *Canadian Participation in Peacekeeping Operations and Related Missions* August 1994 edition produced by J3 Operations, NDHQ, Ottawa; ECMM (9 Aug 1993) "Operations Brief."

14. Sean M. Maloney, *Operation BOLSTER: Canada and the European Community Monitor Mission in Yugoslavia* (Toronto: CISS, 1996).

15. Interview with Major Matthew Overton, Trenton, 14 Jan 1995.

16. Maloney, op. cit.

17. The first operations that Canada participated in were the United Nations Military Observer Group India-Pakistan (UNMOGIP) and the United Nations Truce Supervisory Organization (UNTSO) in the Middle East. See Fred Gaffen, In *The Eye of the Storm: A History of Canadian Peacekeeping* (Ottawa: Deneau and Wayne, 1987) and Burns, *Between Arab and Israeli*.

18. See *UNMO Handbook: Notes For the Guidance of Military Observers and Police Monitors*, UNPROFOR (1 Mar 1992, Field Operations Division, United Nations, New York).

19. United Nations. "Vance Plan: Concept for a United Nations peace-keeping operation in Yugoslavia, November-December 1991."; UN Department of Public Information *The United Nations and the Situation in the Former Yugoslavia (Reference paper 15 March 1994).* p. 3.

20. UN Department of Public Information *The United Nations and the Situation in the Former Yugoslavia (Reference paper 15 March 1994).* p. 3.

21. The 12 countries were Canada, Argentina, Belgium, the Czech Republic, Denmark, France, Jordan, Kenya, Nepal, Nigeria, Poland and Russia. The signals battalion was Dutch, the force engineers were Canadian (construction engineers were Finnish), the medical battalion was British and the movement control unit was from Norway.

22. This story is told in Lewis MacKenzie's *Peacekeeper: The Road to Sarajevo* (Vancouver: Douglas & McIntyre, 1993). See also interview with LCol Jamie Arbuckle, Ottawa, 7 Jan 95.

23. UN Department of Public Information *The United Nations and the Situation in the Former Yugoslavia (Reference paper 15 March 1994)*, p. 3; Department of National Defence, *Recognition Handbook: Former Yugoslavia Revised Edition 18 July 1994*, pp. 11-2/6 and 11-3/6; interview with LCol Marc Lessard, Kingston, 22 Dec 94.

24. Only the primary belligerents are noted because there are too many specialist groups, many of them rogue terrorist or criminal organizations, to mention here. Note that the UN did not recognize the Republic of Serb Krajinas.

25. UN Department of Public Information, *The United Nations and the Situation in the Former Yugoslavia (Reference paper 15 March 1994)* pp. 4, 56-59.

26. Ibid, pp. 66-67.

27. Canadian Participation in *Peacekeeping Operations and Related Missions* August 1994 edition produced by J3 Operations, NDHQ, Ottawa. pp. 3-12-1/4 to 4/4.

28. I have excluded Artillery units from this discussion since they did not provide formed peacekeeping units to UNPROFOR, although 5 RALC contributed an artillery company to UNPROFOR II in 1995.

29. Both armoured regiments and infantry battalions also have squadrons and companies devoted to administration and maintenance. These are not described here to conserve space.

30. Other Canadian APC types include the eight-wheeled Bison and, since 1999, a more modern variant called the LAV III. All of these wheeled light armoured vehicles are made by GMD Diesel Division in London, Ontario.

31. Information provided by Colonel George Rousseau (correspondence with author, 15 Sep 95).

32. Information provided by Colonel Paul Savereaux (interview with author, 18 Jan 95).

33. Information provided by Colonel Gary Furrie (correspondence with author, 9 Feb 96).

34. I am indebted to Captain Scott Arbuthnot for this information.

35. Canada 'gave' UNPROFOR the second battalion 'free.'

CHAPTER TWO

LIEUTENANT-COLONEL MICHEL JONES

Commanding Officer, 1er Royal 22e Régiment Battalion Group
Sector West, Croatia and Sarajevo, Bosnia, 1992

THE FIRST DEPLOYMENT

At that time, we didn't have any maps or anything to do any planning; we didn't know where we were going in ex-Yugoslavia! Nevertheless, we tried to get some maps from National Defence Headquarters and they told us they didn't have any! We told them to go to the Americans, but they said to us that they couldn't do that for security reasons, so we used one of our contacts, who was an Air Force intelligence sergeant in Ramstein, an American, and through him we got some maps, 250:000, 50:000. My intelligence sergeant went down there to get the maps and when he arrived there, the officer was not too sure if he could let the maps go so he called the Pentagon right away and within the following hour they got the answer, which was "Yes, give it to the Canadians." This was under the condition that we could not take the maps to ex-Yugoslavia.

During that time my intelligence officer was doing a small history book on the background of the country and what the political, economic and cultural situation was. We prepared a lexicon. French, English, Serbo-Croat. We prepared a training plan and administrative requests based on the organization proposed by the UN. Everything was going on between the 20th of January and around 7 February at which time General Clive Addy, the commander of 4 Canadian Mechanized Brigade, identified the unit that was going to go. Then all the planning procedures accelerated between the brigade and ourselves and with the Division, Mobile Command and National Defence HQ. We tried to get more information, but that was very difficult. As a matter of fact we received a bunch of draft orders from the national level one or two days prior to our deployment.

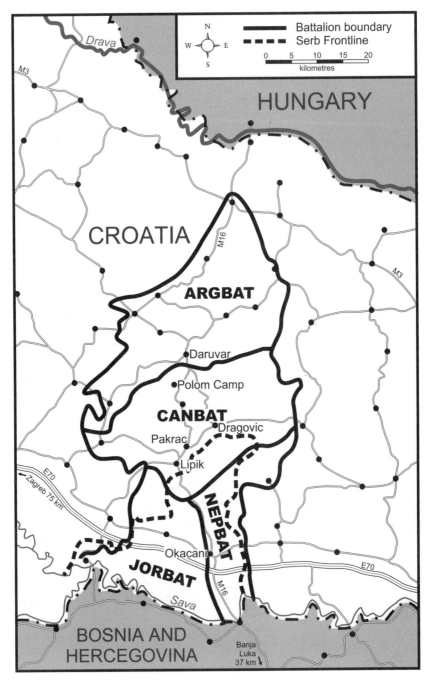

**Figure 6: UNPROFOR
Sector West, 1992**

The unit deployed to Sector West in Croatia on the 6th of April and on the first night November Company, 3rd Battalion, The Royal Canadian Regiment was on the ground and they were shelled. They had to do crash action from their bivouac area and the Command Post of A Company was shelled. Right off the train! The soldiers performed exceptionally well, and they did all the crash action like we trained for and nobody was hurt seriously. That was, in a sense, a good thing. It set the mind of the people; it was not an exercise anymore, that it was real! I explained that to them when we got off the train but when I visited them in the afternoon, I saw they were really relaxed and that set the pace for the rest of the mission.

THE MISSION IN SECTOR WEST

Our mission was to maintain peace within the boundaries in Sector West of the UN Protected Areas *(see Figure 6)*. In terms of belligerent forces, there were two main factions there, the Croats and the Serbs. However, there were extremists within each of those ethnic groups, what they called the Ustashi and the Chetniks. I have to say that, especially on the Croat side, they were not liked too much by their own people but they were used because they were important for special missions. On the Serb side, the Chetniks were a small group that were respected by the other Serbs but we didn't see them that much. There were about 40 men on the Croat side who were Ustashi and on the Serb side the number of Chetniks in our area was difficult to determine.

On the Croat side, there were three Operational Groups. An Operational Group is about the size of a brigade. There were about 15,000 Croats in this area. On the Serb side was the 5th Corps of the JNA. There were about 15,000 on the front line also. The Croats didn't have that much heavy equipment but they had a few tanks, T-54/55s, a few pieces of artillery, heavy mortars, 30mm anti-aircraft guns and the rest was small arms, and anti-tank cannon. On the Serb side, they were well equipped, from combat helicopters to guns, mortars, and tanks; the last version they produced there in Yugoslavia was called the M-84, which was like a Soviet T-72. Morale was low on the Serb side and the Croats were very aggressive at that time. You have to understand that from Christmas to the time when I arrived there in mid-March with the recce group, the Croats launched a counterattack in that area that was very successful and they repulsed the Serbs 150 kilometres.

The fighting was a mix of conventional and unconventional because there were raids by specialist groups who blew up houses. Each night you would hear houses being blown. It was part of ethnic cleansing and was mainly from the Croats' side. The Croat liaison officer attached to us explained it to me. He had been a commanding officer of a special forces unit and had been wounded. He explained to me all the procedures. They would call the family in the day and tell them by such a time in the evening they must be out of their house and gone. Then they would move in and blow it up. If the family didn't follow their instructions when they arrived there, they fired a Kalashnikov on the outside walls and told them, "You have ten minutes to get out, we are moving in and we'll blow it up." General Bob Gaudreau, the Canadian contingent commander, told me that they had found some mass graves and they were waiting to produce all the belligerent troops in front of the international court. Personally, while we were there, we didn't see anything. There were people killed because they were still shooting at each other but we didn't see any major massacres.

When we arrived on the ground, we were the first UN contingent in Sector West in the Protected Area, which meant that in Phase 1 we had to show the flag throughout the area. We established liaison with the Croats and Serbs and the success that we encountered in Sector West for demilitarization was based on the work of the liaison teams. There were liaison teams deployed on the Serb side and the Croat side, there was a communication net organized by radio and line, and at that point there was only one official crossing point on the front line. When we passed it over to the other contingent, which arrived about a month later, there were six official crossing points and about thirty non-official crossing points to allow our patrols to go freely and do what they had to do. Those patrols gathered a bunch of information on the equipment, the personnel, and locations of the same so when the demilitarization Phase 2 started we had the information on their order of battle and deployment so we were able to monitor the withdrawal of both forces very easily. The Canadians, without a doubt, had freedom of action. We were keeping the Sector West commander informed, and he was dealing with negotiators at a very high level, political and military. I attended most of those meetings. I explained how we were going to proceed and all of that.

After the shelling of 6th April, I requested a meeting with the Croatian Operational Group Commander in Pakrac. They were the ones who started the shelling. His command post was in the house where we used to meet. My driver and my Battle Captain, who were fully equipped with small walkie-talkies, looked like bodyguards. I had one of them stand at the bottom of the stairs, the other at the top of the stairs, and I was alone in the house. When the Operational Group Commander arrived at his house, he requested the authorization to come in! Five minutes after we started the meeting, my battle captain moved in with his weapon, looked around the conference room, gave me a nod from his head to make sure everything was all right. They were really impressed because the commander, when we left, looked at his bodyguard and gave him lots of shit.

We did that on the Serb side also. For us, we knew he'd show off. However, when they can see that we are professional soldiers, we're not there to play a game, and we are serious about what we are doing, that sort of thing gave us a lot of credibility.

We eventually had six official crossing sites and thirty un-official. The UN Chief of Staff of the sector told me, in amazement, that I was the only commanding officer that was allowed to do whatever he wanted to do. Sector West was the only UNPA that was completely demilitarized

After stabilizing Sector West in Croatia CANBAT I (a composite 1 R22eR-3 RCR battalion) deployed through a collapsing Bosnia to secure the Sarajevo airport in the summer of 1992. Despite the blue and white trappings, this mission could no longer be considered "peacekeeping." (CF Photo)

and during Phase 3, which was to restore normal life conditions, the Serbs could go on the Croats' side and vice versa and they were meeting each day of the week. It started with a group of 50 people and when we left it was up to 600 people that were meeting there, old friends who were seeing each other again and asking how it was going. The people, the normal population, they're not into this war. I mean it was really the people at the top who wanted to preserve their power and all the privileges that are associated with it. So, that's what was accomplished in Sector West.

DEPLOYMENT TO SARAJEVO

Brigadier-General Lewis MacKenzie, UNPROFOR's Chief of Staff, told me sometime in May 1992 that there was some possibility for the battalion group to deploy to Sector South in the Krajina because there were some major problems there and Sector West was pretty stable at that time. He asked me to start to do some planning without spreading the word around. So I kept it at my level, and we started to think about it. At mid-May, Mackenzie called me again and asked me to send a small group to help the Canadians at the HQ in Sarajevo, in Bosnia, to help move their personal belongings and the normal stuff you see in a command post HQ, so I dispatched Captain Belisle with about fifteen people. When you do that the group has to be self-contained and self-sufficient, so we sent mechanics, medical people, rations, water, POL and that sort of thing so they could cover all aspects because you couldn't rely on anybody else. That was my philosophy. I only relied on people I could trust, my own people. I couldn't trust anybody else because UNPROFOR at that time was not well organized. Everything that we did, we did ourselves and we didn't count on anybody else. We asked for some assistance and all that but all the basic things, combat supplies, munitions, and everything was done by ourselves. My motto was Adapt, Improvise, and Overcome, as simple as that. So that group went to Sarajevo, along with a Public Affairs cell that moved there at the request of General Mackenzie and on 15 May 92, Sarajevo blew up and started to be a nightmare. My people were caught in that and that's where Captain Belisle and Corporal Morin got their Meritorious Service Medals for their actions in rescuing wounded people.

In early June, General Mackenzie called me and said, "Michel, you will probably deploy to Sarajevo. I would like you to gather the people you need and come to Belgrade to do some planning. Then you will move to Sarajevo with me and you will conduct your recce on the ground." So that's what we did. We were about thirty people and again we were self-sufficient. I brought my Orders Group, less a few individuals, and my specialists, medical, logs and so on. We went to Belgrade, did some planning, produced a concept, and I briefed General Mackenzie. He approved it and then I briefed Lieutenant-General Nambiar, the UNPROFOR commander, who approved it also. We went on the ground to Sarajevo after spending about four days in Belgrade doing administrative planning. Operational planning was done on the map within a day or two while the rest was administrative planning.

We went on the ground, did the recce. It went well the first two or three days, and as a matter of fact the Serbs offered to give us the airport, which we did accept, but we didn't have enough people so we took only the main terminal. The rest of the airport was occupied by Serbian soldiers and within twenty-four hours they used us as a shield and the airport became their Line of Departure for an attack they were launching into the suburb of Dobrinja. So I spoke to the commander at the airport and told him that that was unacceptable and if he didn't stop that attack we were going to leave. I called General Mackenzie, explained the situation, and he said "Okay, we don't have a choice, we pull out" and we did. Then after that it was impossible for us to conduct our recce properly because we only had soft-skinned vehicles, and we didn't have any armoured vehicles, so I asked General Mackenzie if we could go back to Daruvar. You have to understand there were a lot of things that happened also at the planning stage in Sarajevo. At one point General Mackenzie asked me what kind of equipment I would like to have and I produced a shopping list, which he approved. As a matter of fact the TOW launcher vehicles and the self-propelled mortars were in the initial proposal I put for the complete

**Figure 7: 1R22eR Battlegroup Deployment
to Sarajevo, 30 June to 2 July, 1992**

deployment from Lahr, Germany to Daruvar, Croatia, but the UN denied it. The main reason for the TOW was for the sights, Thermal Imaging sights, and in addition to that the range of the TOW was greater than the range of the belligerents' anti-aircraft guns that were set up pointing at the airport. We would have been able to shoot at those if it were required. There were a bunch of belligerent tanks also around the airport. We registered a lot of targets when we were there! These were normal, necessary steps for our protection. I also requested APC ambulances, a bunch of ammunition, and defensive stores like barbed wire and trip flares. I didn't know exactly where all the major belligerent equipment was, trenches and all that all around Sarajevo and along the routes. We developed several options for those routes. We needed to know about destroyed bridges and that sort of thing. So it worked out. We did a staff college exercise. It was quite interesting to see the big machine at work and you can get a lot done and out of it *[see Figure 7]*.

Our mission this time was to secure the airport, open it, and to deliver humanitarian aid within the periphery of the city. When I went back to Daruvar, I was sure, personally, that we would never deploy. The situation was terrible in Sarajevo. They were still going at each other and the battle was raging. President Mitterand, the French President, flew into the airport and it changed everything. Within forty-eight hours I received the order to move. As a matter of fact there was a glitch on the command line. I received instructions from Sarajevo, General Mackenzie, to go on 24-hours notice to move on such a date, and the HQ UNPROFOR was now in Zagreb, because they had moved, and was issuing confusing orders. So, General Mackenzie called me on the 29th of June around 1800 hours and said, "Michel we have to move now!" I said, "Sir, I am on 24-hours notice to move, we're not ready to move now." You just don't move 300 vehicles and 850 men just like that. He said, "You have to put something on the road." I said, "Let me check, and I'll call you in two hours." So I called him back two hours later and said, "Okay, I can put out about 300 men and 100 vehicles on the road and the rest will follow twenty-four hours after." He said, "It's perfect."

It worked really well in the sense that we did a lot of liaison in Sarajevo with the belligerent forces and also in Banja Luka and my senior liaison officer there was doing it, clearing and

The UN in New York attempted to block the deployment of Canadian TOW Under Armour vehicles, deeming them "too aggressive." On numerous occasions the threat of force had to be used by Canadian soldiers to ensure the battalion's safe arrival at Sarajevo and the TUA played a key role (Author's Collection).

making sure that the route was okay. When I got back to Daruvar, everything was ready except some of the trucks were not loaded and still needed some equipment. So that had to be loaded and we didn't have the French transport vehicles that were required. They joined us in the evening and at 0400 we crossed the start line. We stopped in Banja Luka for refuelling. I had about three liaison teams up with the recce, my engineers sergeant, and my interpreter sergeant, who spoke Serbo-Croat, to clear the route. At Banja Luka they told me that on the route recommended by the Serbs, there was a bridge that we couldn't use because it had collapsed so I changed the routes right away, which was actually the route I had intended to take originally. It went well until we got to Jajce.

THE JAJCE INCIDENT

Jajce was a Croat town surrounded by Serbs, and my liaison officer did have some problems. They did not get the authorization to go through. The political man, the Croats' man, was not too co-operative so they came back to me and after a half hour of negotiation, I got authorization to go through the town and we went up to a few kilometres before Turbe, and that's where I met the warlord that stopped the convoy.

He was unhappy, and he was pissed. There was a political advisor with him who was cranking him up against the UN and all that. The situation was very, very tense and I negotiated two hours with him but to no avail. He was so pissed that there was no way, so we turned around for about 15 klicks and spent the night on the road. My intention was not to go back to Daruvar, so I told myself I'd wait till he sobers up and then try again. The following morning, there was another Serbian commander and he was surprised to see us there. He said there was no reason to stop us as he did receive the orders to let us go through. He said that he'd try to reason with the warlord. So he went to the command post of the warlord and he came back two hours later and said that there was no way, he won't let you through. He said he'd call the Serbs higher HQ and they'd dispatch a liaison officer that would tell him to let us pass. Finally the LO arrived, went to see the warlord, and told us that the warlord didn't want to let us through. I said, "Well, that's enough. I'm going through." When I said that to the people at the checkpoint, they said, "If you go through, if you try to force your way through, we're going to open fire." I said, "If you open fire, I'm going to respond and that's it!" I said, "Two o'clock. If the warlord doesn't show up, or your boss doesn't show up, we're going through." Finally I told the guy that there are a few elements that were deployed for security reasons, and finally I moved my APC up front. At one point there were some Serb reinforcements that were going to the checkpoint. I told the captain in charge there that if he didn't send back the reinforcements I was going to open fire without provocation, so he obeyed. Then the warlord appeared. I sat with the warlord and there were some very intense moments. At that point in time the weapons were cocked, our snipers were deployed, one of the platoon commanders had done his recce for an assault, the TOW launchers and heavy machine guns had their targets, and all the fire orders were given. Now I was negotiating with the warlord and he said, "Yes I have arranged everything for you my friend. You will take that route." He told me that I had to go back to Banja Luka and take the route that he wanted me to take. I said, "No way! I'm going through. I'm not going 200 additional kilometres." I stood up and he took my arm and he said, "No, no, sit down. We'll talk." I did know at that point that we were going to go through, as he was sober by this time. Finally, after half an hour of negotiations, I wrote in his book that I was discharging him from all responsibilities and all that bullshit. He said, "I'm going back to my command post to give orders to my people and at the same time I'll come back in about thirty minutes to give you some information about minefields that you are going to encounter when you cross the front line." And he did so. Then we went through.

I have to say that the route that the Serbs wanted us to take was recce'd later on in September by one of my liaison officers and he told me after he went that if we had taken that route I would have probably court-martialled him because it wasn't practical for the types of vehicles that we had. Anyhow, we crossed the front line, met with the Croats on the other side, and we were welcomed. They assisted us gladly, it went very well and finally we passed the night at Vitez. The following morning, around five o'clock, we started to move and we entered Sarajevo around ten o'clock in the morning, which was where I met General Mackenzie.

SARAJEVO INTERNATIONAL AIRPORT

Sarajevo went very well. An hour after we were on the ground the troops were dispatched to their positions and they started to dig in. Everything was dug in, vehicles, trenches with overhead protection and all that. Forty-eight hours after we were there, we started to deliver humanitarian aid. We opened six distribution centres; it went very well, that task. There were a few incidents in Sarajevo, and in total we had 18 people wounded in Sarajevo, including a corporal from November Company, 3 RCR [Corporal Reid], who lost his foot and there was another one evacuated, Corporal Smith, who had shrapnel in his leg. There was a lot of negotiation in Sarajevo, and we were able to secure the routes for the delivery of humanitarian aid. There were eight routes we secured for the evacuation of dead and wounded people and we started to negotiate the demilitarization of Sarajevo. I was very close to getting it done. In Sarajevo, at this time, we were only dealing with two factions. I was dealing with the presidents of the Crisis Committees on both sides. There was the Bosnian side and there was the Serbo-Bosnian group. On the Bosnian side, I was dealing with Dr Ganic, who was later the Vice-President of Bosnia, and on the military side was the Deputy Commander of the military force, Colonel Ciber. These guys were both Croat and Muslim; Ganic was Muslim and Ciber was Croat. On the Serb side, I was dealing with Dr Kolovicj, who was the president of their Crisis Committee, and also the military guy, Citic, who was responsible for Sarajevo to Dobrinja and up to the north. So I was quite busy.

During the day generally it was quiet but at night shelling and shooting resumed and there were some small attacks launched by the Bosnians against the Serbs, but more patrols than anything else. I mean it was fighting in built-up areas, so it was hard to operate. The airport was on the southern side of the city, and the forces around it changed daily. You had Sarajevo, itself, you had Dobrinja in front of the airport, and on the other side you had a bunch of small communities that were on the periphery of Sarajevo. When I was talking with the Bosnian government, I had to go to Sarajevo, when I was dealing with the Serbs I had to go to Pale, and it was very challenging. General Mackenzie approved the demilitarization plan that I'd put forward on the UN side and he said to me, "Go ahead and do the negotiation." The Serbs approved it with small changes and what they proposed made sense. The Bosnians, that was another ball game. They produced five options based on what I produced and there was only one that was workable for a starting point. It required a lot of negotiation. My proposal triggered a battle within the Bosnian government. The civilian side wanted my plan to be approved but the military did not. Finally the military won the battle. It was a struggle. Normally I would get an

During the initial battles in central Bosnia, UN Aid convoys had to be escorted under fire by CANBAT I M-113 APCs through Sarajevo's infamous Sniper's Alley, an open multi-lane thoroughfare leading from the airport to the city centre. (CF Photo)

answer in forty-eight hours but it took three weeks for the Bosnians to come forward with their options. When they produced them, it was time for us to leave in July so I passed it on to the UN Deputy Commander of Sector Sarajevo, who was a French colonel.

The French replaced us at the airport and the Ukrainians and Egyptians replaced us at Beaver Camp. The way they worked out the plan was that the French were responsible for the security of the airport; the Ukrainians and the Egyptians were responsible for the delivery of humanitarian aid, with the assistance of the French because they had all sorts of APCs. The main problem was that these three small units had 400 people each and it was a political decision every time they tried to do something. They didn't have enough APCs, less than I had but I had a lot more resources than they had. They didn't have the heavy weapons I had, either, so it was very difficult for them to organize and co-ordinate the delivery of aid.

PERSONAL ASSESSMENT

It was the most exciting experience I have had in my career thus far and I used all the training that was given to me. We shouldn't change our training because it is perfect. I saw soldiers from about thirty-six different countries and there is no doubt that our soldiers are the best in the world. The reaction of the soldiers when shell fragments hit them was fantastic. They went to the UMS for a patch and then they went back to work, even though we told them to relax, they carried on. The soldiers: Canada has outstanding soldiers.

CHAPTER THREE

MAJOR R. W. (DES) DESLAURIER
MASTER WARRANT OFFICER J. M. C. LAPLANTE
CAPTAIN TIM GORMAN
CAPTAIN J. M. CLARK

4 Combat Engineer Regiment
Force Engineer Regiment, Croatia UN Protected Areas, 1992

FIRST IN TO THE FORMER REPUBLIC OF YUGOSLAVIA: DARUVAR, SECTOR WEST

4 Combat Engineer Regiment actually arrived in-theatre two weeks before the 1 Van Doo Battalion Group on the 1st of March and we were the first organized unit of all the UNPROFOR countries to arrive in-theatre.

Our recce party, lead by the CO, had left three weeks prior to our arrival and they had to determine what tasks we would have to do in the FRY, which in turn would help get our organization down pat. We also needed to know where we were going to live. The CO travelled all over and went to all the UN Protected Areas. We originally thought that Banja Luka would do. The recce party got up there and found that the road infrastructure was terrible. It was a mountainous road and the rail lines were broken between there and the rest of the country. We eventually decided not to go there and went to Daruvar instead because Daruvar was central and had good infrastructure and we could deploy easily to all four UNPAs. We also knew that the Battle Group was going to be nearby and it would make resupply easier if we had both units in the same area. We established different camps but they were only a few miles from each other. It was the correct decision, as it allowed us to support the Van Doos and allowed the trains to go to only one location from Lahr instead of multiple destinations.

After we arrived in Daruvar, one of the sections found an old, abandoned ordnance depot, complete with bunkers, that had been bombed and subjected to artillery and had been fought

The former Yugoslavia was one of the world's largest producers of land mines and small arms. Decentralized JNA mine stockpiles were looted at the start of the conflict and were a significant risk to the UNPROFOR troops deployed throughout the region. (CF Photo)

over back and forth. It was very close to where we were located, so our sections and our Explosive Ordnance Disposal teams went in and they found pallets and pallets of mines! They were literally just piled up and thrown helter-skelter because of the fighting. These buildings and bunkers contained examples of just about every type of mine, artillery shell, tank shell, etc. that the JNA had used and had been used subsequently by the belligerents. That saved our bacon because we could get in, x-ray them, pick them up carefully, take them apart and learn how they operated. We then developed lesson packages and comprehensive knowledge that we needed to teach everybody else. Finding this site put us back on track.

MISSIONS AND TASKS IN THE U.N. PROTECTED AREAS

Once both units were deployed in-theatre, the infantry battalion commander, Lieutenant-Colonel Michel Jones, became the deputy force commander for the Canadian Contingent. The force commander was Brigadier-General Mackenzie and he worked out of Sarajevo, then Belgrade and finally Zagreb. We were, however, two separate entities when it came down to work. The Canadian-only things went through Lieutenant-Colonel Jones. 4 Combat Engineer Regiment was a UN Force-level regiment and as such worked directly for UNPROFOR HQ. For work, and for taskings, we received our orders straight from the force HQ based on what the other UN battalions needed done.

In terms of 4 CER's mission, we were responsible for all combat or field engineer, heavy equipment or armoured engineer support for the entire force (UNPROFOR). This included mine awareness training, mine clearance of areas to support construction, and building accommodations. We gave support to all five sectors (including Sarajevo) and supported all twelve UN infantry battalions.

The biggest task that we had was mine awareness training for every single person in UNPROFOR, civilian UN personnel including UNCIVPOL, and for local civilians. Everybody had to know what the threat was and it was extensive. They needed to know what was out there, how to mark them, and how to report them to us. This was all necessary so that our EOD people could go take care of them. The mine-awareness training centre of the house was the most visible and urgently needed right away.

The second task was enormous in itself. This was the actual clearance of mines reported and clearance of the areas that we were moving around and living in. Every infantry battalion in UNPROFOR required an enormous area to operate and deploy into. All the routes from their checkpoints, observation posts, headquarters, and base camps had to be cleared, so we accompanied each battalion as it deployed.

Other tasks spun off from that, like the construction of parking lots and paths for the camps. In many cases the camps were in farmer's fields. We had to go in with heavy equipment, strip off the topsoil, bring in load after load of gravel and build them gravel pads. We consulted with the battalions on local buildings and had to explain to some of the battalions that the latrine had to be down wind from the mess, and things like that, within the camp layout.

We were surprised that many of the UNPROFOR battalions lacked the knowledge and experience in building field fortifications, of how to sandbag, and build bunkers. We had to go to each infantry battalion (with the exception of the CANBAT) and teach them how to do this! Same with checkpoints: "Well, you have your checkpoint here, in this field of two-year-old corn that's roughly waist high. If you move your checkpoint slightly down the road to that open field, it will be easier for us to clear it out." Generally the units were receptive to our advice, but sometimes they weren't. Russians are always right, even if they are wrong.

None of the battalions had worked with Canadians before and I suppose our advice at times was suspect. Some of our recommendations were not accepted, some for tactical reasons, some for other reasons. In many cases we were eventually proven right in the end and we had to go back and sort it out. Our guys, right down to the corporal level, were giving advice to UN platoon and company commanders and sergeants were giving advice to battalion commanders. Once the UN battalions were comfortable with our expertise, they started listening to our people.

The fact that the other countries were not prepared was very obvious. A country would come up to us and request the loan of just a small generator because they had no means of generating power. So here we are down there with all our equipment and we in fact ended up sending sections out to others to help set up. We had to teach them how to get water, and how to get food, the whole gamut. Some of the countries were absolutely lost and would have been completely useless if the Canadians had not been there to help them.

Some of the Third World countries in particular posed many problems for us and created many situations that were very laughable. Having to go in and construct a pen to hold their chickens ... that was different! This particular battalion had live chickens for their ration supply. Other Third World battalions had trouble adapting to the weather. It was May-June and in the evenings it would go down to 15-16 degrees Celsius. We'd run around in shorts and they'd be in a raincoat with a toque on, freezing to death in a pair of sandals. I mean these people didn't even have combat boots. I don't know how they made out in the winter.

Another situation occurred when one of our junior officers was driving down a very narrow road. He was following a tractor pulling a wagon onto which a cow had been tied. When he attempted to pass, the cow panicked and ran into the jeep and the jeep ended up right on top of the cow with all four wheels off the ground! The jeep had to be recovered off the cow. The Nepalese were nearby, came to investigate and they got pretty crazy because of the religious aspects of this. They didn't want us to touch it and they really got upset when we did the recovery!

The one thing that really helped us was our previous experience with working within the UN. A lot of our people had been on many taskings and that helped us help the other people out to a great degree and we also had the luxury of bringing in everything from Lahr by train. We had extra stuff with the close-out in Germany and we were able to give some stuff away to the other units to help them out.

RELATIONSHIPS WITH THE SERBS AND CROATS: THE BRIDGE

In terms of our relationships with the belligerents, we found that the Serbs were generally very professional. They had a better idea of what their capabilities were and they were less likely to start wildly saying that they could do this or that, or making promises that they couldn't keep. They were more likely to tell you to fuck off and there was no way they were going to help. On the other hand, the Croatians were very much, "Oh ho, we'll do that for you, *nema problema,* yeah, no problems" and then they'd turn around and fuck you. We found the Croatians to be flakier than the Serbs in some areas.

When we first arrived, the Croats believed that we were there to help them in their efforts. At first they were willing to do anything for us, and give us anything we needed. That honeymoon period wore off when they realized that the Canadians were down there to work for the UN and the UN was impartial. At first they were very, very friendly. They wanted us to come out for barbecues and they were consistently trying to get us into their social life so that they could argue their point of view on the war to us. It became nauseating to deal with them because they would try to win you over against those devilish Serbs and they were always trying to coerce you into doing something for them.

One of our officers lived in fear of having to deal with a particular Croatian colonel, a confirmed alcoholic. This Croat colonel always showed up half in the bag and he wanted our CO to come out for a drink so he could get us to do something for his side. We had to avoid this guy at every instance.

The really outstanding thing that stands out in my mind from dealing with both sides was the amount of palm-greasing both sides expected. In one instance we were trying to build a bridge in Sector North. The bridges had been blown and they only had one half-decent bridge, but nothing you'd want to send traffic over on. We spent three months trying to build a bridge

Infrastructure seriously damaged by the heavy house-to-house fighting in Vukovar had to be cleared to facilitate the delivery of humanitarian aid and to stabilize the situation. Here a Badger AEV from 4 Combat Engineer Regiment goes to work. (CF Photo)

there. The UN won't pay to make any repairs to war damage so any materials would have to be supplied by the locals and the amount the locals wanted for the materials was disgusting. We told them, "Look, we have a whole squadron here and we'd like to build you a bridge. You get us lumber and Bailey panels, and we'll build you a bridge. You guys aren't going to have this expertise or the money to build the bridge in the next 250 years. There are no construction companies." They stalled for three months and told us, "We'll wait and talk to the next engineer unit that comes in." These guys were expecting us to line their pockets. They really don't care what's happening to the town because food isn't getting through. The town did not get its bridge.

SARAJEVO INTERNATIONAL AIRPORT

Although Sarajevo was very prominent in the media, it was only a small part of the operations conducted by 4 CER. The field troop we'd given to the Van Doos went with the battalion down there. There were three field sections plus a construction engineering section with tradesmen. We attached a couple of Badger armoured engineer vehicles and these were sent down to help dig in the infantry battalion. We sent a lot of tradesmen: plumbers, electricians, and carpenters and these people helped get Sarajevo International Airport back on line. We also established a water supply. The Sarajevo operation wasn't really different from the other work we had been doing in the other sectors. Building and ground still had to be cleared, bunkers had to be built and trenches dug. The Badger really earned its keep there in Sarajevo. The only difference was that there was fighting going on in Sarajevo, as opposed to the relative peace in the other sectors. It didn't affect our tasks and we carried on just the same.

One exception was digging in at the airport. We did have to do this under fire and we appreciated the Badger's armour. We had to rip up parts around the airfield itself to dig in the TOW vehicles and APCs. We tried to find electrical diagrams of the airport, and diagrams of the radar landing system. We couldn't find them and so we were forced to dig the fighting positions in without any knowledge of where these cables were. We weren't responsible for the running of the airport but we were responsible for its defence. In doing so, the Badger ripped out the radar landing system, which meant that no humanitarian aid could land at Sarajevo until it was fixed. The Badger isn't a dainty piece of equipment; it's a 47-ton tank with a bucket and a blade on it, all operated by a hydraulic system that can't tell the difference between granite, clay, mud or electrical cable. We tore up the system in about six places, including phone lines, radar and lighting systems. Everywhere the infantry dug in, we cleared the area, dug them a hole and then turned over to the French technical people who spliced the cables back together. We were able to get the airport up and running again and we did the best we could.

SECTOR EAST: VUKOVAR

We got into Vukovar and the Russian UN contingent moved in with us. Their chain of command was confusing. They really didn't have section commanders since this was supposed to be an elite unit but our guys outshone them in everything we did. They didn't have the same quality of leadership at the corporal, master corporal or sergeant level. They had a coup mentality. The battalion commander is worried about a coup by his second in command so he really didn't keep his subordinates informed. The only person who could make decisions was the commander. "Well, we want to move that garbage bin." "Well, we have to ask the commander if we can move the garbage bin." You had to work for the right person in the Russian organization otherwise you were just wasting your fucking time.

It was an eye opener for our guys to see the Russians at work. We had to keep separate meal hours. They were eating this barley mash three times a day and we of course were eating something a hell of a lot better. It did cause a few problems with their people after a while and they were booted out of the camp for some time. There was one instance where a couple of their young fellows went into our kitchen and helped themselves to a juice. Their whole group was formed up the next morning and the guy who had stolen the juice was literally beaten for about half an hour while our guys stood around. It's a different system. They had ripped the juice off to use as mix for their booze and Russian soldiers were not allowed to drink. These guys got caught. This beating was more than just discipline. Half was for their benefit and the other half was for ours. They were very big into the macho, "This is the Russian way of doing things and you guys are all weak," etc. The Russian commander got drunk one night and came down to our mess to talk with us. He told us that all Canadian soldiers were fat, overweight and useless. We had to take a couple of our corporals aside so that they didn't take him outside and kick the shit out of him.

In Vukovar, once the day was over, and the job was done, that was it. We couldn't go downtown, as there was too much fire going on, which was mostly harassment by local, drunk soldiers who would shoot just for the heck of it. For at least a couple of months, we couldn't leave the camp. We were stuck right there. We did have some RCMP guys from UNCIVPOL with us. They really appreciated the fact that we were there because they could affiliate with us. They joined all our messes, particularly the Senior Non-Commissioned Officers' Mess. Without them giving us that extra side for a social life, it would have been a pretty dull operation there. They were definitely part of the team, a good part of the team.

Once things settled down in town, we started doing work on the buildings and infrastructure, setting up sanitation sites, which was an eye-opener. We had this particular jogging route that we used when we were let out of the camp. We jogged past this particular bridge every day. Just to the side of the bridge, a month after we got there, a young child was playing there and lost his leg to an anti-personnel mine. We finally realized that there was still stuff out there that had to be cleared and then we started seeing dogs uncovering human limbs, legs and arms, along the river near the bridge. We got in touch with the RCMP, cleared the area, and uncovered a lot of mass graves. The Serbs had told us that this area was mined and that we should stay out. There was always some corpse floating down the river. We called them "buoys" or "Bob" in a generic sense. That was the scariest thing, the ethnic cleansing thing. We had people pounding down our gate day after day, telling us that their mother or father had just been beaten to death the night before and they had to sign over their house to the Serbs and that type of thing. People were going missing every day there.

ASSESSMENT

It's a traumatic experience for any unit, battalion, regiment or whatever to go into an area that does not have any infrastructure, that has been set up by the UN and it's the start of mission. The mandate that we were operating under restricted what we could do, and we could only handle things that directly affected us. Although we certainly saw a lot of misery, we couldn't do anything beyond accomplishing our mission. We'd help if we could, or had time, and if our other jobs were done. We'd help if it was a humanitarian issue, but if it was something else, we couldn't. We had to divorce ourselves from the situation so that we could work. You didn't want to get too involved with the plight of the local people. We were there for a specific purpose and we tried to keep that in mind, even when we were dealing with people experiencing misery or hardship.

We did do a lot of extra things in order to help the population. We focused on mine awareness and our teams spent a considerable amount of time at the local schools. Everywhere we went, we tried to gather up kids in schools and our aim was to try and save a few kids' lives by telling them what was what and to stay away from it. Our guys spent a lot of time making rubble out of condemned buildings to help the communities get back on track. Vukovar is an example. It was a complete shambles. The rubble stopped us from providing aid to the citizens so we cleared the roads even though it took days and days. We spent an awful lot of effort on an individual basis with guys trying to organize food and clothing to be brought in from Canada and Lahr. There was a lot of this type of work. The hospital in Daruvar was another example. Serb aircraft had bombed it so we took our equipment down there. The hospital was still standing but it posed a threat to the public in the sense that it was about to fall down on them. In an afternoon we cleared it and took it down. These sorts of things aided the population from our perspective and they definitely liked us for most of the time we were there. We did a lot of extra work for them to make their lives better.

CHAPTER FOUR

MASTER CORPORAL ROB CALHOUN

C-9 Gunner, 2nd Bn The Royal Canadian Regiment Battle Group Gorazde and Srebrenica, Bosnia, 1993

ORGANIZATION AND MISSION

We were the first Canadians in Bosnia, besides November Company of 3 RCR, with the Van Doos who were over when Brigadier-General Mackenzie was in Sarajevo. Our battle group consisted of 2 RCR, with one company, B Company, from 1 RCR, to help augment the battalion, and there were some guys from 5 RGC, engineers, 12 RBC, and other logistics units.

The original mission was to deploy to Banja Luka in Bosnia, south of the Sava River. I believe Banja Luka is where we were supposed to deploy to and from therewe were going to set up a base of operations. Every week we would do convoy escort and then bring humanitarian aid to the surrounding small towns and enclaves that needed aid, like the Croat enclave of Doboj, and I can't pronounce some of the other ones. Once we actually got on the ground and found out we weren't going anywhere, the mission pretty well almost got cancelled.

HURRY UP AND WAIT: LIPIK, SECTOR WEST

The idea was that we were going to go to Lipik, wait, and then be deployed to Banja Luka. We did not know how long we were going to have to wait. We drove there and that's where we got our armoured personnel carriers, in Croatia. We were about thirty minutes outside Daruvar. We were living in tents and sleeping on the ground for the first week. So the living conditions were rather austere to say the least, and we lived in modular tents and that was it. I still say the happiest day of the tour was when I got my combat cot, two weeks into the tour. We were sleeping on sort of a slab of tarmac. That was what we had the company area set up on, with a long length of modular tents. Each platoon had one and there was one for the company HQ.

The Croatian town was somewhat populated but it was really blitzed by the fighting there. The people didn't look too badly off, as at that point there had been no fighting there for several months, six or seven I think, so really they were slowly rebuilding and getting back into the swing of things. It was very quiet there when we arrived. It was obvious that the Serbs weren't going to move back in there or anything and people were carrying on with their daily lives, weren't living extravagantly and were pretty much indifferent to our presence. I think it depended on the individual, some liked that we were there and other people didn't, but it wasn't overwhelming one way or another.

GOOD OLD CANADIAN INGENUITY

The advance party had everything set up. Everything was covered in mud, including the liners of the tents. When we first moved in, there were mice and everything crawling all over our stuff and rats, a lot of big rats because we were in stables. The location of the entire company, battalion HQ and the field kitchen were in a terrible facility. We didn't have a shower tent, so we went into town a couple of times; it was a week before I showered. We went into Daruvar to some little industrial place, a metal factory or something, and we had a shower in there. We did that a couple of times, and then we finally rigged up something on our own. We found some hoses, God only knows what was in them, boiled them, and cleaned them up. We took a bilge pump from an APC, had immersion heaters put inside a Water Buffalo trailer, got a welder and we filled it by hand. Sometimes you had to fill it by hand; sometimes we took it into town where they had a hose set up. We put the immersion heaters in there, stuck the bilge pump in and had nozzles off the ends of fire extinguishers and that's how we showered! It was a high maintenance tasking! We showered like that for four months.

TRAINING, WAITING AND WATCHING

We did road moves in order to keep people from pulling their hair out. We would take the company, with all our carriers, and would do convoy taskings, just to get the company moving, you know, to make sure the vehicles were working and keep them running. I don't know if there was any grand plan or reason for it but we drove around Croatia. At one point we went down to the bridge that we were supposed to cross to go to Banja Luka and we turned back around and came back. These drives were quite peaceful with no problems at all. The only time, it was kind of funny, was the time we went to that bridge. There had been a lot of UN negotiations at the higher levels to let us go, but the Serbs wouldn't allow it, so we drove through this town and there wasn't a soul out, just a company of carriers rumbling through this town. We turned around down by the bridge and came back. When we came back the whole street was lined with soldiers; it was kind of funny, and I guess we had surprised them! We certainly stirred people up; I guess they thought we were going to actually force our way across the bridge or something. They were all giving us a dirty look and wondering what we were doing there.

NEW TASKINGS AND LEAVE

One of the companies in the battalion, Hotel Company, had been fortunate. Since the Banja Luka tasking had been scrapped, the CO was trying to find a mission for us, something for us to do. So basically one of the companies, H Coy, had been deployed to Macedonia as part of the UN Preventive Deployment to help set up a base for the Swedes, who were going to take over that area. Their job was to go there, help them and act as an advance party. They had to go and do something and we were quite envious of them. As it turned out, it happened to be better for us, and our company in particular. We knew we were going to Bosnia, we knew they were going to be headed towards Sarajevo somewhere, but we were unsure and there had been a lot of rumours and nothing was written in stone yet, so we were about 90% sure we were going to go. We packed a lot of things up and got ready to go.

THE ROAD

We went to this port of Rijeka in Croatia and stayed on a cargo ship. It was a loud old rust bucket. My naval terminology is not up to par but it was a ferry crammed with our vehicles and we were in a small hold with a metal floor that was only five feet tall and I had to bend over to walk. We were on this ship for one night, seventeen hours. We moved down the coastline to Ploce and there we disembarked, got on buses and they started taking us to Bosnia. I ended up driving a CUCV [diesel truck] so we drove from the port of Ploce through Mostar in Bosnia, which was where there was a lot of fighting going on now, then through some other small towns, and then up through these hills (I call it the "truck of Hannibal") in the wintertime. It was really slippery, icy, a lot of civilian trucks were getting stuck, and no one else could get up them but we managed to do it. There were these big switchbacks, like in a cartoon, no guardrails or anything! If you went over you went over.

Fortunately, that didn't happen. There was a lot of civilian traffic on the road, and UN traffic bringing aid in. This was the only road into this area that we were going to because the main highway was blocked. It was some of the most beautiful country I have ever seen, mountains were very pretty, and the coastline, if you saw it, was pretty. Mostar, though, was badly blown up and most of the other towns were as well. Ploce was like Zagreb, untouched. The further you got into the country, the more you saw the effects, where more intense fighting had occurred.

KISELJAK: BOSNIA-HERZEGOVINA

Once we got up this hill, we went through a little Croat town called Kiseljak, where one Canadian company, K Coy, was posted with their TOW launchers and everything. Then just ten minutes down the road was Visoko, a little Bosnian, Muslim town, and that's where the battle group was stationed. They started building the camp there. They had only been there a couple of days and then once I got there we laid wire, and built up our tents. We had the tents set up in a big concrete building, which had taken a couple of direct hits from mortars and artillery. That's what we put our modulars in and they were much better conditions than Lipik. Civilians and military worked right out of this place we were in, and it was like an industrial complex. This would be our base where we did humanitarian convoys to wherever for the next three months.

The locals, Bosnian Muslims, thought it was fine, and they were more indifferent than anything. We had incidents where people really didn't like us there and we had incidents where they liked us. There were a lot of people there. We had come from Croatia, where people looked fine and we went to Visoko and people looked, so-so, and then it would get worse as we went along.

This was only about a thirty-minute carrier ride to Sarajevo, so it was pretty close and it was about 30 kilometres west of Sarajevo. At night, up in the hills, we could see firefights going on and hear shooting. We had a lot of mortars land in our compound and close to it. They were letting us know that they didn't like us there. You could see tracers, volleys of machine-gun fire, and .50 cal being exchanged.

THE GORAZDE RELIEF MISSION

There was never any set routine like in Visoko, every day was different, and we prepared for something different every day. We were setting up the camp, doing camp security, and then we waited for our next mission. We had several taskings; we had set up our RRB [Radio Rebroadcast] posts outside Sarajevo, to give us communications with the UN HQ in Sarajevo and we set them up on top of a hill half way between the two places.

One of the other things we did while we were there in Visoko, before we went to Gorazde, included what we called the infrastructure taskings. We'd go into Sarajevo, right downtown, drive through there and we would help out the civilian workers. We'd guard them, provide security for them so that they could repair electrical lines, pipelines and stuff like that which would help bring electricity and water to parts of the city. We did a lot of that for a couple of weeks. We'd do an RRB tasking, and then we'd do an infrastructure tasking, or go out on a relief convoy. It was a lot of juggling.

We did our first major tasking, which was to go to the Bosnian Muslim enclave of Gorazde. They hadn't seen relief in ten months. Our OC and a couple of carriers from our Company had gone with the Ukrainian UN battalion on a recce of that route and the Ukrainians were going to deliver aid to Gorazde. After that our platoon was supposed to go. It was a long, arduous task but we did it.

The Gorazde relief mission was one of the most gratifying experiences that occurred on the tour I was on. We got the order that we were going to be going to Gorazde, so immediately all the preparations had to be made. The Serbs were being difficult about it. Gorazde was a small Muslim enclave completely surrounded by Serbs and they were fighting for their lives. The Serbs didn't like the UN going in and giving them food. In that sense, we knew we were going to be seeing people in bad shape. So we had to get all the serial numbers of every weapon in the platoon, all our ID cards and numbers had to be put on a large manifest sheet. All the weapons numbers, carrier weapons, carrier registration numbers, UN licence plate numbers on the carriers, and every last little detail the Serbs wanted checked, which was basically just to stall us and make it more difficult to get through.

STOPOVER AT SARAJEVO INTERNATIONAL AIRPORT

So we were en route and we stayed one night in the Sarajevo Airport, which was interesting. The French Foreign Legion was there. We stayed on little cots and it was quite a wild little spot with a lot of killing going on. The airport ran in between various factions and it was a vital little piece of real estate. It was also a divider between the part of town that had medical supplies and food, a food distribution centre, and at night a lot of people would try to run across the airfield to the other side to get food and relief supplies. When this would happen, the Serbs would roll in along the hill, where they had a good view of the airport, and they would open up, shooting at them with coaxial machineguns on their T-55 tanks. What the French would have to do, at night, was to roll around in their carriers on the airfield, trying to gather up all these people and return them to where they came from.

These people included just about everybody. "Sarajevians," I guess I'd call them. The airport had big dirt mounds surrounding it like big berms and they would climb over it. We had security on our own vehicles at night and I remember watching, looking around at all these berms, seeing heads pop up and they'd look at me. I'd look at them; they knew I saw them and the heads would pop down. It was kind of comical in a way. Then they would sneak across, if they could, and you could hear the shooting, see the tracers going, the carriers turn around and round them up. A little trick they had was that they'd run across towards the areas they were going to, and then they would turn around and face the way that they just came from, the idea being that when the French picked them up, they would take them to the side that they were supposed to be coming from so when they did this, they would wind up where they wanted to go! It was a nifty little trick they had. The French just sort of turned a blind eye, as they just wanted to get them out of the way. In the morning it was a gruesome sight. They had to pick up bodies of men, women, children, and old people, the whole gamut and it was a mess. Fortunately, the night we were there nobody got killed, just a couple wounded. The night before I was talking to one of the guys there and he said that they had seven wounded and eleven killed.

ON THE ROAD TO GORAZDE

We got up the next morning and had a couple of holes in the vehicles, like stray bullets and stuff. A couple of jerry cans had been hit and diesel fuel was running all over the side of the vehicles. So that was that and then we were on the move again to Gorazde. Our formation included an expanded platoon because we also had an HLVW [10-ton truck], a maintenance group, and an ambulance group. There was a box ambulance, and then an APC ambulance, and we also had a section of engineers, so it was a platoon battle group.

We were escorting a convoy of trucks full of food and medicine but the majority was food. We had gone through several checkpoints en route to the main Serb checkpoint, that would let us go to Gorazde, and once we got there the other big UN trucks, with the humanitarian relief on and food were already there waiting for us. They were Swedish UN and I believe there were about sixteen of those trucks. We ended up waiting at this checkpoint for three days. The Serbs were just being stubborn and wouldn't let us through. We just kept on waiting, waiting and waiting. There was a French convoy supposedly coming after us, but when they got there and saw that we were waiting, they waited for about one night and left.

Eventually we got to move. It was kind of strange, something right out of the movies; I have a twisted sense of humour and I thought it was kind of funny, really. It was a little Serb hamlet I don't know the name and the main guy that was there was this Boris Karlov-type character, who looked something like a Russian Cossack. He had a big beard, and had a leather suit on with the furry collar and the big buttons and he had this AIG leather jacket on. He had a pistol on, like an old six-shooter, a knife, big boots and he had one of these big Russian hats, with no peak or anything but it goes up and comes down. He had an AK-47 with two mags taped together; he was the head honcho there. They had a little bar and you could see them going in there and getting whisky or whatever they were drinking, with a lot of young teenage kids hanging around there.

I think that's one of the main reasons that they have so many problems. The head Serb will say, "Yes, we want to allow convoys through" but the problem is that there is such a loose command and control that you don't have an army saying, "Yeah, you can go through here," but you have each little village that has its own boss and until he gets what he wants, then nobody moves. A lot of times they want your diesel fuel. I know the Ukrainians sometimes give them whisky or something just to bribe them and let them though the checkpoint. Eventually, with no bribes or anything, we got through. They knew that we were going to stay there until we got through and I think they got tired of seeing us. They finally got word that they had better let us through and then we went on to Gorazde.

We were the lead carrier. Our callsign was One Three Alpha, that is 1 Section, 3 Platoon. We started to go through to Gorazde, and the minute we started getting closer, we could hear a lot of fighting, mortars and stuff. We got to this one point where we could see these soldiers, Muslims, who had been fighting up in the woods since April of the year before, and they looked like hell. I remember just looking at the guys, their eyes looked so tired and they were beat to snot. They were pretty thin, and I saw two of them lugging a .50-cal up a hill and then all these mortars started coming down on them. It was obvious that the enemy was watching. The Serbs knew that they were down there and mortars started hitting on the hills around us, and so we drove through there, and a few more minutes we were in Gorazde. Gorazde had been constantly shelled, but when we went in there was no shelling and, I think, that was one of the main reasons why the people there were so thankful to see us – finally, they could go out into the streets safely.

The soldiers talked to some other people who were letting us through the checkpoint. They had the roads mined and they had to move them to let us through. We turned around as we came around this big corner and I looked and saw this big mountain. It was all really mountainous but it opened up into a big valley and there was this great mountain, with green water and a big stone ridge and it was one of the most beautiful things I had ever seen. I looked down and there were thousands of people along the side of the road, yelling and screaming at us, waving to us and they were all crying. It was quite a scene. I really felt like I was ten feet tall, and it was something. I was a C-9 gunner and I stood out of the back hatch of the APC all the time so I could see it.

They let us go through. We drove through the town and then went to a food distribution centre. Once we got there the people were all over the place and we had to keep them out. The food would be distributed, as they were genuinely hungry.

We didn't really see any defences inside the town. The town had been shelled hard and these people were really hurting. I was watching it on the news about a month and a half ago when Gorazde was about to fall to the Serbs and the Brits went in. It brought back a lot of memories because they had the same scenario we had but it wasn't quite as publicized.

All we did was guard the convoy. We got in the carrier, I handed out a couple of rations discriminately to people, because you just didn't throw a pile of rations into a crowd of people unless you're looking for trouble or a riot. You had to do it discreetly. So we stayed overnight in this little office building where there was a picture of Tito on the wall, and his desk and everything was still there. We moved the desk out of the way and it was like everything had been packed up and moved out. We slept on the carpeted floor, got up the next morning and left.

We were the only platoon of our company to get through, and that was the last time anybody got through. I don't know if after we left anybody got in or not.

We headed back to Sarajevo for a rest and the whole trip in total lasted four days.

RELIEF MISSION TO SREBRENICA

It was in *Time* magazine and all over the news that Srebrenica, a small Muslim enclave again, was about to fall to the Serbs. When we rolled in there, the shelling stopped immediately. This mission was different. It was to set up a demilitarized zone, a UNPA. It was just our company with the attached engineer element. I believe there were a couple of call signs from each company, a couple of extra sections.

So we kept going and going and going on this route and we went to Tuzla, where the British Army had an airport. The British Army was based out of there and we were to meet there with the UN Military Observers and then we were to form up and they would take us to the release point to get into Srebrenica and then we would be on our own. So we stayed in Tuzla for three or four hours and then we were moving again and we went through several small towns where you could tell we were getting into more hostile country. People really didn't like us there, as we would get dirty looks, and then it got more serious after a while when people were throwing stones. We went through a small town called Zvornik, and this was just before Srebrenica. There was Zvornik, a dead man's land, sort of no man's land, and then there was Srebrenica. In Zvornik, I couldn't believe it; I was standing up in the track when I saw all these people along the road. I never really thought anything of it and then all of a sudden, I saw these rocks come flying at me. I'm going, "Holy shit!" I got in the carrier, looked up and I could see some buildings with people on top throwing things out of their windows, and you know we had some canteen supplies in our track with us, when we went under this overpass and they dropped this huge cinderblock that landed right in our carrier, just missing a couple of the guys and it took two of us to lift it out. If it had hit anyone, it would have broken his back. A big flat of pop was also dropped on us and it went everywhere. Pop. I couldn't believe it! They threw everything at us and all the wheeled vehicles hardly had any windows left, the Iltis, the MLs, the CUCVs, and a lot of the drivers had bloody faces, bashed up heads, and everything else from these rocks.

I certainly wanted to throw some CS gas at them. That's what it's for, riot control. I consider that to be a crowd-control problem. I think we should have gassed them, but I guess the thought was that we were just moving through, so the quicker we did so the better and it took us ten minutes to get through there.

We stopped in the no man's land. Basically on either side were Serb and Muslim positions, as we passed through the front lines and we were hatches down. The temptation would have been there to shoot at us if we had the hatches up. It was all hatches down and we went through the town quickly. It was night by the time we got there and I remember getting out of the carrier feeling completely disoriented, I had no idea where we were or anything like that. We took over a small building, made a compound out of it and that's where we based. So we went in there for the night, got up and started the job. There was constant gunfire, lots of shooting but no shelling. Once we got there the shelling stopped but there was a lot of machine-gun fire at night up in the hills.

Srebrenica is a small town. It was probably a big tourist area, a lovely little town in a valley. All around, you heard the gunfire going out and returning, by the Muslims and Serbs. Our job was to go outside the perimeter of the town. The basic rule was that soldiers were allowed to go and fight and they were allowed to come back in, the problem was they weren't allowed to bring weapons, grenades or anything like that back into Srebrenica, because it was a demilitarized zone. They didn't even want people to wear combats in town. If they were wearing camouflage, we had to give them a hard time coming back into Srebrenica. It's a strange situation but you have to understand that if we're not there, then they would have been taken over. Those were the rules to play by and we were just there to do our job. Basically, when we did our job, humanitarian relief could come in to them.

These people were hurting quite badly. They were very dirty, and hungry. This is how hungry they were: I remember seeing one woman I handed a ration to just tore it apart. They didn't know what anything was [in the ration pack] and one was a thing of Tabasco sauce that she started feeding to her baby that she thought was food. I grabbed it away from her and told her, "No, no, hot! She didn't understand so I put some on her tongue and she knew then. It was much the same as Gorazde, really.

Then we had checkpoints set up around the town. When people would come in, we'd search all vehicles, the people, handbags, and everything coming in or out. We confiscated grenades, rifles, and a couple of T-55 tanks from the Muslim forces. They were out of gas or the battery didn't work, and they just used it as a static position. As the demilitarized zone expanded, these tanks were in the zone so we took them and the same with howitzers. We took a howitzer, some APCs, and a lot of weapons. We had a weapons cache point that all the sections rotated through – 2 [Section] got one area; the other got another, etc. A reinforced company, G Company, did the whole thing. It was a lot of work and it was go, go, go. I think we did three nights out on the line, and then we'd come back in one night, get cleaned up, and go back out the next morning for another three days. At some points up in the hills we stayed in tents, and then sometimes down in the actual town we stayed in bombed-out houses. Some people let us stay in the front part of their house.

We never saw any Serbs really. There were snipers that would shoot at us occasionally (pretty much every day) but we didn't get shelled there. I was shot at, though. Sometimes I'd be standing at our checkpoint and hear zip! zip! go by and you'd see the dirt shoot up.

Braving Serbian "rent-a-mobs," snipers, and bureaucratic stall tactics, 'G' Company, 2 RCR eventually pulled into the Muslim-held Srebrenica enclave bringing with them a much-needed relief aid convoy. (CF photo)

THE SHOOTING

This was a totally different spot than we had been in before. We had gone out four or five nights before this, gone in for a day that morning and we ended up going back out that night. We were a little upset that we got sent out again. This happened in May and we were supposed to go home the next day. It was kind of unlucky. We had gone out and we were to set up an observation post to observe the Serb front lines. It was really hilly so we were basically on a hill where there was a little valley and on the other edge of the hill we could see Serb soldiers walking around. I could see a foxhole-type deal, a pillbox or something. They were within C-7 range, maybe 400 metres. Off to our left at that OP was an old abandoned Muslim defensive position. Then about a kilometre down the road to our left as we were facing these Serbs was a TOW missile vehicle of ours. So, we got there at around 1830, set up our tents, set up the carrier, and got some wood, as we were going to build a small fire behind the carrier. We weren't trying to hide; we wanted people to know that we were UN. We got there in daylight, and they saw that we had a UN carrier perched on top of the hill, a white carrier, with the flag flying. We weren't going to go rustling through the bushes and give them the impression that somebody was taking over the defensive position or anything. We were there to be seen so that they knew who we were.

So we set this up and it was quite a little ride up there so I decided to clean my C-9 and Master Corporal Stevenson* asked me if I wanted to go look at the Muslim defensive position with him. A couple of the other fellows were going to go with him but I said, no, because I wanted to clean my weapon, as it was dirty because of the dust and I just wanted to give it a quick cleaning. Once they left I started taking my weapon apart and they were only gone for about ten minutes, when they came back and Master Corporal Stevenson said something to me. It just started to turn dark, around nine-ish, we were just talking away, Corporal Keegan* was on the .50 cal turret and I was putting my weapon back together when all of a sudden out of nowhere, all this shooting started, and, you know, it was obvious we were being shot at as I saw tracers going over my head. I looked up and the top hatch of the carrier was open. I didn't have my helmet on, because I was in the carrier, and I looked out the door and I could see dirt being chewed up. I heard screaming and I knew it was

* A pseudonym

When Canadians took over defending Srebrenica in 1993, many wounded citizens were evacuated by the UN. Unlike most of the people in the background of this picture, these lucky few were spared the brutal events of 1995 when Serbian forces murdered some 7000 inhabitants. (CF photo)

Stevenson because of his voice. It was scary, but also a big adrenaline rush, and I knew that he had been shot. Corporal Keegan immediately started returning fire with the .50 cal, one of the fellows was in the tent and a couple of the other fellows, with Master Corporal Stevenson, started firing back with their C-7s. We had a lot of stuff on top of the carrier, like a radio, a starlight [night scope] and another set of night vision goggles, so I immediately stood up and threw all these inside the carrier. I didn't realize that I didn't have my helmet on or anything. My first reaction was that my weapon wasn't even put back together and because I knew other people were returning fire, I thought that by the time I finished putting it back together the whole thing would have been over by then anyway because it happened so fast.

Somehow Stevenson had crawled back to the door of the carrier and I looked at the door and there he was. I grabbed him and pulled him into the carrier but I couldn't really see where he was hit. He was screaming and I knew that was a good sign. When someone goes down and they're screaming, they're probably hit somewhere in the extremities, so obviously he wasn't hit in the head or chest.

All the first-aid training came right back into my mind. I asked him where he was hit and he said his leg. I looked at his leg but I couldn't see anything. He was hit in the right thigh, on the meaty part of the leg. I opened his legs up and I could see some bleeding there. By this time everybody else was starting to pile into the carrier.

This all happened in less than five minutes. So we patched him up and then I called in a contact report on the radio and told them we were en route to the other location. It was combat driving, the driver was just cranking the tiller bars and everything was falling off the sides of the carrier on top of everybody and the engine was screaming, Master-Corporal Stevenson was yelling and I was trying to yell over the radio.

The other guys could see people firing. I didn't see, as I didn't have time. I reacted. Once we started firing back, their firing stopped and by that time we were all in the carrier and we were moving. I screamed over the radio the contact report and between my coming down and pulling Stevenson in, I got on the radio and I said, "Zero, this is One Three Alpha, contact, wait out!" By that time we had piled everybody in, patched them up, we were moving and then I gave the contact report: "Zero this is One Three Alpha, contact grid 183 198." It wasn't a perfect by-the-numbers contact report by any means but nobody complained. I gave the grid and then told them that enemy of unknown size had ambushed our position, we had returned fire, had one man down, and that we were en route to their location.

The drive back was quick and the medic and an APC ambulance met us half way into the town. They called over the radio and I gave them the description of the injury, which was relayed to Corporal Keegan. He had the headset on so he could hear what was on the radio.

We unloaded Master Corporal Stevenson into the ambulance carrier, where he was emergency operated on and they removed the bullet that night. We had to do statements once we got back to the position. Master Corporal Stevenson had dropped his rifle and his NVGs and they were left there. We got to go in and talk to him but he was pretty drugged out and seemed in pretty good spirits. We were happy about that. It was a pretty disturbing experience, especially so close to us going home. The next morning, our section went back. A lot of people said that we shouldn't have gone back but we all wanted to go. So we went back about 0430 that morning to pick up what we left behind. Also, that night we had to do a count of all the ammo we had expended and do a complete kit check to see what else we were missing.

Everything was undisturbed and nothing was touched. We found Stevenson's weapons and goggles exactly as they lay, and it was like visiting the scene of the crime. It was so fast and furious and you came back and looked at everything and everything was just there as it was. It was kind of weird.

It was just light, dawn. We set up in an all-round defence, packed everything up, threw it in the back of the carriers, all the kit, the weapons, everything, and got out of there quickly. They investigated and looked around a bit, and they could see where the shots were fired from, but there were no bodies or anything found.

We don't know if it was Serbs or Muslims. There was a lot of dead ground, and anyone could have done it. A lot of the Muslims will fire at Muslims and blame it on the Serbs just to break a ceasefire or something like that. It could have been done to make it look like the Serbs did it or it could have been the Serbs, we didn't know but it was definitely a deliberate attack on us. There was no question.

A lot of people always wonder how they would react when in a situation like that. That was a thing that all soldiers wondered. My answer would be to not worry about it. I think that it would take care of itself, because your training is really good. I often think back myself and think, what if I hadn't been cleaning my weapon, I maybe could have returned fire and helped in that way. I also look at it and say, well, the weapon had to be cleaned, and there was plenty of firepower within the section to take care of that. I did a lot of other important things, that's what I tell myself. I couldn't do those things if I was firing back. A lot of people say to me, "It's too bad you didn't get to fire back. You didn't get a chance to fire your weapon in anger." Well, I say I don't agree with that because I did my job. That's the most important thing. I did first aid and a contact report and I drove. I feel good about it. It gives me more confidence as a soldier and it makes you take the training more seriously, more realistically. You see the importance of the training. It's an unfortunate way to have the lesson driven home to you but I guess it's things like that, which make people wake up and realize that what they are doing is important. Every little bit of training is important, and nothing's insignificant or should be overlooked.

MEDIA COVERAGE

The way the media works now is changed. Now they get right into it, and they're right there. You're seeing some of those camera people see more action than soldiers do. I think I thought it was going to be worse than it was. With regards to ethnic cleansing, I think that's a big misunderstanding that people don't understand what it is. It's not so much where they take a bunch of people out, line them up against the wall, shoot them and bury them. I'm not saying it doesn't happen but it's not what you would call the par-for-the-course version of ethnic cleansing. Ethnic cleansing more or less is when you were driving through, say, a Muslim town and you were driving along and you saw all those houses which look fine and then you'd notice a cluster of four or five houses and they're all blown up. Then you'd see six or seven more houses and they were fine and you'd go through the town and you'd basically see all these houses where half were fine and half were blown up. This was a Muslim town; so obviously, those houses were Serb or Croatian houses. That's ethnic cleansing, where they threw a bomb at your door and said, "Get out of town!" So, that's what ethnic cleansing was, more or less, and that's the major definition, I'd think. Our platoon found a body that had been in a river for quite some time, a small child who had been shot, but we didn't walk into a village and find everyone slaughtered. That happens, I know, but we did not have that happen because we were dealing on a different scale. We got there before that had to happen and we had been able to intervene and prevent that. But as far as ethnic cleansing is concerned, you could tell the difference between the types of houses. Muslim houses had different types of roofs. You'd go through a small village and you would see all the houses that had Muslim roofs on them were blown up and all the Serb ones were fine. This was a Serb community and they had cleaned out the Muslims. That's ethnic cleansing. That's the best example of what it is.

The media can get a bit carried away. From what I followed, of course, they sensationalized some things a bit but overall it wasn't too bad.

PERSONAL THOUGHTS

It was a very good tour for me; I mean it was a wonderful experience. I would go back. I don't plan on it, but I would. Does the UN accomplish much? Well, I'd say that we were helping in small ways; I wouldn't say we are changing the face of Yugoslavia. We didn't make any broad sweeping changes, but certainly when you can deliver food in any size it feels like you are doing something useful. You can see the obvious effects, people are happy that they are going to live a little longer and I think that any lives that are saved are a success on its own in some respects. Sure, I feel that.

It was a great relief to come home. I was still shaken up a couple weeks afterwards, after the one incident, especially when Master Corporal Stevenson got shot. That's the only one that I can think of that really shook me up. I thought about it. It happened on one day and I was home three days later. I was at home in my house thinking, "Four days ago I was shot at! Ambushed!" It's kind of weird. Suddenly you're in a completely different situation. I thought about that for a little while. No nightmares. I made a lot of good friends and it was a good experience to share. At the same time I wouldn't like to see that kind of thing continue.

CHAPTER FIVE

WARRANT OFFICER MIKE McBRIDE

Troop Leader, Royal Canadian Dragoons Battle Group
Visoko and Gorazde, Bosnia, 1995

BACKGROUND

I'm the Armoured Ambulance Troop commander with the RCD Battle Group. I joined as an infantryman in 1974, and remustered to the medical corps in 1977. I spent most of my career in the field, the last six years on deployment out of Victoria. I figured that it was going to be my base posting and I've been going non-stop since. Our 6B course was a long one and I got that as soon as I was posted to Victoria, which was nine months of the year gone, and then I went to Cambodia, the Gulf, did this operation, I'd been serving as a sea trainer in support as a medical assistant with the Pacific Fleet. There I was, minding my own business at cadet camp last August. On the first of August I got a phone call from the Chief of Staff of the medical organization at MARPAC, and he said, " You're going to Yugoslavia." I said "When?" He said, "You have to be in Petawawa on Saturday." He said, "You asked for it, you got it!" We came off the national tasking brick and off we went. So we formed up in Petawawa, a rather ad hoc organization, with people drawn from all across the country. CFB Wonderful is where most of them came from. Not a lot of field experience, so we had a lot of work to do with the troops. We picked up a few from the field ambulance in Petawawa, but most were base-hospital types.

THE FIELD SURGICAL TEAM

The FST is a kind of neat organization that consists of 54 people. We have a whole surgical team here with us; we have surgeons, and anaesthetists in the surgical section. We have a lieutenant-commander, a staff officer from the navy who is with us, but he hasn't practised medicine in awhile, and he's an excellent administrator. We had a reserve guy here at the start but he didn't do near as well and he didn't have the face value. He was more concerned with the humanitarian aspects than with looking after the battle group and this was the broad consensus in the organization. Our task was to support the battle group and anything else we did, we'd do in our free time, including support to civilians.

We have the surgical team and our surgeons here are both on their second tour. One of the OR nurses was on his second overseas deployment in four years, in the Gulf on the hospital ship, and one of the OR techs was on USS *Comfort* and USS *Mercy*, plus HMCS *Protecteur* with their Canadian surgical team on board. There was a hospital complex on the Operational Support Ships. It was an incredible organization. We had the Outpatient Department, which was really the Royal Canadian Dragoon's Unit Medical Section [the regiment's own clinic]. The FST absorbed the whole RCD UMS, which caused a whole lot of growing pains back in Petawawa when we came in and took over. I think for the most part that they worked around us. We had to control all the ambulances as you can't have ambulances up at each of the squadrons and expect us to look after the other ones here. We needed to control the works.

There were varying standards there, too. With the guys that came in from CFB Wonderful, we started flipping through files and recognizing names and faces. We came up with some very interesting people. One guy used to run the UMS at 4 Air Defence Regiment in Lahr, one of his master corporals, who used to be a Pathfinder with the airborne, had been in the Airborne Medical Platoon, and our Biomedical Equipment Repair Tech had done three tours with the Airborne Regiment as a medical assistant. No shrinking violets here, no way! Even the young medical guys from Halifax were skilled and two of them were divers. That shows the level of motivation in the organization. That's the navy equivalent of the Airborne Regiment. Our sergeant major had been around for a long time, and he came from the alcohol rehabilitation clinic in Kingston, and that paid dividends too. It was funny how it all jelled together but I don't think it was a conscious effort on someone's part to do it that way. Surprise. Here we go!

Myself, I've served with an armoured regiment before too, the Lord Strathcona's Horse, for three years as the recce squadron medic, so I was kind of familiar with armoured operations. I also served with the engineers for three years in Chilliwack as a combat diver, so we could cover all diving medical aspects with the team here. It was just by a fluke, I'm sure, that this talent showed up.

Each of the armoured squadrons, within the regiment, had their medics come over to me and they automatically became crew commanders on the Bison ambulances. We had these back in Petawawa, too, as the prototype was sitting there and we used it for training, which was excellent.

We had the Ward Section, which combined the intensive care unit and the ward. We had two nurses and then three or four medical assistants. The major part of the organization was the Armoured Ambulance Troop, and we supplied ambulances to the OPs on all three sides of the contact line and we did the evacuation as required. We escorted the convoys, we did the Joe jobs around here but we had a lot of fun doing it. In my organization, we had 11 ambulances: one tracked M-113, eight Bisons (the eight-wheeled armoured vehicles) and two 5/4 tons, which we don't use very often compared to the Bisons. We maintained the equipment for the upload UMS, and there was a UMS sitting on the other side of the camp that we used if there was a withdrawal or something happened to our stuff here on this side of the camp. We had to have a bit of separation in there to ensure all the equipment couldn't get wiped out by one shell.

I'm the equivalent of a Physician's Assistant. If there was a requirement for advanced medical care, but not the workload for a doctor, I did it. We did a lot of learning by OJT and our formal trade courses were the best part of a year, plus formal training in the school after all the junior trades training. We did a preceptorship for six months under a doctor. He was an ER physician and you qualified in advanced trauma and life support, cardiac life support and you also did routine sick parade. You put your shingle up just like a doctor does in the hospital or the facility you happened to be working in. You took your own patient load, and your own calls. You did all the minor surgery that came in, along with the admission and medical responses as required. We had medical assistants who were Emergency Medical Technicians, paramedics and they rode the ambulance. They did a three-week ride-along program with the ambulances in Ottawa and Halifax. They were able to do that as privates, as junior crewmembers and after that it became more in-depth, and they started doing sick-parade things. There was a lot of nursing involved in our early training and I had master corporals that surprised me with their skill and ability. These guys had their act together big time. They were very well educated, they were well spoken, and their patient handover notes were clear and concise – but they knew their limitations. They were always pushing the envelope with their trade knowledge and they were good.

When we got on the ground there, we had to go have a real good scope-out of the area and what we had, how were we to support the battle group, and how the Strathconas were doing their job. We took a lot of their ideas and kept them, and threw the RCD Armoured Ambulance Troop twist into them. The last battle group, near the end of their tour, had become a little bit complacent. We didn't have the big bunker complex set up like we did now, and a lot of the stuff was neglected, but you saw that happen when guys had been there seven months.

Out of the 54 people, you'd lose anywhere between 8 and 12 on the leave blocks. We spent weeks and weeks going over how we were going to organize leave back home before we came over here. I guess, with the mixed rotation, it was going to be squared off a whole lot better with staggered leave in 30-person blocks, three weeks home and then back here again. We couldn't afford to have one sixth of the battle group gone at any one time if the crunch came and you could always expect the guys back very shortly.

We also had dedicated drivers for our vehicles so that the medics weren't driving for the most part, but a few of us were qualified on them. Two of my young medics came from the Airborne Regiment, so they had lots of practice with the Bison ambulances in Somalia before they came over here and it gave us a bit of flexibility. We hadn't told the battle group that we could drive the Bisons, as it preserved capability. We needed the capability to do 'surge' if we had to and that's what happened with the Gorazde deal. We got the phone call, had a quick staff check, and we said "We can give you four" and that wasn't leaving the battle group shy of anything. We still supported here and we could have generated another couple of crews if push came to shove.

As a matter of fact, when we got the Bisons over there, one of the guys who made a lot of suggestions was one of our corporals who recommended modifications to the vehicle before deployment. We took the standard carrier, pulled the infantry seats off, put two medical bins in, and we got the capability of supplying oxygen to all litter positions in the vehicle with lots of good storage. There was a big 1,800-litre oxygen tank under the left-hand seat, and we had the only ambulance over there that had that capability. The French unit just went berserk when they saw that. The French used their VABs for ambulances and they were very tight inside. They didn't have a ramp; they had swinging back doors, which made it difficult to load. There had been a French staff officer coming through there for months looking at our vehicles and I fully expect the next family of French armoured vehicles will look quite similar to the Bison. Too bad the buggers won't just buy from us.

You know, I wish we had more Bisons. When I was a young squadron medic in the Strathconas, I would have given my left arm for a Bison ambulance. We've got them now and only eleven exist in the military; one back home in Canada, two in Primosten and I happen to own eight of them! You know there was a contingency plan that if things were worse later on in the month, then I'd inherit the two on the coast. It's the best armoured ambulance in the Canadian military right now.

TRAINING AND DEPLOYMENT

When we did our training in Canada, we had non-medical people doing our assessments, which we objected to and there were some growing pains there. They were concerned about the time it took to evacuate casualties out of armoured fighting vehicles and I guess they hadn't had the experience before. In a secure area if it took thirty-five minutes to take a guy out with a suspected fractured spine, then you'd take thirty-five minutes to take the guy out. You weren't going to risk any further injury to them. They thought that was far too long. If it's a secure area, then I'm going to take my sweet time to get this guy out but they didn't understand that. They figured that it was a five-minute evolution and there was a lot of fear that the battle group was not going to be supported adequately by the FST. We were all new to them for the most part, there was a new doctor in the UMS, and a Militia guy was our boss. If it hadn't been for the NCOs in this organization standing fast, I could have seen additional training going on. We were confident that the guys were ready to do their job and when we got there we proved it. They did the big suck back and re-loaded because of the ad hoc organization that we worked with and in. There were a lot of people who just looked at the messages and said, "This guy's from CFB Halifax, what does he know about the field?" but he's run two UMSs before, he was an infantryman for seven years, and he probably knows what's going on. I mean, a Biomedical Equipment Tech with three years in the Canadian Airborne Regiment? What does he have to be taught about the field? One problem was that we turned up wearing brand new combats for the most part. If we had turned up wearing our other uniforms, we would have had the face value walking in the door as, we had corporals here with four medal-ribbons on their shirts, sub dolphins, the works. We had to prove ourselves and it took a long time to do that.

THE FIRST INCIDENT

It wasn't too long after we arrived, about twenty-four hours. A Bosnian Serb soldier was shot down at observation post Charlie Sierra 2 and it was a half-Strathcona, half-Dragoons medical crew that was down there. We were right in the middle of the rotation and we went down and looked after this guy who had a gunshot wound through his buttocks. We dolled him up, got him on our stretcher and we assisted in getting him down to Ilijas hospital, which was a Serb facility. A Bison was already pre-positioned there but we backed it up with one from here in Visoko. It was the first time we'd seen a gunshot wound in this operational theatre and we were kind of interested in it. We scrambled onto that ambulance to go down there and have a look and that was the start of it. The belligerents didn't mind. We had the technology and capability but they had the most efficient ambulance system in the world here because any vehicle that drove by became an ambulance. There had been numerous occasions where people, civilian and military on both sides of the line needed us. There was an old guy with a heart attack down by Podlugovi and we rolled him down to Ilijas hospital too. We evacuated him under fire and there was some guy taking pot shots at the ambulance. But the guys were cool, calm and collected. "Yeah, lets get him out, get inside the vehicle, we'll be safe and we'll go down to Ilijas."

THE ILIJAS "55"

Then we had the "Guestage" incident with the guys stuck over on the Serb side for fifteen days, held hostage and we had an ambulance crew over there for the whole time. Master Seaman Kendell volunteered to go back twice and he brought one guy back, a guy with a broken arm. He broke it slipping on the cover of the AVGP [the armoured vehicle]. We brought him back here and then Kendell went back to the troops again, the ones being held by the Serbs. Our guys over there were locked down tight. They weren't allowed to leave the positions that they were in, the OPs on the confrontation line and the only things they couldn't get were phone calls and clean clothes. Everything else seemed to work out quite well but it was tense there for a while when the Serbs started dropping rocket and artillery rounds close to our camp here in Visoko. We were confident that those guys were relatively safe over there and there was a lot of contingency planning going on to get them out if we had to but I'm glad it didn't come to that.

There were quite a few medics involved in the contingency planning, which paid dividends too, having a Pathfinder medic in our organization, as he had done special ops before. There were a couple of things that even he picked up on that would have caused a disaster if the planning had carried on without him noticing it. They had a big input in the planning process from Day 1 and the operational security was quite tight around there. It was amazing about how much people didn't know. You'd walk through and hear the rumours and the bullshit talk, but they weren't even close to what was going to happen. There were a lot of ex-shooters from JTF in this organization and the guys that had done some time in special forces organizations be it Airborne Regiment or combat divers training with the SEALs, we all seemed to end up in the briefing room upstairs in the Big Four! The JTF guys had one of their medical guys over here too and that was a bonus on our part. He didn't work for us but we knew there was another medic in the organization and he knew us so that gave us face value with their organization.

Master Seaman Kendell spent the entire fifteen days out there. He took casualties back, the guy with the fractured wrist and the guy with the broken arm and he willingly went back to be with the troops. For a young master seaman, who had been six months in rank and have him go back there, we thought it was incredible. He'd come in and load up with pop, chocolate bars, cigarettes and take the mail in. He was, in navy parlance, "inboard." A young guy we had out there as an ambulance driver, a reserve trooper from Southern Ontario, Chris Boyd, we borrowed him for the day to get us over a crew change. We were short a driver and fifteen days later, when he was still sitting over at Charlie Sierra 2, the big rumour was, "Chris' mom is going to be some pissed off at you!" [Because he couldn't go on leave]. Every time he came with us he got involved with some interesting tasking, and he went to Gorazde with us too.

OPERATING AROUND VISOKO

When there was shelling around and people got hit, the locals stopped and helped. The people that were driving thought it was their patriotic duty to support the cause and they'd pull over. A mortar round landed in a town a kilometre from here. It so happened that it was one of our interpreter's mother's house that the round hit and she was rather distraught about the whole thing. We rolled our ambulance up there, and it was a point of honour for those guys to look after their own unless they were so swamped that they couldn't do anything. We were asked to stand by or roll the hell out of there and get out of their way so that they could get on with their job. We were there in a matter of minutes, primarily because it was a member of the battle group staff who was directly affected by it. We were standing by with all the equipment, all the medications, but UNPROFOR was not the best-liked organization in this country either, as there were such varying degrees of military competency within the UNPROFOR organization. You had the troops from Third World nations, which perhaps were over here for the financial benefit of their senior officers, and then there were the true professional soldiers, the Brits, the French and us, who didn't have a whole lot of hesitation in doing this and we'd put ourselves between the belligerents. One of the deals we had back in Petawawa with the battle group, the commander said that we'd be more pro-active in dealing with things. If we saw someone getting beat up and dragged out of a vehicle, then we'd get in between the two and the CO wanted that to happen. I think they respected us a whole lot around here, but maybe they were scared of us too. I think they knew what we kept inside this wall here – TOW launchers, Cougar armoured cars, and mortar carriers. We were very professional about it, though. We were doing dismounted patrols down in the town, and we guarded their hospitals and their schools as "mortar deflectors." That's what our guys in the OPs at the Visoko hospital called themselves. The locals were pretty intimidated around here. When we locked down the main road in Visoko in October or November, we put up a 24-hour roadblock and nobody moved in this town. They were a little bit annoyed but they backed down.

CANADIAN MEDICAL SUPPORT IN THE VISOKO AREA

The surgical team saved a whole lot of lives in this community here in Visoko. They did surgeries here that Visoko hospital didn't have the capacity, capability or expertise to do. We resected livers and there was a Bosnian lady in here for four days in our intensive care unit after she had her liver resected. We had the equipment to do electrocautery for bleeders that they just didn't have down there. Visoko hospital wasn't a surgical facility until the war started. It was just a clinic and they would use Sarajevo, which was 25 kilometres away. The surgeon there, by hook or by crook got a staff, trained them and away he went.

That was a neat part because the surgical team was able to assist. We took our equipment down there and they brought their patients to us. Last week they did a hernia repair on a six-month-old child and then they did a tonsillectomy on a 14-year-old, which was something that they couldn't do there at all and then the surgeon from the local town was gone, as his family lived in Zagreb. So now there was no surgical capability in this town whatsoever, and we were it. You always kept that in the back of your mind. You'd never see that happen back home even in the smallest towns. We've got access to medical care and helicopters. I didn't see any vehicles up at the village at all, just ox and horse carts and that was it. Those guys are living two hundred years in the past. Their hospitals are probably what I would equate to Canadian small community standards years ago.

OPERATION GOOD SAMARITAN: THE GORAZDE EVACUATION

Have you ever been ready to leave the office, the phone rings, and you ask yourself "Should I answer it or leave it?" and then when you answer it, you say, "I should have just left it." Well,

1530, 1600 in the afternoon I was just packing up everything and getting ready to go do some PT when the phone range and it was the G3 Medical Operations at UNPROFOR's BH Command in Sarajevo. Through his bizarre accent (Norwegian, with a heavy Scottish twist – I understood him, it comes from my mother) he said, "I know you have nine ambulances that are armoured. Would you have any available for a casualty evacuation run?" I said, "What kind of casualty evacuation run? What kind of distances are we talking about?" I wasn't about to commit ourselves without knowing a whole lot more and I said, "Have you talked to our Ops people?" He said, "No, I'm touching base with you first before I make it a formal tasking," which never happened, in fact, and there was never a formal tasking message to send us to Gorazde. So he gave me a quick idea about what was going on. There were 118-plus civilians, both Serbians and Muslims in the enclave of Gorazde. The Norwegians were going to move them but they didn't have the lift capability and they were looking for us to assist them. My 2IC was bending over the phone by this time and he was looking at the vehicle status board to see what we had available. He was showing me four fingers and I said, "We can probably supply four." So he gave me all the details that he had at the time and I said, "Okay, I'll see what I can do and get back to you." I had a quick talk with the OC and our administration officer and I told them what was going on and what they were asking of us. So we bumped it up one higher to the Battle Group ops officer, Captain Rich Moreau. He said, "Sounds good. What else do you need?" The stores are opening now, and we can get whatever we want. I said that we needed a couple of drivers, and that way we could protect our capability back in Visoko. He said that was okay, and what else? I said, "An armoured escort would be nice." He said, "You have two Grizzlies. What else do you want?" "Well, we're going a fair distance, 140 kilometres one way, through some pretty rough territory. A Bison wrecker would be nice." "You've got that too." Within a matter of minutes it was all confirmed.

We had seven vehicles involved: four ambulances, two Grizzly APCs and the Bison recovery vehicle and we could have rolled in a matter of hours. We took the four vehicles off the line, cranked them, did the comms check and the crews were just itching to go because this was the first time we had done a platoon-size operation. Then it was the big hold. We had to wait for approval from all sorts of higher authorities. Eventually the Chief of the Defence Staff, General De Chastelain, approved it. We were ready to roll and we rolled out of the camp at 0600 the

CAN BAT 2's Bison ambulances and medics from the Field Surgical Team based in Visoko were critical in the evacuation of injured civilians from the embattled Muslim-held Gorazde enclave. The Bison proved its worth time and again in this hostile environment. (Author's Collection)

following morning. The weather was the absolute pits and it was raining. We got to Kiseljak and we were in a holding pattern for two and half hours waiting for the CDS to approve the operation. The guys were getting antsy and they wanted to get going. We looked at our watches and said, "I don't think it's going to be a one-day event. We're looking at two now." We figured it was going to be eight hours there and back but we knew that it wasn't going to happen. We just knew it. So about 1030 or so we got the word that we could roll and we went the long way down to Sarajevo.

We went across through Kiseljak and down the back way into the airport and it was quite the sight to see, the seven vehicles going there by ourselves on a Canadian operation. We got into the airport and we were waved right through every checkpoint. The Serbs opened everything up. The paperwork had been staffed through and everybody was putting on a lot of political pressure to make it happen. Everyone wanted their piece out of it. The Bosnian Muslims wanted their people back to say how horribly they had been treated by the Serbs, that they were emaciated with their teeth falling out and so on. The Bosnian Serbs wanted it because they could demonstrate that they were very nice people: "Look, we're letting these people go." UNPROFOR wanted it because they could make some press out of it, and get something back home to everybody's country, which caused a lot of ruckus at the end of the whole program.

We got into Sarajevo as it was starting to snow and our route took us over the side of Mount Igman, and we were up high. There were Serb fighting positions everywhere, and there was three feet of snow so we had to put chains on the vehicle tires. We got to the crest near the former Olympic ski run and the luge run that was all destroyed at the side of the road. There were more guys walking around with Kalashnikovs than I have ever seen in my life! They wanted us off the road very quickly because we were blocking traffic. We chained up and went through Pale, headed for a place called Rogatica and then it started getting real tight on the other side of Pale, in terms of checkpoints. We sat at one for an hour browbeating each other. They just wanted to make sure that everything was correct – all the Ts were crossed and the Is dotted on the manifests. I'm glad they didn't start checking weapons numbers because there were extra pistols aboard the vehicles.

Everybody took two weapons with them for the most part and we all had our rifles and pistols. Everything had to be in the correct order and we couldn't even shift our order of march because if we had shifted, then they wouldn't let us through the checkpoints. Rogatica was known as the hardest checkpoint in the entire theatre. You had to be clear of the checkpoint at last light or they wouldn't let you through and you had to sleep by the side of the road all night. This caused us some consternation because it was 1500 hours and we still had another 60 kilometres to go to Gorazde, get the patients and bring them back, and we knew we were not going to clear that checkpoint. We had visions of staying in Gorazde that night.

We finally cleared the checkpoint. The Mounties were there, as a matter of fact. UNCIVPOL, a corporal from Whitby Ontario who got us through the checkpoint, along with our escort commander, Captain Fleet from Assault Troop, and they browbeat their way through the Rogatica checkpoint into Gorazde. We were escorted by the British unit CO of Gorazde Force there. This guy was a dynamic personality and he got us through. The whole thing reminded me of *Apocalypse Now* when we were going through there as Gorazde was just destroyed.

On the road there had been lots of landslides, and there were huge boulders in the middle of the road, that we had to swerve, deke and cut through. It was starting to get dark and there was this fellow walking around wearing his blue beret, while the rest of us were wearing crew helmets or Kevlar helmets. He had no weapon, no body armour on and he had his RSM and his signaller with him. "We'll go there, we'll go there, we'll do this, and we'll do that." Just looking at him, we knew he had the presence to get us through and we blasted into Gorazde. The Norwegian medical convoy was going out as we were going in. Little did we know that we'd marry up with those guys and become part of that organization. When we got in, I scoped out the place and asked what was going on. They said, "Get your vehicles fuelled up there, and eat over here." The Brits had it well organized and they took down our vehicle call signs and UNPROFOR numbers. I got a briefing on all the casualties but the crews didn't get as detailed a briefing as they would have liked. In retrospect, there probably wasn't a whole lot they could have told us about the casualties, as there were a lot of chronically ill and a lot of elderly. There were also a few family groups in there.

The guy from Reuters asked me what their state was. He said, "What was it like in Gorazde?" I was probably still shocked by the whole situation when he asked me and I said, "I don't know, I was watching for snipers and looking after the crews," but it's funny what your peripheral vision will pick up. The houses were all destroyed. We didn't go very far into town but what we saw around the Brit camp was absolutely destroyed and it reminded me of pictures that I had seen of Europe at the end of the Second World War. The kids were all walking around, picking up candies and they were also begging for food, their clothes were in tatters, and they were dirty. Then we found out what dirty was when we pulled into the Britforce camp. There were two and a half feet of mud in their vehicle park, and we had to drop our chains and then it was a nightmare trying to find them and fish them out.

It was a quick turn-around between getting our vehicles fuelled up, finding the chains and getting something to eat. We weren't there much more than forty-five minutes. I had some reservations about some of the patients we took. We took a 75-year-old lady in my carrier, who was blind. We asked the interpreter to pass on to her that it was going to be a close space, warm, and there was going to be a lot of motion. They didn't pass the message on adequately enough for our liking. Consequently, this woman vomited for ten hours straight just about in the back of the vehicle. We had the medication but we didn't have the interpreter on board. If we were going to do this again, we'd pre-medicate the patients so that they didn't throw up in the vehicles.

These people had been through a lot and they handled it quite easily. They took a lot of interest in what was going on outside the vehicle, especially when we were coming out and they were scared. I was hesitant to let on that we had a load of Muslim civilians when we were going through the Serb checkpoints. Our crew medics were standing in the rear sentry hatches with their rifles up just in case something happened and they did a positive identification check on everybody in the troop. It was tight with the Serbs and it became even tighter going through the Muslim checkpoints because they wanted to see what they were getting and didn't want any surprises.

We came back over the same route and we told the civilians on board that we were going through Pale. They were sitting a bit lower in their seats and they were tapping on the side of the vehicle so I gave them the thumbs up, "Yeah, it will stop whatever they're going to shoot at us!" The other thing we learned, in a nine-hour evacuation like that, was when we married up with the Norwegians – they waited and did one large convoy – that they like their lights and sirens and this attracted a lot of attention to the convoy. We eventually got them to turn them off. Fourteen blue lights flashing in the darkness going across the side of Mount Igman, you know? Somebody might take a potshot at us so we just went with regular lights. If we ever have to do it again, we'll have a secure rest area so we can pull in and protect the casualties so they can take care of their personal business. I felt sorry for some of these old folks, I really did.

Could you imagine putting your grandmother in the back of an armoured vehicle, not being able to speak the language, at night, going through the worst weather that I'd seen in this country since we deployed over here, lousy road conditions, with a bunch of crazy Canucks who can't speak their language other than "Zema!" (It's cold!) and having the medication available and not being able to use it? It would not have gone over very well in the vehicle if we had taken some of this old lady's clothing off and given her a shot of Gravol, as she couldn't take it orally, and pulling out needles and sticking them in. They had probably heard stories that UNPROFOR wasn't there to protect them. We were scared that the Serbs would want to get on the vehicles at Mount Igman. This was running through our minds there and then the weather just kept on deteriorating. The Norwegians, with their Sisu ambulances, were so big they couldn't manoeuvre them very well and they took out a Serbian checkpoint. This was just grand!

If we hadn't tucked in with the Norwegians, we would have finished that mission earlier that evening. The Norwegians didn't have a lot of tactical sense or experience, but very, very good medics and their navigation skills weren't the greatest. We had a Serb guide bringing us through the south side of Sarajevo up to the river and he disappeared on us just as we were pulling into the city. We were coming in down off the hill and one of the funniest things I noticed, the telephone lines were draped with rugs like a sniper screen. I was looking at these beautiful rugs in the lights and thinking, "Those things are probably worth thousands and thousands of dollars back home, but they're probably doing a better job here than people just walking on them!"

We pulled into Sarajevo right in the bad part of town, if there was one bad part of town in Sarajevo, right at the confrontation line. There were weapons everywhere, and nobody wanted to let us through. It took us almost three hours to talk our way through the checkpoints between the last Serb checkpoint and the first Muslim checkpoint and then we had some inkling of what might happen once we cleared the checkpoints. We had to get one of our francophone guys to interpret with the Muslim forces, as they couldn't speak English at that checkpoint. The mechanics jumped off and started to talk to them and that got us through the checkpoint. As we went through there, we saw all these TV camera lights and I said, "Something's going on here and someone's going to make some good press out of this." So we went to Kosovo Hospital, I think that's what it was called, under escort, and as we were going down the road, the one traffic light in Sarajevo that worked was red when we went through! I felt so sorry for this traffic light because there were 21 vehicles in total going through there, and not one stopped. It was 80 kilometres per hour and the Norwegians once again had their lights and siren on; these guys were really starting to annoy me.

As we were going down the road, we saw all these armoured Land Rovers pulling up with TV painted on the side. They had been filming us crossing the checkpoint and they were going up to the hospital for the arrival. It was a circus, a media circus. They had the international press, they had UNPROFOR Public Affairs, they had the local press, and there were cameras everywhere. This made it difficult for us to do our job trying to get the casualties out of the vehicle into the hospital, as the cameras were at every vehicle. We dropped the ramp and if you weren't blinded while you were sitting in there, you were blinded when you were coming back out again. The ramps were slippery and we were helping these old folks off the vehicles. They were so busy taking pictures that we couldn't get hold of an interpreter to brief the blind lady that this was the way she was going to get off the vehicle, so we ended up picking her up and carrying her out of the vehicle.

Associated Press shot a famous picture. If you read in the narrative of the article that appeared with, it identified us as Norwegian medical guys! They were the first guys in, they got the big part of the press and we were left sucking the hind tit. Anyway, it says in the blurb that we were moving this blind lady out by stretcher but I was just trying to place her feet on the ramp. There were some other shots of our public affairs officer but I wasn't very happy with the way things were being handled there, and I wanted them to clear away from the ramps.

There were a lot of family reunions there. One guy met his mother who he wasn't sure was dead or alive. There was a Bosnian Muslim soldier with a Kalashnikov over his back with tears rolling down his face when he was re-united with his mother, who he thought was dead and had been told she was dead for two years. Her name came up on the list in the newspapers and he turned up. One of the neat parts was the little babies that we brought in. One old lady that we brought in was dying of cancer but she wanted to be re-united with her family. She was on a stretcher with the IVs running and we were all sitting around punching each other on the shoulder, as we didn't know what to do. The crews had a good time. That was just about the end of the program for us and we felt that we had accomplished a whole lot. Then we thought about it a little bit more and there were a few of us that realized that nobody actually came up and said, "Thanks!" Not one of the people. It was such a media circus that nobody came and said thanks and it was a bit of a let-down but they guys knew that they had accomplished something.

I think this was a media event. That's the way I feel about it. They used the event to get their press. It was annoying coming from a platoon commander's perspective. My troops worked exceptionally hard preparing the vehicles, driving under those terrible conditions, picking up those people and nobody said, "Thanks!" It would have been nice to get the high sign from one of the locals but I guess being reunified with the family was a big thing in their life but how it happened, they didn't give a rat's ass.

We brought out 28 in our vehicles and the Norwegians got the remainder. They used soft-skinned vehicles, which was something that we were very hesitant to do given the situation up there, and we used armour exclusively. Our vehicles worked exceptionally well and we got our job done. We thought the night was over and we were going to go down to Sarajevo Airport and stay with FREBAT 2. It took us a long time, probably two hours, to get there from the centre of Sarajevo. The old eyeballs were working overtime, as we were worried about snipers, and the Norwegians were still with us with their lights and sirens going. They had a real fixation for it. We were sitting between blocks of apartments, ten or twelve storey buildings, and you could see guys up on the balconies. They were rather annoyed and as everyone in Sarajevo owns a Kalashnikov I was just waiting for them to rain down on us but fortunately it didn't happen. We got to the airport, parked our vehicles, dragged our kit into the old departure lounge and we slept on the marble floor. We got in about 0430 in the morning after the circus was over, nobody was there to brief us on the place, and we didn't even know where the washroom facilities were. I would have killed for a cup of coffee then. I went back to the Bison, cranked up the boiling vessel, had a cup of coffee and sat down to think about what we had done. By the time I got back upstairs, the troops were just knocked right out. They were exhausted. Twenty-five hours-plus standing in the crew commander's hatch and the drivers were just bagged, not to mention all the excitement at Sarajevo Airport.

Operation GOOD SAMARITAN was a combined Canadian-Norwegian affair which included the participation of several Sissu armoured ambulances and their crews. (Author's Collection)

We got up about 1000 that morning and we figured a straight run down Route FINCH to home in Visoko, probably about half an hour. Well, that half an hour turned into another eight hours before we got home. Because we had inherited the Norwegians, the Canadians, being nice guys, said that we'd escort them back to our AOR and they could go their own way once they'd cleared Visoko. So our seven vehicles cleared the checkpoint, but the Bosnian Serbs wouldn't let the Norwegians through the last Serb checkpoint onto Route FINCH because their paperwork wasn't "correct," which was no surprise to us. So we were clear, only twenty-five minutes from home and we had to turn our vehicles around, go back down through the airport again, clear the other checkpoints and come back down the back way past Kiseljak. It was 1600 hours by the time we came back here. For something that was supposed to take eight hours, we were in excess of thirty-two hours and not a whole lot of sleep involved in the whole thing. It was just a hoot.

We got back to Visoko and the boss was antsy, as he wanted to know what had happened to us. He saw us off in the morning to give us the big high sign and he was waiting for us when we came back. We had made the press back home in some news reports. The Canadian Armed Forces Network didn't report a whole lot of it, but the public affairs officer who was with us on the entire journey, Chris Henderson and his photographer, did a good job. It was interesting going through Pale in an armoured vehicle in a convoy and he had this big Betacam sitting out the hatch on my vehicle and I said, "Time to put the camera away. Put it in its bag and hide it under the medical bags." We didn't want the Bosnian Serbs pulling us over for spying.

In the end, despite the let-down, we proved that we could do the job at the Troop level without any effect on the battle group's medical support. The guys came through big-time. Everybody was outstanding, the drivers, the crew medics, and the crew commanders. The drivers and the crew commanders in particular because it was so cold that night that we dropped down in our hatches every time we stopped to get warmed up and the casualties in the back were complaining that it was too hot! So there was a big dichotomy. Did we leave the heaters running and fry those guys or did we try to get warmed up ourselves? I was hanging over the radiator on mine, while the drivers were curled down low in the hatch, and putting their hands in their armpits trying to keep warm. Eventually most of us went hatches down for the last few miles on Mount Igman and we had no night vision, either.

There was an old fellow there, who'd probably lived through the Second World War and all the other stuff that had happened in this country and he was just intrigued. He was looking over my shoulder through my vision blocks to see what was going on and I had the feeling that this guy was probably a tank driver at one time and there he was. I could feel his breath on my back. He was looking out the vision blocks so I slid out of the way and turned the interior lights off. I could tell by the look on his face that he'd done this before. But it was cold, God it was cold! The guys put up with a lot of bullshit from the conditions and the pre-sweetened Brit tea. Anyway, we were the talk of the battle group when we got home. It was the furthest we'd ventured out of this place except down to the coast. Gorazde was way out of our AOR. We looked at the map and, you know, back home this whole operation would have probably taken three hours. But then again people back home don't carry a whole lot of weapons and the roads aren't mined. It seemed that we had gone through twenty checkpoints. Rogatica was another place that stood out. A belligerent guy was wearing Bosnian Serb Frontier Police camouflage uniform, a lot of purples and blues, because it was night camouflage and he had this bright pink scarf on! It was really bizarre.

The unfortunate thing is that we were not allowed to take our cameras with us. The only cameras that were there were the PAFF O's cameras and we reviewed a lot of the pictures. I've seen a whole lot of them and there are some really good ones. One of my medics getting off the ramp of an ambulance, and the cameras were in his face and you can see what was going through his mind, and his hand was out gesturing "Get the fuck off my ramp! Get back so I can do my job here!" The interesting part is that the UNPROFOR photographers were probably the worst. It was flashbulbs and TV camera lights going everywhere.

THE GENEVA CONVENTION AND FST OPERATIONS

Back in October when we had a few minor casualties, not related to the situation here, but guys with high fevers, tonsillitis, guys who just couldn't stay out on the line with this stuff, we went and got them. We'd have to browbeat our way through the checkpoints. Our deal was, nobody messed with the ambulances. We didn't carry fuel on our vehicles, we didn't carry soldiers in our vehicles, we were an ambulance and it didn't matter who you were, we were going to look after you. We'd been trying to beat that into their heads down at the checkpoints for five months but of course it's always the junior guy on at Christmas time and you had to get off the vehicle sometimes and just get in their face and say, "Look, we're not doing anything wrong here. We're looking after everybody and the Red Cross on the vehicle means neutral." They'd start going on about carrying weapons and I'd say, "Well, that's for me to protect my patients and myself and not for shooting at you." Not right now, anyway. But it was amazing.

We really pushed the Geneva Convention over there. We had a few trying incidents with the battle group, as they wanted us to take replacement soldiers across in the ambulances. "I don't think so!" "Well, why not? We do that back home in Petawawa." "Yeah, but this isn't Petawawa." And the next one was, "Yugoslavians haven't signed the Geneva Convention at all." "Well, yeah, okay, but we did!" We had to abide by the rules and they couldn't get it through their heads, a lot of the junior officers and junior NCOs, all newly promoted guys. They were used to back home, where the company or squadron medic on exercise said, "Yeah, I'll drag your kit across for you." Here we stuck by the rules big-time. It was perceived that the FST were not team players and you had to explain to them that it was a violation of international law, not a buddy-fuck. It protected us and if we lost our protection under the Geneva Convention, we would have lost it for the entire tour and we couldn't play as medics anymore.

If that happened you lost all your protection by the book. If you were caught taking fuel or ammunition or soldiers across, that entire crew was marked. They had all our names and numbers, and we'd never get across the CFL [the cease fire line] again. If they wanted to push it, the entire organization could lose its protection under the Geneva Convention. Well, the planners said that we had removable crosses on the vehicles, and thus we could use the Bisons for resupply. Well, yeah, they were only removable because they were put on in Canada. They were used for tactical exercises back there, when the Bisons were not used as ambulances. To be fair to the battle group, it was a nightmare in staff planning trying to get the guys resupplied over on the Serb side and the planners were looking at all the options. Fortunately, the senior minds prevailed on this. I remember one of the messages that came back from Ottawa that if we had to evacuate the camp, non-essential personnel were supposed to man the Ops. Well, a rocket came back saying, "I don't think so and this is what will happen if you guys do that." The CO minuted the message with "Serious Shit!" They'd evacuate non-essential personnel so they could put medics in the towers? It was bad advice that the CO had received from the JAG in Primosten. When the Director of International Law at NDHQ got wind of it, the message came down. It was a peacetime army response to what was going on. Here the learning curve was so steep that you had so much to learn when you got here and things that seemed to be little things actually weren't. They got overlooked. The peacetime mentality was gone from the battle group and it was an operational mentality that we had now. Sometimes the troops got a bit complacent, like a few weeks ago, when the hammer came down. "This is the way it's going to be, folks!"

CHAPTER SIX

MAJOR MATTHEW OVERTON

European Community Military Monitor
The Bihac Pocket, Bosnia, 1993

PERSONAL BACKGROUND AND CALL-UP

My name is Major Matthew Overton, I'm with the PPCLI. I've been in the Canadian Forces since 1977 and joined the regiment in 1981. My experience up until my deployment in Yugoslavia with the ECMM had been principally regimental duty, with one staff tour. I found myself in training system headquarters during the fall of '92, and I was warned that I was to be on the international standby list. That developed into a hard tasking to go to Yugoslavia as a member of the ECMM from March to September of 1993. I was on the list until approximately December, and I got a call from the Joint Staff warning me that I might be going to Mozambique with the ONUMOZ UN peace observation group. In January I got a call asking whether or not I was interested in going to the former Yugoslavia instead. So, essentially a week later a message directed me to finish my clearance and my assignment to the ECMM came through. I had approximately three weeks to prepare myself. All the members of the 12-man rotation went to Ottawa to receive some basic theatre training.

TRAINING

The briefing itself was very much UN oriented. The NDHQ briefers had very little concrete information about what the EC monitors were doing because the EC monitors couldn't really tell them! They said that depending on where you're going you could be doing a number of tasks, anything from humanitarian relief assistance to monitoring ceasefires to political negotiations. The ECMM was spread across all of the Balkan countries in addition to those in which there was fighting, i.e., Croatia and Bosnia. It was also involved in a large number of other countries like Albania, and Bulgaria, and in Slovenia. They also had attachments in Serbia and some people in Macedonia. So depending on your area and what your duties were in your area, you could cover a wide range of tasks. The training that we got in Ottawa was of questionable quality. We were told about medical considerations, we were given some background on the area, we were told about the various operations, who was doing what to whom, our clearance and that essentially took four and a half days from start to finish. And then the Sunday thereafter we were on a flight to Zagreb, Croatia. From there we had five days worth of ECMM training. That went further into depth as to what was going on, where the ECMM was deployed, a very brief overview of the mandate and what the do's and don'ts were of monitoring. Some equipment training on the radios, the vehicles and that sort of thing. Then we were assigned to a regional centre, and then deployed.

ECMM: MANDATE AND ORGANIZATION

The ECMM mandate changed over time. Originally it was put in place to monitor the withdrawal of the Yugoslav National Army (the JNA) from its barracks in Slovenia. As the Yugoslavian problem developed and there was now a problem in Croatia, a new memorandum of understanding was developed that included participation in what was going on in Croatia. And then Bosnia. And so it sort of developed as it went along. It went from a purely 'let's watch the troops leave and make sure they're gone' sort of thing, to a very big mandate which included 'assisting return to normal relations' – at least I think that was the key phrase that we were working under. It covered a wealth of activity that you could justify using this very vague mandate. It put us into a very interesting position in that we termed ourselves as being in the grey zone between the other organizations in the area who had very well defined mandates. We could fill in the cracks. For example, in a number of cases where there was a refugee or person who needed evacuation and according to the organization such as the Red Cross or UNHCR, it was a very valid case but somehow didn't fit within their criteria, they would come to see us to determine if we could work something out. We didn't operate under the same sort of constraints even though people from UNHCR or the ICRC felt that it was a very valid request.

For organization, the ECMM mission had its headquarters in Zagreb in the Hotel "I" in the southeastern sector of the city. They reported directly to the EC presidency on a weekly basis, daily if necessary. From there there were a number of regional centres set up that would deal with regions of varying sizes. For example there was an RC in Zagreb that dealt with the majority of Croatia and the Bihac area of Bosnia. There was an RC in Knin and then the remainder of Bosnia up until central Bosnia. There was an RC in Zenica in central Bosnia, there was an RC in Tirana in Albania, and there was also a ▨▨▨▨▨ RC in the capital. There was also an EC liaison officer who was in The Hague, as well as EC liaison officers with all of the major headquarters of the UN from the command down to the sectors.

Each of the RCs could have a number of controlling centres working underneath it. For example, RC Zagreb where I worked, it had two CCs, one in the Krajina in Sector West and one in Sector North. Knin had one CC that it controlled in addition to its own activities. And then each of the CCs could control one or more teams. One CC that I worked with in Kronac in the Krajina controlled eight teams. A team would be three people, a driver plus two monitors. It more often than not included an interpreter as part of the team. All four of those people were deemed to be part of the EC from the time that they were working for them, including the monitor. We were directed to wear no military clothing at all, and to wear white. That was the distinguishing mark for the EC monitors. We had blue arm bands to wear and also had dark blue EC ball caps with the twelve stars. We had our own communications, we had VHF and HF, as well as the cellular telephone network that we hooked into, the Croatian network when we had a signal. We also had a satellite communication, CAPSAT, which we used for our daily reports. None of these systems were secure.

Each team would send in a report on a daily basis. The report would go to a CC, it would also go to the regional centre as a back-up in case the CC didn't receive it, because sometimes the CAPSAT would take a fair bit of time as there was a lot of traffic on that. Generally, a copy would go to the humanitarian section of the main headquarters of the EC because they liked to see what was going on for humanitarian activities each day. Each report would be broken down into operational, political, humanitarian meetings and other activities.

EUROPEAN COMMUNITY MONITORS AND UNITED NATIONS MILITARY OBSERVERS

Essentially there wasn't a great deal of difference. The biggest difference was the mandate. The UNMOs had a very military oriented mandate where they were to observe the forces in the area, that was their job. If you looked at the various sectors, their job was to monitor the Croatian Army outside the sectors to make sure they stayed out of the 20-kilometre exclusions and that sort of thing, to make sure they were abiding by the terms of the agreement. The EC monitors didn't have that precise a mandate to execute. We had carte blanche. When I was there we had very little direction as to what information was to be gathered. So we would make up our plans for the week, as we could or couldn't have meetings but we would think what we would want to do that week and we would execute our own plan. It could be anything from going to see a relief agency, to talking to a local political leader, to talk to a military commander, go visit a portion of the front line, do a general area tour behind the lines and see what sort of conditions there were, to talk with local economic leaders, to go visit some of the various industries in the area, see what was going on there, if anything, what the state of the manufacturing company was, that sort of thing. That was the largest difference.

ARRIVAL: RC ZAGREB AND THE DAY MISSIONS

For the first two weeks I was at loose ends. I did several day missions. At that time the RC was running day missions to handle the immediate area. RC Zagreb was in the same location as the main headquarters. Most of the contingents consisted of a senior diplomat plus some diplomatic individuals, plus military individuals: a mixed bag, because of the fact that the ECMM was very much evolving into a political monitoring device instead of a military monitoring device. Each of the Heads of Delegation was normally a diplomat of fairly senior rank. Several of them were ambassadors. Certainly, the head of the mission was an ambassador. The nation that had the EC presidency administration at the time, and that rotates every six months, that would be the nation that sent the Head of Mission. The time I was there it was the Danes followed by Belgians, which caused some problems.

What this meant was that the senior staff really weren't the sort of person that you wanted to go out on missions in central Bosnia, or to deploy with for long periods of time. They didn't have the temperament. They would have national duties and would be required to comment on activities to the Head of Mission as to what was going on to assist him as the Head of Delegation in formulating opinion or direction or in reporting to the EC presidency. Also, because they had to fill duties on a national level, they could not leave the Zagreb position. As a result they were usually lumped into RC Zagreb and were used for day missions where they would go out and travel for as far as they could for a day. And that included places such as Karlovac, for example, which were a couple of hours by road plus or minus, to get to where they would patrol for the day, and then they would come back. And they would have various missions assigned to go and look at things. This did not work particularly well. I was assigned to a couple of day missions and went on those with a couple of diplomats, which was an interesting experience.

One was a day mission to Karlovac. It was my very first mission and I wasn't really sure what to expect since I was the junior man on the activity. There were actually three monitors plus a driver and we picked up an interpreter on the way out. When I showed up, being the keen young military person that I was, I was ready to go on this mission and patrol. So I took all my patrol kit, I brought my flack jacket, my helmet, I brought a camera at the bottom of my sack, I brought my patrolling notes that I got from the week's training, and showed up. The individual was a senior diplomat. He had no flack jacket, no helmet. He had a hand-carried camera that he couldn't put into a bag, he didn't have a map, and no patrol plan as to what he wanted to do. We got into a Volkswagen mini bus, and off we went to Karlovac. So I sat there and said "What are we going to do?" "Well, we're going to go down and we're going to see the local refugee centre in Karlovac, the director is a good friend of mine and we'll talk a while, about things going on there. And then we'll have a look at some of the conditions. And then we'll see what happens after that." And I said, "Okay, fair enough." So we get down there and I discover that he hasn't arranged this meeting with the director and the director is not there. So we end up talking to a very harried looking assistant. We talk some very banal details of what's going on, whether or not they're going to see any support, and has anyone come to see them recently, and this sort of thing. I drank my first cup of coffee in the Balkans, which was interesting, because it was Turkish and was very strong. After about an hour of this out we went, and the fellow said, "We'll go and talk to the local military LO." So we went over there and the talk consisted of dropping the interpreter off and then we said "Right, we're going to go visit our friends just over the front line at Krnjak." And I thought to myself this is rather odd, because one of the things we had been told in monitoring was that if you are working one side of the front line, you only work one side of the front line. I said, "Where are we going?" And they said, "We're just going to cross and go to the other side." I said "Okay, fair enough," not knowing whether this was a routine procedure or not. Off I went with him and we drove across.

As soon as we got through the Croatian checkpoint out came the camera and he started taking pictures. I was watching this, and I said, "This is something that I don't think is a really good idea." The reason is that most military installations are very sensitive. They don't like their pictures being taken. They refuse to have it done because they feel it can be used for propaganda. And they're very leery of anyone taking pictures because they're suspicious of your motives. So it becomes a very dangerous thing to take pictures. And that was what this driver was trying to get across to the diplomat, who I found out later had been warned innumerable times about this. Who actually had been stopped by one or other of the sides and had a camera confiscated. He had shown very little understanding of the reality under which he was working. So, it made for a bit of a nerve-racking tour.

I could see the driver, an Italian, looking in the rear-view mirror, and I could see that he was a little upset about this but he didn't say anything. The senior member managed to get the camera back into his hand before we got to the Krajinan Serb checkpoint. We got through and we went to see the Krajinan Serb LO and we talked with him for a while. I discovered that what he wanted to do was to give him some of his own money and receive examples of Krajinan Serb money in exchange. He wasn't exchanging money, he was just collecting. That's exactly what we did. We had coffee and talked for a while of nothing really that important. They introduced me, and he was quite a nice chap and thought that I was great. Then we bundled ourselves back in the van and it was the same thing going back through the checkpoint. As soon as we were through the Serb Krajina checkpoint, out came the camera and he kept on taking pictures and taking pictures. Finally we were on the down slope going towards the Croatian checkpoint, and I started reaching for my flack jacket because he hadn't put the camera away. Just as I was reaching for the flack jacket, the driver stopped the vehicle, turned around and said, "If you don't put that damn camera away right now, I'm kicking you out of the vehicle." So the diplomat said, "Oh, that's no problem," and he put the camera away. I thought, this is absolutely crazy. We got off the checkpoint and I said, "What are we doing now?" And he said, "We're going back for lunch." I said, "Lunch?" And he said, "Yes, it's 1100 o'clock, we have to go back for lunch." Back to Zagreb, another hour's trip back. "What are we doing after lunch?" "Oh well, the patrol's done." I said "Pardon me? When are we going to get together and do the patrol report?" "Oh don't worry, I'll do that." "You're sure." "Oh, no problem, I'll submit it."

So I went back and had lunch and that afternoon I saw one of the fellows that we'd replaced, they hadn't rotated out yet, and still had a couple of days clearance to do. And they knew what I was going to be doing that day, and they said, "So, how was it?" I said, "That has got to be the most ridiculous waste of time that I have ever participated in." And they said, "Yeah, day missions are great, aren't they?"

About three weeks after that, day missions finally got cancelled. They finally resolved the problem of having diplomats there who didn't know what they were doing, were not really interested in monitoring, but were just going through it because they had been told to. The senior diplomats went to do diplomatic things, and all of the monitors went to monitor. They arranged for permanent teams to be stationed in various towns that they were visiting beforehand, who would then take on the day-to-day monitoring. And that worked out very well. But day missions were special.

SECTOR NORTH: EUROPEAN COMMUNITY LIAISON OFFICER

After a couple of days of this, I was then assigned as the EC liaison officer to Sector North because I had no monitoring experience and really didn't know what was going on. But I was a stop-gap. An Italian LO had gone on leave. He was replaced by someone else who had promptly been medevac'd out for tendonitis. His arm was useless and required medical treatment. So I was thrown in as the ECLO and spent a week and a half in Sector North, learning what was going on there from a UN point of view, and liaisoning with the other monitors, and generally getting my feet on the ground. I had no patrolling duties as such, I was required to be in the headquarters during the day in case there were any EC information required, and to make reports back. It was very interesting. At the time, that week and a half, I was quartered with a Serb family in Topusko, which was where the headquarters was.

I was living on the economy. There are no EC units there. Even the hotel where the EC was set up was on the economy, so we were quartered with this family which was very interesting. I had a French driver, as opposed to a full monitoring team. It was a very interesting family. An older mother and father with their daughter-in-law living with them. The son was in the ARSK, the Army of the Serb Republic of Krajina, and was unavailable. So the two of us had his room upstairs, and had three very good meals there a day. They took very good care of us. It was very interesting to see them. We had the occasional chat of what was going on and I learned some words of Serbo-Croat from the family. Generally that was my first introduction to the people. Very simple, rustic people, very friendly. From a cynical point of view that's not surprising. I was providing them with hard currency each week, so it was in their best interests to be friendly. They were decent people caught in a very unpleasant situation, people who led a very simple life. They had a very simple home. Obviously they were doing very well for themselves, which from what I saw overall was a bit of an exception in the Serb Krajina. The accusation by the Krajinan Serbs that they had been neglected by the government and had been locked in basically a rural backwater while the rest of Croatia had developed under the Yugoslav regime I think has some validity to it, but certainly the Slokovics were not suffering and I think they were better off than most of the Krajinan Serbs. They made me feel welcome, as much as they could.

THE BIHAC POCKET

From Sector North I was recalled and sent down to what was going to be a very long haul in Bihac, which is in northwestern Bosnia *[see Figure 8]*. If you think of Croatia as a large croissant, it is the area that the two ends of the croissant would cover if you joined them. Sort of a triangular parcel of land. The town of Bihac itself is in the southwestern corner of that triangle. It was cut off from the rest of the government-controlled area of Bosnia by the Bosnian Serbs.

When I got down there, the situation, although I didn't realize it, had just evolved. Prior to my arrival, there had been essentially a coup. It was still under the control of the Bosnian government, however the individual who had been in charge of the ad hoc regional assembly that had been formed to take care of the area for the Bosnia government had just been deposed. Essentially what you had was the area of Bihac, with an ad hoc regional assembly and its military forces, was surrounded on two of its three sides by the Serb Krajina and the Croatian Serbs, with whom the forces in Bihac had a fairly neutral relationship. The frontier, the border between Croatia and the Bosnia area, was more or less unpatrolled, reasonably quiet. You would find the occasional outpost, but essentially it was an uncontrolled border. No one really paid much attention to it. The fight was not between the Bosnian Muslims and the Krajinan Serbs, it was between the Krajinan Serbs and the Croatian Croats and the Bosnian Serbs and the Bosnian Muslims. So it was in the interest of both the groups on the Bosnian and Croatian border to leave each other alone. There were minor problems. Certainly in the northeastern area of Bihac there were some problems. But because patrolling was difficult in the area and the brigade commander in the area was relatively negative towards the international organizations, we couldn't really confirm what was going on on the other side. That was the Danish battalion area, and they said there were problems but not big ones.

When you went to the southern area of Bihac, the southern front, that was where the majority of the action went on. It was concentrated along the Una River. That is a major river system going northeast-southwest in Bosnia and runs right through Bihac. It is also a major road and rail link and was one of the major links between Serb-controlled Banja Luka in Bosnia and Knin in the Serb Krajina. It is a major communications hub. A lot of north-south travel goes through Bihac. You've got a number of power lines, there are rail lines, several river valleys come in there, there are road links in there. So it's a fairly major centre in a fairly mountainous area. It's a real crossroads for a number of reasons. The Bihac area is also significant as it is the largest and most western Muslim-dominated area. It borders right on Croatia. If you look at the ethnic map, it is almost completely Muslim. In fact all of this area up here, all that triangle is Muslim, and there was a significant Muslim population that was south of the Una River before the war. They were either driven out and there were a large number of refugees in Bihac, or that are still in the area. When the Bosnia Serbs took the area, they pushed all of the people out or kept them in enclaves.

The Bosnian Serbs almost flatly refused to deal with the ECMM, or with the UN for that matter, and it was very difficult for the UN in western Bosnia to make any contact with the Bosnian Serbs, a situation much different from central Bosnia where they were talking to people all the time. In this area there was almost no contact at all. The Serbs had some very bad press as they were still involved in their ethnic cleansing program. If you remember during that time, Banja Luka had a thousand-year-old mosque that was destroyed. The Serbs stopped a lot of people from going to Banja Luka, Prijedor, and all of these areas around there. There had been

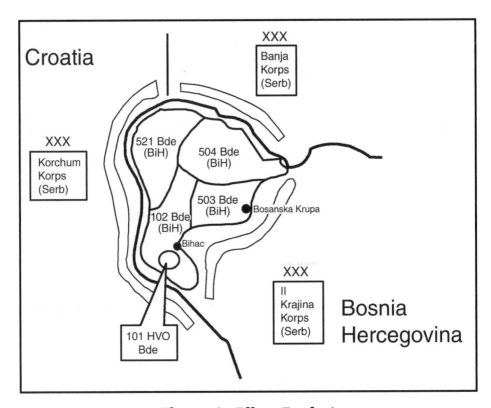

Figure 8: Bihac Pocket

very little UN presence. Even the Red Cross was extremely restricted. For example, I remember talking to the ICRC rep in Bihac, and he was trying to get information out of his counterpart in Banja Luka about some allegations or some information about Muslim refugee camps where they were being kept. He said basically at that time his counterpart was restricted to the city limits of Banja Luka.

It just made it very difficult to deal with them period. You couldn't get any information as to what was going on. Very, very infrequently would they agree to negotiations. In fact, my first experience with the Bosnian Serbs was a meeting just outside Bihac in a little town where we had arranged a meeting between the representatives of 5 Corps, which was the Bosnian army formation in Bihac, and 2 Corps, which was facing them on the Bosnian Serb side. This had happened two or three times before and the head of the co-ordination centre had attended these meetings, had organized these meetings. We arrived at the meeting, we sat down. The first thing out of the lips of the Bosnian Serb representative was, "What is the EC doing here? We made no agreement for them to be here. We will leave if they don't." And this was the third in a series of meetings of which the EC had chaired. From that point the Bosnian Serbs and the Bosnian government representatives argued about whether or not the EC could be there, whether or not the EC could share, who said they could be there, who didn't say they could be there. It just circled around for about two and a half hours. Finally, the agreement was that the EC could attend the meeting, however they would not share and they would not talk. That was the last meeting that was held for a number of months between the two sides. For one reason or another there was a lack of understanding between the two sides. Whether we were there or not it didn't matter, they just weren't interested in talking.

As a side note, by the time I had left the area in June, one of the last things I did was I headed the co-ordination centre. I was acting head for two weeks. I chaired a meeting between the Bosnian Serbs and the Bosnian government representatives out of Bihac. So it had come full circle. It was a meeting that we had organized; we had been approached by the Bosnian side to see if we could organize it. We had made the contacts through the UN with the Bosnian Serbs, they agreed to the meeting, we chaired it, we had subsidiary meetings the day beforehand, and then we chaired the meeting. In fact we chaired a number of meetings. But it had gone full circle from this very hardline stance, this 'get out of our faces' to 'you're the chairperson' attitude. It was very odd. We couldn't pick out any particular reason for this attitude to have been taken. We don't know what inspired that. It shocked the living daylights out of the head of the EC who chaired several of these meetings. He was completely blindsided. The UN observers were completely blindsided by this as well. The one thing I learned was that no matter how well you thought you were getting along with someone, you could be blindsided by them at a minute's notice. They would come out of left field with something.

EC MONITORS AND UN MILITARY OBSERVERS: INFORMATION SHARING

All three belligerents, the Croatian, Bosnians, the Krajinan Serbs, had their own agendas. They were cultivating you as a friend for a particular purpose, or a number of purposes just to exploit you. I was no exception. The arrangement we had made with the UN military observers that were based in Bihac, was that they would operate at the brigade commander level and forward, and we would handle brigade commander and back, though we could transgress in each other's area. It was an informal arrangement, it wasn't anything cut in stone. If we wanted to go over a front line, we were more than free to do it, and we would do it with or without the UNMOs. Sometimes we would join belligerent patrols and sometimes we didn't. But that was the basic arrangement. We would handle everything behind the brigade command and even humanitarian aid, social activities, what were the social conditions, religious, you name it.

It was senseless for us to send back the same reports. This was also in the face of the EC presidency giving some indications to the ECMM Head of Mission that they wanted more politically oriented, diplomatically oriented information. They said, "We're getting all of the military information out of the UNMOs. There's no sense in us having monitors, they're doing the same thing. Let's get some more politically relevant information, get the background, try to get into the heads of the leaders, to find out what the hell is going on there."

We were doing some rudimentary analysis. As I progressed up the chain of command, or the level of command, I got more experience and became more valuable to the mission, as would anyone else. The more experience you have the better you are at making analysis or at least shaping your information to provide relevant information. Certainly when I was head of the CC, which was mid June, and then as the senior duty officer in the RC, they were looking for more analysis. When I was head of the CC the weekly reports would try to tie together the relevant events of the weeks with what happened previously and perhaps do some analysis as to what we thought was coming on. That's what was going on at the RC level. As to what was leaving the ECMM and going to the EC presidency, I don't know. But they were doing some analysis. At the ECMM level they had the legal advisor and also a political advisor working for the head of the mission, who was a diplomat himself. So there was plenty of analysis going on.

The UNMOs could provide some analysis. They would also talk about what they saw on the political side. For example in Bihac we would sit with them during their daily wrap-up. Because we were only one team we wouldn't have to wrap up with anybody. But we would sit with the UNMOs and listen to their team reports, and then provide them the information we had. We would discuss it together so we were all working from the same sheet of music, at least at the UNMO-EC level at Bihac. I know this was going on in a number of other areas where it wasn't as structured because the teams weren't necessarily living in the same hotel as we were when I first got there. The senior military observer at the time who was a very good friend of mine, we had been in the same battalion together before. So, it was a very natural arrangement for us that we had continued. There had been a Canadian in Bihac for the last nine or ten months, so with a Canadian being almost constantly in the Bihac UNMO team, it was a very natural link to make and that they talk to one another. We kept that going even after I left. I know that the EC team would go down the street to the UNMOs when we had changed accommodations. They would go down to the UNMOs on a daily basis and talk to them.

We had a good working arrangement there. I know that at the team level in other areas they had worked out arrangements that had worked very well, where they arranged not to go to see the same person on the same day, because what the individual would do is just see everybody at the same time and make the meeting very short. Which satisfied no one. We sometimes did combined patrols, but we're talking about the exploitation of the information.

WORKING WITH THE BIHAC LEADERSHIP

While I was there, the team made an active effort to carry the attention and co-operation of the regional assembly by the president of the regional assembly, to get known to him, to get him to trust us to a certain extent. Or at least to feel comfortable talking to us. I think we were reasonably successful at that. He had spent some time in Germany, spoke German, and I had a German team member. He was also reasonably young. Ejup Topic was an electrical engineer by trade and fell into politics due to the nature of the war. Certainly, he wasn't a hardline Communist, he wasn't a political hack from previous years. So I think we had some success in getting good relationships. And that was the same with his prime minister, Zlatko Jusic, who was a younger man as well. But I discovered that he was starting to use the relationship for his own purposes. When I was working in the RC I had talked to him a couple of times when he was out of the Bihac Pocket, and I arranged for him to get back into the pocket using UN transport. He came to the EC and myself to get a briefing, which I was very pleased about. At the same time he said that he had a package arriving and he asked if I could get it to the pocket for him. Thinking it was something personal I said it was no problem. The problem was when it arrived, it turned out to be a number of Zagreb cellular telephones. So I at that point had to say no, I wasn't going to do it. Which was very difficult but I also know that I couldn't be used in that regard. And I was disappointed in how he was using this relationship I had worked to build up with him. So, even though you think you get to know people that you give an understanding of what you think you should be doing and what their relationship and yours should be, they will turn it quickly. And I can understand it. They are dealing with a very difficult situation, they will use whatever means they can. It was disappointing to be used in that regard.

They will also try to gain your co-operation or your agreement on certain points of view. For example, I had a very difficult meeting with a brigade commander who I remember writing in my diary had "eyes of fire," very intense burning eyes. He was a bit of a zealot. He worked for about three quarters of an hour to get us to state, while a video camera was there, that the Bosnia Serbs were the aggressors. Of course, we were in no position to do that, we couldn't do that. We danced on that topic for about three quarters of an hour until finally my counterpart, a German, came up with the key to the door and said that we had to work with both sides. You know we do cross lines, we work with various organizations at various times, we are neutral, that sort of thing. If we were to state categorically while we're on one side the other side is the aggressor, the other side will take a very dim view of that, make our life very difficult and we could no longer carry out our mandate. So we didn't state anything of the sort to anybody. It would also have been used for internal propaganda. I'm very certain the tape would have gone down to Bihac TV and it would have been broadcast that the ECMM stated that the Bosnian Serbs were the aggressors. Words could be twisted very quickly.

THE PINK ZONES AND ETHNIC CLEANSING

In the pink zone in the Krajina there were a number of Croatians who were captured in the pink zones and who wanted to leave. The Croatians wanted them back, everybody wanted these people to go, it was in everybody's best interests. It was something that the international agencies hammered out time and time again to assist. The Croatians would say "Help us get these people out." Well, finally it was arranged that one or two bus loads of people were gathered together to be brought across, with the full co-operation of the Krajinan Serbs, who of course wanted them gone. They got the bus through the checkpoint. When they arrived in Karlovac, they found there were press crews and video cameras all over the place. That day in the newspaper was a huge headline to the effect that ethnic cleansing had been propagated by the international agencies including the ECMM. The ECMM Head of Mission pulled in a senior government official and said, "You guys wanted this, you begged us to do it and you've done this to us, and we will never do it for you again." That was modified to some degree in that we would do that on a case-by-case basis. In fact while I was there we tied up a last end to it, because the aid agency and the Croatian agency had been yammering to us about lists and lists of people. So just before I arrived at the head of CC, the incumbent had arranged for an independent medical survey of the people, and had gone through and made a list of about twelve people that we would assist in their departure because of medical conditions. The rest we will not touch. They are in no danger medically, they may be older people but they are in no danger any more so than anyone else and there is no medically pressing reason for them to go. And so we were working with the local Red Cross in the area of Trzac to arrange for people to get out. And that was very much on military authority of some type. So one by one they were being brought out. But not any more than one or two at a time in order to avoid exactly the spectacle that had happened before.

It was difficult to avoid becoming paranoid. You have to be extremely careful in what you say. Even if you're very scrupulously careful of what you say, it can still be turned against you. Negotiations that I chaired at the end of my time in Bihac, for example, I found my words turned against me. There was no acknowledgement by the individual who was twisting my words that I had been there, that I had said the words, and I told him I did not say that, I know what I said, I did not say those words. There was no acknowledgement. It had to do with a body exchange. There were a number of bodies that had been buried by the forces because they were close to the lines and they were looking for an exchange. Well, the whole thing was a mess from one end to the other. Both sides indicated they weren't going to require international observation to recover the bodies, so as a result the only thing they wanted us to do was to monitor the exchange of bodies. There were disagreements on the Bosnian Serb side as to whether or not monitors could come to their side from a different area and approach from the rear so they could see what was going on. They didn't want that. So we ended up with no monitoring at all. The Bosnians said they didn't want any monitoring, the Bosnian Serbs said they weren't going to allow monitoring. So essentially what we did was show up at the exchange point on the day desired to watch and just say yes, the bodies have been exchanged. It took four hours to cross-load the bodies. Almost immediately after the exchange and everyone had taken the bodies away, allegations ripped back and forth about the condition of the bodies, who was actually given over, the number of bodies that were exchanged. It just went from bad to worse. The Bosnian Serbs were upset because the EC monitors and the UNMOs had not forced the Bosnians to give over the number of bodies they said they would. I remember clearly in the negotiations we wanted a monitor to say that the exchange was done. I remember saying that quite clearly. Fine, we'll attend and we'll watch you do this. But neither of you want us to watch the number of bodies, you don't want us to verify anything about their condition, you don't want us to verify anything about where they were, or the conditions. That's fine.

The belligerents would keep their own records anyway and distort them. And the particular individual we were dealing with was a very hardline sort and made the statement that the EC promised that the Bosnian Muslims would give over thirty bodies. I said the EC did not say that, because I was the EC representative. I said I would monitor the transfer of bodies and I acknowledged that a number of bodies were being stated, they were stated as being ready for exchange, or that they could get. He said, "The EC promised that the Bosnians...!" I said, "I was at the meeting, I know what I said." "The EC promised!" It didn't matter. Because you had been at the meeting and because you said you would monitor, they expected you to be the guarantor, when in fact we had no guarantor status, no guarantor ability. They use it to their own purposes. It's to make you look foolish. They do this for their own propaganda. Immediately after the meeting, one of the negotiators was filmed by a Bosnian Serb TV crew coming out of the tent, went and talked for five minutes with people in the background, you know 5 or 10 metres away talking among themselves, and it was obviously a public relations exercise.

Fortunately we were also fairly well squared away from that sort of thing by the EC. There was one time when the Bihac TV wanted to interview the EC, and so the public information office came down and did the interview. He said the questions were fairly mundane, there wasn't anything big about it. But they tried to avoid giving a list of questions. He said he wanted a list of questions before he answered. We tried and tried, and finally didn't get a list of questions until the morning of the interview. He said they were very stock things, I'm sure he'll ask me something different. And sure enough he did. He was prepared for it. Later on ECMM HQ said if someone wants to take a statement from you, just tell us that you're going to do that and we'll let you do it. They were fairly paranoid, because of the bad experiences people had. Unguarded statements at various times in meetings that would be blown out of proportion, for example. They would be very leery of anyone talking to the press, I think for a very good reason. The propaganda intensity is very unbelievable there. It's agitation, it's disinformation, it's hate mongering. It's all there, very sophisticated. They control their press completely. Croatia is no different. The press there is controlled to a great extent. It's not independent, it's not what you think of as an independent critical press. It is very much, we're with the government, we'll do everything in our power to assist the government to make the others look bad. It's very strange by North American standards.

The thing is the nationalist feeling there. You've got to understand that the Yugoslav constitution provided national status to the Serbs, to the Croats, and Muslims. So they see Croatia or Serbia as the embodiment of the nation, the state. It is the nation's state. So if you transfer that national feeling to the state, and so the state becomes the nation, the nation the state. What is good for the nation is good for the state, what is good for the nation is good for Croats. So what's good for Croats is good for Croatia. So it's a very circular sort of thing, very reinforcing thing. It's very difficult to deal with. Where in Canada you have a variety of peoples, not nations, but peoples living here, ethnic groups. There in the Yugoslav constitution they were guaranteed status as a nation in the state. Very powerful. This was carried on into the Croatian and the Serbian constitution. Probably the Slovenian as well. There was a dedication of nations within the state, and Croatia is the expression of the Croat nation. And that's a very powerful statement.

Symbols took on greater importance too. A large problem was the Croatian national flag, which had in it the red and white checkerboard. It's a very powerful Croatian national symbol. It was associated with the Ustashe of World War II, the Fascists, who did some pretty horrendous things to the other nationalities. Now the present Croatian government's defence of the use of this symbol is that instead of starting it with a red square up on the top left-hand corner as the Ustashe, they start it with a white square on the top left-hand corner, which makes it a totally different symbol, which is a fairly silly argument, but it's how they defend it. So you see it's a completely different symbol, because we do that. But the problem is that it still looks like Ustashe, and so the Serbs were very sensitive to this, they are very sensitive to symbols, and they see this as the Ustashe being reconstituted within the Croatian state.

The Serbs use the double-headed eagle. That became a very prevalent symbol. For them also there is the cross with four c's, a cross or an 'x' with four c's. Basically, Serb strength through unity. That is a very powerful symbol for them. The Serb mentality is strength through adversity. I had it stated to me once in the Krajina that the harder the world pushes us, the more we will resist. And they believe that very intensely. If you look back to the Kosovo it's one of their great national moments. It was the slaughter of the Serbs by the Turks. You've got to think, if this is what they take as their great national monument, this horrendous defeat from which they recovered, you have to question the value of pressing them harder and harder.

As for the Bosnian presidency, there was some regional identification. For example, where I was in Herzegovina, there was also an historical foundation for the area of Bihac, in that the boundaries of 5 Corps were more or less equivalent to the boundaries of the partisan organization that operated there during the Second World War. I found this out through an old partisan, who it turns out was actually the political officer of his partisan unit.

All the symbols were powerful and call to mind the Austro-Hungarian Empire. The four c's and the double-headed eagle, very powerful. The Krajina was their military border area. In fact, the area of UN Sector East and further to the west of that was a major displaced population from the centre of Bosnia. Up until the 1500 or 1600s, there was a large Serb Eastern Orthodox population in the centre of what was the Turk-held area, the Ottoman Empire. But during one of the Hapsburg assaults into the area that had been supported by these Eastern Orthodox Christians, which had been defeated, as punishment they were told to leave. And so they were re-populated to the area that I think is now Sector East, along there. So it's very interesting. So the Serbs within the Krajina were very appreciative of the Hapsburg dynasty for their support. But they actually feel betrayed. Once this developed into the Austro-Hungarian Empire, control of various areas of the empire were given back to the locals. And of course the locals of that time, instead of giving the Krajina over to the Eastern Orthodox Serbs, the Catholic emperor turned it back to his Catholic Croats. These things sometimes had a direct impact on our relationships and working conditions. Old battles, old wounds, that sort of thing. But they didn't have a direct impact on day-to-day things. You get an appreciation for why they are there. The Serbs were put there to defend against the Turks. They were built up, provided troops for the various Krajina areas. The terrain certainly favours it. It's a brilliant area defending.

MILITARY OPERATIONS AROUND BIHAC

When I got there Bihac was actually being shelled fairly significantly. There were in the order of seventy or eighty shells a day, that were either direct or indirect, arriving in the town mostly in the southeastern sector over the river. One of the problems I have with that is that because I was working the political organization and the economic organization rather than the military, we deliberately distanced ourselves from that. We said the UNMOs are doing that, they have all the details. We're going to stay away from it. So we did. But we had a general understanding of what was going on. Now the area I understood best was in the area of Bihac, because that's where I spent most of my time monitoring. Surrounding the pocket area on the Krajina side was basically the Serb Banja Corps and Kordun Corps. The reason they're called these names is because those are the military districts when the Krajina was originally set up. All the troops that belong to Banja Corps come from the Banja district. On the southern frontier, which were the Bosnian Serbs, was basically 2 Krajina Corps. Again, because it's a military district. The corps was the formation that came out of the district. They call it the corps, but it could be of varying size, it's not what we think of as a corps ourselves.

Within the Bihac area, it was broken up into essentially five areas. Each of the areas was more or less aligned to an Opstina, the equivalent would be a county, say Yorkshire, that has sited on it the city of York. Same idea. So the opstina was a county area of varying size based on a particular major town or city. In the area of Bihac, there were actually three units involved. There was 101 and 102 Brigade, plus the 101 Hrvastka Brigade or the Croat National Guard of Bosnia-Herzegovina, of varying size. In the area of Cazin there was the 503 Brigade, again in what was essentially the Bosanska Krupa opstina, but because over half of that opstina had been taken by the Bosnian Serbs, it was centred on Cazin, and it was defending the frontier from approximately Ostrozac to the end of the Una River and the Bosnian border. In the area of Buzim was 504 Brigade, and in Velika Kladusa was 521 Brigade. Each of these brigades were of varying strength and equipped to varying degrees. I know when I arrived there you never saw an off-duty soldier with a weapon. Just before I left I came back down to talk to the team in Bihac and everyone had weapons. So there were obviously weapons being obtained one way or the other. Originally they did not have many heavy munitions such as mortars or tanks. Only two tanks had been identified, one which was not a mover, it was on a flatbed that they moved around as basically a mobile pill box. They had a few heavy mortars which they used occasionally, and they had a couple of anti-aircraft guns and a couple of armoured car sort of affairs. And that was about it. Certainly the Serb forces were much better equipped in the way of tanks, artillery, mortars, etc.

The issue we had to deal with was control, essentially. Who controlled the trappings of the nation to allow their existence? Who controlled Bosnia-Herzegovina? One analysis I read said that in Yugoslavia it was a question of the Serbs controlling everyone else. In Bosnia, it was a question of everyone else controlling the Serbs, and the Serbs were not going to allow that to happen. That was a large question. Although they only had 40% of the population, they now controlled about 70% of the country. They controlled all of the major economic areas. All the power-producing areas, most of the general activity, all of these sort of things. They held the military and politically significant areas. Their problem was in central Bosnia, where they had that very narrow corridor in the area of Brchko that traverses the north end of that long finger that heads up into central Bosnia. And they're very aware of that. That is a very strategic weakness, an important strategic weakness they have to improve on. So, that has to be resolved. The nature of the conflict is essentially a low-level conflict with the occasional spurt, very high intensity operations. It is very much aligned along campaign season from late spring to early winter, because they don't have the logistics or the necessary material to support a year-round battle, so a lot of the time in the campaign season is spent in harassing attacks, low expenditure of munitions, low expenditure of personnel, with a slow build-up that is obvious to both sides, and a very short battle to try and take an objective. And then they hang on. They try to weather the counterattack, where the other side responds. Their build-up will not have been as quick or had started as early, so they then have to have the time to respond and fight back. And that's very much the nature of the conflict that I've seen.

All the belligerents have various elite units that they train with varying degrees of professionalism. I did not have any personal contact with them, but I've heard of reports of various training establishments that are supposed to be training these elite forces for insertion into the other side. Certainly there was some indication that that had been going on. There were some odd instances of sabotage. For example in the Krajina, they actually had a rail service operating through UN Sector North back into Bosnian territory, and this train was blown up. So there's obviously activity going on.

ECMM OPERATIONS

We conducted two types of activity. The one that took the majority of time was trying to figure out what was going on. That involved talking to a large number and a variety of people. We talked to business leaders about the state of their businesses. We talked with local political leaders, the mayors, members of the regional assembly and its prime minister and a couple of his ministers. We talked with various military commanders on various issues. We talked with the other agencies, such as the aid agencies, and the local aid agencies about the distribution of food and the problems they were having, what the conditions were. We talked with some agricultural people about what was going on there because there was still activity still going on, to feed themselves, and what sort of level they were able to produce, and what was also going into the front lines.

The other side was direct humanitarian assistance to various individuals. For a while that almost overwhelmed the team. We would not accept people coming directly to us. There were two aid agencies that dealt with the vast majority of refugees, and that was the UNHCR and the ICRC. They dealt with the majority of the cases. A lot of these cases were stalled. In other words, the individual met the criteria of one or two of those organizations, but the evacuation or the refugee relief was stalled because of one of the belligerents or the other. This was extremely frustrating in the case of people who could be evacuated but 5 Corps was not letting them out, for example. It was frustrating.

We got involved in situations where there was an individual or two that could not be helped by one of those two groups because they didn't fit the criteria. For example the ICRC or UNHCR would not accept into the evacuation chain anyone who had left their area voluntarily and showed up somewhere else and then said "I'm a refugee." So if you came from central Bosnia and you managed to get yourself to Bihac, which was a relatively safe area, and said "I'm a refugee, I want to keep going," they would not accept you at that point because you were in a relatively safe area. It was a bit of a Catch 22: if you stayed where you were you would be harassed but you go somewhere safe and you could not get any further. So it was a problem. They had to be very hard-hearted about that, to avoid being abused. We arranged with them, if they had someone who came to them who was, they felt, a deserving individual for assistance, to get out of the pocket. That was the way it worked. As a result we actually assisted a number of people in and out of the pocket.

There was one case of a Slovak who was living in Vrsta Bekovica who started getting nervous about what was going on and was not getting anywhere from UNHCR or ICRC for one reason or another. We managed to evacuate her, which was an interesting experience, driving through the two checkpoints with her. At the time we had an armoured Mercedes car. I don't know if you have ever seen one of these Mercedes armoured cars. They are two-and-a-half-ton monsters. Think of a Mercedes land rover, but with armoured windows, speaker system with mikes so you can listen out and you can talk. They're beasts. In fact all of the vehicles that we had were super. There were already three of us in this vehicle, the two monitors plus the driver, and then we had this little woman in the back with all of her bags. You could not see out of the back of the vehicle, or out of the side of the vehicle, you could only see out front. Of course everyone was nervous as hell because at any time we expected that she would get stopped because she had her Slovak passport, but we expected the worst to happen that we would get stopped and she'd be pulled over and we would have a crisis of some sort. But it was almost like a drive on a Sunday afternoon, just sailing through the checkpoints, they couldn't have cared less, they didn't even ask for her ID, just kept on going. It was unbelievable. All of the angst we went through for months trying to organize this, and then we went through without a problem.

There was another case that was very interesting actually. One of the wives of a soldier in Bihac, I'm not sure whether or not she committed suicide or she was hit by a shell. However the situation was that he was now widowed with two small children and his intent was to get his mother-in-law to take care of the children. He wanted this and she wanted this. The only stumbling block was that she was a Serb who had left there previously and who was living not far from Bihac, but outside the pocket area. It took us over a month for the arrangements to be made to finally get her into the pocket. It was extremely frustrating. We ended up talking with the corps commander who was an ex-JNA captain, now a general. This was not uncommon. Very much political. We had to talk to him, had to talk to the president of the regional assembly, talk to the prime minister, talk with the police. All of whom pointed the finger at someone else being the stumbling block. It was a big circle. We finally managed to get this thing hammered down and it was basically talking to the chief of staff of 5 Corps and saying look, this is for your soldier so he can go back to your front line to fight your enemies. Why are you stopping us from bringing this woman in? And the day after we had the paper. It was bizarre.

There was one group, I think it was the Bosnian Army, that was blocking this old Serb woman to come in. And so, we finally got her in with one restriction. She had to go to the police station and re-register as being back in the pocket. We took her to the police station, we took her to the registry office, they pulled out her file and they said, "You never went anywhere." They had no record of her having left the pocket. And so we said fine, and we took her to her home. We let her family know she was coming and they were overjoyed. But it's just the level of frustration. Sometimes I was under the impression that if they knew something was important to you, even if it wasn't important to them, they would play the power position. They would say no slowly, they would say yes even more slowly. Very rarely would you get a fast yes. In fact I don't think I ever saw a fast yes. And the only time I saw a reasonably quick yes was when they knew the other side was in on it. I'm firmly convinced that the faster that one side says no the faster you know it's not going to work.

We tried to feign disinterest to speed up the process, but it didn't seem to help. They knew they had a power position. If they want it to happen, it would happen extremely quickly, and the international agencies would never get involved. That was the bottom line. If it were in the interest of both sides to happen, the international agencies wouldn't know about the problem or the situation until after it had been resolved. The only time the international agencies were involved in an event was because one side or the other wasn't going to do it. That was it. Time and time again. I remember very clearly that in UN Sector North the UNMOs in the area were advised of a body recovery and exchange after the event. It came up at a weekly meeting,

"Oh by the way, a couple of days ago we got together with the other side and we exchanged bodies." And apparently at this meeting you could hear the jaws hit the floor. You see, these two sides talked to each other all the time, they knew each other. They were friends, they worked in the army together, they knew each other. In fact that was the problem in one of the areas: the two commanders knew each other and hated each other. There were constantly problems in that sector.

I still remember it very clearly, after the body exchange was all over and the trucks were getting ready to pull away and the two sides were separating, during the whole exchange process they were there exchanging information with each other about how people were and stuff like this, and commiserating about various things, talking about the old times. At the end, I remember very clearly one of the senior government officials had in a headlock one of the senior Serbs. And they were both laughing like crazy, and it was being filmed! I thought this is just bizarre. But there they were, having a great time, laughing and joking. They were on very amicable terms. And then the next day, we're back at square one. Yelling about the various atrocities that were performed on the bodies and how they had given all their bodies back in good shape. For a while I was sure they were going to take us into the morgue and show us the bodies, and I thought "I just don't need to see this."

We said, "Look guys, we weren't there when they were dug up on either side. You didn't ask us to verify the condition of the bodies. All we saw was a bunch of bodies going back and forth. We're not helping anyone on this. You made it, you live with it. We refuse to deal with this." We told both sides that, we said this is not an issue, this is your fault, that's it. They saw we weren't going to have any of it, so they stopped.

The majority of the time I spent there was relatively peaceful. We didn't get involved in the front line because of the nature of the mission, though we did a couple of times. You feel exposed the moment you step near a front line when you're all dressed in white. Especially in the height of summer when everything is green and brown and you wander around sticking out like a sore thumb. Your flack jacket was white. You didn't wear green because you wanted to wear white to show you're a monitor. It was a mixed blessing. I know that on one front-line area the ECMM team did get sniped at because we just stuck out. And another time we went to the top of the hill and got onto the forward slope and looked down at Bosanska Krupa feeling very exposed. And every once in a while shots would ring out, harassing sniper shots. Nothing directed to us fortunately. The one time that I felt a distinct unease about putting myself in a position was when I went to a place called Otoka which is right down the Una River and is right on the front line. We sort of fell into doing this. It was a joint patrol with the UNMOs, one of the few times. We had gone down to see the company commander in the Otoka area which was in Cazin Brigade. We got to the company headquarters position which was in the back of the village in dead ground. And he said "Well, do you want to go down to the river?" And we just sort of looked at him and the UNMO just looked at him and we said, "Well we can talk about that in a few minutes. Let's just see what's going on." We sort of eased into it. Eventually we found ourselves more or less boxed into it. The UNMOs had committed one of the cardinal errors, which was they hadn't brought their flack jackets since they were not expecting to go down there. They thought about this for a while and said "Well, we're in for a penny, in for a pound," so we left our jackets as well just to maintain continuity and also to maintain a certain speed as well. If everyone is running at the same speed we'd better too, because we're sticking out like sore thumbs once again. And so down we went.

The company headquarters position was further back and higher, so we were always going down the forward slope with various bits of houses and things for cover. When we first started out what we did was visit the schoolhouse, which is in the basement of a little house. There were about eight children there learning their lessons. The children were there carrying on on this dirt floor. That was a very interesting scene, because people would not leave their houses unless they were absolutely forced to because of the fighting. And so even there right on the front-line area there was still this normal activity going on which I found very interesting. And off we went. I guess there was a pack of ten of us, and of course Murphy's Law operating, the two white guys were stuck at the back of the line. You couldn't put them up front, so if there was anyone watching they had a reasonable chance of not being shot. But down we went and got down to the main street of Otoka which was absolutely devastated. Every building was bombed out. The infrastructure was useless. All the power lines were down, you could see the road had been picked up in places, the sewers were gone. We got down to the river and all you could see from that point was the hill on the other side, because you went about another 50 or 60 metres on the other side of the Una River, and then up to the top of the hill which was about 100 metres, and then I said "Where exactly is the front line?" And they said "Well basically you're on it." Okay. "So where are your troops?" "Well today they're actually across the river." He said from here to the top of the hill is sort of like a shifting front, sometimes we hold it sometimes they hold it. He said you just have to be careful, there are a lot of snipers. I said where do you normally hide out? He said that house and that house, you see that house, we think that's where they are today. You could feel people moving back away from the windows at that point and being very circumspect about how they wandered around. It was interesting because that was one of the first two or three days that one of the new UNMOs had been there. He was a Russian who had just come from Sarajevo. For him snipers were nothing. There were actually a couple of sniping battles going on while we were there and we could hear the rounds going in and out. He was very cool and calm through this. I remember the next day we were in Bihac and we were talking about something, and one of the normal occurrences, we had a mortar round drop in the same grid square as us. He almost jumped out of his skin because he wasn't used to that. He was used to snipers. Snipers he could deal with, but being bombed … I don't like being bombed! It was very funny to see it. No one else moved because they were used to hearing the shells going off in the same general area. But he didn't like that. He got used to it, but it's funny the things you get used to.

We found that very frustrating. For the longest time Bihac was actually under more intense bombardment and more military activity than Sarajevo was, but the only thing that was making international news was seven bombs in Sarajevo. And we said "Well, seven bombs in Sarajevo, wow! We had that by 800 o'clock this morning."

There were a couple of periods there when they really did a shellacking on the hotel. There was one day where the Serbs had built up for an attack, an attack on the Serbianic plateau which is the plateau that actually looks into Bihac, to try and push the Bosnian troops further away. It was the infamous dawn attack. By about a half-hour later it was obvious the attack had failed, so they just laid a pasting on the town, and that started about 0630 in the morning. We were wondering what the hell was going on. All of a sudden there were constant explosions in town for about three hours, over and over. It was unbelievable. Just retribution for not allowing the attack to succeed. "Well we're going to paste the town for it." Unbelievable. At dawn there was an enormous firefight that lasted for about a half an hour. But that was the nature of the war in

Bosnia. Things were nice and calm for a while and then they would blow up for a couple of days and get calm. That's what happened with the area just east of Varoska. That was the attack in April, where the international news media, now it's the Bihac Pocket, Bihac was being invaded. In reality it was a small portion of the northeast portion of the pocket which was originally a Serb majority area. The story was never particularly clear as to exactly why the Serbs left. I wasn't clear on whether or not that had been forced or if they had been pulled out. Both stories have a certain validity. I think it was a combination.

It was "apparently" some of the people who were expelled who decided to take the law into their own hands and get back into the area. They did this through the use of a number of armoured vehicles, fairly heavy artillery bombardment and various other aspects of a fairly major attack. You couldn't convince me that the Serb authorities didn't know about that. It was a fairly transparent cover story. That was a three-day attack, a very odd attack in that the armoured vehicles would advance about 150, 200 metres and stop for a half-hour, then advance and stop and advance and stop. But a company of tanks, about 10 or 11 tanks supported by an infantry company of about 100 men. It was certainly well beyond the capability of the Bosnian forces to hold. But they took back that little slice of territory and stopped. It was about three days of activity and then things calmed down. It did cause a real crisis in the UN in how they dealt with this. It's one of the things I saw time and time again, and that was the UN military was fractured along the political / military / humanitarian lines. From my point of view as an EC monitor, there was little co-operation between those three groups. At times there could be, but most times they went their own way, to their own agenda with their own plan structure.

The military organization was UNPROFOR, which the UNMOs worked for, and there was UN Civil Affairs. The civil affairs group had a separate chain of command that went to UNPROFOR headquarters, but UNPROFOR headquarters did not control both groups. UN Civil Affairs for UNPROFOR took its orders from New York. It made it a very difficult chain of command. The same thing with UNHCR. And then you had the military aspects. So in all these three chains, there wasn't a single joint commander in the former Yugoslavia to control the UN activities. They were controlled in New York. What it meant was the sector commander for one reason or other did not have what I term a good view of the political ramifications of that particular activity. He decided, and I applaud him for this, that he was going to try and extend influence here, although Bihac already had a certain amount of UN influence. Because the French battalion was there just for the humanitarian aid, the sector commander didn't have authority in the area over that battalion, it was commanded by the UN BH Command. Not only did you have an international boundary but you also had the sector boundary. The sector commander however decided that he was going to try and sort this problem out, because the problem had originated from Sector North.

The UN forces in Bihac included French BAT plus the UNMOs working out of Bihac. Then you had UN Sector North in Croatia. Commander Sector North was involved because the probe originated with the Serb forces in Sector North; he was going to try to swerve to the south. And he was going to be the point of contact for the negotiations, try to separate the forces, get things back to normal. The problem was that he didn't understand the political ramifications of the crossing of the border. In fact he wasn't dealing with a body of Serbs all the way through the full breadth of Yugoslavia and a body of Muslims all the way across Yugoslavia. This was Krajinan Serbs, an assault that originated in the Krajina, that went into sovereign Bosnian territory. No matter how you put a face on it, basically the attack originated in a foreign nation against Bosnia. This was a problem from the Bosnian point of view, quite apart from the military aspects of how the territory is invaded or the territory being forcibly taken. It had been attacked from Bosnian Serb territory into the Bihac area, I mean that is a military problem, they've lost in the territory, but this had political ramifications. The UN commander to my mind didn't appreciate, even though he had been warned about this, certainly from the ECLO. I don't know whether or not his civil affairs officer did. But when he came to sit down with the two sides he presented a ceasefire document that did not acknowledge the fact that the international border had been crossed in the attack. The Bosnian commander took one look at the document and said this is not acceptable, and left. The UN commander looked around and said, "What's wrong?" And so it was a real problem, because you have this separation of three groups.

I don't know what the civil affairs person did. But civil affairs is not a political organization, he is more concerned with the civil infrastructure, the redevelopment or the re-establishment of social services, government services, the humanitarian aid. I know the ECLO had a chance to talk to him about some of these things, and we had seen an advanced copy of the document in Bihac and had come up with four or five of these things to say. "You have got to acknowledge this, this is an important issue from the Bosnian government point of view. If you don't acknowledge this sort of thing it's going to be a problem," and he didn't acknowledge it and it was a problem. And it took another month and a half to get sorted out.

FIKRET ABDIC AND THE FRENCH BATTALION

Fikret Abdic is a well known figure in Yugoslav politics who was very active as an entrepreneur prior to the dissolution of the Yugoslav organization. During the stand-up of the Bosnian government he was a member of the Presidency as the economic advisor in cabinet. Now for one reason or another he split with the Presidency in the fall of '91 prior to the Bihac region being cut off and arrived back in Bihac where the majority of his operation is business. He is very much into agriculture and food processing. It became apparent while I was there that he was very much an important figure in the Vance-Owen negotiations, that he had been consulted by Lord Owen at least a couple of times through an intermediary, and that he was also a power figure within the Bihac region. He had supported the pocket during the time it had been cut off by the Krajina, he released all of the stocks that he held in his warehouses to feed people. I understand he sold them, he didn't just release them. In any event he made them available, a lot of them could be sold at cost, but he helped support the pocket through a very rough period of time when they were cut off in January or February. There was no food aid coming in which made it very difficult. UNHCR was not allowed to deliver, but the French battalion was able to get food in as well as Abdic's food being released.

As I spent more time there it became clear that a coup had been organized, a change of government of the regional assembly. It was an ad hoc organization that had stood up when the region had been cut off by the Serbs, to basically carry on the central government administration on behalf of the government in Sarajevo. There had been a peaceful change of power and the new president of the regional assembly and his prime minister had been put in. It became apparent that these were people supported by Abdic. Decent people in their own right, hard working, very committed to sorting out the central government and putting into place all the proper organizations to administer to the region properly and get themselves on a footing so that they could survive, bringing together all of the resources and sharing. But these people were very much Abdic trustees. Abdic was becoming the power force and there was trouble looming on the horizon because General Razim Drekovic, the commander of 5 Corps, was not necessarily an Abdic supporter. There had been some sort of break between Abdic and the central government, and that's why he left. It wasn't clear what it was, and Drekovic was very firmly a central government supporter. I think that was where some of the problems came up over the few months that I was there. The problems we had getting an agreement for people in or out or various other things was a symptom of the problems between 5 Corps and the central regional assembly. At certain times the regional assembly said that they were in control, and at other times they said, "Well you're going to have to talk to 5 Corps about that." So it made things very frustrating. As things developed and the regional assembly took on a more central government-like attitude, even to the point of saying that "We don't care if Sarajevo gives us the permission, we're going to do this anyway." It became apparent that it looked like Bihac was going to go its own way, more than likely with Abdic in control. He had the tacit backing of the French battalion who I believe was assisting him a great deal. Certainly Abdic's commercial enterprises were being assisted by the French battalion. I'm fairly certain they were trucking in supplies to him, which was very interesting.

French national interests were in play there. During the change of command of the French battalion while I was there, the outgoing commander sat down with my Spanish partner and I, and we said to him you're going on your way out and we're going to continue to be here. We'd like to benefit from your experience. Is there anything you can tell us about the French battalion or the area that would be useful to us in assisting us in co-operating? He laid out very clearly for us that he received orders from Paris, from New York and from UNPROFOR Headquarters, the order of priority not necessarily that given. On any given day he would follow the orders of whoever he felt was the most reasonable for the given situation. And that his operating instructions were to, one, establish food delivery to Bihac; two, to use the food delivery in Bihac as a method of putting into place a moderate government; three, to establish food delivery into the Krajina (from Croatia), assist UNHCR, establish a food delivery supply line into the Krajina; four, use the food delivery as a method of levering any moderate government in the Krajina; five, establish food delivery into the Serb-held areas of Bosnia adjacent to Bihac. Now you can imagine, using the delivery of food aid as a lever to establish a more moderate government in the area. This was absolutely astounding. I had been there for about a month, and although we had suspected the French battalion was doing a lot more than just assisting with the delivery of food we had no confirmation of this. Certainly 5 Corps nor the government in the area was going to confirm any of French BAT's activities. Although they were extremely supportive of French BAT, they are a great group, this is the sort of comment we got about them. So to have the commander state this to us quite boldly was earth-shattering. It was a complete revelation to us and it was very interesting. So it was certain that the French were exercising their national interest through French BAT 3 as well as completing their UN mandate. They were certainly assisting Fikret Abdic a great deal. I believe that some of his supplies were being trucked in by French BAT. Independent of the UNHCR deliveries. UNHCR had their own trucks, their own delivery schedule, etc., and French BAT assisted with that.

The Serbs were benefitting directly. I am certain that French BAT 3 was making deliveries to the Serbs. I can't prove it but that's my suspicion. They were making it worthwhile for the Serbs to allow the trans-shipment of these goods. It stabilized the area. They were certainly the most successful organization in the area in getting to talk to people and getting accommodations out of them. For example, the Bosnian Serbs flat out refused to deal with the EC and had very, very marginal relationships with the UNMOs. French BAT 3 quite unabashedly used food delivery as a hammer to get access to Bosnian and Serb territory, to the point where they could patrol. They said they were patrolling in the Bosnian and Serb area opposite Bihac. They had patrols that had gone there and had done things. They basically used it as a real club, and it was with UNHCR's agreement. They were co-operating with one another because the UNHCR rep in the area was a fairly hard individual as far as food delivery went. He said "If I don't get to deliver the food, you're not getting it." This was quite a departure from other areas and other organizations. I can remember quite clearly that he had just come back from a food delivery mission into Ripac, which is not far from Bihac but in the Bosnian Serb territory. He was extremely pleased, because the Bosnian Serbs had been complaining for a long time about the fact that Bihac was getting a steady supply of food and none of the other Bosnian areas in the area were. And this guy said okay, you want food? Okay, let's talk turkey here. They said fine, this is what we want, we need so many tons here, so many tons here, etc. They came up with I think a total of twelve communities they wanted food delivered to. And he said okay, we can only carry so much a day, therefore it's going to be two days worth of delivery. They said okay, this is where you can move to, here first, and here second. He said fine, we're going to bring it in. They said no, you just bring it to the border and we'll carry it. He said we carry it or you don't get it. They said okay, you can carry it. You'll take this route, you'll meet us here. These are the areas you can go to, that's it, you go in, you drop the food, you leave immediately. So the first day they went in and they hit five of the twelve locations. The next day, instead of going to the seven locations, they were going to go to three central locations from which it would then be dispersed. So he didn't say anything. He said what was the load for those three locations? That's what you load, that's it. So when they showed up at the three locations they only had the food for those three locations. And he made the point. He said, "I don't go there, I don't bring the food. We'll see you next time." And he left. And very shortly thereafter they ran some fairly major concessions out of the Serbs about movement in the area, their access to areas, and it was all done through the viability of getting food. And it worked.

The relationship with any of the organizations depended on what you could do for them. If you had something they wanted, you could get agreements from them. If you had nothing to offer or what you offered was of no value to them, there was no deal.

French motives were opaque. I suspect that the French were trying to exert leadership in the EC and in Europe. I suspect it's national leadership. That's the part of being in the EC and the development of Euro-Corps, which is based on the French and the Germans. I think the French and the Germans are taking a strong leadership role within the EC. I couldn't see any other interest there. They were being very unabashed about it. I have my suspicions about the technique, because as was pointed out by one of my partners, he said that a lot of the French army officers, especially the senior ones, have a lot of colonial experience, and they're treating Bosnia and Croatia as a colonial situation. So they were trying to run the thing for them. We were told that the outgoing colonel had said that he had substantially assisted 5 Corps in its reorganization and training. That they had provided assistance to the regional government. They didn't provide weapons, but they helped them in their reorganization and preparation, and probably some training to the soldiers and the officers. Certainly 5 Corps had developed as a fighting organization. It was ad hoc to start with in '91. As I watched they were certainly much better at organizing themselves in their operations as they went along.

The French were in very deep. My suspicion is that the replacement of the French battalion with the Bangladeshi battalion precipitated some of the activity in Bihac. The Bangladeshi battalion was not as strong as the French battalion. It certainly did not have the respect of the French battalion, which therefore weakens the Bihac position.

When NATO aircraft bombed Udbina airfield in the Krajinas, it had some bearing on Abdic's activities in Bihac. Abdic was being supported by Zagreb, the Croatians, and he was also receiving support from the Krajinan Serbs. They could see benefit in supporting him because the French battalion was supporting him and they were given food to allow the convoys to come through. I believe there was an accommodation between the Croatians, the Krajinan Serbs and Abdic. He was not seen as being a centralist government leader, he was essentially rebelling against the central government. I'm quite certain he was making economic deals, commercial deals with them about his resources and the future. When I talked to him in the beginning of my tour in March, I just happened to be at an interview he was conducting with the head of the CC at the time, we were there because we were the team in the area and he wanted us there. He mentioned that he had just completed a major deal outside of Bosnia and it wasn't clear whether it was with Slovenia or Croatia. So his commercial empire was carrying on.

The Croatian government was certainly supporting him. There was no way the food going to him could have made it to Bihac through Croatia unless the Croatian government was aware of what was going on and supported it. There's no doubt about it. I believe that there was a certain amount of co-operation between him and the Krajinan Serbs. Certainly. Where did he go to when he was defeated? He went to the Krajina. And then, there has been this return attack back into Bihac supported by the Krajinan Serbs. That is why the airport in Udbina was used: the Krajinan Serbs were supporting him. The Bosnian Serbs don't want to support him, but it was in the interest of the Krajinan Serbs to see that Abdic gained control of his area again, because they were supporting him to start with. So that's how he wrested support out of them. So that's why it's a different affair. That's why the attack into the Velika Kladusa area was a different affair, crossing the border.

When they declared independence in October of '93, I had been waiting for that for three months. All the indications were there. Certainly my team and I had reported this. We said all the indications are here that they can jump both ways. And as it went on it became clearer, certainly in my mind, and I figured I had been down there and saw what was going on, it was clear in my mind that they were going to jump for independence. It was just a matter of time before they did it. They were completely isolated. They got no support in this area. They had some philosophical differences, they were having arguments in this area. It was very clear that they could jump easily. Having Abdic there, who is obviously against the central government, that just made it clearer in my mind. I'm not trying to make myself look as though I'm the all-knowing god who saw the situation when no one else did, but certainly that's what I predicted further up, and I think that particular view was accepted and certainly supported by others. That this was a strong possibility. They did do it in October and there was the fighting ever since. Originally I had heard that 5 Corps had gone over to Abdic and then of course it turned out it hadn't. Then this summer he was defeated, apparently conclusively, and had all of the refugees up at Karlovac waiting to try to get in. The defeated forces, and I think a lot of families, left Vileka Kladusa and they travelled the 30 or 40 kilometres up to the crossing site at Karlovac and were hoping to get through. Of course they weren't let through, the Croatians weren't interested in that. While I was there I watched the hardening of the Croatian attitude towards all the refugees coming out of Bosnia. Because it was becoming quite a strain on Croatia. They were getting less than the support required from these national agencies for it to be self-sufficient. So Croatia was having to kick in money and food, and it's a drain on the resources. And Croatia is not rich. They are in a very difficult economic position.

COMPARING THE FRENCH APPROACH TO OTHER UN OPERATIONS

The situation here though is remarkably different from what was going on with CANBAT and BRITBAT. French BAT was in a position where the area that they had to deliver food to was secure, stable and friendly. You look at the other areas, you had to cross confrontation lines, they actually had to physically escort the food, and it was subject to attack. The only time in the French BAT area that it was subject to attack or confiscation was in the 30 kilometres that it crossed the Krajina. As soon as they entered into the Bihac area, they had no fears. They didn't have to escort it. And because they were working on the Krajinan Serbs, the requirement to actually physically escort the food was going down. Now there was some harassment of the food and some inspection requirements that dragged on for days. And some of the convoys were turned back for minor discrepancies. There were not major problems. This freed up a lot of the resources of French BAT to do other things. Which they did. They made very obvious patrols to provide a visual presence guarantee for the pocket. Everyone in the Bihac region felt secure because French BAT was there. They thought that French BAT was there to defend them. But the commander had the liberty, because he had the resources, to actually do these physical patrols. And say, "This is our area." He interpreted his mandate of protecting food to say he had to protect the whole food distribution system right down to the individual house. He basically assumed that this was a new UNPA and treated it as such. Or a minor French colony and protected it as so. He had an area to protect and he had the resources to do it. By mounting a visible presence he sort of reinforced the idea that we are protecting food delivery and we are here to do that. He went to the point of, outside Bihac, of putting in a 2-kilometre tank ditch. Because, he said, that is where the major threat is. Right now it is a mechanized attack which could come down this valley. It comes out of the Serb Krajina and down to Bihac along the northwest-southeast corridor. So he put in a tank ditch. And he put his anti-tank vehicles on the forward slope and they were basically nose to nose, they were within 700 metres of a couple of T-55s pointing in the other direction. They had a troop of VAB APCs there pointing the other way. So they had a visual reinforcement. Those are French troops being protected by French troops because we're protecting the food delivery system. They had enormous liberties that they could take in the area because they were French BAT. They had the forces, and they had the co-operation of the local area because they were doing a lot of things for them.

THE ECMM, THE UN AND PEACEKEEPING

Working with Europeans in general I found extremely interesting, because in some cases, it would explode the myths of various European attitudes and government attitudes. Sometimes it reinforced the clichés. There were some very thoughtful people there that had the European experience. I found working with several of the Germans fascinating. Very thoughtful people. Very clear insight. I also gained an appreciation as to why the Germans are so interested in Croatia. If you went to the main cemetery in Zagreb, you would see an enormous number of German names. This is from the early 1800s. Germany had had a very close association, an historical association with Croatia that goes beyond the Nazis. It's a very interesting sort of thing. You understand why there is a national inclination towards interest in the area. There were several other nations that were involved with the EC monitoring mission, because it was at the behest of the signatory nations, that they wanted not just the EC, because I think several of them were suspicious of several of the EC nations. They asked that one neutral, one North American and two eastern block countries be included in the monitoring nations. As a result, Sweden was a neutral, Canada jumped on as the North American, and then Czechoslovakia and Poland were the two Warsaw Pact nations. And of course Czechoslovakia then became the Czechs and the Slovaks, so it turned into seventeen, and it's now back down to sixteen with Canada gone. But certainly the point of view of the eastern nations, the Warsaw Pact nations, is very interesting to get from the Poles, the Czechs and the Slovaks. Very interesting point of view as to what was going on, and how to deal with these people. Even the Slovaks, the Czechs and the Poles found the Bosnian Serbs difficult to deal with. They said they are hardline Communists through and through. You can see the old style Communism in them. They recognized it for what it was and they knew how to deal with that. In fact, one of the fellows who was a diplomat told me, if ever you want to get in for one reason or another, write a letter to whoever it is you want to go and see. And when you get to the checkpoint say, "I have a letter to deliver." He said these people are oriental in their viewpoint. They're eastern thinking in their viewpoint. And the letter is a symbol, it's very important. You as an individual don't count, but that letter takes on significance. Letters must be carried, they have weight of their own. Which I thought was very interesting. Their commentary on various activities, and what was going on, why things were significant, where the western EC nations would discount this or that, the Czech or Slovak or the Pole would say, no this is very significant. This is what they have said, or this is what it applies to. This is why it's significant.

I was thinking about news reports and various instances which didn't seem to have any impact for me, but they would bring out some significance in it. They were also useful because very often they would understand some of the language. And so you didn't have to rely on an interpreter, you could get some independent assessment of what was going on. I can't think of an example right now. There was nothing of critical importance. They just had a different slant on things, how to view events. Where our point of view was the democratic, western way of thinking, theirs of course was the Communist, eastern bloc different background, different way of thinking about problems. Just put a different slant on it. I found that was an interesting way to think of things. It was good for throwing ideas back and forth about what was significant. When intentions were involved, trying to figure out where people were going or what their background was and why they were doing these things, having an individual from one of those three nations there was very useful to get this outside, non-mono bloc opinion. Where if I talked with a Brit or a Belgique or a Frenchman, or even a Swede to some extent, we were looking at it from the west going east. But these people were looking at it sometimes from the east going west. It was just a way of looking at things. And they would bring up some different points and make you think about it a bit differently. So it was good to have them there. It was also good being in the EC looking at the UN. Although I'm sure the monitors and the other people you've talked to have mentioned the various problems within the UN, some of those things came up all the more clearly because I was outside the UN.

We saw the separation of the command structure, the difficulties of their convoluted mandate, their blindness to certain aspects of what was going on. Their bureaucratic focus, their superiority complex. It's very evident. The UN does not believe that anyone can do the peacekeeping as well as they can. The UN, certainly the military aspect of the UN, and even the civil affairs, believe that everyone else should be under the control of the UN organization. They do not like competition. Certainly, UN Civil Affairs did not like the ECMM at all. Certainly the UN did not like the fact that the ECMM had a separate memorandum of understanding with Croatia. Because for example, Croatia essentially ceded control of the Protected Areas to the UN. But they had also agreed with us, the ECMM that is, to let them have access wherever they wanted. So the UN wanted to run the Protected Areas as their own personal fiefdom, but our agreement with Croatia was that we could go there and monitor them and talk to people. But the UN didn't like that because we could go in and we were coming out of left field as far as they were concerned. They wanted the ECMM under their control as much as possible. Some people accepted that very well. Certainly at the monitor level and usually at the sector as well, the UNMOs and that sort of thing, they would understand that and knew what was going on and accepted that. But there were other individuals who did not accept that. Did not accept the second opinion, or could not accept the second opinion of the ECMM whose monitors had been to different places and talked to different people and would often have a different opinion of what was important or wasn't. I found that if you got to the individual commander early enough, for example we went and talked to the Danish BAT commander as he rotated in, and said this is the situation as we see with the UN as to what's been going on between ourselves, and we want to try to bridge that. If you wish advice from us, a second opinion, we're more than pleased to give it to you because we have different experiences. And he was very receptive to that. I found that if you got to the commander early before he could form an opinion and talked to him and try to keep the gate open, it worked very well.

CANADA AND THE ECMM

We were asked to provide national data and would send back a report once a week. As far as I'm aware, once having set up the requirement for the task, External Affairs washed their hands of it. One of the things that was very frustrating for me was that here we were, essentially a diplomatic political monitoring unit, or was evolving into one, the other nations had sent one or two of their diplomatic corps to head the mission and to provide that input from a national point of view. We had not done that, so it left us out on a bit of a side street, where although we sent a full colonel and good people who were competent individuals, reasonably aware of what was going on around them, they were virtually ignored by the Head of Mission. They weren't diplomats, they didn't speak the lingo, they didn't have that experience, they didn't have that background. External Affairs was not interested in sending any people to this. External Affairs assessed it as being important that Canada was there. They saw it as a military monitoring mission. But we saw it as involvement. That there was certainly the weakness at the top Canadian level, not because of the individual but because of his background, that needed to be addressed. They had a chargé d'affaires in Zagreb who was responsible for all of the former Yugoslav area. I said, "He's not gaining any real experience here, he's able to get the Croatian experience but he's getting no Bosnia, he's getting no Serb, he's getting no Slovenian." If we had even one, we had two people there out of the 12-man mission who diplomatic corps background, who could come in and get the experience and find out what was going on. The junior man could go monitoring, there was no reason he couldn't go monitoring because a lot of the things we're doing are not military. The senior man becomes the Head of Delegation and sits in on the council to bring in the Canadian national viewpoint and has the External Affairs connections.

I think the presence of the Canadians in the mission was very much appreciated, certainly from the technical point of view. We were one of the longer-lived contingents. We had six months in theatre, there were a number of nations that were three months or less. The French and the Germans were six months, the Brits were a year. A lot of other nations sent for shorter periods of time. Some sent for longer, the Slovaks and Czechs have been there for years. The first Italian that I met was the head of the RC, he'd been there since the mission's inception. We didn't send thugs. We were a professional army. We sent competent people who had training and experience. Most of us had UN experience or working in headquarters type of experience. That's not the case all of the time. But the majority of Canadians went there and just didn't sit there and wait for something to happen, they went in and made things happen. They went on patrol, they went and talked to people. In the headquarters they looked at plans, they directed people, they made things happen.

I think we were appreciated because of that. We were also appreciated because we came from North America, so we had a different point of view. We seemed to be a bit more neutral than European countries. So when we talked with the belligerents, when they got over the initial shock of "What do you mean you're from Canada, this is the ECMM." You could use that as a card for the shock value. I used it a couple of times. I wouldn't tell people I was Canadian unless it was useful. It also sort of took you out of the European framework, even though you were ECMM, and they would deal with you a bit differently than they would with Europeans. Being Canadian was an asset. The same thing with the Swede, to a lesser extent. He's still a European but to come completely outside Europe to be in the ECMM I think was an asset. If nothing but for its novelty, people would talk to you for a while. And that was a big thing, getting people to talk to you. If you get people to start talking to you, you can keep them talking. If you couldn't get them to start, you weren't going to get anywhere.

The belligerents, on the other hand, weren't impressed. The only time I had any discussion outside of affairs was one night we invited the police chief of Bihac to come and have dinner with us. He brought one of his deputies and we talked for a while. We were talking about the frustrations they were experiencing with the UN and the EC, to get them to do anything. He said "You and your democracies, you don't do anything." And so they sort of look at it from that point of view. The democratic nations just couldn't make a decision to save their life, so we talked about that for a while, the point of view and the expression of different points of view, the resolution of these points of view, the synthesis. Which they don't like. They like the central authority, one man speaks, everyone follows. They were very disparaging. But it was interesting working with the Europeans to see the European point of view from within a European organization. It was very useful.

PERSONAL ASSESSMENT

Oddly enough, during one of the discussions I had with a Brit who had come down as part of a medical assessment team, we got talking about dissolution of states and then came around the question of Quebec. She said she was a member of an international student organization that regularly got together. One year the organization almost blew up in their faces because the Canadian delegation was complemented by a Quebec delegation who insisted that they be treated as an equal partner of this organization and that they consider the Quebec question. And it almost blew the whole thing up because this organization was only supposed to represent states in being and considered questions of the states in being, and the whole thing almost fell apart because of that. It sort of brought the point home to me along with meeting this ex-JNA officer who had been an UNMO in the Gaza Strip, that the dissolution of the state by violent means is not such a foreign concept to Canada as Canadians might believe it is. I watch all of the things going on about heading towards referendum, the possible separation of the state, and it seems to me to mimic a great deal what was said and being done in the former Yugoslav republic. And for me that's a very frightening parallel to draw. On the other side, I look at the Czechs and the Slovaks who were able to have their referendum and draw apart. But they did that amicably where both sides indicated they wanted to do it. Here we're dealing with a situation where a ruling group is being tossed over by a minority. This JNA officer said, "I never expected that I would have the UN in my country." And it's not such a foreign idea, when you consider in those terms, that the potential is there. There are a lot of extreme opinions being expressed. A lot of idiotic statements that have been made in Canada about separation. Inflammatory statements that should hold a lot of concern for people, and I think for those who have been in Yugoslavia and seen how easily something like this can tear a nation apart very quickly. In some regard, the new Yugoslav republics have more claim to statehood than Quebec does, based on their history. They have had this incredibly debilitating, violent war, very cruel war, and I find it very frightening to look at the Canadian situation. I suppose that's one of the things I've drawn from it.

As far as my personal experience is, it showed me that in some regards our training as a military officer is not covering peacekeeping as well as it should. At least my experience in training has not covered it as well. There is a growing need for an awareness of the impact of a peacekeeping operation on more than just military terms. Somalia pointed this out, Yugoslavia is pointing this out, Cambodia I think is pointing this out. Cambodia I think, despite the fact the overall end was not obtained, I think it has been a reasonably successful mission in combining the political, economic and military aspects under one commander to be aware of those aspects, and then to tailor your force's actions towards that. I think we have to move towards that much more effectively than we've done. Is the development of military peacekeeping doctrine to take into account these other areas?

CHAPTER SEVEN

MAJOR PAT STOGRAN

United Nations Military Observer
Sector North, Croatia and Gorazde, Bosnia, 1993

UNMOS AND SECTOR NORTH

My tour started on the 1st of June 1993 when I deployed out of Calgary, leaving the 1st Battalion. After six days training in Zagreb, military observer training, we deployed. My role was in Sector North, deployed to the town of Plaski, which is a Serbian-held area of Croatia. Plaski is actually part of Sector North which is the area south of the cities of Sisak, which is Croatian, and Karlovac, Ogulin, that are Serb. My first team was originally in the town of Slunj, but I was quickly sent over to Plaski where a new team had opened up. I was there for just under a month when I was pulled out of the team and sent to the Sector HQ as the UNMO Operations Officer in the once-resort town of Topusko. I should just point out that in the UN mission, within the military observer organization, Canadians are often put in key roles such as information or operations, that type of thing, because of our experience, background and training. So I was very quickly seconded to the HQ where I spent a period from July to September as the ops officer and then was appointed as the Deputy Senior Military Observer in Sector North *[see Figure 9]*.

During that time things were very tense in the June-July-August time frame between the Serbs and the Croatians, particularly in the area of Plaski, where I was originally deployed, and also the cities of Karlovac and Sisak, where the Serbs were regularly shelling the Croatian side. During that time the Croatians were actively infiltrating into the Krajina, the so-called Serb Krajina. I was not a witness but my teams investigated sabotage of a Serb train. Shortly after the Serbs received diesel oil or managed to get diesel oil and get their locomotive refurbished; it was running between the town of Glina and Vojnic. There was an infiltration group – we believe it was infiltration – it may have been warring mafia factions within the Krajinas, but it's impossible for us to say. In any event, three anti-tank mines with toggle switches were laid on the track and blew those trains right off the track, vaporized five women, and twenty-five women and children were seriously injured. There were numerous ambushes in the area of Glina, Petrinja, by Croatian infiltrators, defiantly in these cases, and as well around the town of Plaski. There were continuous infiltration activities by the Croatians. We never witnessed them but there were Serb soldiers that were killed by them. There were several instances where I suspected that the Serbs perhaps killed their own people and blamed it on the Croatians. Just suspicious circumstances, like a truck that drove over a mine, where the truck had no business being there and the Serbs blamed the mine being laid by Croatian infiltrators. There were ambushes that were, in the estimation of the military observers, clearly Croatian aggression. The Croatians, who were apparently the underdog in the world media, were being the aggressors against the so-called rebel Serbs. In early September, in the town of Plaski, the Croatians got particularly aggressive. Normally the Serbs would, for lack of a better term, shell the shit out of the Croatians in the town of

Figure 9: UNPROFOR Sector North, 1993

Karlovac and it was always getting shelled. Military observers would always mediate a cessation to hostilities and calm things down and they were a regular occurrence in June-July-August. I should add that the Croatians' response to it was, "If we take one more round, we are going to retaliate with all available rockets and artillery!" For the new military observer and the new UN troops that were deployed in the area, it always looked very tense. However, the Serbs would fire a hundred rounds and the Croatians regularly would answer with one or two of their own, or maybe a salvo of rockets and there was a considerable imbalance in indirect fire support.

Coming up into September, around Plaski, the Croatians became extremely aggressive in their counterattacks. They had tanks forward in the positions, while the Serbs in turn had reinforced with what our military observers estimated to be 300 troops and they appeared to be Serbian regular troops. I investigated and confirmed that there were strangers in town. I knew most of the people in Plaski, it being a small sort of hamlet, and there were definitely an influx of Serb soldiers that had no respect for the UN, not the sort of relationship that we had garnered amongst the people. As I said, the Croatians were actively retaliating and in many cases they were initiating.

UNMO ORGANIZATION AND RELATIONSHIPS

Within Sector North, there were UNPROFOR troops. There were three battalions, actually two and a half because the Nigerians were being sent home. They were, quite honestly, a shambles, and a hindrance to the UN, so in order to fill in the gap, a company of Argentineans was brought down from Sector West, the Danish battalion in the east took up a bit more area and the Polish battalion in the west filled into the centre. During my tenure, the Argentineans pulled out and a French Battalion came in and occupied the centre. We had on the left flank, the Poles, centre was the French battalion, and on the right flank was the Danish battalion. A Danish officer commanded Sector HQ in Topusko and he had a Danish staff and Dutch communications. It was a joint HQ where the UNMOs worked side by side with the UNPROFOR troops, which was not an enviable working relationship. The UNPROFOR troops thought we were spying on them. In actual fact I guess we were spying on them. We weren't targeting them but we would certainly relay incidents that occurred between the warring factions and the UN troops in our SITREPS, incidents that perhaps the UNPROFOR chain of command would sooner not have gone out to New York.

Initially, when I first got there, the UNMO organization was totally independent from the UNPROFOR troops. We had our own chain of command and we had our own deployment areas. The operations staff in Zagreb tried to rationalize the UNMO deployment with the UNPROFOR. That worked to a degree but there was still this "we-they" attitude. You know, "UNMOs cannot go there!" We used to press the point, as we had our own mandate, which was to observe and report. The way the UNMOs were deployed, we had a team on the Croatian side and a mirror team on the Serb side. The rationale there was that we orient ourselves around crossing points on the frontier, whether they were opened or areas that we hoped to turn into crossing sites in the future. We would have a stronger presence on the Croatian side, because the UN troops, the UNPROFOR troops, I mean, were not allowed to operate or patrol on the Croatian side whereas the UNMOs had some sort of a mandate on the Croatian side.

Our role was to mediate problems immediately, and we worked with all of the higher-level HQ with liaison officers. As well, we liaised with the UNPROFOR commanders on the ground. We would mediate hostilities when there were flare-ups, and bring points to the attention of the commander. We served as a direct line to the Sector Commander when there was a problem because our line of communication was a little more streamlined than the chain of command within the UNPROFOR battalions. It went straight from our UNMOs to our HQ, to the ear of the Sector Commander. We had teams on the Croatian side in the cities of Sisak, Karlovac, Ogulin and we eventually took over the town of Ottocac. There were some boundary changes that changed back, which is neither here nor there. On the Serb side, we had teams in Glina, Patrinja, Tucilovic, Plaski, and a team in Plitviz Lakes. This latter changed back and forth.

On the Croatian side we tried to patrol twenty-four and seven. We were strapped, as we didn't get enough UNMOs to have the proper amount of shifts and, quite honestly, the work ethic of many UN representatives from different contingents was lacking. Thirty-three countries contributed. Basically we had people in there collecting a lot of money and not prepared to risk anything. I was a bit of a rebel. Up until I took over as the Deputy Senior UNMO, the policy was that there would be no night patrols, as it was considered too dangerous. UNMOs worked from nine to five and then they went to bed. If there were a crisis they would go direct to the HQ and liaise. I took a different approach from the day I set foot in the Krajinas. I went out to try and meet people and I urged the UNMOs to patrol at night and when there was a crisis UNMOs had to be on location.

PROBLEMS IN SECTOR SOUTH, REPERCUSSIONS IN SECTOR NORTH

It was very hairy to start because I arrived shortly following the heels of the Croatian attack into Sector South where UNPROFOR troops failed to hold up their end of the bargain. The Kenyan battalion were holding a dam, a power station and an airport in Sector South when Croatians overran them. They mounted a deliberate offensive in January 1993 using the whole works, including mechanized and armour. They apparently overran Kenyan positions and French UN positions where not a shot was fired to protect those installations and they fell to the Croats. Up until that point, under the Vance Plan, the Serbs had actually turned in their weapons, and they had demobilized their commands, apparently. I actually found this hard to believe because the Serbs were very aggressive and very belligerent when I was there, all armed to the teeth, and all in uniform.

Up until the 23rd of January, they had allegedly disarmed themselves. I spoke to Croatians who said, "Yes, but they didn't turn in all their weapons and they were continuing to fire on us. The UN did nothing about it so we had to settle the score." I personally think that was a crock of shit, but I can get on to that later. So the attack went in. UNPROFOR's name was mud. UNPROFOR had let the Serbs down and when I first arrived in Plaski, the Serbs were very aggressive and very ignorant towards me. I used to go out at night as a military observer. You often had to drink alcohol because that was the Serb way of socializing. I used to go out at night and see where the lights were – those were the mafia guys who had the money. A Norwegian, whom I had taken over the ops job from, told me that those were the guys you wanted to get in with, because they had their finger on the pulse and I got in with them. It was very scary to start off with, because I would have to sit by myself, and nobody would talk to me, as I was UNPROFOR. Over three or four weeks, buying people drinks and giving little gifts and all that sort of thing, they figured out I was a neutral, a professional soldier and I would not deal in the black market. They respected that. I was given gifts of Canadian Club whisky that they were having shipped in to them. It was an amazing world!

The risk to United Nations Military Observers was also high. Consequently, many teams were forced to move around in armoured Land Rovers. UNMO's frequently operated with the belligerent forces at key flashpoints, sometimes on both sides of the line, attempting to defuse incidents before they escalated and trying their best to provide information to the UN in New York. (Author's Collection)

For me this was like a local intelligence net. By the end of my tour there, I knew all of the special forces guys. I would drop by their HQ and they would give me smoked meat and rakija and they would tell me what they were up to. They invited me out on patrols to the Bihac Pocket. The Croats were far more professional and the Serb people are very rural people. They're warriors and they'd fight to the death. They enjoy fighting, and they love it. I have many friends there, but I still think they're savages, all of them, the Muslims, Croatians and Serbs, but the Serbs are a very giving people. The images that are portrayed in the press, I get very irritated with because very few reporters would go onto the Serb side. They were on the Muslim side or the Croatian side, but they would not go in and get to know the Serbs.

RELATIONSHIPS IN SECTOR NORTH

Let me tell you a couple of anecdotes about the Serbs. I was driving along one night with a Russian guy who was Senior Military Observer. Things really opened up to me when I started working for this Russian because he could speak the language fluently and all of a sudden I had a full-time interpreter so I really got to know the people first-hand. A Serb car had flipped and was in the ditch and some Serbs were trying to get it out. There were about 20 of these special forces soldiers trying to pull it out. The Russian and I offered the use of our car to pull this thing out and we started getting this Volkswagen Golf out of the ditch, but it needed an extra boost so 20 guys were getting together to pull this thing out. I went over to give a hand, being a soldier into physical activity, and I was roughhoused by these soldiers. They grabbed me and pulled me away. I was pissed off. I said "Why are they treating me like a woman?" I was very protective of my image, because UNMOs working nine to five weren't really gung-ho airborne troopers. I wanted to come across like a professional dedicated soldier, not afraid of anything, but those guys pulled me away and I was pissed off. "I can lend a hand, I'm a man, and I can do as good a job as any Serb asshole!" I was quite ignorant with those guys, and they loved it too! They loved my honesty. Through the interpreter they said, "We appreciate you coming from Canada to try to stop the killing. We like that. We don't want to fight anymore but we will fight and we don't want you to die for our country." That was their attitude. On the other hand, there were occasions where UNMOs thought the Croatians were being put in dangerous situations in order to have the Serbs kill them, for propaganda purposes.

I got to know Croatians and I made a point of it. Individually they are very good people but they were bound and determined to destroy the Serbs. They wanted to kill every Serb. Speak to the people in the coffee bars, people who had grown up with Serbs, they wanted to annihilate them. Now they're very aggressive. They didn't like UNPROFOR and they hated the UN being there. We'd get snowballs thrown at us, we got spit on, and I had guns poked in my face, by the peace loving Croatians. I knew some of the commanders and they were very much gentlemen with me and they would treat me very well. I made a point of trying to get to know everybody on the ground on both sides and the Serbs would speak to me like we're speaking right now. Croatian commanders, the one in particular I was making inroads with, he had a political officer sitting beside him, right out of Soviet doctrine! This was the new democratic republic of Croatia and they still had these political officers. I would speak with Commander Lukatic, with whom I was trying to open a crossing between Plaski and Vojnovac. I had a brilliant relationship with this guy because he had many of his relatives here in Toronto. He was eager to try and work along with me but the last word always went to his political officer, somebody that was from Zagreb. This guy was an ignorant asshole. Serbs, on the other hand, never fucked with you. If they wanted to kill Croatians, they'd say, "Pat, get out of the way. We're going to work."

Croatians had formatted pieces of paper to complain about Serb ceasefire violations and I suspect that many of the Croatian claims were falsified. They were always pulling our chain, trying to get attention drawn to what the evil Serbs were doing and they had it down to an art. They knew exactly how to work with the UNMOs to make propaganda gains. All our SITREPS went to New York and they knew this. We would report that the Croatians told it, but we were totally objective in our reports. If it was reported confirmed by an UNMO, then that was validated.

They used the UNMO organization to influence New York. To them, they're fighting a war and everything is used to support that. It's part of the propaganda effort, deception. We view the Croatians as being these peace-loving people but I take every opportunity to tell people that that's not the case. They are fighting a war, I respect them for that and I don't begrudge them. But this is the way I worked with them. I treated them with respect. I understood they were fighting a war and I didn't want to mess with that. I just wanted to report it the best I could. That's the difference. The Serbs, on the other hand, had a lot to feel guilty about, as they were the aggressors.

I went with the Serb commanders and I told them, "Croatians are using UNMOs, and you guys are ignoring us." They said to me, "We don't want anybody to fight our war." I said, "You're being too narrow-minded." They complained all the time about Croatian propaganda abroad and how it caused the sanctions on the Serbs while the Croatians were still living well and that it was the world's problem. I said, "No, it's your problem. When there's a ceasefire violation I'm not asking you not to fight them. I'd prefer you didn't. But I'm asking you to use us. Otherwise we are wasting our time in the Krajina." After awhile they started reporting those things. They were still belligerent with the Croatians and would retaliate in grand scale but they started using us. After being in the sector for nine months, I actually developed this relationship and we were very successful. The Russian helped since he could speak the language and he was a very dedicated, hard-working soldier so it was a very rewarding experience.

The Serbs were fighting amongst themselves and in fact a very good friend of mine, when they had their first elections in the Krajina, said, "If this guy's elected in Knin, then I'm going to take over Vojnic and it's going to be my area!" I said, "You're calling yourselves a republic and you're acting like a bunch of barbarians! That's just not the way a democracy works." The thing is, they're not the educated, cosmopolitan people of Croatia. I don't want to denigrate the Serbs, they are brilliant people, but they are rural people. They are like our aunts and uncles who live and work on the Prairies and they are the salt of the earth. I remember one night I was in Glina. It was dark because there was no electricity and I needed an interpreter so I went to this house that I thought was the interpreter's and I knocked on the door. It was the wrong one. Everything was dark except the inside of the house and this old guy answered. He said, "Ah, Canada!" and he brought me in. This guy was as poor as poor can be. He was an old man, and he had a little girl with him, his granddaughter. He brought his wife in, who could speak a little bit of English. The floors were wood and they were dirty and they were struggling for an existence. They cut me meat, and they cut me bread and he insisted on drinking schlivovitz with me. He wanted me to tell him about Canada through his wife. Brilliant people one-on-one. I once had a Czech officer say something. I was gaining an affinity for the Serb people, not the fighters but the general people when he said, "Pat, if a Croatian ever buys you a beer, I'll give you a hundred dollars." Basically, though, the Serbs hate Canada because they feel that Canada was premature in recognizing Croatia'sindependence, and that we were premature in recognizing Bosnia too. Now, they love General Mackenzie, the Serbs, because of his impartiality but the Muslims can't stand him.

ETHNIC CLEANSING: SECTOR NORTH

As a military observer, I lived with the people. Of course the rebel Serbs are blamed by the world for being the aggressors and having started the war. We, the UNMOs, rented houses from the people to support the economy. I talked to these people about how the war started and my landlady gave me her perspective. The stories related to me by the people was that Croatia was starting to flex its muscles for independence and several countries in the world followed Germany's lead and prematurely recognized their independence and at the time Tudjman was establishing a constitution that recognized the Serbs as a minority, making them second-class citizens. Milosevic, at the same time, was flexing his muscles trying to make an independent Serbia and he realized that the Serb population was concerned about a resurgence of the Ustashe. As they are second-class citizens, the Serbs would be persecuted, so Milosevic fuelled the fires of fear and he was pushing the powers that be in Knin, saying that this was going to happen and to open your eyes. They got concerned about it and started setting up barricades and started to be a bit rebellious. This was in 1991. Now that's what I also gleaned from a couple of the corps commanders who were involved in the decision-making process at the time. My landlady told me that about that time, life was going along normally for the people until truckloads of Croatian paramilitary police were sent in. I assume they went into Knin, but they went into Koronica, Topusko especially, and into Patrinja and Glina. These were areas that were predominantly Serb. They went in and started burning, destroying the houses of the influential Serbs. This old lady hid up on the mountain of Petrova Gora for two months while this was going on. Her house was partially destroyed and she showed me where it was rebuilt. Many of the houses in Serb areas were destroyed by those Croatian storm troopers. The more influential or wealthy that you were, the more they destroyed your house. This lady was "just an old lady" so they didn't wreck her house that badly but they tried to burn it down and there were some bullet holes in it.

SECTOR SOUTH: UNMOS AND THE PRELUDE TO THE CROATIAN ASSAULT ON MEDAK

It was common knowledge that when the JNA pulled out of Slovenia, there were many Serbs living in Croatia who did not take up arms and didn't fight the Croatians. They had farms in the area between the Karlovac-Ogulin highway and the Slovenian border to the north. From our estimations, demographic estimations, there were between 5 and 10,000 Serbs living in that area. You could tell a Serb because they would wave at the UN vehicles. We were not treated so hospitably by many of the Croatians as a unit of UNPROFOR because they thought we were supposed to hand the Krajina back to them and, in the eyes of the Croatians, we failed to come clean with the goods. This corridor at Ogulin was a strategic part of the area. Had these Serbs taken up arms and started fighting, then the Croatian commander of the area between Karlovac and Ottocac would have been fighting a two-front war.

Things started to heat up in Plaski, where the Croatians were being far more aggressive than we were accustomed and I was the acting Senior Military Observer at the time. There was an extreme build-up in the area. The UNMOs had identified this and there were all sorts of indicators that something big was coming down from the Croatians in the area of Ogulin and Plaski, Ogulin being on the Croatian side and Plaski being the Serb side. We reacted to those indicators and the Danish Sector Commander, General Hasselberg, confronted the commander of the Croatian Army, and said, "The UN knows what you are up to. Something's happening there. We've never seen tanks on the Ogulin side before, what is happening?" We were at war stations and I was sleeping in the office by my radio. I was travelling out to Plaski, I had a two-and-a-half-hour drive, and we knew something was happening. It was very tense. The Serbs were shelling the shit out of the Croatians and Karlovac was getting a pummelling, and rockets were being fired off.

So we confronted General Bobetko. I remember it vividly. General Hasselberg came to a morning briefing on the 7th of September and he said "I confronted Bobetko and I have been assured that he has no offensive intentions in Plaski." I relayed this to the UNMOs who were at our weekly meeting that day. I said to the guys, "I don't want to sound like Neville Chamberlain, but this is what Bobetko said, that he has no offensive intentions in Plaski." Everything went quiet there. It was amazing as everything stopped dead, so to speak.

Within three days of that agreement, the Croatians attacked into the Medak Pocket and ruthlessly slaughtered every living creature. I mean every living creature! I got this from an RCMP war crimes investigator that went in afterwards that there were as many as 60 Serb bodies piled up, old women, children, chickens, and they levelled every house before they left there. It was a war crime and I'm really shocked that more of this was not publicized to the world. I know that the world press was invited in by UNPROFOR and I thought we were going to make a big exposé. I went to the Serb commander and said, "See? Canadians went into Medak Pocket and you can be sure that we are sending the truth out to the world. The world press went into Medak Pocket and saw that the Croatians were the aggressors!" However, I understand not much news of Medak Pocket actually got out.

THE MEDAK POCKET OPERATION

The Medak Pocket was a Serb-inhabited area on the boundary between the Serbs and the Croatians. It did not have an UNPROFOR presence and the Croats attacked and destroyed the villages of Citluk, Bilaj and I can't remember the third village. The Croatians went in there shortly after we had their assurances that they were not going to attack into Plaski and they annihilated those three villages. Subsequent to that, our teams on the Croatian side were told by some of the locals that the primary objectives of the Croatian assault was Plaski but the plan had been compromised and so the backup plan was activated. I feel fairly confident that that was what happened. The Canadian battalion went in there and very aggressively drew a line between the two sides and once they got the go-ahead from the Force Commander, they went in and seized a line [see section two of this book]. The Serbs told them, "You're not far enough forward," but the Canadians wouldn't compromise. The Croatians said, "You've gone too far!" and they got an equal response. It was something that Canadians should all know about. I was at a meeting subsequent to this with three Serb corps representatives – two corps commanders and a deputy commander – and they said to General Hasselberg that the Canadians were being too aggressive and not being diplomatic enough. These Serbs said that, to the contrary, the Canadians set the standard for UNPROFOR, they had redeemed the faith in that area and that the Canadians were professional and they were very objective and committed. The Serbs respected that and things calmed down after that. The Canadians went into Medak, down into Sector South and Sector North was dead quiet. It was boring!

THE VOJNIVIC CROSSING INITIATIVE

After that things really quieted down and I started an initiative to open the Vojnovac crossing, which was between Plaski and Ogulin and we actually made fair headway. Initially it was a heavily mined barricade. Through negotiations, I worked with the Croatian side, because they liked Canadians (because of Canadian politics) and the Serbs loved the Russians. We came very close to opening a crossing. The Polish battalion actually tore down the barricades and established itself in no man's land. But the belligerents were busy playing their war games and they never actually opened it. We almost got this crossing open. However, the politicians [the Croatian authority in Zagreb and Serbian authority in Knin] when they heard about it, said "No" and closed it down. They would not open it because Knin said that the Croatians were infiltrating. Once this Contact Group was established between all sides, at the political level the Serbs and Croatians were told, "This is it! There is going to be a ceasefire line, and Serbs, you're not going to get recognized as a republic, and Croatians, we're not kicking them out!" Overnight, Vojnovac Crossing was opened and the ceasefire line was established. The politicians made the peace. We made war and kept the peace once it was made. That was what happened in Sector North. I then went to Bosnia.

BOSNIA: THE GORAZDE SITUATION

I went down to Bosnia in February because I wasn't going to be appointed to a senior position and so I wanted to go somewhere really hot, a good job. I didn't want to go to a headquarters, so I went down and negotiated with a Russian who was in charge of the area around Mostar and the Canadian who was in charge of the area around Sarajevo. I met with Major Roy Thomas in Sarajevo and I said, "Look, I want a good job," and he said, "Sorry Pat, all my HQ billets are filled, I can't bring you in here." I said, "No, you missed the point. I don't want to be in the HQ, I want a good job!" He said, "Well, I've got a team in this pocket around Gorazde where I've had some real problems with team leaders. It's really stressful because the Bosnian Serbs are playing games down there. You are your own boss, and you'll have eight UNMOs. You may be in there for the duration of your tour and not get much help." I said, "Perfect, that's the job I want." So I went in there purely on speculation. I was a bit dismayed, during my last days in Sector North, as I was watching the situation in Gorazde because it didn't look terribly hot, as it did in the sitreps.

I deployed just before the NATO ultimatum where they put in the Sarajevo Exclusion Zone. Gorazde was a Muslim pocket that was southeast of Sarajevo and Sarajevo was our lifeline. We would go once a week, if the Serbs would allow us. Sometimes it was once a month, and sometimes even longer than that. The Serbs had a series of defensives around it, and the city was surrounded. However, the Muslims, up until the offensive in late March, had regular infiltrations from groups going between Sarajevo and Gorazde. We were never up to our full complement of eight UNMOs; there were only five of us at the best of times. I spent a month in the Pocket and then I went on leave to Vienna with my family. During that time, CNN started reporting that a Serb offensive was going into Gorazde. I was clinging to the TV at every opportunity and quite upset that I was missing out on the action, also upsetting my wife at the same time. I was keen to go. I finished leave on 1 April and was sitting on the edge of my seat getting into Gorazde [see Figure 10].

THE JOINT COMMISSION OBSERVERS

General Rose did not believe the reports, at least he came across to the world's press saying that he didn't believe the reports coming out of the Pocket, and that they were being

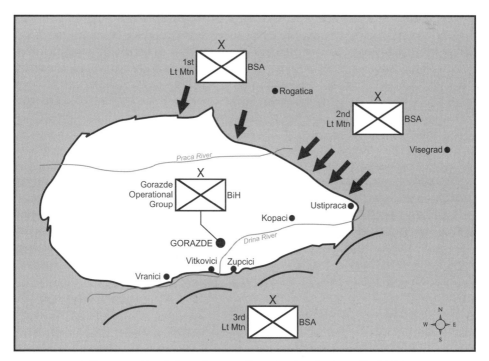

Figure 10: The Gorazde Pocket, April 1993

exaggerated. Why, I have no idea. On or about the 6th of April, General Rose had negotiated with Dr Karadic and General Mladic, to allow his so-called Joint Commission Observers, read "SAS forward air controllers," to go into the Pocket. That was their official term. What they were were special forces groups operating independent from the UN on General Rose's behalf. General Rose, from my point of view as an observer, didn't trust any UNPROFOR units except for the British battalions. He superimposed his SAS throughout the mission, and it started in Sarajevo with the exclusion zone. He superimposed his SAS guys on the mission to feed him information. They wore blue berets but they carried weapons, which was a big, big difference to the rest of us. As UNMOs, we carried no weapons whatsoever. We were totally impartial, as we were not one of the warring factions. We were not UNPROFOR troops, so we were unarmed. I was concerned that calling these SAS "observers" might compromise the impartiality of the UNMOs and recklessly endanger them.

THE UNMOS IN GORAZDE

When I went into Gorazde, I knew that the UNMOs were viewed as Muslim military observers because they were on the inside of the Pocket and the Serbs, quite honestly, would have nothing to do with them and so there was a hostile attitude. My first mandate, when I went in there in March, was that we were going to get to know all the Serbs on the outside. One way to their hearts was through alcohol and all our whisky was reserved for that. I started with Serb checkpoints and I got friendly with them, then I'd go further on down the road. I told the UNMOs, "Look, when I'm on leave you will socialize!" The first time I met with the Serb brigade commander in Visograd, I put down a bottle of Canadian whisky. Itwas ten o'clock in the morning and we talked until midnight. He had actually severed relations with the UNMOs three months beforehand and I had to fix that. I was trying to understand their problem but I was at the same time a professional, impartial soldier sending impartial reports out of the Pocket. I used to stress to them that the only way I could do this was if I had the Serb input on this. I also told them that I had a lot of Serb friends in the Krajina and I liked to get out and talk. Interestingly enough, this brigade commander that would have nothing to do with UNMOs previously was all of a sudden now calling me for meetings. The meetings would be before lunch and we'd start out drinking and we'd talk until the wee hours. It even got to the point where he would put me up in the local hotel overnight so that my driver could drink and drive back sober the next morning. I established a very good working relationship with those guys.

On the 1st of April, as I was returning to Sarajevo after leave, I stopped in to see some of the Serb LOs I knew in Topusko. I was warned at that time to not go back to Gorazde by a Krajinan Serb (and they're different from the Bosnian Serbs) despite the fact that General Rose was making it public that he didn't think anything was going to happen in the Gorazde Pocket. I was told to wait two or three days because they were going to conquer the city, so stay out of the way. That was his friendly advice. So I knew something was coming down and that was in Topusko, which was how many hundred kilometres away?

THE JCOS: ON THE ROAD TO GORAZDE

So I was on leave and General Rose is concerned with what's happening in Gorazde. He went public stating that he didn't believe that the situation was as serious as it had been conveyed by the UNMOs in the Pocket and he negotiated with Karadic and Mladic to send in his special guys.

Originally I wasn't in the plan to go in with them but I had established good relations with the SAS soldiers, who were super soldiers and great guys. I managed to convince them that they needed a good hard-core grunt like me in there as team leader because the deputy team leader, Mike Norman, was a C-130 Hercules pilot from the New Zealand Air Force. An excellent man but his credibility was suspect because General Rose was attacking his reports. So I was this professional soldier that was going to go in with them after they convinced Rose, who in turn convinced Mladic. On 6 April, we started our drive to the Pocket on a verbal clearance from General Mladic and Dr Karadic.

Normally everything had to be done on paper so I thought it was a bit strange that we were given verbal clearance with no hard copy. Just as we were leaving, the international press was interviewing General Rose and Rose, with the media, were going to Gorazde to see for themselves but at the last minute Mladic and Karadic said "No." Only your Military Observers can go. General Rose made a statement outside of Karadic's HQ to the world press and I was standing right beside him when he said, "I believe that the situation in the Gorazde Pocket is not as serious as being conveyed by the present reports, so I am sending in a special team of Military Observers to verify the situation." He didn't call them JCOs he called them UNMOs. I thought, "Holy shit! He's already calling them UNMOs." So we started off and we had to go through several checkpoints to get into Gorazde.

At the first checkpoint, which was Pajugorea, we had some problems. We didn't have an interpreter with us but between the SAS guys and myself we managed to convince them that we had permission from Pale. The Serbs were great at this. They would tell you one thing and they would become "less efficient" if it suited their purposes. We were held up for a couple of hours, which was extremely uncommon at this one checkpoint. We usually bluffed our way through. We got to Rogatica where the Serbs were particularly hostile towards the UN; apparently a lot of people had lost property and loved ones in Gorazde to the Muslims there and they were not sympathetic to our needs. They did a thorough search, took serial numbers, counted the number of rounds that the JCOs had with them, and checked us out top to bottom. The head of security was going through our stuff when he asked a very relevant question. "Look, we've been working with Military Observers for a long time. Why are they armed and loaded to the teeth with specialist gear?" That's where I came in. I said, "Look, they are special, they are Joint Commission Observers, they are not UNMOs. They work directly for General Rose and we work for the UN. JCOs work only in Bosnia." They cleared us finally but wouldn't allow us to take the normal route because of the fighting that was going on.

We used to take a direct route down through Mededa up through the mountains because this was the front line and then to Ustipraca, which was the front line, and then finally to Gorazde. But this time, as the Serbs claimed, the direct route was targeted by Muslim patrols and there was fighting going on. In actual fact, I figured they had large concentrations of Serb forces that were about to attack Gorazde so they took us on a roundabout route. We arrived in Visograd after dark at 2000 hours where we were greeted by the LO who I had come to know through my excursions out of the Pocket and Mila, their interpreter. They had a table set for us with a three-course meal and all the alcohol we could drink, and they put us up in a hotel room, as it was too dangerous to cross the front line at night. Mila, who I knew well, said, "Look, you should not go into Gorazde. We are going to take it. If you wait three days, we can escort you in and guarantee your safety." I said, "I appreciate it but we have our orders from General Rose just like you have your orders from Mladic and we've got this window. It's approved by the president, so we're going to go in." So they let us go in the next morning.

We crossed the front line and I could see that more artillery positions had been put in and there were stockpiles of ammunition. When we arrived at Mededa it had been attacked. Now, I don't know if it had been set up by the Serbs to make a statement that the Muslims had been the aggressors or not but there had definitely been artillery rounds coming down on the houses and the checkpoint house was burned down but it could have been a drunk checkpoint guard. I made this clear to the SAS guys but they were convinced that this was offensive action. I said that all we could confirm was that there was a house with some shelling around it.

As we crossed the line at Ustipraca, the soldiers that I saw there were not the ones I had come to know and they were actually very hostile towards us. One guy, a stereotypical Serb with a big beard, who was missing an eye, spoke aggressively to me. I said to Mila as we were driving away, "What was he saying?" but she started edging herself away from the confrontation. I suspect he was telling me how he was going to dismember me when he saw me in Gorazde. He was very belligerent. We made it through there. The Muslim positions had not changed and we went through the same type of security at their front lines except the police checkpoint, which was behind the military checkpoint, had been vacated.

THE GORAZDE SAFE AREA

So we went in and I started patrolling immediately with the JCOs. They went to all of the humanitarian aid personnel and they went to the hospital. They verified the humanitarian situation, which was exactly what the UNMOs had reported up to that point. Had General Rose gone through our sitreps he would have seen how much UNHCR relief stuff was not making it in, but Rose didn't trust that information. The JCOs validated and collected information in the same way the UNMOs had and we also patrolled the front line. I was asked point-blank by the JCO team leader, "What is your estimation here?" I said, "There is a fucking major offensive going on." We could see off in the distance villages burning, smoke rolling over the top of the hills, and artillery down in the low ground. Even as we were approaching the Drina River from the high ground to the north, we came under shelling. They were pouring out tons of ammunition. I told him that I was convinced that there was a major offensive going on and what was reported was accurate based on what I saw on the ground. I don't know if the grids were the same because I didn't commit them to memory but certainly the pressure that the Serbs were putting on the Pocket was depicted accurately in the UNMO reports.

Then things started heating up. On or around 9 April there was a bridge down across the Drina River in Sadba that was the focus of the Serb attack. Apparently, the Muslims were telling us that it was their aim to take down the bridge that crossed the Drina onto the south side of the river, on what they called the Right Bank. We watched tremendous fighting going on. We could see over the course of a couple of days, the burning villages coming closer, and it was big-time eerie! The bridge never did fall and I thought that was curious. If the Serbs wanted to attack into Gorazde, why would they take down one of the crossing sites? I didn't think their aim was to take down the bridge but the Muslims were adamant that this was what was happening.

On 9th April, I went out to confirm the situation with Mike Morgan, my 2IC. As we were driving out, two tank rounds vaporized houses beside us as we drove along, so it was pedal-to-the-metal down through Vitkovici. Nothing was happening at Sadba, though I planned on making a night patrol out there because I thought that if an attack was going to go in, based on where the BSA were, they would do a night or a dawn attack. I was going to sit up there during the night. As we were driving back, there was all sorts of gunfire coming from the Left Bank. I thought it was Muslims who were pissed off that the UN was ineffective and they were firing over our heads to scare us. I then realized that it was not outgoing small arms fire; it was the crack of machine-gun fire coming at us so I turned to Mike and I said, "Mike, we're under fire from the Serb side." He was crouching down and I thought he'd been hit by machine-gun fire, so I put on the brakes in order to give him first aid and he said, "What the fuck are you doing?" and I said, "What are you talking about?" He said, "We're under airbursts!" and there was light artillery airburst going on about 2-300 metres down the road, and we could see the flashes. So I put pedal to the metal again and just drove out of there. They never fired in salvoes, and only fired individual rounds so we figured we had about thirty seconds to get out of there while they were reloading. It was the big joke amongst the Muslims that the UNMOs were no longer safe here. Apparently as we drove away, anti-aircraft rounds were impacting behind us. So that was our first real close brush with death there and incidents like that increased my confidence.

It was outstanding. I performed the way I should have and I was proud of myself. It was a rush, a big adrenaline rush and the whole experience was great. Mike on the other side, being a Herc pilot, hadn't conditioned himself for fifteen years looking forward to combat. He went straight to the bottle of Rakija, the moonshine, bashed back a couple of snoutfuls and told me that was the last time he was going on patrol with me. He overreacted. He was very brave and faithful and backed me up several times after that.

The Serbs continued to close but the bridge never did collapse, to my knowledge. The SAS guys and I did a couple of cross-country tours to Sadba. The road down through Vitcovici along the Drina River was cut off and we had to go inland and come down 90 degrees to the river to get a look. We were still shelled sporadically every time we went close to the river. I saw some really good scenes there of the Serbs getting into position, digging fire positions with bulldozers, Muslims trying to engage with single-shot tank rounds, single-shot anti-aircraft, and single-shot mortars; they really conserved their ammunition. We heard what we thought were guided weapons, like SAGGERs. They were trying to take out these trenches being dug by the Serb bulldozers on the other side of the river. We ended up having to cease that because things got too hot around there. Even the Muslims had to infiltrate on foot at night and they were taking their lives in their hands. The Serbs had closed up to the town on the right bank at Zubcici and they had tanks, and artillery. They were firing at will, destroying houses within the suburbs of Gorazde.

On the 10th of April the hills around Gorazde on the right bank were being threatened and that's when the UN called in their first close air support (it's politically incorrect to call them airstrikes) and it slowed the Serbs down. The SAS "UNMOs" called it in and that was what Mladic thought. It slowed the Serbs down nominally, but they started up their offensive again on the 11th so the second airstrike went in. About that time the skies closed up and it was pouring down torrential rains. All those homemade generators that the people of Gorazde had put in the river and streams to generate electricity (the Serbs owned the power station up river) were washed away. Mountainsides were down across the roads, and it was really a desperate situation so the Serbs slowed down. I guess they are fair-weather warriors. On the 11th they started pulverizing the city again until the 14th.

In the intervening time, I had told the UNMOs that we would support the SAS into patrol positions, but I would only do it on a volunteer basis. I wouldn't order any of the guys to go and they were not to go near the front lines. On the 14th I did a patrol with the SAS to the hill feature on the right bank of the city called Gradina. As we were going up the Muslims were taking casualties down off the hill, stomach wounds and that sort of thing. We arrived at the battalion position and we were told that they had just repelled a Serb probing attack and they were expecting mortars to fall on the position any second. So we dashed into the HQ and waited out the mortar attack. When things were all clear, we packed up and headed off down the hill, as we knew that this position was under a lot of pressure. As we were going down the hill, big- time artillery stonking hit the hill and a lot of the over-wash of the shells was hitting all around us. We ran like sons of bitches with those things going over our head and it was quite exciting.

While this was happening, the area around Ustipraca, the in-route, there was a tremendous volume of AA fire, machine-gun fire, tank fire, and heavy artillery, the whole bit. When I went back down to Gorazde and met with the UNMOs, I said, "Look guys, none of us are leaving the city. From now on we patrol within the city." The next day the SAS went out by themselves, and not even I would go with them, as I found an excuse to stay in town. That was the day they patrolled out to the area of Urbuksello, which is north of the in-route, the Gorazde-Visograd road. They went with two patrols. The first SAS patrol put in a static OP and the other wanted to go forward to the battalion HQ they had visited the day before to see if the situation had changed. While they were driving up to the position, the situation had changed. The Muslims had been overrun, the Serbs had overrun the battalion HQ, and the JCOs were driving right into the middle of a Serb attack. They tried to turn around and drive out of there but the SAS driver took a bullet in the back of the head and the other got it in the arm. So we started to do the evacuation procedures.

Interestingly enough, the whole war ground to a stop. Once we got this guy down off the hill, there was mass confusion. I was down talking to a Muslim ham operator who was the only guy with eyes on in the area. The SAS communications were not working, and they had intermittent communication with the static OP that they had established. These were direct communications to Rose as they had secure satcoms. One SAS trooper was fatally engaged and it was, I guess, the Serbs who authorized General Rose to do his casevac. At the time we also had some women and humanitarian aid people living in our bunker with us. I tried to get them evacuated but the Muslim authority said "No" and they put an armed guard on us. I had a shit-fit when I heard this but we couldn't get the girls down to the French Puma helicopters.

The young SAS officer, who was wounded, got lost in the evacuation and we couldn't find him. He was wounded in the arm and he decided that he wanted to stay in the Pocket. I ended up evacuating the young trooper who was fatally wounded and we tried to wait to get the other guys down to the aircraft but the crowd was getting hostile. I said to the chopper pilots that they had to go or they'd wind up grounded too. So they got out and we heard on the BBC later that Fergie had died. The young SAS officer had a very serious arm wound and he needed external stabilization, like a pin through his arm and it was shattered big-time. He was a real problem for us because of the lack of medical facilities.

The Serbs continued the attack and on 16 April, a Harrier was shot down. We thought the end was near. We were able to get the pilot, who ejected over Muslim-held territory, and he thought he had to escape and evade. You can't tell the difference between Muslims and Serbs, because they all look the same so he didn't realize that he was in Muslim territory. He had his pistol out and he said that he was going to fight to the death. The Muslims treated him like a local hero and they wanted to turn his ejection seat into a monument and some of the wives wanted to bring him to bed for the night. He came back to us drunk. He was so drunk that the stitches that Mary put into his chin didn't need any anaesthetic. He told us the story and the Muslim who brought him to our HQ actually came with some moonshine and some meat so we had a bit of a party.

Prior to that the SAS guys relayed to the local commander, this was in their words and I don't know who they were talking to, but General Rose had said that if one more round fell into Gorazde, General Rose was going to go to war with Serbia. My jaw dropped when I heard he told the Muslims this. I was sure that if they were told this, they would use their own ammunition on themselves. They were going to drop a round, right where it could be seen, and sure enough, shortly before we flew that airstrike, a round landed in downtown and we "went to war with Serbia." Up until that point, the local people had told us that Mladic, after the first airstrikes, had put together a plan which he called STAR 94 that was to shoot down a NATO aircraft. He moved air defence resources out of Serbia, which was taboo, into the area to shoot down a NATO aircraft, which is in fact what he did.

On the 17th our morale was in the dumps. The SAS called together the local authorities and myself and discussed when we were going to leave. It was decided between myself and the SAS guys that they had to leave. They were combatants and they had said that the Serbs would not take them alive. We had two options. If they did a covert extraction where they didn't have to fight, then they were going to take the aid workers and UNMOs. I would remain behind but Mike Morgan volunteered to remain behind in my place. That was the plan if it were done covertly not under fire. If the SAS had to fight their way out and do an escape and evasion, they were on their own. We agreed at this meeting on the morning of the 17th that now was not the time to leave. It was still premature, as the city had not been surrounded and it was not so tense.

That night we got the message from General Rose, apparently. The SAS team leader held a meeting and he said that the UN and the Bosnian forces had lost the war. He said that the Serbs were dictating the terms at all the meetings, they were in control and calling the shots. He went on to say the Serbs had agreed to a ceasefire immediately and a medevac next morning at 0800 hours. Now the local authorities thought this was bullshit. They laughed and said that it was not going to happen. I tried to maintain a professional approach. It was agreed that we couldn't put together a medevac the next morning so we asked if we could delay it. I don't know what the SAS boys did about that. After we did as much as we could that night, I crashed around 2300. The SAS team leader waked me up at 2330 and he said, "We've been ordered to pull out." So I said, "Okay, should I get the Red Cross and UNHCR people? Are you going to take them with you?" He said, "I'm sorry, but we've been ordered to leave alone."

So Rose abandoned us in there and that was the way I read it because they were ordered to leave alone. I don't know the SAS story as I never saw those guys again but I was pissed off. I saw some of the SAS guys that had set up the operation and I stopped just short of punching them in the face. My gut feeling is that it was Rose behind it. He was ex-SAS and he did not want to be the guy responsible for having his guys captured or killed. He superimposed those guys to fight his own little war over and above UNPROFOR. When those guys left, I had mixed feelings. First of all, I was disappointed. All the British resources left, and they just left me with the UNHCR personnel. I'm really bitter over that, as they were our only protection against the Muslims. I thought there was a bigger threat from the local Muslim group killing us than from the Serbs, as my immediate threat was the Muslims. On two occasions I had to physically throw somebody out of the building who came in with a Kalashnikov to demand our cars for casualty evacuation.

I was also relieved because no longer did I have to answer to Rose, no longer did I have to subordinate my activities to those of the SAS, as I didn't necessarily agree with some of the things they did, for instance, telling the Muslims that one more round would do it! That was stuff we should have kept to ourselves. We were on our own at that point and that's when the shit really hit the fan. I would now decide when we were going up into the hills. Quite honestly, I had as much experience as the SAS did and I think I had a better feel for the war than they did. The next day we heard on BBC General Rose saying that Gorazde was now calm and that he has extracted all UN military out of the pocket. I don't know if you saw my wife on TV. I was sending her sitreps through satellite fax, and she knew that it was not calm in Gorazde. I sent a fax immediately to her and to General Rose saying that I don't know whose sitreps you have been reading but it was not calm in Gorazde! It was the first time I got insubordinate.

CC UNPROFOR really didn't know what was going on. My wife was getting duff information. She was following with the sitreps I was giving her, as I was sending the duplicates back to Canada in the event I was killed so that the truth would be known. She knew the real situation and NDHQ was totally in the dark. They told her that I was not trapped in Gorazde, that I could leave whenever I wanted to and I was doing that because I was a professional. To her credit she did not kick up a fuss because she knew I was doing what I wanted to do. She just wanted the world to know, Canada to know, that this was not a bloodless situation. On 20 April the Serbs signed an MOU [a Memorandum of Understanding] that really didn't amount to anything. They agreed to allow the Muslims to stay on the left bank and agreed to a three-kilometre exclusion zone on the left bank but they never mentioned the right bank and I am convinced they wanted the right bank of the river, which was the south side of the city. They were fighting vigorously to get in there and they were trying to destroy a Muslim ammo factory in the north that had been established there under the Tito regime. Multiple objectives: cripple the Muslim war effort; seize a main supply road from Foca to Cinica. They already had the Ustipraca high ground, they had free manoeuvring room and it was Gorazde where the Muslims were living. This was a legitimate military application, and they were not just going in to wipe out the Muslims in Gorazde. They had other objectives.

The NATO ultimatum came in on 22 April, when the Serbs were told to cease fire by midnight on the 23rd. Fighting on the morning of the 23rd was more vigorous than ever, and they were just pummelling the shit out of the centre of the city. According to the Bosnian Muslims, the Serbs were trying to take over the entire ammo factory complex to destroy it. Fighting was vigorous on the right bank of the city. They never did gain entry but they took the outskirts and some of the suburbs and were trying to lay waste to it before the ultimatum took effect. I thought they were going to completely ignore the ultimatum but sure enough by midnight of the 23rd they cleared out. The next day I went over to meet with the old Serbs that I had come to know and they told me they were worried about my welfare and I tend to think they were sincere. They wanted me to relate what had happened. We were having some problems getting the Serbs out because they were pinned down by Muslim sniper fire and it was the job of my UNMOs to mediate with those guys. I personally evacuated a hundred Serbs that wanted to get out of the NATO exclusion zone post-haste and we were successful in doing so. I was pulled out by the chief Military Observer and sent off to see a shrink at the U.S. Army MASH unit in Zagreb, much to my chagrin, because I wanted to stay there and see the restoration of the status quo in the city.

Part II

A Peacekeeping Infantry Battalion at War: 2nd Battalion, Princess Patricia's Canadian Light Infantry at the Medak Pocket, Croatia, 1993

CHAPTER EIGHT

LIEUTENANT-COLONEL JIM CALVIN

*Commanding Officer,
2nd Bn Princess Patricia's Canadian Light Infantry Battalion Group
Sector West and Sector South, Croatia, 1993*

MISSION IN SECTOR WEST

The mandate of the battalion, according to the Vance Plan, was to disarm the protected area that we're in and to assist the civilian police into returning the sector to a more normal lifestyle. As a result, we took over what was a very well maintained sector at the time. The previous battalion had done a first-class job in disarming the two sides. They had a well organized system of checkpoints, and they had a fully developed plan for doing not only static checkpoints and fixed spots, but putting in mobile checkpoints to keep the two sides a little off balance and keep the initiative. They also sat there and gave us a well developed system of 'just cause' rationale for conducting search operations, whereby we still protected people's civil rights but if we actually saw someone carry an illegal weapon into a house or saw through a window that there was an illegal weapon there, then we would co-ordinate a search operation with a local police representative and seize their weapons. So, I wouldn't say it was a safe area. The mine threat was pretty big and there were a lot of mines all over the place. We had cleared all of the trails and there were certainly still a lot of weapons around.

OPERATION SPIDER WEB

A good example of an exciting operation was Operation SPIDER WEB, which was done by B Company. We had the two sides within our sector, Serb and Croatian. We controlled one of the most sensitive areas of Sector West, which included the towns of Lipik, Pakrac and a long road called the Dragovic Road, where the ceasefire line ran along, that was a major resupply corridor for the Croats. Well, about two months into our tour, the Serbs brought in some specialized units, who were sort of trained in long-range patrol, and they started sending 3 and 5-man patrols across the confrontation line, well behind the Croats of the front line, about 15 kilometres in and they started shooting forestry workers who were doing work up in the hills. We were spread pretty thin and we couldn't protect every little group that was doing work, especially when somebody was 15 kilometres behind the lines. So I asked my Bravo Company to come up with a plan to try to stop them from coming across the confrontation line, and see if we could actually intercept them. Major Verdin, the B Company commander, developed a plan where we set up a series of standing patrols on all of the major walking paths that we could find along the confrontation line. We would have them lay up there for seven days at a time, taking their IMPs, set-up with all their vision devices, and just watch to see if they could find people coming along. About two weeks into the operation we had our first contact when one of our OPs ran into one of their patrols coming across, and they actually had a minor firefight that lasted about thirty seconds before everybody ran off into the woods. Shortly after that, one of our patrols, a 4-man detachment, actually succeeded in capturing a 3-man patrol that was coming across the line. These guys were loaded up with Claymore mines, a sniper rifle with silencer, and grenades. They were pretty well loaded for bear, and they wore special stuff that you don't see on every Tom, Dick and Harry over there. Our guys captured them. Four guys surrounded three, had a standoff, and the belligerent patrol dropped their weapons.

This is when we actually changed the rules of the game and I had a long talk with the Serb brigade commander. While we were holding them I said, "I'm tired of catching guys who are doing things wrong and then sending them back home with a little slap on the wrist." At the start of this operation – that had actually killed two or three workers behind the lines – I said, "We have to make an example of somebody to stop this, otherwise they're just going to go back, get another set of weapons and tomorrow they'll come back across. Let's make a rule that if they come across with weapons that look like they're meant to seriously injure people, or more than a thousand metres across the confrontation line so that they obviously know where they're going and not just lost, we turn them over to the other side, as criminals, and they're no longer prisoners of war or on a military operation, they're just bloody terrorists." And he said, "Fine," and we turned these three guys over. Of course all hell broke loose over that. You know, "What do you mean you turned them

Sector West operations conducted in the CANBAT I area of operations by 2 PPCLI included the detaining and disarming of extremist groups raiding across the Confrontation Line who were targeting civilians. (courtesy of 2 PPCLI/LCol Shane Brennan)

over to the opposite side, you're supposed to be UN peacekeepers!" And I just told them, "Look, they were coming over to murder civilians and as far as I'm concerned they're just criminals and terrorists and they're not professional soldiers. They obviously weren't working on your orders and were probably doing things that you wouldn't want them to do anyway, so we'll turn them over to the other side. And if anybody comes across from the other side and we catch them and they're a Croat, I'll give them to you." After we set up that policy, nobody came across. The rules changed.

In terms of our UN Sector Commander, It took a little bit of convincing but he saw the reason in that one. He was a little concerned and we had to make sure that our RCMP, the civilian police that we had for the UN, monitored the judicial process so they just weren't taken over behind the corner and shot. We had people monitoring back in the cells and found out when they were going to be tried and monitored them. They got twelve years each, so this was not a slap on the wrist.

THE ERDUT AGREEMENT

The Erdut Agreement was really the reason that we began to move from Sector West to Sector South. What happened was that General Jean Cot, the UN force commander, had thought that he had achieved local agreements in Sector South to create buffer zones between the Serbs and the Croats. It really dealt with four positions, one was at the Peruca Dam, one was at the Maslenica Bridge, another one was on the Molavaki Plateau, and the other one was at the Zemunik Air Field. These were all areas that the Croats had taken in a limited offensive in January of 1993. The Molavaki Plateau is important. The critical thing about it is that if the Croats own it they can shell Knin, the Krajinan Serb capital. If the Serbs own it, they can cut off the major highway that goes down the coast. The importance of Zemunik is obvious; it's an airfield. The Maslenica Bridge, the pontoon bridge, is critical to the Croatians for the coastal route. At one time the Serbs owned that and the Croats succeeded in pushing through and opening it up. And the other one is the Peruca Dam. Now it's been blown and that's just a big hole in the ground right now down to about there, so the thing is a dried lake. It was important before because it provided all of the electricity for the whole area here, and the Serbs controlled it. So the Serbs controlled the Molavaki Plateau, the Zemunik airport and the Maslenica Bridge. In January of '93 the Croats conducted limited offensives in all of those areas and seized them all back. They pushed back up to about there and took over Peruca Dam, took over the Molavaki Plateau, got the bridge and they took over the Zemunik airport.

At the time there were UN units in Sector South. The French battalion had the Maslenica area, the Velabat Mountains area, and the Zemunik area. The Kenyans had the Peruca Dam and the Molavaki Plateau area. I'll give you some background that will lead into why we eventually got transferred full-time to Sector South. There was certainly the feeling by the Serbs that the French, at the time, knew that the Croats were preparing an offensive and at the time of this offensive, the Serbs in Sector South were disarmed, the same as they were in Sector West. All their weapons were in storage houses and so they were relying on the UN to sit there and protect them from the Croats. So the Serbs were walking around with no weapons while the Croats, being outside the UNPA, had all of their weapons, and there was evidence that the French knew, or at least allegations that the French knew, that the Croats were preparing an attack. What happened was that as soon as the Croats attacked, the French buggered off and the Serbs said, "You didn't defend us! You didn't stop them from coming in! And you didn't warn us so that we could arm and defend ourselves!" So the French battalions that were there had no credibility with the Serbs; they were just despised and they were not allowed to go anywhere. Their freedom of movement was restricted because the Serbs got all of their tanks and artillery out of the storage sites and they said, "We're going to do this ourselves."

The Erdut Agreement. This agreement was General Cot trying to get buffer zones in these four areas of the Peruca Dam, the Molivaki Plateau, the Zemunik airport and the Maslenica Bridge, so that we would keep the Serbs where they were now and we would back the Croats off to where they were before, creating UN-controlled areas in these four very sensitive areas. They thought that they were going to achieve this in all four areas, and so in order to monitor that, because they only had the Kenyans down here and the French up there, and the Czechs up there, the forces in Sector South were spread pretty thin. They said we need to have some more people and me, being the force commander's reserve battalion, he said "All right, move half of your battalion to Sector South." So we received the word to go on the 18th of July, having been warned a couple of days earlier. I began moving on the 20th of July and I did a 550-kilometre road move from Sector West with about 150 APCs and in thirty-six hours we arrived in Sector South ready to begin operations, which was quite an interesting thing, because I had been counselled by every staff officer within all of the UN headquarters who collectively said "Oh no, what you really want to do is you want to do a rail move from here to the coast and then a boat move on a ferry down to Split, and then from...." I said, "I don't want to do that, I'll lose control of my forces, I'll lose control of my administration, I'll lose control of everything. I will drive my APCs there and I will get all my own stuff down." I needed a couple of trailers to transport ammunition, and we arranged it so that every company had one and towed it behind a 5-ton truck. We had a reefer trailer that's segmented into twenty days of fresh rations and we just moved out lock, stock and barrel.

In thirty-six hours we arrived ready to do our job and General Cot couldn't believe it. He just about kissed me. They gave us the Peruca Dam area for the first of the month, and for the next month we were sitting there ready for the Erdut Agreement to be implemented and it never came to pass. We were given a small AOR in Sector South, and we began monitoring all of the incoming and outgoing shelling, and we started opening up more patrol routes, because the Kenyans really didn't have a lot of APCs and they were a little bit afraid to go to the areas that were patrolled by the belligerents, so we used the old Canadian "we're coming through" approach and we started doing all of the patrolling.

THE MEDAK POCKET OPERATION

We then got into our most interesting and certainly our most dangerous operation during our stay there, the Medak Pocket operation. It was almost a repeat of the Croatian attack that happened in January of '93. At the time it was hard for people to determine why it happened. On the 9th of September, the Croatians launched a major attack into the Medak Pocket [See Figure 11]. The Medak Pocket is a euphemism for a salient that the Serbs had into Croatian territory around the town of Medak and the Croats launched a major mechanized attack into this salient in the area of Medak. The Serbs had this large pocket all the way out to here and from here they were actually mortaring the Croat supply lines and that was pissing the Croats off in a big way. Remember, on the 9th of September we were still moving forces into the area, and we were still establishing the AOR. We certainly weren't firm in all of the areas, and the Serbs, because the French had just moved out, were still looking at us and saying, "Who the hell are you

Canadians and why should we trust you? You're just another bunch of UN soldiers." So we had just established a platoon house in the town of Medak twenty-four hours ahead of time. This house had good old 9 Platoon in it with 25 soldiers. We were still trying to force ourselves up to the front lines to see what was going on when this attack happened, and we hadn't really fully developed the whole AOR.

The first thing that we found out was that there was an attack going on about 5 kilometres further up. Shelling began all across the whole of the sector, all the way from Medak in particular straight through all of our OPs, over top of the Maslenica Bridge, and all the way down as far as the Maranji Crossing site down in B Company's area. Everybody was getting shelled. Shells fell pretty close to my battalion headquarters, which was 30 kilometres behind the lines

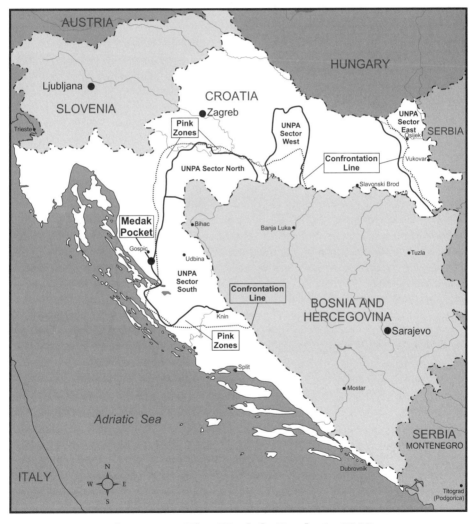

Figure 11: The Medak Pocket, 1993

in the town of Gradcac. There was this hell of a shelling barrage going on that lasted 24 hours. In fact in the twenty-four hour period, the 9th-10th of September, 9 Platoon, with reserve Lieutenant Tyrone Green, in the house in Medak endured over 500 shells that fell within 400 metres of the house. They counted all of the shells. They were sitting in this house in the basement writing a little diary, every line so many shells fell, at what time they were, and what size of shells that were falling. Every time a house would get hit in the town of Medak and somebody would come wandering into the UN house saying, "Oh, my kids are in the basement of this house," good old Tyrone Green or Sergeant Trenhome would hop in the APC, drive up to the house, get the kids out of the basement, and take them over to the Serb bunker and put them in there, patch them up and come back to the house again. This happened for a good amount of time on the 9th of September.

It carried on and we finally established an OP up in this area on the hills overlooking. It was the closest we could get a point of observation, and we set up a patrol up here with a guy named Sergeant Bijima, who was a Canadian, just outside of Ribac, and for a while, this sergeant, with a pair of long-range binoculars, was the sole person who could actually look at some of these towns and determine whether there was still fighting going on. For probably about a 24-hour period, he was the only means of knowing what was going on in the Medak Pocket. He'd send it up to 9 Platoon, who would send it up to the company and send it up to us, and we'd fax it off up to Zagreb and they would fax it to New York. So old Sergeant Bijima was telling old Butros Butros Ghali what was going on there for quite a period of time.

Things all calmed down by the end of the 10th of September. The shelling quieted down. By this time what happened is that the fighting had ceased. What really happened during the actual battle is that the Croatians did a pincer movement, and with their tanks and infantry out of this salient from the area of Ornici and a town called Ridnik, they moved a bunch of special forces up into the mountains and they succeeded in fighting and pinching off a pocket like this and taking over the entire hill of Novosalo and all of the little towns nearby. In the twenty-four hours of fighting they mustered in excess of 1,000 soldiers and probably twelve to fifteen tanks, a bunch of APCs, a lot of artillery, and they succeeded in taking over this area. Then the Serbs reinforced. The Serbs didn't have a lot of forces to be able to handle all of Sector South, so what they did is they moved forces around wherever they needed them, and they did it on a rail line. Within twenty-four hours a train pulled up behind the town of Medak with about 10 or 12 tanks on it, off-loaded them and about 800 soldiers, and maybe 1,000 more soldiers got trucked in. They suddenly moved in and reinforced the area and they succeeded in stabilizing the new lines in this area here, just about four klicks forward of the town of Medak. The two sides sort of squared off and dug in new trench systems and got their tanks all in position. So at the end of the actual attack, the Croats had succeeded in taking over about 22 square kilometres, 5 or 6 kilometres long and 4 or 5 kilometres wide.

You have to remember that ethnic Serbs inhabited this area of the Medak Pocket. Now these were Serb farmers who had lived there for hundreds of years, and family after family had passed down the farmlands. Although this is all Croatian territory, they're all ethnic Serbs who lived in the Pocket and so they took over all of these little towns and assessments were that there were about 1,300 ethnic Serbs who lived in that area at the time that the Croats took it all over. So by about the 10th or 11th, the lines had stabilized. Then there was a pause and every-one started negotiating and the UN started negotiating. The Serbs wanted the Croats to pull back, give up the ground and give back the people. The Croats didn't want to pull back. There was fighting going back and forth, and the Serbs started shelling Zadar, and there was a lot of this stuff going back and forth. The UN was trying to broker a ceasefire agreement. And then on about the 12th or 13th, the Serbs got the Croat's attention, because they fired a Frog 7 missile and they hit the outskirts of Zagreb from up near the Bihac Pocket!

Well, Croatian President Tudjman suddenly became very attentive to the Serb's demands because, of course, this was his capital city. So they came to the table, and they got an agreement signed. The gist of the agreement was that the Serbs would have to hold in their current positions where they had been pushed back to, the Croats agreed to move back to their pre-9 September line, and we would set up a buffer zone in between the two sides that the UN would control. I set up a few regulations, such as no weapons, like we had in Sector West. We would disarm anybody who came in; it would be UN controlled, etc. So this was the agreement that was reached. It paralleled the Erdut Agreement, only a different area.

The next thing that I knew that happened was that I was summoned up to Knin. I was in Zagreb at this time seeing my Colonel-in-Chief off, who had just made a visit to the battalion. In the throes of all this artillery shelling and stuff like this, she decided she wanted to come and pin some medals on the boys. We had her in town for about forty-eight hours and I was just seeing her off at the airport when I got an urgent telephone message at the hotel from my ops officer saying that you have orders to be in Knin at 0900 tomorrow morning. I was about to get orders about monitoring the withdrawal operation. Luckily I had a map in my pocket so I started studying up on the area and I caught the next plane back at 0800. The funny thing was, on the helicopter ride down there I sat and started thinking, if this is like a normal UN operation no one has really thought a lot about the details of it, so I'm going to write down the points that I want included in the withdrawal agreement, so that I can eventually manage this thing after all. I put down no weapons in the Pocket, tanks withdrawn 2 kilometres behind the line, artillery back behind this line, all these little regulations, and I presented them to the general when I got in there.

I arrived in Knin, got taken down for the 0900 Orders Group, and received orders. The orders were co-chaired by General Helmus who was the senior UN Military Observer in the force and General Cot's representative, Colonel Michel Maisonneuve, and my sector commander General Bollo, who chaired the meeting. At this meeting I was told that the agreement had been signed as of twenty-four hours from the O Group and I was to be prepared to go in and supervise the withdrawal. The Croats were going to withdraw to the 9 September line, the Serbs were going to stay where they were, and I was going to set up a buffer zone between them. To do this operation I was going to get two companies of the French Army under my operational control and they would arrive later on that day. One of the company commanders was actually at the O Group, which was a great thing, so I got a chance to chat with him. We received no more direction than that. No sort of detailed timings, no great plan, just develop your plan and tell us what it is. By 1030 I had had a quick chat with the French company commander and I said, "Here's what I want. Go back and get your troops. I want you to come with this kind of ammunition, and these kinds of weapons." They had the French VAB, a large wheeled APC, and each platoon had four of those plus they had one VAB support vehicle. On the four troop-carrying vehicles they had .50 cals and in each platoon they had one VAB that had a 20mm chain gun on top of it. They came with small little Panhard armoured cars for their platoon commanders, each with GPS in them. Each company, thank God, came with a built-in engineering platoon within the company, so they actually had about a two or three-section platoon of engineers within each company and each one of these companies was in excess of 225 men, much more robust than ours and very well equipped. They also came with their own front-end loaders and small engineering plant. It was quite a nice organization to suddenly be reinforced with.

Certainly there were some command and control problems. Mine was an English-speaking battalion and they were Frenchmen that didn't speak any English. None of them spoke any English except maybe a smattering from one of the company commanders. So I automatically had a linguistic problem and fortunately I had two officers in my liaison cell that could double-duty with some basic French. Our radios were non-compatible between the French and the Canadians. So what I did is I plunked my liaison officer in a jeep and I put him right beside each French company commander, and I passed all my orders to him who then translated it roughly into French, told the French company commander what to do, and it worked out fine that way.

My immediate time and space problem was that I had to start moving a lot of troops up to the Medak area. I assessed in time, on top of the two French companies, I was going to need two Canadian companies, and I saw this as a four-company operation when I did my estimate. So that meant that already I had one company up there, which was Charlie Company's platoon, and I could automatically move Charlie Company in there because it was really their sector anyway. I was getting two French companies, so that gave me three, and I had to somehow pull another one of them out of one of the areas that I had already given them. Now the type of the operation dictated to me that I automatically had to have somebody in APCs, so that ruled out the company that just arrived down from Sector West, because we were in the process of downscaling the whole primary operation from four companies to three, and I had been ordered to hand in all the APCs of that company back to Sector West. They came down on buses so they were a foot-mobile company and they weren't available for the operation, so basically I had to give a warning order out to have them take over Major Dan Drew's company AOR, and basically baby-sit that AOR since they had no vehicles to patrol it, free up him, with all his APCs, and his mechanized capability to move up into the Medak area. So within a period of twelve hours, from the warning order, I had companies moving everywhere: two French companies moving down from Sector North and the Bihac Pocket, one Canadian company moving down to take over D Company's area, and D Company picking up and moving up there. My other defence platoon and my recce platoon were way in the south handing over to B Company the two protected villages of Ranici and Bruca, and moving up into the Medak area. Everybody was on the move.

So from getting off the airplane at 0830 in the morning, attending orders at 0900, giving out the warning order for people to move, having done your brief estimate in the car driving back from Knin to Gracac, getting people moving around and then suddenly giving orders at 1600 that afternoon, it was quite a hectic day. The one lesson that I can say absolutely is that Battle Procedure works. The way we learn Battle Procedure, you know, receive orders, liaison with your company commanders during those orders or the attachments you're going to get after those orders, tell them where you want them to go, what they can expect, so that they go off and do their thing and do a quick map estimate, give a warning order out to start preliminary movements back and forth, at the same time you're fleshing out the details of your tactical plan and then giving formal orders later on. It actually works. We did a tremendous amount of movement around and when people know you're going into a real operation, no one questions the little detail. You give broad details to people and you say get on with it and make the decisions that you have to do to make your force ready, because I'm not here to baby-sit you. People just assume a lot of responsibility, they make great decisions, they get on with the problem, and it's really good to see that.

So, I gave orders that afternoon about 1600, oral orders other than a field message pad, because there was not time to do it. My ops officer, a first-class man, Shane Brennan, actually typed up confirmatory notes afterwards to hand out later, but they weren't ready at issuance. So I stood there, my second French company commander had not arrived yet, so I had to give orders to get everybody going now. I would catch up with him later when he got in. It was raining hard when we started the operation. I gave basically orders for a four-phase operation. The first phase was to interpose two companies in between the Croat and Serb lines to stratify the two lines, and that would show the Croatians that I wasn't going to let the Serbs press any advantage when the Croats withdrew and it would stop the shooting between them. My second phase was to establish a crossing site on the main hardstand route in between the two sides so that I could have an access point to the other side. My third phase was to move companies over onto the far side and take over the Croat front lines to allow them pull back and to move them back to the 9 September lines. The fourth phase was to sweep the entire area and record any evidence of any wrongdoings, clean up any bodies, and just establish what happened and we knew right off the bat, or at least I had assessed right off the bat, that I would have to do a formal report on what had happened in the Pocket.

I hadn't anticipated the degree of ethnic cleansing that was going to happen, but I felt certainly there would be something that would have to be recorded, so we were prepared for that. I actually established a special team made up of the company commander of that foot-mobile company that I told you about, Major Craig King. He handed over his company to the 2IC, and he established what we called the Sweep Team, which consisted of two sections of engineers, with my engineer troop commanders with some back hoes to dig out graves and things like this. Some UNCIVPOL, some UNHCR folks, my two doctors and a half a platoon of soldiers to clean up, record buildings, search buildings, pick up bodies, and do whatever they had to do. I thought he would be my main media spokesman as well. Talking to the media, we have to do that kind of stuff. So, with that in mind everybody flashed off. People were moving by 0900 on the following morning, the 14th. I had two companies in the town of Medak, Charlie and Delta Companies, and in fact the French company arrived, so I had three mechanized companies there at 0900 [See Figure 12].

The next couple of hours were pretty interesting to me, because we were all sitting there, and everything was quiet. Remember, we were coming in from behind the Serb line, so we had a good chance to tell the Serbs what we were going to do and they nodded their heads. Now remember, there were a lot of Serbs there, a lot of tanks, a lot of artillery, a lot of soldiers, and they said, "Okay, you're going to go out in front of us and establish the zone and that's fine." They knew that an agreement had been reached between the two sides, so they thought this was going to be okay. Thank God General Cot came down to visit. He came to the town of Medak and for the next hour and a half or two hours, we wandered up and down the streets, and he and I had a little commander-to-commander chat. He told me exactly what he wanted to do. There were two things he emphasized. The first one, it was essential that UNPROFOR have a successful operation. He said

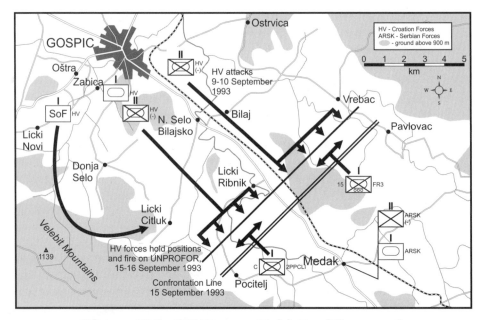

Figure 12A: HV Forces Hold Positions and Fire on UNPROFOR, 15-16 September 1993

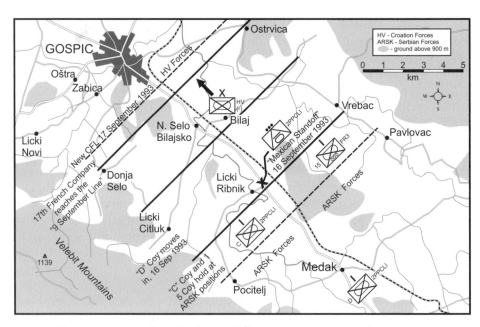

Figure 12B: Final Dispositions, 17 September 1993

that we have had nothing but minor failures all along. Any time we tried to impose our will and to get something done, we have never been able to be successful, and that it was very important for us to have a successful outcome here if we're going to have any credibility to UNPROFOR.

The second thing that he told me was that he doubted very much whether the Croats had told their soldiers what was going on. Because, as he explained to me, it's been a reluctant agreement by the Croats to give up this territory to the UN, as the soldiers had just won the ground at a price, and soldiers don't like to be told by their bosses that they're going to give up ground that they've just taken over. So he said, "Be very careful when you move in there because it could be very unsafe." After more discussions, he said, "Move at 1400 hours." So I briefed my boys. I told them that we were going to have to do this but we were going to have to be cautious in our approach and I told them how important it was for us to be successful. C Company jumped the gun and went in at 1330 and took the left-hand side of the road, and my first French company took the right-hand side of the road, and they moved ahead of the Serbs between 1330 and 1400. And just about immediately, C Company in particular but to a lesser extent the French company, came under fire.

It started off with small arms. I think Tyrone Green, the reserve lieutenant from the Seaforth Highlanders, and his platoon who had already been shelled in Medak for twenty-four hours a couple of days before, were the first guys who came under fire. The company had one platoon that went up the road, one company that came in the centre, which was Tyrone Green's, and one company that came over to Citluk, which was Captain Dave McKillop's. Tyrone moved out into the middle first and as he moved a couple of shots came pinging off his APC. At the time they thought it was a mistake, and that the Croats didn't know who they were, so they hoisted the biggest UN flag that they could on top of the antenna and moved the APC out further into the clearing, and a machine gun fired on them. So they decided that maybe this was not an accident anymore, and when the next burst of fire came at them they started to return the fire. That was one little firefight that happened.

At the same time, over on the far left-hand side in the town of Citluk, Dave McKillop and his platoon started moving into a real dicey area, because as I said the special forces would come down out of the mountains and the Croat special forces, they were pretty thick. We're talking about interposing my company in between two front lines that are only about 800 metres apart, and maybe in some places only 600 metres. So when you have to put forces in between them you're not talking about long ranges and Dave McKillop's platoon came under fire five times in five separate firefights. Some of them were as short as one or two minutes, but there was one that lasted ninety minutes. When you talk about the ammunition expenditures here, we're talking about not just magazines we're talking about cases of ammunition. Remember all of my APCs had full basic loads of ammunition so that platoon in particular was subjected to all types of machine-gun fire, rocket grenades from rifles, and 20mm cannon fire and they responded with everything they had in their arsenal. They responded with C-7, C-6 machine gun and .50-calibre machine-gun fire over extended periods of time. So over fifteen hours that one platoon had five separate firefights, with some of them of quite a magnitude.

I had TOWs all along the ridge, particularly in the centre area. Rules of Engagement are a topical sort of thing. I gave some pretty specific ROE here. For the soldiers, it was always you respond in kind. Make no mistake, after somebody's fired at you with a machine gun, I'm not going to sit there and quibble if you respond with a .50 and he's shot at you with 7.62. When you're in the situation where suddenly there are all kinds of people firing at you and you're just trying to sit there and respond, I'm not really saying, "Oh he's only fired five rounds and you fired fifteen." There are no ROE when you do that kind of stuff but I had given specific ROE to my TOWs. I said that I would retain permission for them to open fire. They had to call me personally and ask permission to open fire, with one exception. They could always fire if somebody fired at them. If a tank fired at them they could shoot in self-defence. I would never ever take that away from anybody, no matter what weapon system. If they'd positively identified which tank was fighting them and a round had impacted close to them, they could fire but if they saw a tank fire at someone else, they couldn't necessarily open up. Because I can only respond if he's fired at me, and if the tank has just fired somewhere else and he's seen the tank that's firing, it could have been firing at a Serb or maybe even just retaliating. So in that case, they still had to call me so we could at least identify it. If he fired at another Canadian then we'd pop the guy, but it wasn't just a case, because he saw a tank fire, that he could open up. That may have been overly restrictive but I thought with something like TOW you have to be careful about just letting people with a 3,000-metre wire-guided missile hit somebody just because he saw a tank fire. I had my TOWs all up here primarily around this area that they moved in, because most of the tanks were down in this area and they'd have most of them sited.

If I'd had a TOW over in the area of Citnik when that 20mm cannon opened up, I would have popped the 20mm cannon, even if it took a TOW to do it, because a .50 calibre doesn't reach as far as a 20mm cannon and I didn't have anything else that would have gone that far. We didn't get close enough to see whether it was a dual or a single, but the Croats had about ten 20mm cannons all along this line. We saw about ten of those things dropped out when we actually finally got over to the other side. This was not a small amount of firepower, and they had about ten or twenty tanks. At least ten, maybe more, of these 20mm cannons sitting on the bridge line posed a lot of firepower.

For fifteen hours the French came under fire as well, but they had the advantage of having that 20mm cannon mounted on their VABs. In their own words, they said, "Once we fire a 20mm, nobody shoots back." It was on a well-stabilized mount on top of their APCs, and they hit what they were looking at. They had a good optical site, they had a good cannon, and they just saw pieces flying off things when they fired that thing. So people didn't shoot at them more than once if they had that 20mm cannon around. They loved shooting back with that weapon.

So, after fifteen hours on the 14th, things calmed down a bit and as dark was falling I got a transmission from the UNMOs, who were floating around the Croat side, that the Croat general in Gospic wanted to have a meeting and so I said, "Fine," and they said come to Gospic. I replied, "How do I get there?" They said, "The meeting is set up for 2000 hours tonight, so cross on the main hard stand." I agreed, so literally at 1900 hours I went up there and parked my jeep. My RSM wouldn't let me go without him, so myself, my RSM [the Regimental Sergeant Major], and Major Drew, who was going to be the guy who was going to be the first company across on the other side anyway, went. I wanted him to go, and I also took the head UNMO that I had with me, who had the Motorola talking to the Liaison Officer on the other side, and after dark we started walking across the paved road towards the Croat side that had been shooting at us for the last fifteen hours. We had a little red flashlight that we would flash and then we'd see a flash from over there, and the guy on the Motorola talking and giving our progress. It's funny to think of it now but at the time you're saying, "We've got to be idiots."

We had a staggered formation on the road. In reality, you'd think that you're pretty safe but it is kind of ludicrous to be walking towards the bastards who had been shooting at you for fifteen hours straight, and now in the middle of the night you're hoping that somebody's got more control over them at night than they did during the day. We made it across without incident, and after we got over, they let us call our vehicles and after we established communication the vehicles drove across, picked us up and we went off to Gospic for our meeting there. There was a rep from Zagreb that attended, and we basically finalized the plan. We found out one thing was true, the Croats had not told their soldiers what was going on and in fact, they had not even seen a signed copy of the agreement. As ludicrous as it may seem, I had to bring a photocopy of the actual agreement showing them that President Tudjman had signed this agreement before they would agree to pull back. You're not talking about professionals here. Anyway, they said, "Fine, we will move back." I tried to press for 0800 the next morning. They succeeded in convincing the rep from Zagreb that they needed until noon to get the word out to all their other soldiers. It was just a bunch of hokey quite frankly; they were just stalling for time. So we agreed that at noon the next day I would be permitted to send my first companies across, take over the Croat lines and they would start to move back to the 9 September lines.

The one thing I did force on them was that I was going to establish the crossing site, which was my second phase, that night. I wasn't going to go all the way back across and then have to fight my way across again, I'm going to establish my crossing site now. I waited on the Croat side after we got back to the crossing site, and I sent Major Drew across to get a couple of his APCs, bring them back across and establish our link on the Croat side so that we actually had a free spot to cross. About 0200 in the morning I went to bed, because I was getting a little tired at this stage in the game. I figured we had earned our pay for the first day and that the next day was going to start off a better day.

We were wrong. The next day started off worse. The first thing in the morning we got up and as soon as the sun rose, there was smoke coming up from all of the villages. Fires started burning and you could hear explosions going on, which turned out to be ethnic cleansing using anti-tank mines with a timed or electrical fuse, and they link a daisy chain mine around all of the walls on the buildings. They'd put five, six or seven mines around all of the concrete block walls and then they'd blow them all at the same time. This levelled out the bottom floor and dropped the top floors right in on the floors below and just collapsed all of your building. So between the explosions, the fires and the small-arms fire that we saw coming out of the Pocket, it was pretty evident that ethnic cleansing was going on. Unfortunately for the UN, and the Canadians in particular, in having made an agreement that we wouldn't go across until 1200, we had to sit there and watch this going on through our binoculars for the better part of five hours until noon came around. But sharp at noon we rolled across and got to the far side. When we got there we linked up with Major Drew's vehicles that were on the other side, where we found that the Croats had put dragon's teeth and more mines across the road and they weren't going to let us through.

This is where we got into the next very tense situation, which is when I had my whole D Company line up behind Major Drew on the road, with TOWs, and APCs with .50 cals on them. You could see mines on both sides of the road so you couldn't walk anywhere. There was a Croat company dug-in a couple of hundred yards just on the right-hand side of the road, and you could see the trenches and all of the soldiers sitting there with their rifles along with a couple of anti-tank guns. There was a tank in the low ground down off to the left, although we didn't see it until we actually ventured across the crossing sector, and there was a tank down there ready to roll up. This is where we got into a big argument with the Croats on the ground. We said we'd got an agreement and we're going to go through. We were held up there for the better part of an hour and a half but in the end what got them to lift the mines and to let us through was using the media. Because the media, when they got wind of all of the stuff going on, flocked in pretty thick. There were a lot of camera crews around. I had a talk with the camera people alone and I told them I needed their help. If we were to get through and stop the ethnic cleansing, I would give an interview right in front of the mines and I would start calling down the Croats and telling them how President Tudjman had reneged on his agreement with the UN and that this general is killing people over in the Pocket. I would make it sound really bad, and I wanted them to start filming me. I wanted President Tudjman to know that he would look bad in front of the world press. We started to do that, and the Croat general immediately called his soldiers and starting lifting up the mines, and said he would honour the agreement. That's how we got through but there was a long period there when it was pretty tense. I finally got two companies through. Major Drew's company went right in along the Croat front lines and started relieving them and they started backing their tanks up.

So we succeeded in getting across and Major Drew moved his company to occupy the Croat front lines, and the second French company moved along to the town of Ornici. Unbeknownst to me, the negotiators that stayed in Gospic from Zadar had changed my basic tactical plan without consulting me. Instead of me automatically going and occupying the 9 September line with one company and the front line where I had a firm grip on the whole area, they said I would move forward in phases from line to line. It was a little short-sighted on their part because that automatically meant that people could ethnically cleanse ahead of me on every phase line andI wouldn't be able to stop them. So be that as it may, that was the agreement that the Zagreb people signed.

We went into Ornici where I had to remain in accordance with the new rules until 1800 hours with my second French company and that was just up the road from this town called Liki Citluk, which was a major centre for the ethnic cleansing. We were sitting there for about another hour and a half waiting, and at 1800 sharp we pressed up to Liki Citluk and that's when we started seeing the ethnic cleansing close up. It was just getting dark; between 1800 and 1900 it's dusk this time of the year around the end of September. The fires were still burning in all of the buildings with most of the roofs caved in and there was a loathsome smell of death. You didn't know what it was then but you sure found out later on when the bodies starting showing. All of the cattle had been killed and were lying on the roads and fields. As the sun set, with all of this smoke hanging in the air, burning buildings, and bodies around, it was really a bizarre scene to drive into.

Initially you were a bit awe-struck at the systematic destruction. We're not talking sporadic houses we're talking about every single building that we saw had been levelled to the ground. It was a very systematic thing. You're looking around and you're just picturing twenty-four hours or forty-eight hours before people were living all around here, and now it's just total destruction. After about the first hour or two you started to get an anger that started building up in you, which I have to deal with later on. That armed people, military people, were killing civilians who had no means to defend themselves. It was just such a violation of everything that you'd been taught. Armies make war on armies; armies don't make war on civilians. We have this sense of fair play about this thing. I think all of the soldiers shared a deep sense of anger over what the Croats had done but in any case, we moved in. As soon as we got into Liki Citluk I gave orders that we would hold here because it was getting dark, we knew there were a lot of mines around, and we weren't going to go wandering around in the dark. We actually succeeded in rescuing three Serbs who came running up to one of my APCs. My adjutant, who was acting as my battle adjutant, my APC actually, between he and the recce platoon commanders actually saved these three Serbs because the Croats were still operating out of the area after ethnically cleansing it all. They basically got these three Serbs, threw them in the back of one of our APCs and saved their lives. I tasked the recce platoon commander and the engineer officer with actually finding an interior route out of the area through the minefields that night so in the middle of the night they spirited these Serbs out of the area. We found a couple of bodies that first night, a couple of women who had been burned to death in a basement of a house. They had just been killed before we moved in by the looks of things. They probably had been held as some kind of a sex toy thing for the boys for the four or five days of the occupation. Basically a jerry can of gas had been put in this small basement room with them and ignited. When we got to them one was without legs, they had been burned off, and the other one was without an upper torso. We just saw charred flesh and the stench was overwhelming.

They were so hot we had to pour water on the bodies before they could put them in a plastic body bag or they would have melted the bag. It was pretty gruesome stuff for the troops to see.

The troops in the line companies weren't so bad. The ones that were affected the most were the ones that were actually part of the Sweep Team that went to every single site and had to watch the forensic guys doing their examinations, of how did they die, how long were they dead, and then picking up the bodies, because maggots and vermin start chewing on these things within twenty-four to forty-eight hours and we're talking about five days. Some of them might have been killed initially when the Croats first went in. After five days some of these bodies got pretty ripe with vermin. We had to rotate some of the people on the sweep team so they weren't there all of the time. It got pretty bad. They did a super job but it was pretty draining on them.

So we spent the second night in Liki Citluk and the Croats did back off. The next day we pressed on at 0900 and I ordered the French company to move forward to the area of Stranici and Foliarmi. At that point, I did a forward passage of lines and I took the French company, who by now was in quite a quiet area, and I pulled them all the way back down, pressed them forward and had them finish off by securing the top end of the Pocket and move them up around the fire. So I actually withdrew them and moved them up to the other French company. We succeeded in actually taking the entire Pocket. There was a bit of pushing of the Croats to get them back. Even though they were withdrawing they were resisting quite a bit and they were still trying to do some ethnic cleansing. We had quite a few confrontations between Canadian, French and Croat soldiers. I don't mind saying that our guys handled themselves very well, even though they had a tremendous amount of anger over what they'd seen in terms of ethnic cleansing. They could have easily done some bad things.

Myself, my RSM and my track driver went for a drive around to see where the lines ended. I ran into a Croat checkpoint. In my assessment they were too far into my buffer zone. I said, "You have to move back" and they said, "No we were told to stay here." I told them, "Move back or I'll call my soldiers and we'll move you back" and they replied, "No, we're staying." So I got on the radio and called them up and shortly a couple of platoons of the French Army came along with their VABS and I told them "Push them back 1,000 metres" and they said "Yes sir!" People starting pulling their guns, but we had more guns than they, and we didn't shoot first. We never shoot first, but if any one of them would have shot we would have killed them all, there's no doubt about it and they pushed them back 1,000 metres, bulldozed over their roadblock, pushed them all back and escorted them back out. This was not a bravado thing, but everybody has to understand what kind of mental attitude that we had to establish. I told my people that I wanted them to establish dominance in the area and one of the ways that I told them I was going to establish dominance was that I was going to tell the Croats where the buffer zone was, and that they weren't going to legislate it to me. When I told people that I wanted to move the Croats back, they were to move them back. The reason for this, in simple soldier's mental attitude, which I think most of my soldiers understood, is that the Croats had just had a big victory. They came in, killed a whole bunch of Serb soldiers, and then they killed a lot of Serb civilians. They were walking around with their chests stuck out a long way. My battalion was going to come in here and we were soon going to hand it over to the brand new battalion that was coming, in about another two weeks, who were going to come in brand new on the ground. If I had to hand it over to a green Canadian battalion when all these Croats thought they were a bunch of big heroes and that they were the toughest guys in the valley, it would have put the UN in a real world of hurt for the next six months, because these Croats were going to think that they were the best soldiers around.

Well, in a very short amount of time I had to show them that they weren't the best soldiers. My guys were better than any one of them, and they better pay attention when the Canadian soldiers say that they're going to enforce the buffer zone. So I said, "We've got a short amount of time to do this and one of the ways we're going to do it is we're going to sit there and show our will right off the bat" and when I said, "Push them back," we pushed them back. Nobody shot at anybody, but there were quite a few of these tense situations. By the end of the next two days every Croat soldier knew that the Canadian soldiers and the French soldiers were not people that were going to be screwed around with. When Calvin told them to do something, they got the job done and the Croats better watch what was going on. A good example of this – immediately after we established the buffer zone, a 16-man Croat patrol came wandering over the hills right into the buffer zone. The first guy who saw them happened to be my operations officer. He stopped and told this 16-man patrol, "Stop, you're in the buffer zone, lay down your weapons." This is a 16-man patrol with machine guns and everything. They said, "No way, we'll go wherever we want." My boys got on the horn, called up the battalion headquarters, and they sent a French platoon from my French 3 Company to surround them with their VABS and .50 calibre machine guns. The Croats put all their weapons down, we confiscated all of the weapons, put them all in the back of the truck and we delivered them to the edge of the buffer zone and told them, "Don't come back." But that is the kind of thing that you have to do right off the bat after one of these sorts of things.

We established checkpoints all the way around the buffer zone. We swept every grid square systematically, grid by grid to record every building that had been destroyed, and every body that we could find. We found that every well had been poisoned, every single building had been destroyed, and all the livestock had been destroyed. I think we found twenty bodies, but the worse thing that we found was that everywhere were surgical gloves. There were just hundreds and hundreds of surgical gloves everywhere. The best thing that we could figure was that there had been a mass execution, they loaded up the bodies and had taken them out. Between the people that had managed to escape that they counted up in all of the refugee camps, and the 1,300 people that they thought were in there, there is a discrepancy of about 500 people. We only found twenty bodies and to this day I'm still a firm believer that the rest were trucked away. It was so systematic in terms of the professional fire bombing of the houses and the exploding of the houses. All of the bodies that we found looked like they were found in out-of-the-way places, that they might have forgotten them, or those two women that the Croat boys kept only for their little goodies and then just killed them at the last minute. They weren't just lying near a house or something where they'd be easy to find, they were sort of in hidden places.

I personally was so demoralized that an army could do that to civilians. I live in a rural community. The area that I saw the ethnic cleansing reminded me a lot of Wolfe Island, quite frankly, just like it is here. Farms separated apart in little clusters but everything levelled. You could picture the civilians who had been living there trying to build up a life. When I think that some of these thugs and hoodlums that I saw carrying AK-47s had just marched into their courtyard, put them on their knees and then plugged them and threw them in the back of a truck, after all of the years of working on the farm, it just made me sick, quite frankly. I espoused that to the Croat general up there, when I told him that I was going to get him fired with my report. I said, "In my country armies do not make war on civilians. We make war on other armies. I don't consider people brave who sit there and go in and kill civilians who have no weapons." He couldn't understand it, he said that the Serbs did this all the time; we're just doing what they do. I said, "That doesn't make it right." I think every one of my soldiers at the end of the operation had very little respect for the Croats. We wouldn't have had any respect if it had been Serbs or if it had been Muslims. In the end, when the final body count was done, the Croats said that we killed 27 Croats. My soldiers and other people who came back afterwards, who were in the MO teams and everything else, said we could have killed over hundred of them, but the Croats didn't want to say that.

Within my battalion group I had ten casualties. I had 3 Canadians who were wounded with artillery shrapnel and I had 7 Frenchmen who were injured due to mine strikes and a couple of them probably will never walk again. About two or three French APCs hit mines and one French front-end loader backed off the road and hit a mine. In the end the report that I wrote on the ethnic cleansing actually got the Croat general replaced. He was canned as the operational zone commander for the Croats.

In my mind it was a unique operation in that it was almost like an offensive operation. Even though we still had to work within the rules of engagement initially, we actually interposed ourselves between two sides, and one side decided to open fire on us, at which time most of the rules of engagement became void, because we were literally in a mini war on the ground fighting for our lives. And again, I try to tell people this. For a soldier on the ground in his 200 square yards, when somebody starts firing at him, this is the rule of engagement. He is in a war and he has to react just like it's a little war. Yes, somebody might fire on him first, but you don't expect to give them two or three times at it, and he uses his good training and he reacts as he's supposed to react.

CRITICAL INCIDENT STRESS MANAGEMENT, POST-MEDAK

Before we went over, on the advice of my padre Bob Sparks, we trained fifty-five guys within the unit in what they call mille level stress facilitator techniques. The first couple of times I was pretty sceptical. I wasn't a big believer in this stress thing, I thought we're all manly men, we can handle all this shit and it won't really bother us. Well, that was a wrong philosophy and I'm converted now. Stress gets to everybody, and you've got to have a way to deal with it. What we found was that the first couple of times when we had a mine strike with an APC and we had to get everybody together in this little 'holding hands' session, it's a venting of your feelings.

What we found were a couple of interesting things. First of all is that things start getting to a soldier when he thinks he's different than everybody. Most people, if they've gone through a near-to-death situation, lose a little sleep, have a few nightmares, and have trouble eating. It's just a normal reaction when you think that you could have lost a leg, a major body part or died. So when suddenly Johnny Tentpegs starts not being able to sleep and he has nightmares, well he doesn't go to his buddy and say, "I want to cry on your shoulder, I've got some real problems." He holds it inside. When he goes to one of these group sessions and he's forced to sit there and he's asked, "Well how do you feel, how does this affect you, how are you sleeping?" and he says, "Well I've had a problem sleeping," and Johnny Canuck over there says, "Well I haven't been able to sleep since it happened too." Then another guy says, "Well I've had a bunch of nightmares about it and I haven't been able to eat and I haven't had a shit for the last few days," well he finds out he's just normal. Everybody is affected the same way. Especially when a couple of guys he really respects, like maybe a section commander says, "I've lost a couple of night's sleep over this too." Suddenly, when he realizes he's normal, all of the nightmares disappear, and he says I'm just one of the boys again, we're all the same, and he's not different anymore. That will get you through a lot of low-level stress builders. It's just a constant release thing.

So that's why we made everybody, whether you watched a vehicle accident, whether you had a mine strike, whether you had a shooting incident, or any of those kind of things, go through one with one of their own peer group. That sort of kept us on a pretty good plane until the Medak encounter.

Nothing really prepares you for a Medak operation. It was a combination of the shootings, the ethnic cleansing that we saw, and living in mud and rain because it was miserable weather in September as we were carrying on and then the last thing that happened was Jimmy DeCoste's death. On the 18th of September, just when the Medak thing was winding down, we hadn't had anybody killed. We had a couple of near misses with the artillery shrapnel and the mines, but nobody had died. We had swapped all of these bullets with everybody and we'd gone through all this crap where people would try to kill us, and then suddenly the vehicle accident happened and Captain DeCoste died and it flattened our unit like you couldn't believe. We had people who had no energy, no desire, and people were just demoralized as hell that suddenly they lost somebody in a dopey vehicle accident. After all of those times that we could have accepted death, because you know people were trying to kill us, you know, it wasn't there. So, yes, stress is a real factor. We had one example of stress right at the end of the Pocket operation.

My problem with it was that it happened so close to the end of the tour. Suddenly we didn't have any time to get people on the straight and narrow. The Medak operation ended the 22nd, 23rd of September. The Van Doos started arriving on the first of October, a week later. We had to hand over and all the equipment checks to do. We did a little bit of critical stress stuff. Then by the 10th of October everybody went. My reservists didn't come back to me so that we could talk about it afterwards; they went home. They had nobody to talk to and also they went back to a Militia unit where maybe nobody else had been over in a situation like this. Who are they going to talk to in the Militia unit where they go out to do compass marches, when he's just been through the biggest action the Canadian Army has been through since Korea? Who's he going to talk to about firefights and all this stress-relief stuff with? Nobody. My soldiers could at least go to the mess and talk with one of their buddies and say, "How are things going?" But the reservists didn't have anybody. At that stage of the game we weren't very good at it. I try to write letters to the guys that had been over there with us just saying, look, if you have any problems just call us, do whatever. We sent a couple of company commanders out to a few of the units where the COs called up and said that some of the guys were doing some heavy drinking that were over with me. Maybe I could send some guys out to talk to them. I'm still certain that there are guys out there that are still suffering some emotional difficulties. We have to get better at it. I think we're slowly getting better at it, but it's going to take some money. I think it will probably in the end take a couple of lawsuits where suddenly the army is put to task to have a long-term follow-up, particularly with the reserves because there are some problems. If you go through something like we did, there are bound to be some problems.

THE NEED FOR IMPARTIALITY

I think it's important, and I don't think Canadians really need to hear this because we know it, but it's important not to pick sides over there. Even at the end when we had gone through this thing with the Croats, they were not our enemy. Our guys were able to sit there and determine the fact that yes, they were shooting at us and they tried to kill us. They were the enemy and we were going to try to tune them before they tuned us. But as soon as that was done and we set up our check-points, the Croats were no longer the enemy. We didn't like them but we were now a professional army doing a professional job. We treated them the same way we did the Serbs. There wasn't any love lost between us because of what they did to all of the civilians and the fact that they had been shooting at us, but still they were not our enemy. They were just another side and we were this side, and you have to keep that always in your perspective, even if somebody takes a shot at you, or the shelling is happening and you figure it's coming from one side. If you can't stand the heat, then don't go into the kitchen. Prepare yourself before you go over that there are some things that you just have to accept. A peacekeeper will always accept the first shot. We say that you always have the right to self defence and that is absolutely true, but over there nobody comes walking up to you pointing a rifle at your head and say I'm going to shoot you so that you can get the first shot at him. It's always a shot that comes out of the blue. You just have to hope that you're always aware enough that you're not presenting yourself to be a big target, and that he misses with the first one. Or it's just an intimidation shot. Because in my mind there are very few circumstances where the first round won't come from one or the other sides and if he's really going to try to kill you, he's probably going to kill you if he's any good. The key thing is that you'll have to be ready to react if he does give you that break and he misses, that you are well prepared to react and return deadly fire so that he knows he better not try it again.

So peacekeeping has a mentality all of its own. I don't say it's an impossible task but it does have its own stresses. I'm not saying that every day is a Medak Pocket operation either but a unit that goes over there has to be prepared. We may go through another ten years before a Canadian battalion is at the right place at the right time to go through a Medak Pocket operation. We have to assume that the next one happens in a Canadian sector, that an agreement is reached, and that Canadians are there to react. That may take ten more years, but it could happen tomorrow and so every unit that goes over there had better be able to react and to do that kind of a job. I'm not a big fan of the worst-case scenario all of the time because I think it's badly abused, but good professional training in live-fire dismounted infantry skills are really needed. And I'll say this at the risk of people getting angry at me, it's one reason that I really disagree with the philosophy now that they're saying that any combat or arms unit can go over to do peacekeeping tasks.

CHAPTER NINE

MAJOR TONY KADUCK

Company Commander,
2nd Bn Princess Patricia's Canadian Light Infantry Battalion Group
Sector West and Sector South, Croatia, 1993

PREPARING TO DEPLOY

We got the unofficial warning order in about October. At that time I was OC Administration Company and obviously we immediately oriented everything that the battalion was doing towards going over there for the deployment. So of course we had the usual hectic things trying to get us organized but we had our reservists start arriving just after Christmas leave in the first week of January. Then we deployed down to Fort Ord, in California, starting on the 2nd of February. The reasoning behind that was that we had so much training to do in such a short period of time that there was no way we were going to get that done effectively in the winter in Shilo or any place like that.

The Americans were receptive and thought it was the best thing going. They could not differentiate between Croatia and Bosnia, so finally we stopped trying to tell them we were going to Croatia and we said Bosnia. When they found out we had a mission and we were going to "Bawsnia," they were great, and they couldn't do enough for us; 7th Light Infantry Division were super. They basically kicked a whole bunch of their units out of programmed training in the training areas so that we could do all the training we needed to do at once.

The advance party flew out [to Croatia] on the 26th, 27th of March as I recall. We had also done a recce in January with the key staff. Things were pretty spooky because when we got there, they [it was 3 PPCLI] were in the process of having a couple of big fights with the Serbs and in fact, while we were there, they had an APC hit with an RPG. It was miraculous that nobody was killed, as it penetrated through the armour.

MISSION IN SECTOR WEST

That's always been a bit nebulous. Essentially our mission, as we understood it, was to maintain the Vance accord in Sector West. The difference was that various Vance and Stoltenberg accords and so on in Bosnia never actually had any effect. In the four sectors in Croatia and particularly in Sector West, the Vance accord was relatively being respected, which meant no weapons inside the protected area. It was the one sector where the UN forces had complete freedom of mobility and were actually enforcing the situation, so we did a lot of stuff. The basic tasks were things like mobile checkpoints to stop people and search for weapons. If we had reason to suspect that there were weapons in a place, we'd do a cordon and search and check it out. Now, we knew there were a lot of weapons out there but they were generally kept well hidden from us. We searched for them but we never really found any big caches, but overall we did confiscate a large number of weapons when we were there and we also did the usual low-level UN negotiations between the different sides.

In land area, Sector West was about 50-50 between Serbs and Croats and there was an actual dividing ceasefire line. There was Kutina, which was just outside the borders, Daruvar was essentially the north end of our responsibility and the south end was basically south of Donje Kaglic, which was about the southern-most part in our Delta Company area and then sort of over to here to include Pakrac and Lipik, and Pakraca Poljana was the western edge of it, which made roughly a square. The sector itself went down to the Sava River but we had the Jordanians on the southwest and the Nepalese on the southeast and then the Argentineans on the north part of the sector. The ceasefire line was almost totally inside CANBAT's area. Daruvar was just inside ARGBAT's area but that's where our UMS [the Unit Medical Station] was, as well as Sector HQ. The sector commander, when we came in, was Argentinean and he was replaced with a Jordanian, with lots of Canadian staff to support him and they did try desperately to support him. The Jordanian sector commander was basically a waste of time, which was a shame, because the previous guy, who was an Argentinean, was super. There were Argentineans and Brits in the same area and sometimes they had soccer games, because there was a British medical unit in Daruvar as well inside ARGBAT's area. It was amusing from time to time....

Anyway, CANBAT was in Pakrac and Lipik here, because that was the centre of gravity in Sector West, if you will. The ceasefire line basically ran along like that and in this area were B Company, and essentially Delta, and Charlie. Charlie Company was the one company that didn't have any pieces of the ceasefire line and they were also the battalion reserve and were able to be deployed forward. So you had D, B and A Companies on the ceasefire line. The ceasefire line went right through the towns of Pakrac and Lipik, which were the major towns in the area. 'A' Company was almost an urban company, as a lot of the problems were within Pakrac.

SECTOR WEST: BELLIGERENTS

As far as we could tell the threat were 99% local forces, 1% outside. There was a Croatian police chief in Bjelovar who was both politically active and I would estimate that he was part of the security apparat before in the Communist regime. He had a lot of minions who were always operating in our territory and he kept his nose very carefully into all the business that was going on down there. Likewise there was a fellow on the Serb side who was nominally the security chief for the area but these two were actually good friends but sworn enemies! They were both

In the early phases of the war in Croatia, belligerent forces used cached stockpiles of weapons and vehicles, some of them dating back to the Second World War. Here a Canadian patrol passes a derelict T-34/85 in Sector West. (CF Photo)

security-type operators with their own private armies and these guys weren't under any central control from Zagreb or Belgrade. Nominally the police chief was under central control from Zagreb, the other guy was under control nominally of the Knin government of the Krajinas but he did, as we saw, run his own show to a certain extent. On the ground level with the Serbs and Croats, relations between them and us were pretty good. As good as they could be when you are talking about the fact that these people had just been butchering each other in very recent living memory, so they had a lot of hatred and no trust at all on either side. There had been ethnic cleansing going on, not perhaps in the Bosnian sense, but there had been entire towns in the B Company area, which I was to take over halfway through the tour, where all of the previous Serbian farming villages had been completely de-populated, and we found some bodies and basically a lot of people had disappeared. They had done as much as possible to push the Serbs to the side and the Croats onto the Croatian side, so there were refugees and displaced persons everywhere.

UNPROFOR THIRD WORLD BATTALIONS

Nepalese Battalion (NEPBAT), for better or for worse, whether this was a reasonable decision to make or not, they had this theory that they should just send their troops and everything would be provided for them by the UN and so they had no vehicles at all when they arrived. They had personal weapons, with about 30 rounds of ammo each, no machine guns, no anti-armour weapons, and very light on the ground. They were put down in control of the Stari Gradiska Bridge, which was the only significant bridge left over the Sava River and therefore the route of reinforcement from Bosnian-Serb held territory to the Serbs in the Krajinas. The bridge was critical. They were given control of it and they didn't have the equipment to provide any kind of realistic control of it. The will was there. I think they were pretty good soldiers but they were just boggled by everything, had no experience with the UN, no equipment, and they knew that if it ever came to shots being fired, they would be overrun. They were put out in these exposed positions and they had no means of defending themselves.

The classic problem in Operation HARMONY was that you can send a Canadian battalion over there and the guys aren't going to get involved in the black market. What would it be worth to them? They get paid reasonably well. But, when you send Third World battalions over, essentially what most of the governments do is take the thousand dollars per month that the UN provides for the support of each individual soldier and they put that into their national treasury. So the Nepalese were making about a dollar a day from which they were expected to buy whatever they wanted to buy there plus send money home to their families and they were poverty stricken as well. Not to blame the Nepalese in particular but most of the Third World battalions were heavily involved in black marketeering. They'd sell their gas off and look the other way when certain things happened, in exchange for kickbacks. It was a terrible situation for the soldiers because they weren't eating well. The UN supplied the food but they had a certain package that they deemed to be monthly support for X number of men and they attempted to set this package up so that it would appeal to all the different nationalities, so of course the Nepalese never got enough rice, or enough spices for the things they eat. We, of course, got far too much rice, noodles, not enough potatoes, and too many spices (our cooks didn't know what to do with them). In fact, the Canadians wound up supporting the other national contingents. From the Canadian government we were getting three dollars per man per day in an additional food thing that was under the control of the chief cook and we used that to set up delivery contracts with food suppliers in Europe so we could get the type of fresh food and produce that our guys expected. We also ate more than people from Third World countries, because we're bigger.

We wound up supporting NEPBAT and the Jordanian Battalion, JORBAT, particularly in terms of maintenance. JORBAT was reasonably self-sufficient but NEPBAT and ARGBAT were weak on second-line maintenance, so we did a lot of maintenance for them. I probably shouldn't admit this, but we gave them a lot of parts from the Canadian government, APC parts as the Jordanians had M-113s as well but that was another one of those things. The mission statement of requirements said that each battalion was to be an infantry battalion with one mechanized company of 15 APCs but, of course, we brought 86 APCs. We're not stupid enough to believe what the UN deems to be the requirement. One of the reasons why we were the hammer in Sector West was because we had a mechanized battalion, and we could kick some ass if the requirement came. The Jordanians had one company of M-113s, the Argentineans had one company of Marders, and they call it a TAM MICV. It's a Marder with a different turret. A great piece of kit, though very maintenance intensive. The Nepalese were eventually given a company of OT-64s, Czech eight-wheeled APCs with no main armament. They didn't really know what to do with them, as they had nobody trained to maintain them or anything. They kept them shiny and you could go see them in their hangers so we provided a lot of second-line maintenance to these guys, and we also provided a fair amount of under-the-table food transfers and that sort of thing. Our contribution was a lot more than what we really say. We were carrying Sector West.

SECTOR WEST: OPERATION BACKSTOP

Operation BACKSTOP was an operation the intent of which was to defeat, no, too strong a word, oppose any attack by military forces into the UNPA. For military forces, read Croatian, because they were the likely threat at the time. What had happened in January of 1993 was that the Croatians had attacked in Sector South in the area of the Maslenica Bridge and Zemunik airport and this was to have a great impact on our operations later on. Apparently it would appear that the French and Kenyan battalions got wind that the Croats were going to attack and their job was to defend the UNPA against any military forces coming in so what they did was get out of the way and didn't tell the Serbs what was coming. The Serbs were basically hit by surprise by a Croatian attack, I think on the 22nd of January, and the attacks made quite a bit of progress in the first couple of days moving towards Gracac up towards Knin before the Serbs organized themselves and were able to beat them back to where they came from. UNPROFOR had zero credibility in Sector South after that, which is why eventually we were sent down there later on in our mission.

Anyway, we went down in the beginning of April, talked to the French battalion in Gracac, and set up this operation that didn't actually come to fruition. That was my first war story in the first week of the tour. Beyond that things settled down into a routine the first months we were there and we went about doing our job. We did a couple of rehearsals of Operation BACKSTOP, which was to create UN credibility in the UNPA. We physically went down there, practiced our counter-move operations, our deployment into the UNPA, and we dug and revetted complete defensive positions in JORBAT and NEPBAT areas. The threat was that the Croats could send forces essentially from the area of Novska and Nova Gradiska and just attempt to pinch off the salient in the area Okucansci, cut that off and capture the bridge. There was a major highway, the Zagreb-Belgrade highway that they would be able to move along. So that was BACKSTOP. It was a blocking operation east and west along that highway. For visuals, our mission was, and what we attempted to sell to the Serbs, that we would defend the UNPA against anybody that would come into it but the moment that they started taking their heavy weapons out of controlled storage, then we would bug off. So the deal was, rely on us to defend the UNPA but if you don't believe us and start taking your weapons out, then all bets are off. Their heavy weapons were in a storage compound at Stari Gradiska where they had tanks and artillery and the Nepalese watched the place.

The Serbs didn't have formations, they had people dispersed within the population and they had to be demilitarized and demobilized. They did have local defence stuff but no actual formations that we could see. Anyway, we dug these positions and we had to dig them forward of the existing Serb positions. The Croats were quite unhappy about this because they said that this was evidence of UN bias, "SERBPROFOR." The fact was that the Serbs were not attacking out of the Krajinas, as they just didn't have the power to do that, but the Croatians had forward-deployed armoured units in places where they could be used on short notice and so we ran a number of BACKSTOP rehearsals. We actually impressed the hell out of the Serbs and the Croats when they saw us come screaming down the road with a tracked battalion!

In fact, we know that they went and walked our positions afterwards. The first time we did it they stole some of the revetting. So we went down every week and fixed them and after awhile they stopped screwing around with it because they really started to see that our intention was to maintain these positions and defend the UNPA. Now, the thing was, BACKSTOP was not a viable operation, I mean, it was a blocking operation and we could have imposed probably six hours delay on them but that was it. Enough to get information back to the world. We had big UN flags on the positions. We were only able to deploy three companies down there, a mortar platoon and the anti-armour platoon to defend two approaches at the same time, so we were a thin crust with no reserve to speak of. Or course the Argentinean Marders were superimposed on that as well. For all the beating I've done on Third World battalions, the Argentines were super when they were there, with no experience as a UN battalion but a clear commitment to doing a good job, because I think they wanted to improve their view to the public and the world, and they did. The first battalion they sent over was a conscript battalion, as per usual, and it was very unsuccessful and the 3 PPCLI guys had a low opinion of them. But as we took over the Argentineans replaced that battalion with a handpicked one with volunteers and the private soldier positions were held by NCOs. They were an excellent battalion. I really think that Argentina will become one of the A Team countries in UN peacekeeping, which is good.

PROBLEMS IN SECTOR WEST

Things went on, we practiced BACKSTOP, and things started to fall apart in about June. What happened was we had been maintaining the PA as a weapons- free zone and then the Serb Krajina government in Knin decided to have a referendum about seceding and joining Greater Serbia. So they had this referendum in June and a week before the referendum came out, they unilaterally decided to re-arm. Now understand in the other three PAs, both sides were armed, and there was no Vance accord. In Sector West, nobody was overtly armed, so they started bringing the weapons out of storage. I felt they did this mainly as a means of reinforcing in the mind of the public that they were under threat and that they were reinforcing, in the mind of the public, that this was still a police state, and there was a way to vote and a way not to vote. At any rate, they made that decision and essentially that's when things started to fall apart in Sector West. The UN sector commander was wholly unwilling to take any kind of determined action to shut this down, and in my view if we had acted within the first week or so and physically gone down and made a demonstration, gone to some bad place like Donje Caglic and kicked ass and taken the weapons away by force, that they would have probably backed off but the longer we went on, the more the Croats were after us. "How come if this is an unarmed area, the Serbs are armed and you're still seizing our weapons?" Which we were, because that was the direction we were receiving. So things started to fall apart even in Sector West at that point in terms of co-operation from either side, in terms of increased incidents and so on. I can only blame the sector commander. What direction was he getting from higher? Was anybody interested in what was going on? I don't know. We were extremely frustrated, particularly at the soldier-section commander level. Guys were bitterly frustrated about the fact and they said, "You gave us the mission, told us that it was a demilitarized PA, but there is a guy with an AK, what are we doing about it?" Well, nothing. We're not allowed to do anything about it. "Well, what the fuck are we doing here?" I wouldn't say that morale suffered but the battalion's sense of what its mission was supposed to be certainly suffered.

SECTOR SOUTH HEATS UP

Anyway, that went on until July. Now what started to rise about this time was that again, they were talking. Now they were talking about a new agreement about the Maslenica Bridge but the force commander, General Cot, had identified in his own mind that Sector South was the centre of gravity of the operation. Sector South controlled the Croats' supply lines all the way down to the coast here at Dubrovnik and Split. It was just one road and it was also the area where there was the heaviest concentration of actual tanks and artillery on both sides. There was more going on here than in Bosnia. The media was there and not out here and the whole war happened in Sarajevo according to CNN. So he thought that if we could establish credibility and a presence in Sector South, we would be able to get some kind of meaningful agreement and it would sort of 'osmote' out into the other areas. As a French general, he was also aware that the force that was in place at the time had zero credibility so, he got us interested in this. I have to admit that our CO was active in selling this as well and that we ought to go down to Sector South, as we were the guys that had the toys and the experience and we would bring the rule of law to the place. So the month of July was pretty much spent in going to and fro and lots of recce, deciding what to do about the new sector.

SECTOR SOUTH: KENBAT AND THE SERBS

At about the end of August, we moved B Company down to Sector South while the rest of the battalion was getting organized. We got down to Gracac by doing a road move with the complete company. We displaced the French and the Kenyans down here and we took over half and half. The Kenyans stayed there but we took a chunk of their territory and the Czechs were somewhere up there as well. The Czechs were pretty squared away and they had a pretty tough job. It was completely different here; this was a situation that was very close to war. Those ceasefire lines were in effect armed no man's lands like World War One, in which every day there was constant shooting back and forth, with everything up to heavy machine guns, and most days there would be artillery shoots back and forth. Some days they would have big stonks and they'd whale away at each other with everything: tanks, anti-aircraft guns, artillery and so on. When we came down the idea was to get the battalion down there as close to the ceasefire line as we could get, and then ultimately, with a view to getting in between the sides as a buffer zone, in fact, and that's what happened.

I save special ire for the Kenyans. There was a company HQ down there, and I met the company commander when I came down. I asked him what he did down here. He explained to me how they ate and where they got water. I wanted to know what he did operationally. "Well, sometimes we do a patrol. If you want to do a patrol, you have to make sure you tell the Serbs at least a week in advance where you want to go so they can tell you whether you can do that or not." How often do you do patrols? "Oh, once in a while." So in effect, my read on the situation was that they sat in their camps and only left the camps to sell black-market liquor in Benkovac, which they were doing all the time, or to have fun with the local women or to basically do nothing. They had no operational role at all as far as I could see, so we moved in and patiently waited for the Kenyans to leave. It was interesting when we rolled the company down to this place, the first thing we saw was a big demonstration by the locals at the gates to the camp. They really liked the Kenyans down there because the Kenyans were providing them with electricity, fuel, cheap booze plus they were not getting in the Serbs' way and the kids had the run of the camp; it was one big happy family. The other thing you have to understand about the government of the Krajinan Serbs is that in effect they did not have an army per se, they had a militia. It was a true militia in the sense that the local battalions had elected their leader, who was the local plumber, and he got to be the battalion commander. A local botanist got to be the 2IC, because they were in effect self-elected like the Americans in the Revolutionary War. It was fantastic, actually, because you could see that this was how people determined their leaders when they had nobody telling them what to do. They had heavy weapons, tanks, anti-tank guns, and artillery.

So this was great but the other thing was, because of this and because of the national character, there was no control of anybody by anybody higher. Orders in the militia of the Serb

Krajina were very much a basis for discussion. If you wanted to make subordinates do something, you had to physically get down and harangue them, pound the table and convince them that the order was a good thing. At all levels! So their chain of command took forever to do anything because the division commanders had to be convinced that they should do something, and then they have to go to each of their brigade commanders and convince them by force of personality that they should do it, and so on down the line. Clearly the Serbs had not been able to get the message down that this change was happening among the UN battalions, though the UN had been completely up front about it. Or they had been reluctant to say anything because they knew it would cause a blow-up. Anyway, we arrived there where there was a big scene with a wall of women and children in front of the gate so we couldn't get in and the Kenyans couldn't leave because the people didn't trust us and all these local guys were gesticulating with their AKs and so on.

It was pretty weird. It was not like it was in Sector West and things were different here. There were also three tanks parked 100 metres outside the front gate with a battery of anti-tank guns down there, and we'd seen all this kit coming in, and heard the rumbling of artillery in the background. You could see where one of the Kenyan trailers had been hit by a 120mm mortar shell. We weren't in Kansas anymore. We had this meeting and of course, the way things were settled down there, there was a big guy, a colonel, came in from somewhere, dragged all of the local armed thugs, local militia guys, into the KENBAT OC's office, where they proceeded to pound the table and, you know, eventually convince them that this is what was going on. We had all these armed guys inside this company HQ and neither the KENBAT people nor us were involved in this discussion that took place totally in Serbo-Croatian. I could see guys at points get menacing and start to finger their weapons. It was a really weird situation. Eventually he convinced them that this had to happen, so the Kenyans were allowed to flee, which they did, and we took over the area.

KRAJINAN SERBS AND THE RIGHT OF SELF-EXPRESSION

The first night we were there, about 2300, one of the locals who obviously didn't approve of us, came up and fired a 30-round burst over the top of our camp. Of course we went to battle stations and everything. What we came to understand eventually was that in Sector South, this was a means of expressing displeasure, firing rounds over people's heads. Right out of Misha Glenny's book, that a man was not a man without his weapon. He was absolutely right when he said that the mountain Serbs were a gun-worshipping culture. They've got the guns. We thought it was an attack but it wasn't, it was only somebody expressing that he wasn't happy and they do this all the time. You have to get used to it. We went to dinner once at the Benkovac Hotel with Graham Muir, the RCMP officer with UNCIVPOL. We're sitting there in the Benkovac Hotel, as it was the only place that had power. They had a generator because the UNCIVPOL was living there and this authorized them to get fuel to run their generator. They were very communal people; because they had a TV, and everybody in town would come in, thirty or forty people every night, to watch the news. Anyway, the generator went out for some reason, and there was a lot of grumbling – as we were eating our dinner by candlelight – when we heard some arguing going on and suddenly about five feet from us on the other side of a pane of glass, this guy picked up his AK and fired thirty rounds straight up into the air. None of us hit the floor and we all kind of went on with our meal. You had to get used to that, as it was a means of expressing themselves. The first time it happened, though, was a little weird.

SECTOR SOUTH: A NEW SHERIFF IN TOWN

Anyway, we got in there and of course, needless to say, we got ourselves sorted out and we started patrolling the area in our APCs going everywhere, and sticking our noses into things. We got bitter complaints from Serbs, people telling us we couldn't do this, and we had weapons pointed at us, but hey, we're the UN, its our job. I admit in the six weeks I was down there, just about every day I went to see the Serb brigade commander in Benkovac to talk about stuff. We were really trying to say, "Hey, this is our job, we must patrol the area." And we were patrolling the area so we could see what was happening. We couldn't control the situation but what we were going to do, as a minimum, was to provide a non-biased third party witness to what went on. Shortly after we got there, the Croats had a patrol into this one village on the Serb side that had only old men and women living there. They butchered about six or seven of them and just fled. Of course there were all kinds of artillery casualties, as they were shelling everywhere. We were there essentially as a witness to say that we saw this happen, such as old women being knifed in their sleep. I think they started to see that this was a good thing and I got this in retrospect and from other means.

We had a policy in the company – in fact most of the battalion – when you drove around, you waved at the local people and smiled, even if they pointed their weapons at you, and the funny thing was, that had a tremendous impact. When the French came in the first time, they ran their whole mechanized battalion through Benkovac in a show of force with everybody up manning the guns and this did not go down too well! Most of the time, I drove around in my jeep and I never used my APC. The funny thing was the Serbs and the Croats were very friendly people and they tried to be rough and mean but it was almost like they couldn't resist getting to like you if they got to know you. So eventually we had good relations with the locals and with two of the three battalions in the brigade; the other one was run by a bit of a wacko. The people started to appreciate us, we were doing our job and we weren't in there black marketeering. We had to cut off a lot of things that the Kenyans were doing and we expected a lot of resistance but I think they respected us a bit more because we were going to do what we were supposed to do. I dedicated one guy as my "Kenyan Chaser" and his mission was to go chase Kenyans out when they were black marketeering, which was all the time. Every time they did something, he would show up in his jeep, start taking pictures and notes and they'd scurry off.

So we started to establish OPs. Once we had been there a couple of weeks we had a lot of fist-pounding sessions with the Serbs because they really didn't want us to patrol in certain areas and I told them that it was my job. The compromise that we worked out, which I was surprised at, was I would man OPs in certain places that would give me 100% coverage of the ceasefire line. Once we manned the OPs, we pushed the platoon's houses and sections forward, right onto the confrontation line. We were overlooking the confrontation line itself, and we could see the Adriatic. We'd push a section up here, a platoon house up there in the area of Donje Biljane, Smilcic, so that we could overlook the Zemunik airport. We had a huge fight over this one platoon house because it was the place we had to be in to see what was going on, and those were the orders I had from the CO, to push as close as we could. This area was really exposed and was shelled all the time.

There was a school up here near Obrovac in the D Company area that overlooked the Maslenica Bridge. The thing was, I think they were legitimately concerned that if a bunch of us got wiped out in an artillery attack, it would reflect badly on the Serbs. They had this vision, and very rightly, that nothing they did as Serbs would ever be viewed in any kind of objective light in the world media. In fact the world media demonized the Serbs from the word "Go." The Germans had a big influence in that, CNN also but the fact is they really felt that it would cause problems if we had guys killed. The second thing was that there were still some Serb guys that didn't trust us because they equated us with the French who had bugged out when the Croatians attacked. The third thing was they didn't want us to see that they were initiating a lot of the artillery duels themselves. So there was a lot of resistance. Unfortunately, the big fight about this happened during the time the Medak Pocket operation was going on. We had three companies north of the mountains involved in the Medak operation and there was part of A Company here, about a platoon-plus covering off this area, and there was us down here. The problem we ran into, and I'm not complaining, because obviously Medak was the schwehrpunkt, and we were hanging out on the edge here with nobody to back us up. That was the biggest stress factor there, the fact that we had to push these guys all the time to accomplish our mission, but if they decided to turn on you, you'd be beaten because they had tanks and there was nobody to back us up.

There was one particular night when it reached the culminating point. The Serbs sent this military policeman around 2400 hours and he told us we had six hours to be out of there, and out of this house. So the platoon called me up, and I talked to this guy, but he was an MP, you know, "I have my orders, I'm not discussing that." So I had to get one of the battalion commanders out of bed, had a couple of drinks with him and stuff. That was the one night we actually had called up A Company and said, "Have your platoon on ten minutes' notice to move to reinforce us," because our company itself was spread out and there were places where, if we tried to reinforce this platoon itself, there were obvious defiles we had to go through manned by tanks. Again, I think that without making this into some macho story, both the Serbs and the Croats operated in a kind of way where they are contemptuous of people who are weak, who don't say, "This is what I'm going to have, goddammit! End of story!" You built respect with them by treating them as equals and working on a reasonable basis with them but also saying, "I'm a soldier, these are my orders, and if you don't like it talk to your division commander. I'm going to do what I've been told to do." That worked with them and it was critical but it hadn't been done prior to us getting down there.

Anyway, during the time the Medak Pocket operation was on, there was really heavy shelling going on all along the line, particularly in our area. We counted in one six-hour period about a thousand rounds of artillery came down between Donje Biljane and the company HQ area. They used multiple rocket launchers, 120mm mortars, 105mm guns, and lots of rockets. They used to use MRLs against Benkovac a lot and the shelling was going both ways, too.

THE MEDAK OPERATION

Somewhere around the middle of September, there had been a lot of shelling at the Croatian town of Gospic by the Serbs so the Croats decided that they were going to do another operation. Their assessment was that they could bite away at the Krajinas piece by piece and get away with it, incrementally. The world didn't know that there was a war going on in Croatia and if they did know, they'd support the Croats. They launched an attack into this area with no warning with a spearhead going down the road in the direction of Medak towards Gracac itself. Shortly thereafter, we got the word from General Cot, the Force Commander of UNPROFOR, to be prepared to go back and take over this area by force if necessary. This French General Cot, bless his soul, understood what needed to be done there and he was perfectly prepared to launch us in there and kick the Croatians out. He in fact attached two French mechanized companies to us so that we were able to go in with a four-company battalion while retaining control over the rest of our area, and those guys were under Canadian command.

I'm telling you, if guys like General Cot ran the UN, we would be able to sort things out. I don't mean a big macho display of power, but sometimes that's what has to be done. You've got the forces there, but if you are not prepared to use them, what good are you? So he gave us the preparation order to go in and retake the Medak Pocket. Meanwhile, at the national level, he started putting intense pressure on Tudjman and his government to back off and I think essentially they used the sanction hammer. This would be death for the Croatians as they are essentially not under economic sanctions, which boggles my mind. You have to look at the Zagreb-Vienna-Berlin axis to understand that one. So eventually within a few days, the Croatian government said, "All right, we'll pull our forces out." But when it came down to the brigade commander, he chose not to obey his orders or the orders were couched in such a way that it was understood that he would not actually pull back, so we had the battalion geared up. The op order was issued that we were going to go in and kick these guys out of the Medak Pocket, and I'll tell you, it was understood to a man that we were going to go in there and physically kick these guys out by a deliberate attack with all the means at our disposal. It would have been touch and go, as they had tanks. We had the shock action of a mechanized battalion and we knew what we were doing and have trained and are ready for this.

The unit was preparing to move and there was intense negotiation going on. As we rolled up to the start line, my understanding is that through a series of finger-poking sessions of the CO or the OCs against whoever was there, they basically pushed by those roadblocks; they trained their TUA at the Croat tanks and deployed the troops. There was a series of these pushes, the Michel Jones concept, and there were two or three cases during that time where we were actually involved in sustained firefights with the Croats. We used all weapons up to and including 20mm cannons of the French and on the Croat side involved HMGs, small arms, mortar fire, and so on. We had no serious casualties but there were a few guys hit by shrapnel and so on, and the Croats claimed that we killed 25 or 27 of their solders, depending on the source. I understand that it was true that our guys killed some of them, and we saw guys being hit. In one case they were under heavy fire and pinned down, and we were able to roll out some of the French APCs with the 20mm cannon and they essentially cleared off the top. We were in white vehicles, blue helmets and kicking ass. People wanted the UN to go out and make peace, and this is what we were doing. The thing that was terribly frustrating was that it quickly became apparent that the Croats were stalling because they were doing ethnic cleansing in the area. You could hear the gunfire in the villages, see the smoke pouring out of civilian-held villages and the Croats were resisting us as we tried to push forward. The frustrating thing I know from the battalion HQ, the CO and Ops O point of view, is that there were times where we were held back, we were deliberately, explicitly held back by UN HQ [in New York], and by UNPROFOR, because they felt they didn't want negotiations to be upset by us pushing forward. It was tremendously frustrating for guys to be held back from going into a town and then when they got to the town, sure as hell, there was nobody left, every building in the salient was destroyed, and there was not a living thing, except for one horse. All the livestock had been killed, and we found 27 bodies, but the whereabouts of 300 people has never been explained.

HANDLING STRESS

I sensed that there were still a lot of unresolved feelings about it among guys who were involved. One of the best things we did in the battalion was based on 3rd Battalion's experience with the Critical Incident Stress Debriefing business. We geared up fifty of our own people to be peer councillors so that they could do the actual debriefing after a critical incident.

What would happen is, whenever we could get a group of people pulled off after one of those things, that they'd sit down immediately in a section group with, maybe one of the padres there, Padre Bob Sparks, and he was one of the guys who really pushed this thing, plus their own peer councillors, you know, a section commander from another company or the Sergeant Major. Somebody they could talk to, and they'd basically talk the incident through. That was essentially all you did. You talked about the incident and what you saw. One of the things that became apparent in this sort of thing, in fact to go way back, the first time I saw this critical incident stress debriefing done was when we had a guy killed on an exercise in Suffield in '92. He was run over by an APC and when they did the debriefing, I was there, and there was a group of people who were there. We were ordered to go into this debriefing, which we didn't want to do, but we sat around with 30 guys. The thing that really struck me was that everybody there in the twelve to twenty-four hours since the accident, had worked out in his own mind how it wouldn't have happened if only he had done X and that therefore he was responsible. Everybody! Including a guy who was a rifleman on the far right flank of the battalion attack into this town, who thought "If only my section had fought through faster, then this guy who was on the enemy force wouldn't have been able to jump out in that street and get run over by an APC." That's the basis for this, to talk it out just so everybody gets a chance to see that they are not alone and that everybody else is shocked or horrified about what they saw.

It really went against the macho image we built up in training but the basis for this came from the Israeli army experience. I met a guy who was the chief psychiatrist in the Israeli army and he'd been a platoon commander in '67, a company commander in '73, and so he had a lot of real infantry experience before he did this. He said it struck him after they did an attack, they immediately pulled the unit back, and they'd sit around and talk about it. They'd rant or cry or whatever but everybody got their feelings out and that's what I think the genesis of this thing was. It was tremendously useful. It gave everybody a chance to say what they felt, for once, with a bunch of other people who were there. "This was what I saw and this was what I felt" and it was done on a you-and-me basis, no rank.

The more we go on in UNPROFOR and Somalia, the more that sort of thing is becoming institutionalized. It's absolutely necessary.

CRITICAL INCIDENT STRESS

I had problems when I came home. Everybody did. To give you my own example, every week we go out and play this trivia game at the bar, my wife and I and some friends, the NTN trivia game. Just over a week after we got back we were playing in this bar and after the game we got into a discussion and one of the guys on the team was discussing something with a Polish guy. This guy was going on and on about how stupid Canada was, how great things were in Europe and how much better it was there. I have never been closer to punching out a complete stranger than I was that night. I'm not a person who gets into fights but I could barely control the urge to grab this other gentleman by the throat and beat the living shit out of him, and that's not me; that was a stress reaction. There's no question. It's funny to laugh about it because at each period after being back a week, a month, Christmas time, we'd all go, "I guess I'm over that now" and then something would happen. I guess I'm not really over it. We've all had that experience, certainly the guys that I'm close with. I think that we're probably 99% over it now but I still find that, of the guys who were on the course who were in Yugoslavia, on the course I'm on now in Staff College, we can't seem to get away from it. It was strange. We had to give a five-minute speech at one point and all of a sudden we started talking about Yugoslavia. We kept getting into it because it was such a significant event and it really changed the way you thought about a lot of things.

I also think there is still a residue of feeling that the public does not really know what happened and doesn't appreciate what we did over there but it's not for want of appreciation. Members of the public that I talk to invariably want to know, desperately want to know, why they have been poorly served by the media and the politicians in explaining what was going on over there. I've done a lot of speeches to chambers of commerce and people like that, and at the civilian level, they really want to know and they are damn proud of the job that we're doing. We don't get that feedback unless we get out there. The media sits in Sarajevo or they worry about Somalia. There is no positive feedback at all. It's not like WW II were they came back and people patted you on the head and told you what a good job you did.

I think we were the first battalion to come back who was really assessed over a period of time, using different measurements, to see what the level of post-traumatic stress was. They say that 12 to 13% of people coming back from these missions in Yugoslavia are, six months more or later, showing signs of what you would call unresolved stress-related problems related to this. Not surprisingly, the guys who did the study said we were a couple of points below other units even though we were arguably involved in at least as bad stuff as anybody else. He thought that it was because we were the first unit to really extensively and as a matter of policy, make use of this stress debriefing business. The makeup of our battalion was different. We were almost half reserve, and nobody before or since has approached those numbers. That's where the real problem is, you know, there's lots of assistance for the regular guys to keep an eye on people and see if there are any problems, and even for the reservists that stay in their unit, there is at least a means of contact there, but for the reservists who go back home and quit the reserves, they're just out there by themselves and there are not a lot of guys in Buctouche to talk about Yugoslavia with! That's a problem. I know that the powers that be are aware of that and are doing what they can but it's difficult to see how we solve that one. It goes against the grain and guys who are in the army are not, by and large, people who like to talk about their feelings and it's insidious. This is something I found interesting. I'm 36 now, and I've been around long enough to get a better idea of what's going on in my own mind, but still there are times that you do something and you reflect and think, "That's not the way I would normally react to that," so it's not like it's looming over your head like a cloud but you think that everything is straight and narrow and good-to-go and then you say, "Wait a minute, maybe this hasn't quite worked its way out yet." The problem is of course that guys are going back there for Tour 4, and the long-term result of that I don't know.

BLACK HUMOUR AND STRESS RELEASE

This is in fact an example of real black humour; it shows the way people got by during the last month. We had a couple of dogs in the company, strays that guys had picked up and they really liked having them around. They were good watchdogs but over there, dogs are not something you keep, nothing you'd get emotionally involved with. When we were down in Noraygornia, we had these two dogs, Pivo (which means beer) and Fucky. Anyway, they used to bark at the Serbs as they went back and forth on the road. One night, Pivo got out and was chasing this guy and barking at him. He was walking along, the dog ran up and barked at him, he pulled out his pistol, and cocked it. Pivo stopped, and then he put the pistol back into the holster. Pivo started chasing him again, so he plugged him, cleared his weapon, and put it back into his holster as though he'd just sneezed or something. Well, they were really shocked about the fact that somebody would cold-bloodedly shoot a dog and it really bothered them. Again, from the guy's point of view, having been at war for two-three years with his buddies being killed everyday, what's a dog? The black humour part of it was that they didn't know what to do with this dog so they eventually threw her in there and burned her. It wasn't long thereafter that the little signs started to show up around the camp saying, "Pivo Sleeps with Jimmie Hoffa!" The real sort of cynical humour but I can't remember most of it. We used to laugh about things that really weren't that funny and it was just a stress release.

PERSONAL ASSESSMENT

In Sector South, during that period in September when things were just going to hell in a handbasket, things were really tense, you'd look around and the thing that amazed the hell out of me was that we had this battalion made up of guys from all across the country, half of them reserves at the rifle company level, and it would bring a tear to your eye. The people that were over there were professional in the way they reacted to things. From private soldier up they had just the sort of confidence and sense of teamwork we needed. The fact that we were there and nobody really believed that anything could happen to their company because there was this sense that we were there doing a job that nobody else could do and in fact, I'll tell you, the UNPROFOR commander sent our battalion in there because he thought that we could sort out this situation that nobody else had been able to sort out, including his own army. When we were going to leave, the night before we left, General Cot had the CO, all the company commanders, and the Ops O and so on up to Zagreb so that he could take us out to dinner on his own hook and tell us this. General Cot sat down and said, "You guys are the best battalion in UNPROFOR, you are the only battalion that could have done what you have done and you guys have done something that's going to change the future of this country." If you look at the fact that there is a buffer zone in Sector South, patrolled by the UN, that didn't come out of the air. It came because we came down and opened the door to that.

Are we doing any good? I think we are [in Croatia]. Personally, not having been in Bosnia, it's questionable what we are doing there, because I think that the fact that we are roped into a humanitarian support mission without the ability to defend ourselves effectively means that we are hostages to fate. We've had to make all kinds of deals with the devil just to get the food through. I question whether that mission is achieving anything, but there is no question in my mind that the mission in Croatia has achieved something. There are a lot of people there who would just be dead if we were not there. It's not as if everything is going well but I think that in that part of the world, that mission is doing a good job.

I think that the thing that most of us would like to see is a little more interest being evinced by the people that have sent us over there. In the time we were over there, we had visits from three Members of Parliament, two Conservative cabinet ministers, one who wasn't running for re-election, Barbara McDougall. She was just there to have a look around, but she was interested and Tom Siddon came by. Then there was one NDP Member of Parliament, who sadly was not re-elected, from Sault St. Marie. He came over on his own money, by himself to see what was going on, because he felt that he had a responsibility as an MP to know what was going on. So he came over and showed up relatively unannounced. That impressed the hell out of me. By and large, having committed us there, we'd kind of like to see some more interest being shown in what's going on. You'd like to see the media portraying it a little more, but you don't and you can't control what they do. That's just a fact of life and I think that's the biggest thing.

I would send tanks in if we could, no doubt in my mind. The Danes brought theirs and now of course they are in demand by everybody. It comes to a point where you get to a standoff with somebody and he has a tank and you don't, and that you have limited ability to push them around. I don't think we'd see a lot of tank on tank engagements, but we would see that we'd be able to back up our people. I don't recall his name, the guy who was killed by the anti-tank round [Cpl. Daniel Gunther]. When you have a deliberate hit, then you go and shoot one of their bunkers and that's tit for tat. It seems silly but as I say, when you have a bunch of people who have been fighting a particularly ugly war for a couple of years, have really reduced the amount of compassion for humanity, there are a limited number of things that they will understand and one of them is that act that if you hurt me, I'll hurt you back. They're not going to stop, but that language they will understand.

I have no time for those who want to have a constabulary UN force go and do this. Totally ludicrous. If you want to see the effectiveness of a constabulary UN force look at the effectiveness of some of those weird battalions that are over there from the Third World. How effective are the Kenyans or the Nepalese? They just aren't able to cope. If you bring a knife to a gunfight, you are not going to be able to get your point across and they just don't respect weakness.

I had a new appreciation for the importance of loyalty upwards, which is something in a peacetime army that comes under a lot of strain. The fact is, the hardest thing I found was the fact of being alone and sort of boss of my own area, and therefore, although I didn't have complete authority to do whatever I wanted, there is no question that I was responsible for what happened there. You really felt that pressure because of the fact that people were looking to you to say "What are we going to do now?" and if something goes to hell, you are the guy who is going to be on the spot to make the decision and live with it. That is a lonely position and I think it caused me to appreciate how lonely it is to be a CO, because I had five other company commanders and an Ops O that I could go and talk to and I had a really good 2IC and a super CSM. The CO's making the big snaps and he's got to have loyalty. It's so critical both ways, upwards and downwards. If you really want to take all of these things, truth, duty, valour, integrity, honesty, but loyalty is the thing, and it is the difference between us and those various rag-tag mobs of ethnic militias or even the other UN armies. That is the critical thing. Professionalism is important, but the key thing is loyalty upwards and downwards. That's my perspective.

CHAPTER TEN

CAPTAIN DAVID McKILLOP

Platoon Commander, 2nd Battalion PPCLI Battle Group
Sector West and Sector South, Croatia, 1993

ORGANIZATION

On 4 January 1993, I had a platoon comprising 54 all ranks, Senior NCOs and a truckload of corporals and privates. The workup training was set up in a step fashion, and at various points in time we would see who had made the cut, and proceed to the next bit of training. By about the end of January I had a normal rifle platoon size organization.

During March the platoon changed slightly as we finally hammered out who exactly was going to deploy. But when I did deploy, I deployed with 24 reservists and 11 regular force soldiers. My Platoon Warrant Officer was from the reserve and right down through all levels to corporal and private. Our equipment was standard for mechanized operations: four M-113 carriers with .50 cal machine guns, and 84mm Carl Gustavs, one 60mm mortar per platoon, one C-6 machine gun per platoon, two C-9 light machine guns per section. Everybody else carried C-7s, the warrant and I carried pistols as well as C-7s. My carrier was jammed to the top with ammunition!

My Platoon Warrant Officer was Dave Desbarres. Quite an individual. He's a master warrant officer with the Nova Scotia Highlanders who volunteered to drop his rank to warrant officer to come over and serve as a rifle platoon warrant. I can't think of a better guy to have as a platoon warrant. I'd take him back in a heartbeat. As a platoon warrant, as a CQMS [the company quartermaster], as a sergeant major, any one of the Senior NCO positions I'd take him. I've never seen a man fight so hard day in and day out for the welfare of his troops. In terms of platoon administration completely squared away. One of the few people who can run a platoon, administratively, out of a field message pad and one single file. He'd been a used car salesman on civvy street. Very diplomatic, very switched on in interpersonal relations, very aware of the limitations of regulations and standard operating procedures, and all that nausea, and perhaps too aware of how to get around that, but always for the good of the soldier.

THE SITUATION: SECTOR SOUTH

It was around the end – before I went on UN leave, if I returned to theatre on the 11th I was gone for eighteen days – go back eighteen days into August, which would have put it roughly the middle of the last week of August. We got our orders and we had already done some recces to deploy over to the area of Sveti Rok, up to Gracac, to take over from the French battalion that was there and the story I was given is they had blown it when Maslenica Bridge was seized by, I guess the Croatians, and the Serbians had no trust left in them. Whether it was to give the Canadian half-battalion down there something to do or to actually appease the Serbs and get the French out of there and then get the Canadians – who perhaps are perceived as a little more trustworthy in terms of actually accomplishing the UN duty in there – I don't know. Suffice it to say we deployed to Sveti Rok. My glory days of being separated from Company HQ and free of continuous observation ended. I became reserve platoon right in Sveti Rok. The best I could do was get a section 2 kilometres away up in the hill overlooking something or another valley down on the Croatian side. We lived in Camp Sleepy Hollow for about three or four days, while the French were busy moving out. It was like another holiday, and we didn't get into any more trouble there. I left on UN leave before we even took over any of the buildings. I'm not sure what happened in the next eighteen days, but I know the platoon was busy rebuilding bunkers and everything at Sveti Rok, because it's an old ammo compound, down right there. Unless you're right on top of it looking at it you'll never see it.

I can't remember what they called Sveti Rok. I always called it Sveti Rok. But we built the Dearing Bunker there which was this huge two-storey bunker built up on the hill. I say we: they did it, as I was on UN leave. I think that my platoon warrant got into a little bit of trouble again. He mentioned something about it. There were some grumblings at Company HQ afterwards, but I was never given the full story by anybody. So obviously it had been looked after before I got back.

On 9 September just before I returned to theatre, the Croatian forces launched an offensive towards Medak, from the area of Gospic. My interpretation of it is that the Serbians fought a fighting withdrawal just trying to hold on to each village. I think it was sort of an informal assessment or belief amongst the battalion that the Croatians wanted to do nothing more than ethnically cleanse the area, level it, make it inhabitable and then they were quite happy to move back and let the UN step in and set up a buffer zone. As sickening as it sounds they've gotten rid of the Serbs, killed a lot of them, ruined their villages, their crops, everything and now the UN's going to be nice enough to step in between the Serbs and them and keep the Serbs off their backs.

I never actually saw the CNN broadcast or whatever it was and I never heard the story first-hand, but Colonel Jim Calvin asked our public affairs officer once, "What's going to get me on international TV should the opportunity arise [so we can get the press in to put pressure on the Croats]? And what do I do if I swear inadvertently?" There was some line of question to that effect. And the PAFF O said it's all right to use a swear word in the right way to emphasize the right point. And the story, as I heard it first, second, third or fourth-hand or whatever goes somewhat along the lines of Colonel Calvin's being interviewed by some news agency which managed to get us on CNN or equivalent and he was being asked his opinion what was going on or what had to happen or something like that. The key line that he thinks did it for him, got him worldwide coverage as it happened, was "This bullshit has got to end." That's exactly what it was. Anyways, they started on the 9th, and they were stopped on the 11th or the 12th. 9 Platoon was in Medak itself. They were forward of the company, observing.

WARNING ORDER

I got back on the 12th. We were given an initial warning or order almost immediately to stand by and move in and set up a buffer zone. No later than the 13th we were given a warning order. No later than the 14th we were actually given an updated warning order, if not actual orders that night. Now we may have had orders on the fly the next morning, the 15th. But I know the morning of the 15th we were packing up and moving, we were going very light. All the good stuff, TVs and everything like that all stayed behind us and would be retrieved later. So essentially we deployed with carriers, soldiers' fighting equipment, weapons and basic rations, water and stuff like that. Three platoon commanders and the OC left early enough to get all the way in. So we drove from Sveti Rok to Medak, which was nothing. The first place we went was up through the bottom part of the pocket to Citluk. It's only a small village before Citluk, but only 800 metres short of that, which is where I was going. In a left-right sense it was on the left-hand side of Charlie Company. Knowing we were UN and had to show that we were there, we had to show that we were not afraid of either side and intent on doing our job, regardless of the fact that the Serbian troops were ducking and crawling. We rather boldly walked straight forward, taking due caution of course, past the school in Citluk and right up as far as we could go, right to the forward farm where the barn became 2 Section's house. This was as far as we could go. So we determined that this was the edge of the buffer zone.

There was the main road that went from Gracac through Medak to Gospic. That was the MSR [the main service route] that Colonel Calvin wanted open. However, when we went in through Citluk, you come up around the corner through this other village. This is a hard-top road. It's tarred or paved and you can drive tracks without warning because if there was a mine there you'd know it. There would be disruption in the road surface. Citluk, or "main street Citluk" as I called it, was a gravel track about 90 degrees to the MSR with a bakery there, a little house here, barn and farmhouse here. This was all fenced in as one property.

Just back of that outbuilding was the school which was L-shaped in this manner. Then there was Sniper Alley 1, Sniper Alley 2. There's a house and I can't remember how many houses there were, but at least one, two, three, four, then the road became very overgrown and stuff in here, and there was another track that ran along here. There was another village over here and they all met and went up against the mountains out this way here. Open field with a hedgeline here, a row of trees, a house back here and then just back of that was another village. So this part here was Citluk, and this area back here. They were all so close even on a 1:50,000 map. We in Canada would call it all just one village.

8 PLATOON AND THE MEDAK OPERATION

So we waited out for the OC. Just outside of Medak we got the green light. I then bumped into I wish I could remember his name, a big heavy-set Serbian fellow who wanted nothing more with the war but spoke a little bit of English. He took us up past this. We were on foot at this time and they wanted us to scurry around the school, which all made good tactical sense. We got in behind this building. And we were given through the broken English to believe that this was the edge of the buffer zone. So I said, "Fine, no problem. I'll move in and the Serbs can pull back behind me." *[See Figure 13]*

I wanted them to pull back because there was a bunch of Serb M-84 tanks back here. There were four of them. It was kind of interesting to drive by them every time I went to Medak. We knew they were operational because we knew they moved around. So we went in. We were back in Medak area in time for me to meet my platoon at 1000 or just short of 1000 o'clock in the morning. I remember saying to the OC "I'm going to do this one step at a time, and do it slowly and do it properly." And he said, "No, I want you in by 1000 o'clock." So I must have met the platoon just

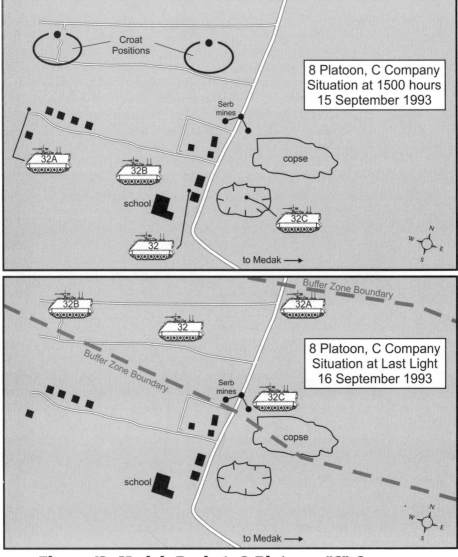

**Figure 13: Medak Pocket: 8 Platoon, "C" Company
15-16 September 1993**

before 1000 o'clock. So, normal battle procedure, while the OC is forward, the platoon commander is doing all this. Like he dropped me off there and took off with 7 Platoon or 9 Platoon Commander and went around to the other side of our area of responsibility. It wasn't much more than a kilometre in a straight line from me.

They went over and did their recce and the company was waiting just short of the Medak house, Company HQ house. I gave them a radio call, they came forward, I jumped up on the lead track and away we went. I rolled my carriers up to this point where the tanks were, met the same Serbian fellow who spoke the broken English, and away we went. I got about 800 metres forward to this point here, at the edge of the rush line, and they wanted me to stop there. They were afraid, I believe, that if I just rolled right in, the Croatians would go haywire and open fire on them. You can understand the misconceptions. They were afraid that the Croatians would believe that I was fighting with the Serbs and would just fire on everything. Understand, of course, that these Serbian fellows had just had their homeland devastated. I said, "Well, that's all fine and dandy." In fact, I brought the platoon up in behind the school, there, bearing in mind that the vehicles were spread out a bit. Got down with the section commander. The warrant said, "You want these vehicles spread out a little bit?" and I said "Yep."

I wanted to get into the farmyard, first, because I knew that this was the farthest forward I was going to get. So, me and my section commanders walked up to this house. That's the point in time when Sergeant Dearing said "Fuck it, Sir. We've got to get on with this." He just walked around the corner and had a look at things. So he went right forward into this spot here with his carrier. Parked it right up in plain view, sprang the antenna with the UN blue flag on it. This was after some haggling. There was a big pile of logs here which was kind of interesting. The Serbs were all groaning and saying that you can't do this so fast, you can't do this so fast. And I said "I got my orders and I'm coming in." And then just showed up here.

So I wanted Sergeant Dearing, 2 Section Commander, in that farm area, the farthest forward as we're going to get. The Serbians were a little antsy with what I was doing, the reason being is that about twenty-four to thirty-six hours later we figured that the UN buffer zone came to this trail, not the other trail, in Citluk. They wanted us forward, however, so they could have more territory.

When all was said and done Citluk was just outside the buffer zone, enabling the Serbs to stay there, and the UN was out of that trail, establishing the buffer zone. This was the basis of a lot of arguing and discontent between me and the Serbs over the next twenty-four hours. So I said "To hell with it. Sergeant Dearing, I want you in there." He said "Right on, Sir!" There is a little pile of logs there that he could have driven around if he had wanted to. He told the driver to go right over the top and away we go. I brought my carrier in to just behind the bakery, right here. 3 Section, they set up in a depression.

My task was to co-locate with the Serbians in an effort to present a UN presence. To be UN, to be obvious, and maybe that might be a deterrence to the Croatians pushing any further or any harder. Meanwhile, over on the MSR that Col Calvin wanted opened, 7 Platoon was going out to the checkpoint, 9 Platoon going into the middle. So we had 7, 9, 8 Platoon and Company HQ back, with a plan that Charlie Company would establish this edge of the buffer zone, Delta Company would push through towards the Croats and eventually we take over everything. Delta Company and Recce Platoon pushed through, widened the buffer zone and A Company eventually got tasked to go in and do a detailed search and sweep to assist with the removal of bodies.

The effects of ethnic cleansing operations by Croatian forces in the Medak Pocket included the complete destruction of civilian houses and their inhabitants. Smoking ruins like these were a common scene which the men of 2 PPCLI encountered, somewhere near Liki Citluk. (photo courtesy 2 PPCLI/LCol Shane Brennan)

I hadn't had a chance to look at these four houses yet. The reason was Sniper Alley. You could look right down this, and this was an area that the Serbs were very cautious with and darted across. You could see right down here that they were very cautious about crossing here and here. So, I went out the other end of the village and I could see the area up into the mountains and everything, all this area from this point of view, I turned to the Serbians and said "I'm bringing one of my APCs up there." They said, "Oh no, no you're not." I don't know how long it took, but I talked with the company commander about it and all this, and he said you have to go ahead and put them in there, and I advised him that the Serbians were blocking me. I don't know why they were blocking us. They didn't want to give an inch of ground. I'm sure that's the reason. Maybe I thought it was just their hard-headedness or something.

In the end I came straight up the hardpack road, and down the trail. I got to about the third house there and in typical fashion over there, whether Serbs or Croatians, they put out a human roadblock. All the soldiers just stood out in the way, and there was my carrier, filled with the section, the driver, the [engineer] troop commander. A big pile of Serbian soldiers, about 20 of them, and me and the platoon warrant on the other side. They're stopping me and they are not going to let me get through. [I get on the radio to the company commander and say] "I'm going to take this by force if required." "Three Niner. Roger out." I wave at the driver to come forward slowly. Click, off go the tiller bars and you start the engine forward. There are not too many people in the world that will stand in front of 13 tons of steel for a long time. We got past there, unfortunately damaged a fence, no big deal. They went out and established themselves there. So when it's all over, my little portion of Three One left, Three Two Bravo sort of centre forward, Three Two at centre rear, Three Two Charlie right. Observing, primarily down the hardpack surface there, and started to dig in.

Along comes a sergeant from the engineer section. He said "I'm here." I said, "I'm not expecting you," and he said "Make use of me, Sir, 'cause who knows when I'm leaving!" I said "Warrant, please take the good sergeant and his crew away, and let's get some work done with them." So we got Three Two Bravo dug in, and their vehicle run up; Three Two Alpha, Three Two Charlie were good because they were down in the depression, then we dug in Three Two. 2 Section had this house with the basement for a bunker. 3 Section with a mad dash could make it into the school, which was about 3-foot solid stone walls, sufficient to withstand artillery fire. 1 Section could get in too, I was in behind the bakery being Platoon HQ and low priority and all this, and if we really had to we could crawl forward to 2 Section, and if I had to we could cut the door down there, which we eventually had to, anyways. So we started digging a bunker over here, just the other side of Three Two Alpha's position, with the dozer. We figured this was the edge of the buffer zone. We were going to live in this village, occupy these houses, modify them, lay electricity, and the whole nine yards. This was it and what we were going to do for the next three weeks. You never know when you're going to get an engineer and bulldozer back, so we were going to dig out the bunker, lay in the timber and backhoe it all ourselves.

At 1500 hours, it happened very quickly. As my guys were digging shell scrapes, the Serbs and Croatians would exchange fire. There was a Serbian position with their mortars, there were Serbians intermingled with our forces. So from the Croatians' point of view it looks like the UN has moved in right beside the Serbians who had been fighting. All day there had been exchanges of small-arm fire between these Serbians and the Croatians. We were no more than 50 metres away from them, and they were exchanging gunfire. All I could hear all over the position was my troops, every time it happened, would lean back on their shovels and yell "Yee Haw!" Given five months doing mundane work in Sector West, and sitting around getting into trouble for a month, now they are actually seeing something happen.

That ended about 1500 when either a sniper or a well aimed rifleman shot at us. Warrant Desbarres and Sergeant Jantz were over here digging in the bunker. It struck the tree right behind them. Everything happened in a flurry of activity, but we pieced together amongst us what happened. The round hit the tree right behind them. Of course the round hit the tree. The warrant turns around to the .50 cal gunner on the APC, and says: "Fire in that general direction and let them know we're here." At the same time the Croats' fire opened directly onto 2 Section.

Through foresight, planning, training or whatever you want to have it, or just good luck, Privates Simmonds and Bombard, they were lying, as they should have been, back in their shell scrapes, observing while the remainder of 2 Section was working. The bulk of the fire came right down, over top of 2 Section, cut the fence over the top of those two soldiers at about 18 inches – we went back and had a look at the path of all the bullets– went through the farmhouse, and we could track it all the way down, right down past the bakery, right in through the schoolhouse, through both sides, right out the other side. It was smaller-calibre fire, to begin with.

And whatever point in this brief few seconds, 3 Section was also engaged. Sergeant Dearing said for the first time ever under effective enemy fire, all training went out the window. His orders were something along the lines of "Kill them! Get them!" whatever. He'd been fired at. It was obvious, there was no doubt about it, the closest Serbian was easily 50 metres away, and there was enough of a massive gunfire, or small-arms fire, to know that it was directed at us. All said and done, it had to last close to a minute, because the Croats dropped a mortar bomb in. Corporal Pendlebury was just in behind the farmhouse and it started. So he scrambled to get around the corner. He dove behind the blast wall which they had put up in front of the steps that went down into the basement. At the same time a mortar bomb impacted about 10 metres away. The fact that he got down in behind that blast wall, which was set up by Sergeant Dearing, under the direction of Warrant Desbarres, and to this day, I thank God for that, that Warrant Desbarres had that done, or otherwise Pendlebury would be dead or seriously wounded by now. So he was saved.

Corporal Mosier, from 1 Section, was coming along the trail here, with his C-9. All hell broke loose, so he scrambled. You always hear your trainers harping about getting down behind anything – I'll tell you that much, 12 inches of a rut will save a man, because Mosier got in behind that, he identified the weapon signature, about 75 metres away in the bush there, aimed directly at him. Same story: another fence and tree, they were literally cut in half behind him. He laid his seeing eye onto it, and returned fire with exactly 14 rounds, because he picked up his casings after that. So, it got a little hairy there. We figure that they didn't quite expect us to fire back, because, at whatever point in time, they opened up with something else much heavier calibre. I'm back in behind the bakery walls, here, all hell breaks loose. No more than five feet away, it sticks in my mind as being able to see it, but of course I wouldn't have been able to see it, feel it more than anything, the percussion of the rounds flying by. It's a pretty good crack-thump exercise. I'm scrambling for a headset, I can't remember exactly what I was doing. Afterwards I was seriously exposed – I was back, I couldn't get forward.

The next thing I know there's an engineer beside me, revving up the chainsaw, which afterwards I found out was under the direction of my HQ Master Corporal O'Brien. We didn't want to touch the bakery, it had been boarded up, obviously, in an effort to come back to it in some future day. He told the sapper to cut the goddamn door down. So next thing I know I'm talking on the radio, to Company HQ. There's this sapper beside me with his foot up against the door, like this, with the chainsaw in his hands. Chainsaw noise, rounds flying by and you can hear, and I don't recall actually hearing, but you must have been able to hear two mortar rounds drop. The next think I know he's poking at this door and knocks it down and we drop inside. We wouldn't have scrambled inside if it had just been small-arms fire.

There was Mosier, Pendlebury, Simonds, Ray, and that door. We figured they opened up with a 20mm cannon fire or something in an effort to extract the Serbians. Maybe they expected us to fire back. When that stuff opened up it opened up right over the top of 2 Section. That was what tore a hole all the way down through that, and it took seeing-to-believing to convince some people that they had actually been up to something that day. At that point in time Dearing said "To hell with it boys, get down, ride 'er out." So they just hunkered down in the shell scrapes, in behind the dirt and all that and then it ended. It was dead quiet.

So we just went back to work. I now had a place to go. We slept in the bakery that night. Throughout all of this and especially from that point on I was constantly negotiating with the Serbs. I wanted them to pull back behind me to this area back here, so that they were out of sight and there was just me. They said "No, no, no, no." I couldn't figure out why until we finally determined that I was 100 metres short. I couldn't get up there, because there was a mine necklace, a Serbian-laid mine necklace. I wasn't going to cross this farm field here, unknown mine trap. The only way I was going to go forward would be on this hard surface right here. It was wide open. There is a hedge along this trail, which is what the Croatians had to have used for cover. There was a trail that came along this way, to a gap in the hedge there. And the mine necklace was in two parts. It covered the main road. The C-6 crew, covering from the top of the barn, were the ones that spotted it and I confirmed with the Serbs that it was theirs and I said "You got to move it." They said "No." Not on your life, buddy, type deal.

I intensified my negotiations on the ground to try to get these Serbians to pull back. Of course the OC's too busy with the overall company picture. The battalion commander is too busy. The Serbs kept setting up some sort of big gun here. I was constantly over there to tell them to "take that bloody thing away. Just get it out of sight. You're antagonizing the Croatians." And they even had, I thought it was some big news agency, but I guess it was a Serbian news agency, videotaping me. I wasn't thinking what I was saying. I was saying "Listen, get out of here. You go and stay behind me, I will stay and fight." And they try to speak as little English as they can. They waffle with you. All of a sudden I realized this camera just came right on to me, you know. He was right there. I was thinking to myself, "OH, SHIT!" So, I started watching what I was saying. But I kept pushing the same point. "I will stay and fight, I am UN. This is my job. You move behind me. Let me set up this part of the buffer zone." Of course, "No, no, no, no" etc. At some point in time I was coming back across this open area here. There was five or six rounds of tracer which meant another four rounds for every one round of tracer, about 15 feet over my head, but enough to make you go flat. I beetled my way back to my carrier. Then they hit us again.

There was a 60mm mortar there. The Serbians hadn't used it yet. There was also a machine gun there which they fired every once in a while. They had a limited field of observation the way they were set up. I had 2 Section looking out past the woodline there, and I had 3 Section primarily observing this wide open area. And not knowing the full layout of everything yet, there was nothing in my mind that would preclude the Croatians to come around in a typical flanking.

It was a little after dinner, because my pork, or whatever we were having, was cold. Which was fine. That was no big deal. The medics were there, and they were the first of the unbelievers that I'd come across. They didn't quite believe that we had actually been under effective enemy fire. Of course, they were made into believers shortly after that. Then it must have been 2100 the Croatians hit us again. You could tell, even after two engagements, you could tell what was going to happen. They were going to hit us again. There was a single round, the gunfire seemed to swerve around like this. Remember, I'm sitting here in the area of the bakery; it seemed to swing around this way, and open up full force and then my guys would open up, and it would go away. That happened, every time for the second, third, and fourth, and fifth times. After that time they hit us, we got faster, and faster, and faster at reacting. After the incident at 2100 or 2200, call sign Three advised me that the UNMOs wanted me to go over and tell the Serbians to stop firing at the Croatians, and stop antagonizing them. I said, that's fine they understand that, but I think that I tried to impress upon them that the Croatians were firing at ME, not necessarily the Serbians.

A story within a story here. After the first one the Serbs finally got through to my platoon warrant, through broken English and all that, how impressed with the Canadians they were. He said, "Canadians go, Serbs no go. Good Canadians." And my warrant thought that they want us out of here, and he kept pursuing that line, and he kept saying "No, no, no, we're not going." And he said "Yes, yes, Canadians go, Serbians no go." What they meant was, when they hit us, that Canadians got down behind their guns, stood their ground, and fought back. The Serbian's 'no go' meaning that they got into their bunkers, and just rode it out. So that was a shot in the arm for the platoon, from the Serbians.

As a platoon commander, as an infantry officer, I always wanted to know, but never wanted to have to find out, if our training was sound enough to work. I found out. It works. The training is good, it's sound. The Canadian doctrine is sound. After the first incident, Dearing got down to business, all three of them got down to business – anticipatory fire orders, and all that, so much to the extent that Louis Leblanc called him on a C-9 for 2 Section the second time – the story goes, from the boys in 2 Section. There's little Lou behind his C-9, just givin' er, eh? He's been told, that if we get hit again he's to fire from there to there with his C-9 back and forth till someone tells him to fuckin' stop. So away he's goin', firing away. And he's ridin' the gun up. So we reach up, we grab him, and we anchor him down, and say "Lou, stay down!" Cause Lou don't care. Not even cracking a smile or grimacing, there he is, just firing away.

In particular, I wanted to note what this platoon, this group of 30-odd people, could do it together, and I found out yeah, we can do it together. In retrospect, I was amazingly calm at the time. It never even dawned on me that I might, that I might take casualties that day, that night, at any .... it never even crossed my mind. There was a job to be done and we just got on with it.

From a pure leadership point of view, and I might be faulting myself too much, I maybe could have done more, and got around to the troops more, and down beside them and talked to them more. Then again, I didn't have the time or, maybe, subconsciously, it was a self-defence mechanism not to do it yet, just to get on with the matter, see this through. I don't know, but, in terms of the job, I was busy with the Serbs. Sections were digging in, and I was with the Serbs trying to get them out of there, behind me. I was convinced that if I could get them the 800 metres back, nearer these tanks, things would come a whole lot calmer. I wouldn't have them to worry about for one thing, and I could get on with the job of setting up a UN checkpoint for my part of the buffer zone. That day, the 15th, from the time we got the platoon in right through to about 2000 I was constantly with the Serbs. I don't know how much Rakia I drank that day. It had to be too much, but I was constantly with them, other than the periodic break to have a coffee or something like that.

We had another one at 2100 and the one at 2200. Call sign Three told me that the UNMOs wanted me to go over there and tell the Serbians to stop it. And, it had gotten down to my troops at this time, that our people elsewhere weren't convinced that our platoon had actually been under effective enemy fire. Take that from a soldier's point of view who has been under enemy fire, he's fucking pissed off! And I said to call sign Three, "No, I'm not going to do that." And I was told by call sign Three that, yes I am going over to do that, and I said, "Listen, who do I take my direction from? From the UNMOs or from you?" All I heard was "Uhhh, call sign Three, wait out. Got to go find the duty officer." The company officer comes back and says, "Three Two, I want you to go over and tell them this." In the interim, I figured out that I hadn't told the company HQ that I had this sort of nighttime standing agreement with the Serbs, that we wouldn't move around, the reason being that the Serbs didn't move around and they shot anybody without question who moved around, other than the patrol that was out there.

We suspected that there were Serbian infiltration groups all over the place. So my warrant had sort of negotiated for us. We have to move around. If we are going to move around, we the Canadians will mutter in English, and you the Serbians will mutter in Serbian, and if anybody out there is moving around and is stupid enough to mutter, then obviously it's either Serbian or Canadian. If somebody is out there not muttering, we the UN are not going to shoot them. You the Serbians, well, we advise that you don't shoot them either. Good deal! Had I told call sign Three about this beforehand, perhaps I wouldn't have had to have this radio conversation. However, at some point in time I told call sign Three to tell the UNMOs that if they wanted to talk to the Serbians, they were more than welcome to come out to Citluk and I would escort them over to talk to the Serbians. I found out the next day, and it kind of made me feel good, that the troops were all huddled around the radio, just listening and waiting to see what their platoon commander was going to say next! There was this eruption of cheers all across my platoon, quiet subdued cheers of "Right on!" type thing. I finally realized that I had transmitted things.

The last engagement that night at 2200, or whatever time it was, it was either 2200 or 2300, Sergeant Dearing himself was on sentry duty at 2 Section's location. He happened to be on the C-6 himself, and his fire-team partner, Private Simonds, was watching and there was a short burst after the lead-up, and for whatever reason, his C-6 was waved right on the weapon signature from the

Croatians, which was right about there – about a hundred metres out, maybe a little bit more, a little bit less. So Dearing just came on to her, about a 20-round burst from the C-6 and that was the last we heard from the Croatians until morning. We went out, out of morbid curiosity, and found the tree he had torn apart. Checked all the bullet scars and everything. We went digging in the trees for bullets.

At the first light they hit us again. I am convinced that it was the Serbs that started that one. At about 0600 a couple of mortar bombs got launched out of this tube over here, and they erupted into gunfire, and then the Croatians erupted into gunfire, and then they were on to us again, and we got on to them. That was it. It was over. That was the last gunfire exchange.

The OC came out before 0900 with the CSM, maybe not yet fully convinced that we had been under effective enemy fire. I walked him through the position, explained everything, showed him all the damage, and he walked away from that a believer. At about 0900 the Croatians dropped two mortar bombs on the position. That kind of convinced the CSM that it was a little bit interesting around there. That was it, 0900 on the morning of the 16th.

As that day progressed the word got down to me that the UN buffer zone was actually another 100 metres out. I got to the Serbs, said, okay, I understand the deal now. Here's the way the deal stands. Your mine necklace is out there. I can't do anything with that mine necklace in place. So they went out. Have you ever watched a bunch of nervous Serbs trying to remove their own mines? It's kind of funny. They were all tilt-rod mines and one of them was tipped over, on the rod, and it hadn't exploded yet. But they disarmed them all. There was a bunch of dead cattle out there too. I told the commander I was going to move down and do a recce of the area. I stood the platoon to, walked out with 3 Section Commander and myself, and his section on the road, right down the road, and had their carrier follow us down the road. So I got the remainder of these two sections stood to, watching us. We walked all the way down to about here, and turned around and without leaving the road – I wasn't going down these gravel paths yet. Now perhaps I should have, because I'd driven straight down this one and driven straight down that one, cause I knew the Serbs were there and they wouldn't plant mines on their own street, not yet, anyways. So I figured okay, here's my plan. I'm going to put a section here at this corner of the woods, which eventually ended up being Three Two Charlie. What I am laying out now is basically the way I left it, when I left it. It's the way it was for a few days at least. We'll put Three Two Bravo here, because my orders were when I could to get out there, turn around, face the Serbians that way – being inside the buffer zone, looking out at the Serbians.

At the same time Delta Company managed to push through on the MSR, through intensive negotiations, or whatever. They were busy over in this area, widening the thing out a little bit. Put Three Two Bravo over here, Three Two Alpha here facing into the buffer zone, just in case. I moved out into this area where that Croatian that Sergeant Dearing had the C-6 laid on and fired. That was my plan, that was where I was going to go. I told the company commander that I had my plan, I was ready to go, I was just waiting for the word. He comes screaming along and wants to have a look at things first. He stops his carrier. I figured we were going to do this slowly. He says "Jump on." "Okay, Sir, can I have at least enough time to have the platoon stood to again just in case?" "Yep, do that." Okay! Jump on the OC's carrier and away we go, just roaring down the road, right down this hardtop road. Well, here goes nothing, as I disappear around the corner. All fine and dandy. We go about another one or two kilometres towards the Croatian lines.

We hit almost the identical setup at the other end, except it's a Croatian mine necklace. Stop the carrier, and he says "Let's go. Sergeant Major, you stay with the vehicle." We get down, step over the mines, keep on walking, and come to broken debris and telephone wire and stuff just thrown across the road with a wire running through. Yeah, it looks like it could be a booby trap. We'd passed an anti-personnel mine on the way and we saw Delta Company about 50 metres rolling along. So we knew the buffer zone was being expanded. That was a little bit of a load off my mind. We stepped through this debris and stuff, careful not to touch anything, walked up, and right at that time a Croatian army truck comes roaring around the corner with two guys up front, slams on the brakes when he sees two UN guys with the weapons slung just walking along. They turn the truck around and fuck off at the high port.

We walked down and find somebody from Delta Company who is stationed there, figure out what they're doing and say okay, this is good. He had the bigger picture, so okay, I'm fine, I'm happy, so okay, let's go back and take a quick look at what you got. We go roaring back to this position. I say "I'm going to put a carrier here, a section here looking out." He says "Okay, good. What are you going to do before that now?" This trail is not quite right. Actually the trail is right but the woodline is not quite right. And Three Two Charlie would have been there. When we get to this junction here I said, "I'm going to put a section up here (meaning Three Two Charlie) and that will become the checkpoint on this road." He says, "Good. Where are you putting your headquarters?" Down this trail. He tells the driver to go and I try to tell him "What about the mine threat?" He says "It looks good to me." So I crossed my legs up on top of the carrier, I'm sitting right up on top of the carrier. So I think, okay, I got the bottom of the carrier and the top of the carrier, and it's a relatively hardpack gravel surface, I should be okay. So we go screaming down there, he said, "Yeah, okay, Platoon HQ looks good," down to here, "Yeah, this is good for Three Two Bravo," he zips down this little one, which is sort of sandy and I was a little bit worried about that, then we hit this one which was hardpack, and came screaming back out this way. Fine, up here, he drops me off and I asked him, "When do you want me in?" He said, "By last light." I looked at my watch and I have fifteen minutes. Have you ever heard of giving orders on the back of a cigarette package or anything? Well, I've done it, for real. I grabbed the section commanders and basically, it was nothing more than saying you're going here, here, here, and here. Are there any questions? "Yes Sir, what about the mine threat?" I said, "The company commander, through his good graces, has cleared a track for us with his track." Okay, that answers that. What about getting off the road? I said, "Gentlemen, use your initiative." If you want to prod, prod. If you don't want to prod, use your initiative. Just get your vehicles off the road so that we can put the battalion through here. We're having so much problem over on the MSR over there, nobody wanted to budge an inch over there and we might have to use this road as an alternate. It eventually became the MSR for the battalion for a while, at least for a few days.

Dearing had it set because nobody was going to roll over his position. He just parked his APC right on the spot, and then there was two mounds of dirt there that he just threw a tarp over and he slept there. It was Dearing that asked when they had to be there, and I said, "You've got about ten minutes." The last question was the order of march. I gave out the order of march, and in anticipation everything had been packed, and the next thing I know, I am walking down the road, and said to the warrant "I'll walk out." My carrier just rolled by me. It was kind of cool, actually. The boys went ahead and set themselves up. I don't remember what Master Corporal Roberts did down here. He got his vehicle off the road. He was good to go. Dearing, like I said, wasn't too worried, because he just stayed on this hardpack trail over here. Sergeant Defner, he walked his troops down because it was only a matter of 50 metres, and he had them stand well back and sort of manned the checkpoint, by standing there. And he told his 2IC to keep them back. He jumped in the vehicle himself, Sergeant Alan Defner, and said, "Okay boys, don't look directly at this, cause if she blows I'm blown with her," and away he went with his track and tore the shit out of the area. He turns all over the area until he had an area off the road big enough to park his troops and his vehicle. That's initiative, eh?

So when all's said and done, we're sitting there at night. I went back to talk to the Serbians, and said "Listen guys, the short of it is you've seen me stand and fight against the Croatians. If you fire in the general direction of the Croatians, I will consider that firing at me and I will fire back at you." "Yeah, no problem, great Canadians," etc., etc. Three Two Charlie had a spotlight which was the deciding factor in giving them the checkpoint. We gave them the biggest UN flag that we could find. They flew it on their antenna, lit up the blue flag. It pissed the Serbs right off, because they didn't want a light on the position. The rest of us took little handheld flashlights, set them on top of our carriers, illuminating our little patch of blue. And that's the way we spent the first night. It was kind of interesting, 'cause we were over there, the warrant and I were having coffee and I think it was part of recce platoon escorting somebody through here, and we sort of looked and said, there goes the first part of the UN other than us to go down and use this road.

Morning came, and we had no engineer resources, and we had to dig in. We got the engineers long enough to build a vehicle run-up for Three Two Charlie. The plan was that if anybody tried to storm through there with vehicles, we were going to park that vehicle on the road. That would be it, a .50 cal trained down the road. Same deal over here, and they also built up a little bit of a wall around Three Two Alpha, because they were in a flat field, for them to get down behind in the event of direct fire. What happened, though, was that in all of these little villages over here, now that we were here, the Serbians felt confident enough to move forward again into these villages which they had just left a few days before. All of a sudden, I'm just losing control of the situation.

In the end all they wanted to do was move forward to their villages again. They had a very clear understanding about where the buffer zone was. These villages were, in fact, in the buffer zone. The end result being I had to move Three Two Bravo way down into an open field here. Take our chances, clear it slowly, walking along and having a look for obvious indications of a minefield. I parked them out in the middle of a bald-assed field just to observe these guys. Three Two HQ and Three Two Charlie took up the responsibility of watching Citluk itself, and we had Three Two Alpha sitting over here. So I actually got back to Battalion HQ at Gracac, Camp Bedrock, and actually got a chance to look at the whole trace and see the whole shape of the buffer zone. It made sense the way it was laid out. So it wasn't bad. It was two up and one back, type deal, with HQ in the middle, that was by pure luck more than anything else. These poor buggers had to stay out there, I think it was damn near a week. I was out here living in my hootch, I think it was about a week. Three Two Alpha was out there. Then things settled down. During this period I was keeping an eye on what was going on. Things settled down, and checkpoints started to go up with barriers, the whole nine yards. We got the generator out and the halogen lights were trained, one down the road, and one trained directly across in front of the village. On top of annoying a bunch of Serbs it lit their village right up. And, eventually we moved and manned a checkpoint with a section, Three Two Alpha came back and became my reserve and foot-patrol section, and

Three Two Bravo out, way out to what I call the outpost and took up a lonely outpost position on the edge of the buffer zone, from the French. A Canadian section went over and took over an area from France – a platoon command. They were just dumbfounded that I would do this with just 10 guys. I said, "Listen, that's the way I work." They said, "Well, how are you going to support these guys?" and I said, "Well, these guys will be fine."

To me this means that on a personal level, that the training as in existence now, and the ninety-day workup period, plus some experience in the theatre, that I could actually accomplish it, that I had it within me to think it through and to control the whole thing at the platoon level. Canadian doctrine and training is good enough, sound enough, actually excellent that the sergeants and master corporals we have in the regular force, reserve force, everyone had the training required to get the job done. (Master Corporal Robinson is a reserve force sergeant who had voluntarily dropped to the rank of master corporal – he was the section commander for various other reasons.) We could do it, and we are good UN peacekeeping forces. We achieved the aim. We pushed the Croatians back, they pulled out of the buffer zone. Hostilities ceased between them, in that little piece of Croatia, hostilities ceased, and we were able to get on with the job of doing patrols around the area.

Somewhere in the Garrison newspaper, there was a picture of a Serbian or Croatian soldier – you can't tell them apart unless you know them – and it said, "Get to know this man." If you understand them and what it's about to them, and then to understand your mission is a UN mission, you are impartial, you can start to understand a little bit, and it becomes a whole lot easier. I could rely on my soldiers to get the word back to me what was going on. We used to have what we called the "Sasha and Allan Show." Two Serbians who spoke really good English would show up at the checkpoint every night at about the same time, and shoot the shit with my boys. And they called it the Sasha and Allan Show. We got all sorts of good information out of these guys. None of it really useful, but just good information to have. What it meant to me was, the biggest thing, was we had done something. Yes, we were too late, perhaps, in getting in to save Serbian lives, but perhaps we hadn't been given the orders in time to do that. That's a way up beyond the battalion level. You know, someone way up there had to say, go in and set up that buffer zone, but given the word to go, it meant that we could do the job, and it was great.

I had a duel-installation radio set in my carrier, and having no other radio than the BBC, I had one tuned into the company and I had nothing to do with the other one, so I switched it over to the Italian command net. One night we were sitting there listening and it was just like watching TV at home – there was nothing else to do, we were sitting there listening and Zero, of course being the control station, calls up Niner [the battalion commander] who's out somewhere where he should be, in the buffer zone, fooling around, making things happen. It was a bit of a shot in the arm to hear it and I tried to pass it down to the troops. "Niner, this is Zero, there's a number of high-ranking Serbians here to meet with you to negotiate this, that or the other thing." And Niner's response was quite simply something to the effect that "Tell them that they are going to wait, because I am here and I am busy running an operation and I will see them when I have time. Niner out!" I said, holy shit, right on! It was cool.

MEN UNDER FIRE

My men were outstanding! Outstanding to a man. Nobody second-guessed their section commander, or their next higher supervisor, whatever. Not once. Everyone just got on with the job. Somewhat later when we were set up in this area here, there were a couple of incidents, one in particular. I decided to go back to Sveti Rok with four men to man the gate there, which was a good deal. The four guys got to go back, had a hot meal in the kitchen three times a day, watch a little bit of TV, and get a good sleep on a bed. One of my soldiers went back there and there was a very serious incident involving him and another Canadian soldier, and by rights, on the surface of it, my soldier should have gone away to the detention barracks for a long, long time. The more I dug into it the more I became aware that this was critical incident stress. I went and saw the doctors, who of course had seen him. They confirmed my suspicions and they confirmed critical incident stress. It came down to the point where myself, the company commander and the two doctors were standing at Gracac, Camp Bedrock, in front of the CO. Basically, it was me and the two doctors, lined up against the OC and the CO, and the doctors carried the day. It was made quite clear to me, directly from the colonel, that I was responsible for this man. He returned him to me, and that I was responsible for him in everything he did until the end of the tour. Suffice it to say, we did just that. In fact at some point in time our two beer per man per day (perhaps) became available again and stuff like that. This individual soldier was allowed none of that. Including, the platoon smoker at the end of the tour. In fact he told me afterwards that he actually had a good time remaining dead sober watching the rest of us acting like absolute fools. We got this man back to Canada, back to his unit and he was happy with the way things got sorted out. There was various levels of actions still taken, but I think both sides walked away from that happy. That was the most obvious incident, the most evident incident that I am aware of critical incident stress, and it does exist.

I had another soldier who stood at attention at port arms on the checkpoint for eight hours straight.

I had another soldier who normally carries the day with his good humour and his ability to cheer me or anybody else up. He had nothing but a thousand-metre stare on for two or three days straight. And as I became aware of these things, I became aware of the fact that my sergeants, with all good intentions, keeping it to themselves and trying to handle it – I grabbed the sergeants, sat them down, and I said, "Listen, you've got to let Warrant Desbarres and me know what's going on. We, as a minimum, have to know and we can get help for these people, and get things sorted out."

I had another serious one. One man (I became aware of it after the fact) had been sleeping in his sleeping bag with his flack jacket on and telling stories that were literally scaring the younger soldiers in his section. His 2IC just came right on to him one day and said "That's it, you're going back." We figured that getting him back to Sveti Rok would have been sufficient to get it out of his system. Of course, that's where the incident happened. I saw the Padres or at least the medics at least once a day, somebody on that sort of net. He had to be completely removed from duties. He was involved in the firefight. He's the one that said to me afterwards "Sir, we have determined that if anybody is going to leave this country alive, it's going to be us." I had sent 2 Section out to the outpost, right on the edge of the Croatian part; 2 Section took the brunt of the fire.

I don't know what did it for him. I don't know even what did it for me. I left theatre on the 7th of October. My stayover at Sveti Rok was good. I got myself cleaned up, and got my kit packed up, started the out-process and all that. I was lying in the open sun, a little breeze, a little chilly there, listening to this godawful diesel generator going off about 20 metres from me, just waiting for the bus to come. I wait my turn, went over and bought my bottle of rum, stuff like that, I was fine. Got on the bus that night. For the bulk of the trip I was fine, and then it got dark. I remember when it started. I was sitting at the window seat on the bus on the oncoming traffic side of the bus. I saw the headlights coming, the way you do on any bus trip anywhere. As the headlights got closer and closer there was this point where I just literally flinched. I had no control over it. I just turned away. I shook my head and thought, "Get a grip on yourself. Stop being stupid!" It was involuntary, until I fell asleep. It was every time: flinch, flinch, flinch.

I got back to Canada, back to my wife. I was tooling around through Winnipeg and I don't know whether on purpose or by accident but I didn't drive for a few days. Anywhere we went, she drove. I remember once we were making a left-hand turn, I am in the passenger seat and all of a sudden I get really tense and nervous, afraid she is going in the wrong spot. I had absolutely no control over this tenseness. Somebody changed lanes in front of us, or was making a perfectly legal left-hand turn in front of us, and I flinched. My wife asked what's wrong. I don't know but I think that it is just critical incident stress. If it gets worse I'll get help. From what I've been told, it's to be expected, and it will go away in time. Other examples are waking up in the middle of the night and can't remember. One time here in Kingston, about six to eight weeks after redeploying, I'm lying in bed and all of a sudden I sit bolt upright, on the edge of the bed, I'm listening. Annette says to me "What's wrong?" I said, "Machine-gun fire out there." She says, "No, David, there's no machine-gun fire."

You see all the Hollywood movies, and you hear all the special effects, from the flashbacks and all that, and unless you really experience it, you might dismiss it, saying, "Well, no, you won't actually have a vivid, real, flashback like that." I tell you when I sat up and put my feet on the floor at the side of the bed, I heard machine-gun fire. It was not in my head. It was machine-gun fire in my neighbourhood, period. Critical incident stress does exist. On the flip side they were doing some roadwork about a kilometre from my house here and were setting up dynamite and stuff like that and you see everyone else in the neighbourhood turn and say "What the heck was that?" I didn't even notice it. Somebody had to bring it to my attention.

It improved. It took two, maybe three months. When I first got here to the Princess of Wales' Own Regiment in Kingston, they asked me to speak to troops about what we did in Croatia and that's when, it was somewhere around then, the end of '93, it was really vivid. But I think that everyone will suffer from critical incident stress to a certain degree. I know I did. I never went to see the doctor or the Padre about it. But I knew at that level what it was. I was reasonably confident that should it get worse then I would have the need to go and see someone. But also, I was educated enough to know that it would probably just pass and it was a normal reaction to an abnormal situation. That's what they always tell us.

Every time I tell the story – we all want war stories, and this is my best war story – I always try to tell it chronologically as that's the way it sits best with me. Tell it step by step. The only thing I have to add, should it ever show up anywhere for the people to know of, is that that platoon that I served with – 34 other guys and myself, 24 reserve soldiers and 11 regular soldiers – 35 Canadian Forces soldiers have been the best platoon I have served with anywhere. You talk a lot now about Total Force and I'm not convinced we know where we're going with it yet. It's very much in the infancy. It will work, it has worked. I beg anybody to try and differ. I'll tell them this story. I commanded a platoon. Total Force at it's best! It's been the time of my life so far in serving with that particular group of soldiers, as a soldier right alongside of them.

CHAPTER ELEVEN

CORPORAL ANDREW OPATOWSKI[1]

*Rifleman, 2nd Bn Princess Patricia's
Canadian Light Infantry Battalion Group
Sector West and Sector South, Croatia, 1993*

I joined the military for a number of reasons. There was, of course, the money. I also like going into the field, shooting weapons, and that's basically it. My brother joined before I did and he used to bring things home from the weekend and I'd read up on it. I thought it was pretty interesting so I put my name in and that was that. I was in air cadets at the time, and I've been in everything, cubs and scouts and all that stuff so I thought, well, I'd better keep going and try this. I liked it and I stuck with it.

I tried to get into university but I didn't make it. After I graduated from high school in 1991, I did upgrading and got my physics and calculus, but I decided that university was not really my thing. By that time it was mid-summer and the call-out came for Yugoslavia, so I put my name in and that was it. We really didn't think much of Yugoslavia before we went, just news footage and what not, and then the call-out came to our company. They asked us, "Who wants to put their name in?" and I didn't really expect to be picked. I had no intentions of going but I decided that it was something to do, I guess...

We knew there was a lot of shit going on but the news mostly covered Bosnia and the hot spots and, you know, we were going to Croatia and so we didn't know really what to expect. I knew it was basically another Cyprus except a little bit hotter – 1964 and 1974 were hot spots in Cyprus and I pretty well gathered that it would be the same in Yugoslavia. We expected to get shot at but we weren't sure. We thought our basic mission would be escorting convoys and trucks and transporting people out of the hot spots into safer areas. I thought that was going to

---

1. All of the Canadian personal names in this interview are pseudonyms.

be our mission but it turned out we were wrong. Before we left we had no idea who were the good guys and who were bad guys. It turned out there's no way of telling over there.

ZAGREB, DARUVAR AND CAMP POLOM

The battalion flew Tower Air direct from Winnipeg to Zagreb, Croatia. It was wet. The winters over there are very wet, and we got there around spring, their spring. It was raining, a very wet, miserable day. The airport was fully intact, and Zagreb was untouched. The head UN guys were there at the airport making sure everything was running all right. They met the CO and everything was passed down okay. There were a lot of Croatian cops there, but no Croatian army, because the Army's not allowed in there.

We took a bus from the airport to our position. We didn't even go through the city of Zagreb, as the airport's in the outskirts and it's about a half-hour drive from the town itself. We got off the bus and we ended up in Camp Polom. It's like Gagetown, and it's where all your pay clerks are, your Canadian log wogs. Just your pay clerks, your supply guys, postal, ammunition depot, and stores. It's like Base Gagetown. We ended up there and took a different bus. We were there for a half hour, and they said, "Welcome to Camp Polom, this is your base" and all that stuff, and they gave us a tour. There was everything there, a few tents, but mostly buildings that were untouched and it was ringed with barbed wire and sandbags. The first people who went there in 1991, I guess, were 3 RCR and the Van Doos went over, and they did all that.

AREA OF OPERATIONS: SECTOR WEST

We were at Camp Polom for about half an hour to an hour. Then we got on the back of a deuce to go to our position. From Camp Polom to our position was about a half-hour drive. That's where the head platoon house was and then the company was split up. A platoon was just down the road from us on both sides, to our left and our right, and they had checkpoints set up there and another platoon was about 15 kilometres away to our north.

The accommodations were called AQUA trailers that are almost little mobile homes, which two to three people would sleep in each one. I was with a 3rd Battalion guy, on his second tour, and I stayed with him for the duration of the tour in Daruvar. We were on the Daraguvic Road, which is just outside of Daruvar, but Daruvar was the main town that we were located in. We moved to a different location after five months of being there. They did do a "walk-through-talk-through" deal and the first thing that we did was a tour of the whole facility, the kitchen, the bathrooms, the platoon house itself, where the officers would sleep, and where the transport would sleep. We had our TV room and our bar with real Canadian beer. So we did a tour of our perimeter.

We started the next day. Our first day we were patrol section and all we did was hop in our carriers and ride around while our section commander would point things out. Actually, it was a pretty long day because our section commander wanted to get a look at everything in the whole area, so we were gone most of the day doing patrols. We drove everywhere. It was mostly up in the mountains. We had the largest area, out of everybody, to cover. It was about 100 square miles and there were so many little roads that all led to the same road, which I guess was the main road. It was all farm country and all houses had been destroyed along the whole length of the Daraguvic Road.

There were hardly any civilians. There were Croatian cops, who were the only people allowed in there with weapons and they carried 9mm pistols. They weren't allowed any assault rifles, like AK-47s or sniper rifles, or anything like that. There were also some 'forestry workers,' or at least that's what they said they were. In reality they were ex-army and they had weapons in the houses but we did a clearing of that later on.

Anyway, all the houses were destroyed. When the war took place this place that we were at was a Croatian village before the Serbs came in and burnt everything. A lot of fighting had gone on, so when the families packed up and moved, they burnt everything, smashed the windows, and tore the whole place apart so the Serbs wouldn't have anything. There were a few houses still intact but nobody was living in them. On the Serbian side, to our south, there was a small little village with Serbs living there. They were mostly just old people, roughly in their 40s to 80s. There were no military personnel allowed in there because this was a United Nations Protected Area.

It was a desolate place. What is there to do around here? It's going to be a long six months, I thought to myself. But that's all that there was. We drove around for three days, using different routes and then we changed over and did a rotation every three days. You'd be patrol first, and then after your three days were up you'd go to your "hot-dog stand" where you'd just sit at a checkpoint and any vehicles that passed through you'd write down the licence plate number, the make of the car, how many people, the colour of the car, and which direction they were going (it was either east or west). We didn't search the cars because we had a checkpoint to our left and one to the right about 5 kilometres down each way maintained by a platoon and that was their job. They actually took the people out of the car, and went through it thoroughly and when they come down to us, we'd just let them through and they'd get down to the other platoon checkpoint and they'd be searched again. There are many back roads and they could easily pick up weapons and pass our checkpoint. At first, we'd sit outside and one guy would motion them to slow the vehicle down and the other person would have a clipboard and he'd write down the information. Actually, most of them would stop and get out of their vehicle but we'd say, "No, No, No" and just wave them through. They were probably just civilians. There were a few people trying to get in that were Croatian Army and you could tell by their licence plates, which were yellow. We would stop them and ask them for ID. When they'd show their military ID, we'd tell them to turn around and go back, but that was really rare. Sometimes the first checkpoint wouldn't take notice of the plates or maybe this guy came down through a different route and he didn't think we were there. They'd get all angry and we'd have to get the interpreter out.

He was Croatian, a young guy, about 17. He was very nice, and he was hired by the Canadian UN or the UN in general. We'd say we need the interpreter and he'd come out along with us.

During our first few days of doing the hot-dog stand, we were pretty nervous, just getting to know everything. Actually the hot-dog stand was very boring. You'd do six hours on and with ten people in the section you might get about one shift a day, so you're on for six hours, and the rest of the time you might have off or you might build bunkers on the perimeter or just clean up the platoon house.

We took over the platoon house from 3 PPCLI and the platoon house was in rough shape so we had to fix that up. So we built a new hot-dog stand, rebuilt all the bunkers, and we built three more new bunkers. All in all, we filled about 10,000 sandbags throughout the whole tour.

We did three days patrolling, then three days hot-dog stand and then we were on standby, where we waited around for something to happen. Actually, when we first arrived there, the very first day something happened but we didn't have to go on it. The advance party went on it and it was, I guess, somebody saw some civilians running through the fields. The track went to go look at it but they were gone by the time it got there. It was probably some civilians collecting grapes for their slibovich or raki, which is like their moonshine. But on standby you just wait around for something to happen, and if there are shots fired, you have to go out and investigate.

On standby, twenty-four hours a day for three days, there was no PT or any of that stuff. They told us we had to sleep in our combats, and for the first two months we did, because you know, "flinch factor" is way up there, about 100%. So we would take our boots off and sleep in our combats but after the two months we'd take our combats off because it only takes about five minutes to get dressed.

When we were on patrol, it was pretty slow. We'd go out in the morning and go out for about two hours, come back, relax for a bit, eat lunch, go out around 1330 for a couple of hours, and come back in. We were looking for people who weren't supposed to be there. We'd stop the carrier, get out, and look through the houses. We wouldn't see much, mostly clothing, some mattresses, and stuff the civilians had just left there. You could tell they had been looted, probably by 3rd Battalion guys, or people coming back collecting more stuff for the Croatians or Serbs, whoever, or even tourists. We caught a few tourists going through the houses. Tourists! From Vienna, Austria!

There remains no substitute for rigorous, realistic warfighting training and the confidence and teamwork it builds. Without it, operations like those conducted by 2 PPCLI in the Medak Pocket would have been impossible. (photos courtesy 2 PPCLI/LCol Shane Brennan)

RULES OF ENGAGEMENT

We worked on our Rules Of Engagement in certain situations if you can shoot or not. First, you have to shout out, "Stop or I'll shoot!" or *Stala Ily Putsone!* which is Croatian for "Stop or I'll shoot!" For the ROE, certain situations will dictate how to react. If UN property was being threatened, the land or people in the UNPA, if the army was hurting them, touching our vehicles in any way, or anything like that, we were allowed to shoot. We fired shots over their heads, first, and you'd say, "Stop or I'll shoot!" If they kept on doing what they were doing, then you said, "Centre of Mass." That was their little saying, "Centre of Mass." That was it, and then you'd kill them. We did a bit on language training and learned a few basic words like, " Hi," "goodbye," and stuff like that.

THE CANDYMEN

I guess I felt the best when we helped the kids out. The kids smiled once in awhile when we gave them candy. We'd have to do fuel runs into Camp Polom, fuel up, and we'd come back and stop and give candy to the kids. There would be about fifty or sixty kids run up to us and gather around and we'd pass out candy. We were called "Candymen" in Daruvar. That was pretty cool. I liked doing that, and that was the main reason I was there, for the kids. I really didn't give a shit about the Croat and Serb soldiers. For all I cared, they could be all shot and killed. I was there for the generation that wanted peace.

THE FORESTRY WORKERS

It happened in the middle of June when we were on a four-man patrol. We went out and stayed out there for seventy-two hours. During the day there wasn't much movement because the only people that really knew about this patrol was the OC, the section commanders, and the troops, but nobody else. The interpreter didn't know about it, just in case he had a big mouth and Croatian friends. So we went out and the first night nothing happened. It was just a foot patrol, so they dropped us off a vehicle at around 2100. We went out into the woods and we slept out under the stars. It was total darkness, as we weren't allowed any light, and no hootches, so we just pulled our sleeping bags out. We were in an all-around defence in our sleeping bags, and we could all touch each other pretty much, like the man beside us and the person in front of us. We were in a valley or a small gully, actually, and we just did an hour on guard with one guy on at a time. If something happened, we'd just hit the buddy next to us and our weapons were right next to us already loaded.

We were looking at the 'forestry workers.' We suspected something but we couldn't really barge in because we weren't allowed to do that. So two of the guys, Jameson and Duncan were out there and they thought they heard something that sounded like the cocking of weapons. Around 2300-2400 hours [on the second night out] they came back and got me, I strapped on the radio and went back out with them. We called in Platoon HQ and at that time they were already out doing another search at a Croatian cop station, where they confiscated weapons, so we had to wait till they arrived to support. About a half-hour later, we were already in position waiting for them guys from another one of our platoons.

The forestry workers had a house that they would sleep in. During the day we would watch them [from an OP] and then we'd sneak up to their position, at their house about 200 metres away, and watch them. All they would do was sit outside and drink, and have a little barbecue going, cooking pork or whatever. There were roughly about 12 people there, and with our binoculars, we could recognize what each person was wearing. We wrote it down, so by the time we thought we had everybody, there were about 12 or 13 people there. Really, they didn't do anything suspicious. They didn't patrol, no sign of weapons, and they wouldn't take any weapons out or in, but we were suspicious anyway.

We were waiting about 50 metres away when we got on the radio and our reaction platoon said H-Hour is going to start in two minutes. Two minutes later five carriers arrived, as everybody dismounted and surrounded the house, and in a matter of five seconds, paraflares went up from our position. There was a five-man team that went into the house, cleared everything, and brought all the people outside. The Croats were all in bed! We busted down the door, and took no chances, as everybody was locked and loaded. We hauled them all outside and put them inside a big circle, and made sure everybody was in a tight group so that nobody escaped. They were in their pyjamas. The search team was inside gathering stuff and about an hour later they came out with 2 or 3 AK-47s, several M-80s, which was a rocket launcher, grenades, and RPGs, which is a rocket propelled grenade, anti-tank, and rifle grenades fired from an AK-47 with a blank round, and that was it. We took the weapons and then let the people go on their way, and back to sleep.

After that our guys left, and we went on our own way off into the darkness, as we were still on patrol and we were still out there for another twenty-four hours.

We went back to our hide and Jameson and Rouse went out and did a two-hour listening post at the forestry workers house, just in case they got a re-supply of weapons, or anything like that. They came back, as nothing was going on and it was all quiet, so we went to ground until 0700. We did the same thing again, and went out to watch the forestry workers. As we were watching, the head honcho came by driving a Mercedes-Benz. He was quite important, wearing a suit and tie, and he was throwing stuff around, he was so pissed off because his weapons were taken away from him, and he was throwing water jugs around and yelling at people. We couldn't understand what he was saying (he was yelling in Croatian) so we wrote all that stuff down, packed up and left at 1400 hrs.

THE CROATIAN COPS

The next big event occurred when a Serbian force ambushed eight Croatian cops in early July. It was during lunchtime, when it came over the radio and we were on Standby Force at the time so we went out with the medics and we found four killed and four wounded about 5 kilometres away from our position. By the time we got there, the Serbians were long gone, and the Croatian cops were all lying around bleeding.

They were just driving along in a little valley, and the Serbians were up on a little knoll when they spotted the vehicle coming through, and they dashed down and started firing at the vehicle. The driver and co-driver were instantly killed, two other people in the back were killed, because they were only protected by a tarp, and four were wounded when they crashed into a ditch. I guess the Serbs really didn't want to kill everybody because they just shot and took off. So we went to the location and had the medics patch them up. Later, a Croatian ambulance came by, picked them up, and took off. We sealed the place off and we were on patrol that night and the next morning. Then we heard around noon that the Nepalese were to take over from us.

In the late afternoon, 1700-1800 hours, the Nepalese came in and took over our positions, set up checkpoints and patrols around the perimeter, while the rest of us, 4, 5 and 6 Platoons were on 24-hour notice and we went out non-stop for eight hours trying to find any signs of Serbs kicking around, but we didn't find anything at all.

UN LEAVE AND BACK TO ZAGREB

The next interruption in our routine was when we moved down to Sector South, and had to pack up and leave. August the 18th was our day to move, but that really didn't affect me because I was going on my seventeen-day UN leave, so I wasn't there when they had to pack up and actually go down to Sector South. I went to Greece and had an excellent time. I went to one of the islands called Eos, where there were Irish people, British, Americans, a few Canadians, but there was hardly any Greek people. It was just a tourist spot and the place was all bars, and topless beaches. It was a good break. We were planning on doing a little sight-seeing in Greece, and go visit the Parthenon and Greek ruins but I guess we had other things planned, like drinking for seventeen days.

We got back on the 17th of September. We took the long route. There were two routes you could take; you could fly directly from Zagreb to Greece and that was $625 two ways but they also had another thing that you could go from Zagreb to Vienna, Austria and then from Austria to Greece and that cost only $325, so we went that route. On the way back we went from Greece to Vienna to Zagreb and then we took a cab into the city, and stayed there overnight and had a little last bash. While we were sleeping, three FROG 7s (they're like SCUDS) hit on the outskirts of Zagreb but we didn't hear anything, as they were way, way out.

Other than that it was pretty safe because there were a lot of UN forces there, mostly higher ups, like the UN observers that were there. But they didn't mind us. You would walk down the street and see UN vehicles parked everywhere. There was also a Canadian travel bureau. We felt pretty safe. There was a Hard Rock Cafe there, but they wouldn't let us in for some reason. They knew we were military and didn't like us.

We went back to our position by bus, military bus and we went into Camp Polom (it was about 5 kilometres away from the train station) because we took a train from Zagreb to Daruvar, and then when we got there we stayed a couple of days because our position was being hit in Sector South. We couldn't leave right away but a couple of days later the buses picked us up to take us to Sector South and that was about an eight-hour drive.

TIME OFF

There was one girl, Brzenca, who'd bike by WC 2 all the time. She had big red hair, really hairy, and she actually didn't have a bad-looking body. One time she smashed into the track because she was looking up smiling, crunch, right into the side and then us, which was pretty funny. One of the guys from our section slept with her and he was slamming her there for a while. We had beer that the CQ would bring to us and they had pornos and beer for our leisure. So we drank a bit off duty and did a lot of PT. That was good. The best moments were on leave. I went to Croatia, on the Adriatic coast and you couldn't tell there was a war going on. It was like four hours away by bus, you crossed over the mountains, and there was no sign of war at all. It was like a big resort area, casino, bar, strip places, whorehouses, and all the essentials. We had Canada Day celebrations; there was a band that came over, and girls singing from Quebec, who were performers on a stage. That was a good time and we all got drunk. We were in the base and it was safe. They weren't nude or anything just gorgeous girls, dressed in tight clothes, teasing the guys and singing. It was a good show.

AREA OF OPERATIONS: SECTOR SOUTH

The unit was set up in a big platoon house where we had cots set up inside. It was supposed to be a motel, but when the war started the construction stopped and it was 90% completed. They set up beds and stuff and then a checkpoint, and they started building bunkers, all the same routine. We didn't do too many patrols, as this was a hotter spot. The war was actually going on. There wasn't a UNPA established there yet but they were trying to set one up and so mostly what we did was standby and the front gate hot-dog stand and we did three-day OPs where all we would do is sit there and just watch. Our OP was about 10 kilometres away on top of a house with a flat roof so we set up our hot-dog stand on top, with sandbags on the roof. We had four guys, and we'd be there for three days straight and do two men on for six hours, some off for six and the other two would go on and do that for three days.

We had a carrier there just in case we were hit. There was a Serb T-72 tank about 100 metres away and they would fire once in awhile. We'd have to call it in. We had a NODLER, which is a night vision device, with about 2-kilometre range, and it picks up on heat from your body. You'd pick up animals or anything that gives off heat, so we just turned that on once every half-hour, because it makes a lot of noise, and we'd just do a scan over the area to see if we saw anything.

This area in Sector South was Serbian. We were pretty well surrounded by Serbian forces, but the sector itself was surrounded by Croatian territory. About 5 kilometres away there was a gas station, a few little shops up there, flower shops and grocery stores and it was still populated with Serbian civilians. The town itself was still intact. The town had a few buildings blown up but other than that, it was still standing. The people looked reasonably well fed – well they were mostly farmers, who had sheep and chickens, or cattle, and there was a lot of farmland there, but I don't know if they actually grew anything.

There were also soldiers and they'd walk by our position all the time. They were our age or younger, you know, 16. I saw one who was maybe 10 or 11, carrying an AK-47, in civilian dress, but he was carrying a weapon. Soldiers were still allowed here since this UNPA wasn't established yet. We had a Serbian mortar team about 100 metres away, and about 100-150 metres away, we had a T54/55 and a T-72 in front of us, and they would move them once in awhile and fire. Incoming fire would come in then and we'd have to go into the basement and wait it out until the firing would stop. It was different!

The first day, when Kinross and I got there, it was nighttime and we were in the back of the deuce going to our position when we had to stop because our position was being hit. Bravo Company was being hit, and we had to wait on the road for about ten minutes. We turned around and saw an MRL [a multiple rocket launcher] firing off into the air, so that was pretty cool, as we usually didn't see anything like that in Sector West.

The Serbians were pretty well equipped. These guys had been fighting for a number of years now so they knew what they were doing. As for discipline, they drank quite a bit, and then they'd start shooting. They'd shoot at the Croatian positions, which were about 10 miles away on a mountainside with tanks and mortars, and they would just shoot. The Serbs would shoot at the

Croatians, and they'd fire back, and just do that for a couple of hours and stop. A ceasefire would last for maybe a couple of days or hours, depending.

We hardly saw any Croatians. They were equipped about the same with tanks, and mortars, but we didn't get to see them because they were on the mountainside and our sector didn't go that far. That was another Canadian company's responsibility down there and I think it was Delta Company in that area.

THE DOG

The difference between Sector West and Sector South was significant. The first place, we were protecting a UNPA, and the second place we were trying to set one up and we just watched the fighting. In Sector South we saw more army than civilians. The Serb army really didn't like us at all. They even shot our dog.

I was on leave at that time, but a Serbian army guy walked by with an AK-47 and shot our dog, Buddy. He just walked by, locked and loaded and shot the dog. He shot it with a regular ball round and we had to put it out of its misery. Lifter Payne intended to do so, but he shot the dog with a tracer round by accident. He didn't mean to and his eyes lit up in surprise and the boys thought that was pretty funny. He reloaded and killed it. We couldn't shoot back at the Serb, because the dog's really not part of the UNPA. He was just a pet. Oh yeah, we wanted to shoot him, but we'd end up like Private Brown from Somalia: two years less a day in military prison.

GETTING SHELLED

There were other incidents with the Serbs. There was one with another section which was on the three-day OP and a mortar struck about 50 metres away. That's pretty close and there weren't any targets near by. We don't know what they were trying to hit but all these military observers came in and the Serbians were talked to, you know, "What were you guys doing?" Nothing was around us except for the tank that was about 250 metres in front of us. When a mortar round lands almost in front of you, you kind of start wondering, were they shooting at me or what's going on? There were no houses around us, really, except to our left and right and that was way, way down the road. So the observers came in and the Serbian army observers and they got together and had a little powwow. We were still shelled at least once a day. Sometimes they'd take a couple of days off.

I guess getting shelled the first time was pretty scary. The scariest moment was the first time being shelled, but after the first time, it really doesn't bother you. You'd just hide in the basement and play Fussball, poker or read and just ignore it until it was over. Sometimes we'd be there for maybe fifteen minutes or two hours in the basement. It really didn't make an impression on me, I guess, not after being shelled for the 15th day in a row.

MEDIA COVERAGE

The media is way out. They only do coverage on Bosnia and they only do coverage of something that really happens like if a Canadian soldier is wounded. Not too long ago a Canadian soldier ran over a land mine and he was wounded along with the officer, and the media covered it extensively but on a day-to-day basis, something is happening everyday. There might be a small incident but there is always something going on, and there are always shots, but the media don't report it and don't really do a good job.

LETTERS FROM HOME

There was actually this one letter that went to our CO and he photocopied it and spread it out throughout the whole unit to everybody from this women out west and she said her husband was killed somewhere on peacekeeping duty (I think it was Cyprus) but she said I'm very proud of you guys, and what you are doing over there is hard and we Canadians look up to you, and your peacekeeping abilities. That was pretty good, but we also got letters from kindergarten classes, Grades 1, 2, and 3. They'd colour pictures, and we'd write to them, saying what our job was and what we did and we'd thank them for sending letters. Of course, we wrote to our families and friends and whatnot, and told them what was going on.

GOING HOME

The battalion was supposed to be out of there in October, and the beginning of October was my leave date to take off but the Van Doos wanted to have more time with their family and friends so we had to stay there another week. So I was on Main 2, and everything was postponed one week, so I left on the 12th of October.

Our section sat down with stress guys, who came from Canada, over in Yugoslavia and they basically said, "How do you feel about this? How do you feel about that? What was your worst, best experience?" They told us that one out of every ten guys has combat stress but I don't know, I guess you have to take everything in stride, and try not to take everything too seriously over there. What you did you did to the best of your abilities. We flew to Winnipeg and stayed there for five days, before we had to clear out and turn in our weapons. Then I got on the plane for home.

Did we accomplish anything? Yeah, you know, every little bit helps I guess. You know the war's not going to stop in twenty-four hours let alone five or six years. I'd do it again, but definitely not right away. It was good money and a good experience. I'm glad I'm home. Anyway, I feel sorry for the people over there that have to live through it every day for God knows how many years, and I'd go over there a second time.

CHAPTER TWELVE

CORPORAL MARTIN DRAKULIC[1]

C-9 Gunner, 2nd Bn Princess Patricia's
Canadian Light Infantry Battalion Group
Sector West and Sector South, Croatia, 1993

THE CALL-OUT

What made me join the Forces in the first place? My brother, mostly. I saw the stuff he was doing and the kit he had, so I joined it. He told me a lot and he helped me avoid a lot of the crap you had to go through like the harder stuff that comes with the good. I was always playing war as a kid and now I wanted to go for the real thing here, or the next thing to it. Then I heard about the call-out. We went to Winnipeg in January, but before that I had to wait three months, which was quite a while as there were three or four lists submitted to the armouries before any names were actually picked. I was a prime candidate for it because I was a corporal, had been in a few years, and had some experience, so that's what they were looking for. In terms of pre-conceptions, I knew there wasn't much on the area I was going to, and there wasn't much publicized about it, so from what I heard, you know, it would be pretty rough, you'd see a lot of destroyed houses, but that we wouldn't really come under fire or have to return fire.

DEPARTURE ASSISTANCE GROUP, CFB GAGETOWN

It was about four or five days, which was paperwork, and PT. The paperwork was easy, PT test was no problem, and the medical was good. A lot of guys showed up, and a few got cut there due to medical reasons or personal reasons. There were some guys fit but there were a lot of guys out of shape, you know the Militia's not a full-time occupation, as such a lot of guys

---

1. All of the Canadian personal names in this interview are pseudonyms.

get out of shape, and they were the ones that got cut after the DAG if they got through the paperwork. They were weeded out during the three months prior to training, which is what that time period is for.

TRAINING WITH 2 PPCLI: WINNIPEG

It was cold! Your nostril hairs froze as soon as you breathed in and you could feel them freeze! The land was flat as that was the farthest west I'd ever been. It was a really big city, the biggest I'd ever been in. A bus met us, and then we drove to the armouries, Campion Barracks, but it was not right downtown. When we got there it was on a weekend, so we didn't see anybody for two or three days before we actually got divided into platoons and companies. We did lots of paperwork, the AAG. We did more of a DAG there, getting docs up to date and getting issued any kit you needed, going to stores and stuff like that. They told us in the briefing about what you were going to be doing. It was a three-month prep for operations over in Yugoslavia and a lot of people would probably be cut, due to their own reasons, so just do the best you could and play the game.

We did a lot of classroom work. We basically started from scratch, and we did tests on the C-7, C-9, grenade, M-72, and all that stuff. We drove to barracks in Winnipeg, a naval Militia barracks, Chippewa; you know where everything was "on the deck" and things like that and we went there for the classroom. We didn't go to the range that much in Winnipeg, that happened when we went down to California where it was basically a Battle School run down there. The thing with this call-out, there was a lot of artillery, armoured, guys like that, it wasn't just infantry, so a lot of guys hadn't even seen the weapons or fired them. A lot of guys needed refreshing, like myself, just to get caught up on everything. In addition, we learned basic phrases in Croatian, we did cordon and search, how to search a vehicle properly, and how to deal with the people if we were ever confronted.

After two months we went down to California for three weeks, then we came back for about two weeks, then we went home before going over to Yugo. The first two months was a lot of PT, lots of running, push-ups, sit-ups, jumping jacks, and we did three PT tests in three months, which you had to score a certain amount to pass and I did well on that. A lot of guys got cut because they weren't liked. If they didn't like you, they cut you or if you screwed up on one big thing, they cut you. People got through who shouldn't have, and people got cut who shouldn't have.

TRAINING IN CALIFORNIA

We landed near San Diego and it rained! It rained the whole time! The drought officially ended the three weeks we were down there in the field. It rained so much they broke the seven-year drought, which was the official word from the mayor. Fort Ord was a really big base and they could fit all of the Canadian Forces on that base but it was pretty much empty when we went there. They were closing it down, I guess, because it was a really old base. We had one day off, which we spent in Monterey, as it was the only town we could get to. It was actually sunny that day, and the first few days we had off, we watched the ranges on that base before we went into the field for an extended period.

We did do FIBUA training, and MOUT teams. We did a couple of day's worth but we didn't really get into it as much as we would have liked. However, we learned a lot.

We learned how to enter into a place, how to cover this and that, team fire and movement, how to hold your weapon properly, and help each other into buildings. In some cases if you knew the enemy was there, they taught us to blow everything up when we went in. They said that they did that a lot. The sergeant instructing us was in Panama, and he said that they made a lot of mistakes down there that they shouldn't have, and they shot a lot of the time when they shouldn't have. A lot of innocents were killed in Panama, which there was still a lot of controversy about, because they shot before they looked. They said to look first but if the enemy are in there, then don't take any chances but basically, it depended on the situation.

ROTATING WITH 3 PPCLI

When we arrived in Croatia, most of the 3 Pats were on their way out. Main 2 of 3 PPCLI was still there when our advance party arrived, and then their advance party left. They would switch when our Main 1 got there and then Main 1 of theirs would leave, so when Main 2 of our guys came, their Main 2 guys left. There were guys in the bunkers when we got there and they showed us the ropes, what to do, how to be comfortable, and how to deal with the locals. They told us to be firm, don't be shy, assert yourself, and don't take any shit off them, as they'd try to dick you around. They warned us about the kids who would always try to rip us off. Yeah, little kids were at our outpost all the time, like, these two Muslim kids who'd run down to the town and buy us cokes, we'd pay them to fill sandbags for us, and stuff like that. They had a good time, learned English and got some money. We later found out when we went to Sector South that all the Muslims from that town had been run out, basically kicked out of town.

CODE WORD: PHANTOM

We were in Dolanyi, a Croatian town, and the mass graves nearby were Serbs. The site was just an indentation. You could see the length of it and it was just dirt, with no grass growing on it and there was clothing strewn about everywhere and the graves were behind it. There was a little side road that went into a field behind some trees and that's where it was. It was strewn around, shredded and it was cut up. Not military clothing, but kids' clothing, sneakers and that sort of thing. One thing that I remember seeing was this one sneaker. That was the first day we were there and they told us that there were mass graves in there that we had to patrol and the code word for it was PHANTOM. It wasn't really an operation but that's what the code word was on the radio. They were saying, you know, if there were people gathering there at the gravesite, moving the bodies or things like that, PHANTOM was the code word for the site. We could tell if anybody had been there. It was straight down the road, we had NVGs, and we could do without light. They had been there for about a year and a half and the town had been quiet for that amount of time. It was a really well established town. The mayor was high up there and he knew the generals in the Croatian Army. I wondered how those people could live with themselves, you know, it was just down the road! They drove by it every day with their tractors and saw it but we never talked to the people about that, as we didn't get that close and they didn't think that we knew. That's why it was so hush-hush. When it was finally found out that we did know, I guess the mayor got in a lot of trouble for that. Nobody will probably ever know what really happened. It was a pretty hush-hush thing and we weren't even allowed to tell the other platoon but everybody knew it was there. It was a nice town, Dolanyi.

THE RIOT

Well, we had our ROE, Rules of Engagement, and we were made extensively to memorize them. That was what you were supposed to follow if it was picture-perfect, what was happening. A lot of times they went out the window. The first thing you did was cock your weapon and said, "Stop or I'll shoot!" in Croatian. You just let them know that you were getting pissed off and to stop what they were doing. Usually if there are enough of you and you were firm enough, they'd respect if you were firm. They respected strength very much. We had to do that. Oh yeah, we had one section in a platoon that did a cordon and search and they seized a whole bunch of weapons. My platoon was in the area when a whole bunch of Serb farmers showed up and were really protesting, so we went there and formed up. A riot broke out, people were shouting, pushing, and kicking, but we had the order to charge weapons, you know, as soon as we showed we weren't going to mess around, they backed off.

During the riot I shoved guys and kicked one guy cause he was rioting. I was a C-9 gunner and I shouldn't have even been up there pushing because my weapon was slung across me. They were grabbing hold of that and shaking it, and it was attached to me! So I pushed them off. It was like a mass thing and they all started pushing, people were punching and things like that. Then we had the order to charge weapons and that calmed things down a bit. One guy tried to run through us with his tractor. We stopped that when we locked and loaded. It was a big intimidation factor when you heard forty weapons being cocked! The Big Click! There was a track right down there with a .50 cal and it was pointed right at them. You could hear that being cocked. It was a heavy click and hearing a .50 cal being cocked is really comforting!

This was in this one little Serb area surrounded by Croatians. I could see why they would be pissed off, having their stuff taken away, because they were surrounded by Croatians, but as it was, they were in our safe zone, the UNPA, so they weren't allowed to have them.

RULES OF ENGAGEMENT

Our ROE included what we were supposed to do, you know, stick to this and this will take care of all things that will ever happen to you. It was a crock of shit. A lot of times we didn't have warning, they just pointed their weapons at you. We were really taught fuck-all. There were seven of them that I memorized one time. Like, some were, that if they persisted, charge your weapon, and put it on safe. If they kept doing it, fire a warning shot in the air, but this was later on. The first ones were the right to carry weapons, the right to enforce certain conditions like, if you were working and they were harrying anyone under your protection, you could fire. We were allowed to fire if we were fired at first or if our rules of engagement said that we were protecting someone. Like, before we went over the French were protecting Croatian officials and the Serbs opened the door of the track that he was in and shot him while the French sat around and did nothing. They had every right to fire back to protect him because they were there for his protection but we never had to do that. We were told that if we were fired at, we had positive confirmation and we could see them, then we could return fire, or if someone was firing at us or attacking us, we could fire once in the air, and if they kept doing it, or threatening you, then aim for the centre of mass, and just plug them. We knew we had the right to fire back if we were threatened or if one of them took our weapons, and we were told that there would be no questions asked, just shoot them right off the bat.

There were a couple of incidents of Canadian soldiers being captured and turning over their weapons. They were asleep and that was why they got caught. The Serbs walked right in. They should have been operating under the same rules of engagement. I know some guys that worked with them, guys who came back, who had been over there and you heard what happened. I can't see it any other way. If they were approaching our bunker with intent to capture us, we would fire back. I would have. I would have been court marshalled and thrown in jail, but I'd never give my weapon up. If some guy grabbed my rifle and tried to take it, I'd shoot him and then fire one in the air after he was lying on the ground and that would have been my warning shot. That was unofficial policy but you could pretty much assume and that was what our company commander told us.

SECTOR WEST: PRESENCE OPERATIONS

At checkpoints, at WC 2, we had people coming in who didn't want us to search the car. Usually you lowered the gate, were firm, told them to get the hell out of the car and they would. We worked on the language, like, "Stop or I'll shoot," "dobro vetchie" is good evening, "dobro utro" is good day, "dobro danje" is good night, "Uh, mon tia mon" is motherfucker, "Phutch kin sin" is son of a bitch, and "yevy cec" is fuck you. You know, phrases like that and we could tell when they were swearing at us! When we were searching their vehicles, you know, they'd mutter, and we knew what they were saying, because they were common phrases and then we'd really tear them apart. So, a lot of times, if we knew the guy was giving us a hard time, we'd search him, search the car, and tear everything out, you know, go crazy on him. Most were pretty friendly, they'd get out and we wouldn't even have to ask them. They'd even open the trunk for us. We were on a back road, so we knew a lot of the guys coming in but we still searched them, of course.

In my experiences, the Serbs worked easier with us at the time. When we were in Croatian areas, there weren't many Serbs so when we did work with them they wanted to be on our good side, and so they were but the Croatian police dicked us around a bit. Yeah, in my experience the Serbs dealt better with us.

We did twelve-hour shifts at the checkpoint, if you were on "12 to 12" you had twelve-hours on twelve off. When you weren't on shift, you'd have, if you were lucky, twenty-four to thirty-six hours off. You cleaned the section house, maintained your weapons, and things like that. When people were doing shifts we all did patrols at that point and we'd go do that. There would be two guys on at a time, nine of us in the section. Everybody did it, section commander, 2IC, and they all did their turn, no more or less than anybody else. The first vehicle we stopped, the guy had a pistol but he was a cop. What we did with cops, you know, they'd give you their gun and you checked the serial number to see if it was stolen. I was really nervous trying the new Serbo-Croat that I learned. First thing he did was roll down the window and hand me his pistol. There was a guy on with me, a 3 PPCLI guy, and he was laughing because he knew the guy. Then he handed me his police ID and then we checked the weapon and handed it back to him. He wasn't wearing a uniform and that was why he took me by surprise. Like the very first car I searched and the guy handed me a pistol!

There were a lot of drunks. One guy must have been about 14, drunk and he was driving. One time he went into the ditch by our checkpoint and his car slid in so we had to push him out. There were a couple of guys that gave us a lot of problems and they were just ignorant pricks to us. They were Croatians and that town was Croatian. They wouldn't do what we told them to, and they'd sit in the car or they'd swear and stomp. We'd be really firm. "Okay, you're not going to get through. Go back!" It was just the fact that we were there searching them. Especially the police had to be searched. They were the ones we searched the most because it irked them so much and they were the ones that gave us the hardest time. They didn't feel that they had to be searched and they would resist and say no. They'd just be obnoxious.

The first weapon I seized was an AK. A vehicle drove by us and in the back was an AK, where I could see it. They were two police officers, which were allowed to have pistols, but no automatic weapons. So I pointed it out to Harper and he searched the vehicle and found it and they wouldn't give it up. So we called it in and everybody else showed up. The platoon commander got hold of the company commander and pretty soon everybody showed up but that was an overreaction. Meanwhile, we were arguing with these police and they called their guys and more police showed up. In the end we took all their weapons. These guys were in uniform this time and we seized all kinds of pistols, and Harper seized a really nice chrome pistol. The next day our CSM had it on his hip. Those guys, when their weapons were confiscated, were allowed to come and pick them up but nine times out of ten they weren't returned, which was good. I mean, why give it back to them? We don't need to have all these weapons hanging around.

We also seized RPGs and their rockets. They'd have them in the trunks of cars and underneath the seats. You'd shake the door, the panels came off and they had weapons in there.

We did weapons seizure near Lipik. There was a Serb defensive position facing that town, a smaller hamlet where the Serbs were and that was where we found a weapons cache. My platoon was just doing an exercise in the area, and there was another section from another platoon there. They were confiscating the weapons when all the farmers started to show up. We were the closest in the area, so we were called on the radio, "Get your ass over there and support those guys" and then we showed up. They found the weapons in a house. A lot of the big stuff was found in old houses. You'd observe suspicious people going into houses a lot, we'd do foot patrols, and look for suspicious people. We did these every so often and we did quite a few but not much usually happened. There was a train that we called "The Great Train Robbery" and we would ride from one town to another on the train, to make sure nothing was being smuggled there. The trip was about half hour, forty-five minutes. It was nice to just sit back and enjoy the countryside and know the ML was waiting at the train station to take you back. It was a change to get into the big town as well, as Daruvar was the biggest town that the train went to. There was a train station in Dolanyi, that was where we got on.

LOCALS, ROTATIONS, AND TASKINGS

We really didn't have too many problems with the locals. We had so much more money than them and we were good for business and they'd stay open until we left. They normally closed pretty early but we played pool with them and we never had any problems. The local beer was Pivot and they drank it warm. We liked it cold, so they had cold beer for us. It was a good beer and you got used to it.

Later on, when we rotated with the company HQ, the callsign was Yankee One Four, and it was about half an hour away from WC 2, where the other platoon was. We all rotated. We manned the gate coming in at the company HQ, just one man during the day, and that was where we did most of the patrols from because we were in a well established base. We did vehicle patrols, with one carrier and one section at a time, and pass through the town. We'd also do foot patrols and we were looking for trouble and suspicious things going on. For instance, lots of people congregating in a destroyed house, or a lot of soldier-type young people hanging around but our patrols were pretty uneventful. We'd walk through destroyed towns, and it was weird, and really eerie. In terms of ethnic cleansing there were, of course, the mass graves but Sector West was really uneventful when we were there.

EQUIPMENT PROBLEMS

Our tracks were junk and we needed new vehicles over there. A lot of them kept breaking down because they were really old. When we took them over they were still in their positions so they weren't cleaned and maintained. We got our vehicles from 3 PPCLI but it was not really their fault, as their tour ended while they were still in position and they really couldn't do much about it. Tracks would pop off, and engines blew on a couple of them. The track drivers could tell you what went on but there were a lot of engine problems and electrical problems. You really didn't think about it much. In my section my track driver was Regular Force and he was really good with it. He really knew his track and could keep it up. A lot of guys had problems, and had to get new parts. Jokingly we'd say that, if we were under attack we could get away in time. They're slow as hell. I think tracks were good for over there because mines were set a foot off the road in the ditch and that was why a lot of French vehicles got mined, because they had the big-wheeled vehicles. In order to turn around to manoeuvre they had to do a three-point turn, where with a track you could swivel right on the spot, so I think that's what saved us too a lot of times. They were good in that sense but they were really slow, and couldn't go more than 70 kilometres an hour on an open stretch of road downhill.

When we turned them over to the Van Doos, we took them back to the base where we tore them apart, changed everything that needed to be changed, washed them out, washed all the parts, and all the stores and we left them 100% better than when we got them. As far as our personal weapons and things, our kit, we maintained it and kept it up to standard. C-6s worked well but we really didn't use them much, and .50 cals were mounted on the tracks at first and we left them there all the time. We covered them the first month we took them down from the mounts and we kept them well oiled, covered all the time. We went to the ranges a few times over there but we didn't get a chance to fire them.

THE KRAJINAS: SECTOR SOUTH

About mid way I went on my UN leave when we were up in Sector West. I went home for seventeen days, which was a good break, and came back shortly after that. The last two months we were down in Sector South because the French asked for us. We heard rumours long before it happened. And because of all the trouble down there, the French lost a lot of face value and they weren't respected enough. It was the same area where that guy was shot and the French did nothing about it. The sector commander asked for Canadians down there because we were the most respected peacekeepers. The move was a really long convoy and it took us nineteen hours to get there. We stopped at the border and there was a big hassle there.

Arriving there was weird. It was a lot different than Sector West, and a lot hotter. We saw a lot more. There was a French LOGBAT set up in a base there and we were across the road from them basically. Depending on where we drove, there were Croatians, and five minutes down the road, Serbs. There were no real front lines separating any group of people. We saw a lot of artillery positions, which was the big thing. We'd drive down the mountains and see them set up, the guns, and the tanks. They were not amateurs and were well set up. Their vehicles, tanks, and BMPs weren't in the best shape though.

THE CHETNIKS

The Serbs had a lot of different units. Up to that point I saw a lot of militia units and we saw some Chetniks. Chetniks in general were guerrilla groups and they were little groups that did their own thing. They were not under anybody's control, either Serb or Croatian. They did their own thing and they were the ones causing the problems. A soldier was a soldier, like, Serb soldiers won't shoot unless ordered to but the Chetniks would do what they wanted. They worked for the regular army but they really were on their own. We bumped into them moving down south. One guy told us, "Hey, we're Chetniks" and this one guy spoke really good English. We had stopped every once in a while during the move and there were soldiers all around us in vehicles. We moved into the Serb positions and five minutes down the road was a Croatian position. Anyway, he came over to our track and was talking to us. I was in the C-9 gunner's position and he was asking about our equipment. You know, "What calibre is that?" He asked what we were doing down here, where we were from, and things like that. Basic curiosity. He had a beard and a Dragunov sniper rifle. There wasn't a set military uniform, but they all had the same webbing. He did have a camouflage uniform but not the regular Serbian military stuff. They had badges but this guy didn't really have one on him and he didn't tell us anything, he just asked us about our weapons. We wanted to be careful when we were talking with these guys.

SECTOR SOUTH: THE SCHOOL AND THE BRIDGE

We drove through the town, Obrovac, and it was the weirdest town. The valley went down and it was built up all along the side of the hill. That was a Serb-occupied town and it was a military town. There were soldiers everywhere, hanging out here and there, and on the other side was where the school stood.

It was just outside, an hour away from Obrovac and the schoolhouse was beyond that. We were there for a good two weeks. Like, we'd rotate, one platoon would stay back, we built our own little base across from the French and we would rotate. We built up the area. There was a Serb artillery position around us and we were in the middle of it. We cut the trees, and prepared the houses. We put barbed wire around the stone fences and we made our compound, which was a lot of work. We built the "Super Bunker from Hell" at the schoolhouse and my section worked for three days straight. We got the shaft for some reason. I worked nineteen hours straight and then six hours off and then another twenty-one hours straight, filling sandbags, day and night. We didn't stop, just to build this one bunker. It was a huge bunker that the engineers had designed because they knew we were going to get artillery there.

We sat around a lot of the time and there were no car checks. We were watching the Maslenica Bridge at that point and we had to count the traffic going over it. We were very far away and we had the NODLER but if you have ever looked through that, you saw a white bridge and car, a little black dot, would come across. We had to distinguish transport, cars, write down the stuff but we were more than a mile away and the NODLER was stretched to its limits. There were no troops at the bridge but there was artillery there. The bridge was a white thing, a pontoon, and a big flotation thing. I never saw it with my naked eye, just through the NODLER! They'd bomb it and then repair it, and arty it again. Finally it was totally destroyed and that was the only thing connecting the two islands.

We did crash harbour a few times. We had an RV spot and if arty came in we'd get there as fast as we could. We got shelled at that bunker at the schoolhouse, where a shell landed about 15 metres away and it just shredded the whole side, four-five sandbags deep. One landed 200 metres from our first position, and that was where those guys were kicked out of the bunker and I was there for that. When we were getting shelled, the adrenalin just started pumping! We were told to stay in our tracks and then they changed their minds and said to get into the bunkers. We were really close to mine. You could hear them... SHHHHHHHHOOM. Like firecrackers or you'd hear them going over you. Then, BOOM when they'd land! Some guys would freak out. I was never really scared and I was like, "Wow! Cool!" You know, I never thought it would happen to me. It was good to have that attitude to a certain extent. If you were always worried about it, you'd be stressed out all the time and we got shelled once a day. The time we were filling sandbags it lasted two days straight. When it was right in the area, we could time it and we'd crash harbour from there. The shelling would go on for a half hour, twenty minutes, a whole day. We got harassment fire and they'd fire above our heads, just to see us scramble for cover. My platoon never had to return fire and I don't even think our company did. I think Bravo Company was the only one to have had a firefight. Mostly, we were under artillery fire.

WORKING WITH UNPROFOR ALLIES

We dealt with the Nepalese, the Jordanians, the Czechs and Slovaks, and I have to be careful there! I didn't see too many British but saw a lot of French and they did not impress me at all. They were mostly conscripts, a lot of queers, and a lot did drugs. We saw this at the French LOGBAT in Sector South. We saw them patrolling on their vehicles. They didn't impress me at all. There were a few soldiers, the lifers. They were well dressed, well turned out, professional looking and acting but for the most part they were conscripts. The Jordanians were drinking coffee all the time. Apparently, I heard that they were only issued six bullets and that's all! Jordan is, of course, a Third World country and they couldn't afford it, I guess. They had C-7s, the same rifles as us. The Slovaks had some cool stuff, the engineers. They had tanks, T-72s, and they had mine-clearing tanks, with the big roller on it to set off mines. The French had cool rifles, the ones with the magazines at the back, the MAS. We had a couple of days where we saw all their kit and they saw ours and we drove each other around in each other's vehicles. The French were well equipped, their vehicles were really nice, and they were like our Bisons, really. They had a 20mm cannon on top, which was a good piece of kit to have. Our personal kit was good, the best weapons going, but our vehicles were hurting. The tracks are good if they are new. I know you're going to have problems with anything mechanical but it could have been worse.

THE MEDAK POCKET

We didn't think we would move any more but I guess we were volunteered for it. We were just told to get in and off we went and it didn't take long to get there, as we always had our track packed up. We moved as a company and it was a good long convoy. There were a lot of trench lines, with tanks facing the Croatian lines. We'd see the tanks at the side of the road, and then we'd see the Croatians with their tanks facing the other way. There were a lot of Croatian tanks, and gun positions. It was the most armour that I had ever seen in one place at that point and they were professionally dug in. You could tell by the signs on the tanks and the different uniforms. Within five minutes you were in different territory and we couldn't see back to the Serbs. From the positions we could see Charlie Company, with the flags and the carriers and we pulled in at the same time. They were right behind us, the artillery pieces, 150 metres down the road.

We moved into the Medak Pocket and there were two lines facing each other, and our company, Delta Company, was with the Croatians and Bravo Company was in the Serbs' position. It got worse and worse as we got into the thick of the fighting and it was still going on when we pulled in. The Serbs pulled back and we took their positions. We were facing each other across a field, two UN flags. The Serbs were behind them, and the Croatians were behind us. We were watching those guys, and they watched us. We were facing each other and they had us patrolling. We had our machine guns and mortars set up facing the other guys, which I thought was rather odd. I thought we should have been facing the other way. It's like we were going to shoot our own guys before we got to them!

Medak was a Serb area, but the Croatians occupied it. That was where we found the Serbian bodies. Initially, we heard more than we saw. A couple guys found bodies, women who were killed, and there was one lady out in the field with her genitals cut up, and her stomach slashed open. Two were found in a chicken coop, where they were raped, shot, and burned. I saw the bodies of the soldiers that were executed and they were the first bodies that I had seen. I was on a body recovery team carrying bodies down the mountains. These were Serb soldiers that we body-bagged and carried down. I know that shit happens in war but there were also women and children who were killed. In Medak, when we first came in, the town was still burning. They pulled out and we pulled in with dead animals everywhere, horses, dogs, cats, chickens, goats, etc.

The town was burning and there was a smell of smoke in the air. It was really muddy, hilly and we were in a valley, with forests, huge hills, and big trees. There was a mountain up there, where we put a listening OP. One section was up there and you had to trek through the woods to get there. We had to carry everything on our backs, as you were miles away. If anything happened you'd be screwed up there. Everything was destroyed and still burning. It wasn't a city; it was more like a series of homesteads, a group of little hamlets. There were a lot of dead animals at that time, and then when we looked closer, we found a lot of dead bodies. A lot of women like the ones in the chicken coop, the old lady in the field, and the lady in the lagoon. These people were Serbs. We found executed soldiers who had been captured and used as labour up on the mountain to carry stuff up and down. When the Croats were done with them, they shot them. One guy just had a piece of skull left and a neck and the trees around him were just chipped. They must have put the whole magazine into him and his stomach was gutted open from bullets. A full magazine must have been pumped into him. One guy was shot in the eye and the back of his head was gone and another guy was shot in the back of the head. They looked like rubber, sort of. They had been there three days already, so they were a bit ripe at that point and somebody got sick and was vomiting. Once we got them in body bags it was okay. We joked about it a lot. It was natural to deal with it that way and we'd see who could carry a body down the hill the fastest. The guy I was carrying was about 250 pounds, really heavy. Of course,

Few bodies were recovered from the ethnically-cleansed villages in the Medak Pocket: several hundred people disappeared while the area was under Croatian control and were never heard from again. The remaining corpses revealed high levels of excessive force. The man pictured above had an entire AK-47 magazine emptied into him. (photos courtesy 2 PPCLI/LCol Shane Brennan)

we were going down little goat trails on the mountain. You couldn't be that gentle, and sometimes you were dragging it. By the time we were at the bottom of the hill they were all twisted up. It couldn't be helped. One poor guy had his leg unattached.

The saddest moment of my tour was that day with the bodies. We found one body by itself and the feeling I got was a feeling of loneliness; this one body out here, what was he thinking before he died? You know? That went through my mind all the time. He was here by himself. You know, you thought of him still as a person, just up on the side of this mountain, lying there dead in uniform.

There wasn't a lot of gunfire. There was a sort of ceasefire, because we were there. I guess one night a Serb or Croatian patrol bumped into the section up on the hill and there was a huge firefight all around them. They were just dug in and they could hear the patrol in the woods calling, "Hey, UNPROFOR! Hey UNPROFOR!" and from the other direction they could hear others coming and all hell broke loose but no bodies were found. You could see flashes, and it was like a platoon encounter.

HANDLING STRESS

I read a lot and I wrote in my diary. I started the diary and never bothered to finish it. One guy in our section had Dungeons and Dragons books there and we'd flirt around with that off duty sitting in the track. And sleep. At that point we couldn't work out, and we were always on standby. We had shrinks show up just before we came home to tell us that if we had any problems, we should talk to our buddies about it. It was normal to feel that way, and you were not alone. A couple guys were stressed out. It was nothing big to me and we'd talk about our own shift work. At the point when I left, our section was really close and we were on first-name basis with our section commander. You were that close the whole time and it was just, like, you ignored rank. I read a lot and we'd exchange books in the section.

I really didn't have bad dreams about what happened, no nightmares. Right after I got back, I had some dreams, though. I'd wake up and think, "Wow!" Over there, no dreams except a couple of wet dreams maybe. Not really. A lot of times, if you were woken really quickly, like before going on shift, I'd wake up and start talking. I guess I'd be talking for about ten minutes when some guy would wake me up. I was sort of dreaming and talking to him about snakes flying in the air and things like that, which was total nonsense. Things like that happened all the time. Especially when you're woken up really quick. I don't remember dreaming much over there and nothing sticks out in my mind. A lot of times we were just so exhausted, you just crashed out.

COMING HOME

At the end of October we went back to the Charlie Company base, and it used to be an old JNA base. That's where we cleaned the tracks, did this and that, and got ready to go back home. Ninety percent of our people left in the Advance Party, and I was on Main 1, which was the luck of the draw, I guess. I got to Winnipeg and took three days just to clear out. I was 18 when we went to Winnipeg and I started drinking in Winnipeg, a lot, because the drinking age was 18. When I came home I bought a car, had three girlfriends, and lived at home. It was a hell of a change. We'd talk all the time with the guys, about our experiences. Even now, stories come up.

MISSION ASSESSMENT

I'd go back. First, I'd wait at least six months before I went back again and I could do the next tour comfortably, but I didn't want to go back right away, as I was just sick of it. When sufficient time has gone past, I'd go back. The next tour is RCD, and there's one company of RCR going with them just to guard the armour. The DAG's coming up in June and 2 RCR is going after that and that's the one I want to go on. There's a good chance I could, too. The RCR is having a big recruiting drive, like the PPCLI did so, hopefully, I'll get in on that. Did the UN accomplish anything? Oh yeah, for sure. Like, even if you saved one person's life, I'd be there. A lot of that controversy over peacemaking, and peacekeeping, well, when we went down to Sector South, up until that point it was just another exercise. It really wasn't that hard as far as the stuff that I saw and did but the big-eye opener was the move to Sector South. It was right beside Bosnia, so it was closer to all the fighting. There was just as much fighting going on there than anywhere else in Bosnia but it was just not publicized as much. The world needs to know what was going on but the press just doesn't cover it enough.

There was only one exception. When we came back from the body recovery, by the time we had carried them down to the first checkpoint, we were all quiet and grim, and there were some reporters looking at us. We weren't smiling or nothing, because nobody felt like it at that point and it was like, they were looking at us through the cameras. It wasn't a proud moment but it was just look, see, we're actually doing this and my mother saw me on the news loading bodies on a truck! It wasn't a proud moment but it had to be done and they were looking at you sort of, "Wow! Those guys are doing that!" It was a good feeling to know that you had some recognition for what you are doing, even the guys that didn't go up with us. We came under fire up there, had to hump all the way down this mountain and all the way up, and they were thinking, wow, we don't want to do it. We came under fire just as we got down, but it was just pot shots over our heads to see us scramble.

They said that we weren't doing anything over there, and making no difference there. This was from some guy who was never over there, or just repeating stories of what he heard. The reporters weren't where we were, didn't know what we went through, what we did, or what we accomplished there. Until they are actually digging the trenches and getting their heads down away from artillery, they shouldn't be making those evaluations and we definitely made a contribution. As it was, after we went to Sector South, a few weeks later, it erupted again in Sector West! People were getting shot; shit was going on, things like that, because we left. The Canadians are by far the premier peacekeeping soldiers in the world.

It was a good do, and I'd go again. We are making a difference over there, despite what people say. Even if one person is saved, you're doing your job. I think we should take a more aggressive role. We should have more armour, and more artillery. The RCD is going, and that's good. Air strikes are good and things like that. The belligerents took us for fools a lot of the time because we'd say we were going to do something, which was a bluff, so they'd call it and we wouldn't do anything. That didn't happen when the PPCLI were over there, and we sort of kept our word like we said we would.

CHAPTER THIRTEEN

CORPORAL KENT CAMPBELL[1]

C-9 Gunner, 2nd Bn Princess Patricia's
Canadian Light Infantry Battalion Group
Sector West and Sector South, Croatia, 1993

DEPARTURE ASSISTANCE GROUP: CFB GAGETOWN

We left for the DAG in December of 1992 and there were about 7-800 guys there. The DAG in Gagetown was just for the Atlantic Militia Area, that is, Newfies, Nova Scotians, Cape Bretoners, Prince Edward Islanders and New Brunswickers. We did some PT, an 8-kilometre and a 12-kilometre march and we did circuit training in the gym. We also did the medicals, the eyes, ears, nose, and mouth thing. We did no weapons handling, no weapons handling test whatsoever that I can remember. In terms of physical fitness we all looked pretty much the same. Actually there were a few guys there who were active all the time and were pretty physically fit. We had a sergeant there who was from one of the regiments out west and he could do push-ups and sit-ups like nobody's business. He had arms on him like you wouldn't believe!

There was some cutting at Gagetown. I knew a couple guys, friends of mine, who were cut for reasons like their blood pressure was one point over what it was supposed to be or something like that, which was ridiculous, and another guy because he smoked too much. Just silly things like that and then they'd turn around and let somebody go who was so grossly out of shape he couldn't keep up with us on an 8-kilometre walk. To me that was arbitrary but the decision was made by Base, not by 2 RCR, but by base medics.

WORKING UP WITH 2 PPCLI: WINNIPEG

I travelled with a bunch of friends to Moncton on the bus, where we stayed for the night, got up, went to the airport, got on the airplane and were on our way to Winnipeg. We stopped

---

1. All of the Canadian personal names in this interview are pseudonyms.

once, I can't remember but it was probably Toronto, and then we were in Winnipeg. It was nighttime and very confusing, but we had an AAG there, the Arrival Assistance Group, and we got cleared in to the post office, ammo, clothing and all that right there on the parade square. It was about 2300 hours before we got to the barracks and then we had to unpack. The next morning they still had to clear us in, and we still had to have certain things done before we could continue on. Then they gave us a basic breakdown on what was going to happen to us. They told us they were going to do a selection phase of their own, but there were a lot of you people here who weren't going to make it, this that and the other thing. Basically the people they started with when we first arrived were basically the people who went over. The only guys who didn't go over were the guys who busted their legs or punctured a lung or something like that. As soon as we hit the ground they broke us up into our companies, and who we were going to be with. They'd call out a list of names, "You guys come with me."

My platoon was pretty much all militiamen. Now a lot of those Regular Force guys moved right out of the platoon and out of the company, because when we went down south they only wanted them if they had their TOW qualification or sniper or mortar, some weapon skill. There were only a dozen Regular Force that were in our company, not including master corporals, sergeants and above, maybe less than a dozen.

Training in Winnipeg was hectic. We did circuit training, we did running, sit-ups and push-ups. We did that for about two or three days and then they did their PT selection, where you ran around the gym twenty-six times, and you had to make a certain time, you had to do so many chin-ups, or pull-ups, so many push-ups and so many sit-ups. You had to do so many in a minute. They didn't cut right away, and then they turned around and said, "Well, we'll do a six-day work-up and the people that fail this time will be in remedial PT class." So they did that and then we were tested again.

We also did the weapons handling lectures, C-7, C-9, C-6, the 9mm, the mortar, hand grenades, and M-72 Light Anti-Tank Weapon, the basic soldiering equipment. We went to a navy militia building in Winnipeg for the second or third week, and we started weapons training. As far as I remember, and some of it's so blurry, it was just: non-stop. Well it wasn't quite like basic, as my particular platoon did not have room inspections, however, a couple of the other platoons did. I did a show parade, I think, once when our section commander left our 2IC in charge and there was nothing for us to do so we had to do a show parade. That was a week before we went overseas and it was really just killing time then.

On the whole, we didn't have room inspections; in our particular platoon, our room inspection was open the door, look in, no dirt or mud prints on the floor, the walls were cleaned up, and no busted furniture. They treated us as responsible adults and left us alone. They spent less time doing that and more time on the soldiering, as they didn't want to screw around with petty things because they knew we were responsible enough. They saw within the first couple of weeks that we could take care of ourselves in terms of hygiene and all that stuff.

Our training focus in Winnipeg was section attacks, big-time! We started in Winnipeg and we refined our skill in California. In Winnipeg it must have been minus 40 and we had snow up to our knees but it built good, strong legs, I'll tell you! We also did hasty roadblocks and it was done with a track with all the kit in the back. The track drives up, you pull the equipment out of the back and set up roadblocks. We had the orange lights that blink on and off, we had the tire things with the spikes sticking out like dragon's teeth or whatever, and we had a .50 cal on top of the track and they were set up so that a car could squeeze through them without speeding past them. We'd stop the car and do our thing.

They taught us how to check a car, and then we did mines. They had a couple of engineers there, who showed us some film footage of the mines with the engineers clearing the fields and stuff like that, the PMRs, the TMAs and all that stuff. They also showed us types of mines and how the letters represent what the mine is made out of, plastic, anti-personnel, blast-type mines, or whatever.

We did a day's worth of language training where they gave us papers, pamphlets and stuff, you know, and it's just like any language, you get reading it and you remember it. It was useful training to learn how to pronounce certain letters and stuff, because their alphabet is different, as they have the Cyrillic and our style of letter forming alphabets. I remember some of it, like, "kako ste," "moline" and "fallah," which means "please," "thank you," "open your jacket, open your hood," "hands up" and stuff like that. Once you got a grip on it you learned new stuff to say.

MORE WORKUPS: CALIFORNIA

We had three chalks and a rear party or Main 1, Main 2, rear party and advance party. We flew there by Hercules and Airbus. Scare Air! We flew down by Airbus, and when we arrived at San Jose airport it was just spitting rain. The weather was different but the boys were relaxed and everything because it wasn't cold anymore. The next day it wasn't raining at all and it was pretty sunny out. The OC and the CSM [the Company Sergeant Major] ran us down to the beach and back, just a small early morning jaunt, four or five-kilometre run, just enough to get you going before we had breakfast. After that they discussed what was going to happen. We were going to do section attacks and platoon attacks until we got them right. For three or four days it never rained, for the week that we stayed in Fort Ord. Anyway, we moved from one barracks to another, and they only gave us one day off the first week we were there. They came out and psyched us out too. "Why aren't you people in your webbing? Don't you know we are doing a 12-kilometre march? Let's go! Come, on, what's wrong with you?" and they started ragging on us really hard. Then they said, "You got two minutes to get upstairs, get your civvies and sneakers on and away." And then they left. The boys were gone!

Everybody was down at the bus stop waiting to head into Monterey and they told us to stay out of Salinas and Seaside, which were bad areas, as there were a lot of drive-by shootings going on. It was like the movie Colours you know, red and blue. Naturally, we didn't stay out. It was different. We got a lot of stares. We were on the bus and there were a couple of 15-year-olds that got on the bus and they were packing as we could see pistols sticking out of their back pockets, "Oh wow! Nice piece!" It was different. There were eight of us sitting in the back of the bus and we were just sitting there minding our own business, and nobody's going to do nothing if you're minding your own business. Anyway we knew that nothing was going to happen because we were on a bus. There were two guys busy yelling at each other anyway, "Motherfucker" this and "Yo Mama!" and stuff, so anyway, Monterey was nice, and we went down on the pier where they had all these little shops on the pier and we were looking at the birds. It was really nice down there and it was well worth the day off.

We got back to camp and the next day we humped everywhere. The only time we didn't walk was to the shower point at Fort Hunter-Liggett, and that was it. Basically, whenever we went to the ranges to do our PWTs [the Personal Weapons Test], we walked but it was good. We had some good little humps up to the British PWT point, which was an interesting walk, and there was a lecture about black widows, scorpions, snakes and stuff. At the time, we were having hot weather, which was fine. We did our Carl G, our M-72 on one range, we did our grenades, and we did our C-7s, C-9s and our C-6s. We did a work-up for section attacks, you know, this is what I expect from you and we'd do them up and down a couple of times, have a drink of water and carry on back to the shacks. If everybody gets their stuff together, we can go home so why screw around? If you know what you're doing, we'll leave you alone. That's what happened on that day and we weren't in the field longer than ten days.

We didn't work as a battalion, just as a company. When we arrived at Fort Hunter-Liggett, it was sunny. We got off the bus, took our kit off the bus, humped into our bivouac site, set up our hootches, and didn't have any timings. Then the next day it rained and it never stopped the entire time we were there. The last day we were in the field doing our platoon attacks and getting assessed for it, what it was, if you failed platoon attack, you had to stay in the field, so basically you were doing them to get out of the field, and the CO was marking them. That was the first day it stopped raining and that's when we were leaving the field and going back to Fort Ord. We did section attacks on section attacks upon section attacks upon platoon attacks. The platoon attacks were the last thing we did. We didn't do any patrolling, but we discussed it, if I remember correctly, we discussed patrolling and that but we never did them.

We also did FIBUA [Fighting in Built-Up Areas] and MOUT is what they call it in the States [Military Operations Urban Terrain]. We had American instructors, who were just amazing and they were decent guys that knew their stuff. The American idea of FIBUA was different from what we were used to, and it was pretty neat to see. The way they did it was rather than kick the door open, throw a grenade in, wait for it to go off and then go in spraying, they don't do it that way. Once they get into the building, they have to search each room properly, and they do like a listening type deal if they can get the door open. Even if they can't get the door open, they'll listen, look and peek and stuff like that. If they have to enter the room, then one guy will search high, one will search low, one is crouched and one's standing up and they walk into the room, one left and one right, look around and if they see something, they double tap it and leave the room, or throw a grenade and boom! It's totally different. We did this for about a day or two and they did a demonstration for us. The thing was, they don't work in a building, they work in a city. They have a whole town of concrete buildings with blown-up cars and stuff to do their training in, and it was made specifically for FIBUA. It was amazing to see this. When we walked up I thought we were walking up to a town but it was their FIBUA site with cars flipped over, and bullet holes everywhere. All the Americans were in the MILES gear [which uses lasers and sensors to tell you if you've been shot] and some of our guys got to do MILES gear, but we never did.

We went back to Fort Ord, and we were there for about a week, so guys were allowed back into Monterey, we cleaned up our gear, went back to San Jose, flew to Winnipeg, landed. We had a man from the RCMP, who was over in Yugoslavia, come by bringing some slides with him and he showed us pictures, told us some stories, told us to be careful, and don't trust anybody but it went in one ear and out the other. You take in what you think is important and I took in the "Be careful" part! I wasn't going to go in there half cocked, thinking I was Johnny Rambo or anything, I just went there, did my time and came home.

When we got back to Winnipeg, they wound us down hard, because the recce party had to go to Yugoslavia and recce it out. The OC, the 2IC and a couple of the other guys went over, while some of the other officers and senior NCOs were over there recceing out Yugoslavia, where we were going to be and what was going to happen. We did some PT, but nothing hard-core, no "pick up Mister Log, he wants to go for a jog" stuff just long-distance light jogging and relaxing for a couple of days.

TO CROATIA: AREA OF OPERATIONS, SECTOR WEST

We took off for Yugoslavia on April 6, directly from Winnipeg to Yugoslavia on an American Airlines 747. We landed at Zagreb where we saw two FISHBEDS, MiG 21s, which were grounded. We got to see some of the countryside as we were coming in and it was like it is here, same parallel, and not really much different from Canada except people are shooting at each other. It was, of course, confusing. A lot of guys were there from different companies, know what I mean? We landed and they said, "B Coy over here, D Coy personnel there." We got on a bus from there to one point and then we got off. The guys from 10, 11 and 12 Platoons in D Company got on a deuce and went from there to callsign 4, which was our Company HQ. There were two towns in the area, Pakrac and Lipik. We were there for a couple of hours and then they said, "Okay, put your kit on the deuce, we're going to Lipik." When we got there our Platoon Warrant Officer gave us the scoop on what was going on, and told us what we had to do. It was going to be a busy month, as we had to fill sandbags, paint the platoon house, do this, that and the other thing and that's when the tour started.

We did OPs and WCs. 'WC' stands for West Canadian, Sector West, and a Canadian checkpoint [whose callsign was Whiskey Charlie 5, or 8, or whatever]. When we first got there, I was put on the list and I was told that I was going out first thing in the morning at 0800 to 1800. So I had my breakfast, I got my kit together, and they told me what I was going to need, webbing, rifle, and helmet. I carried a C-9, so I grabbed that, got on the deuce, met John Corwin from the artillery and then we went to WC 5, which was an OP consisting of sandbags, a white building, and a UN sign. We had two guys during the day and three during the night. We had binoculars, compass, map, and radio. You sat there at the gate, and you stopped people as they went by. We'd do vehicle checks (hardly any vehicles came to us at WC 5) and it was like the farmhouse out in the middle of nowhere. We saw some civilians, but they didn't live there. Behind us was nothing and in front of us there were some Serbs living in buildings and Croatian buildings in front of us all blown to pieces. The Serbs weren't starving to death but they were mostly farmers and they were a hard, pretty shoddy -looking group of people, with missing teeth and poor hygiene.

Our mission was to keep the peace and we were basically keeping the UNPA war-free. We'd hear shots now and again but it could have been hunters or somebody trying to start trouble. When we heard shots, we had to get our compass out to take a bearing, establish a distance, and report it in on a grid and send in a shotrep. Time, bearing, and distance, then somebody from our Y 17 would go out and investigate this and callsign 4 handled roadblocks. We had a platoon at Lipik and a platoon in Pakrac and then we'd rotate. Callsign 4, Y 17, and Y 14 would rotate and we would put a platoon in callsign 4, a platoon in Poljana and a different platoon in Lipik. At the time we only went to Y 14, that was in Pakrac/Poljana, and Russ Pages' platoon was in Y 14, which was in Lipik, and Malak was in callsign 4. It was just the same thing all over again, we were just in different areas.

SECTOR WEST: WEAPONS SEIZURES AND ESCORTS

I don't think I seized any weapons personally. However, there were a couple of friends of mine who had an incident where they stopped a guy and asked what he was doing. He said he was going fishing, and they said, "Hold on a second. Open your trunk." He opened up his trunk and there were explosives in there; grenades, and DM-12, which is like C-4 it's a plastic explosive but a different type and they seized the stuff. "Going fishing?" Not a very good fisherman! Buddy insisted that he was fishing and they called it in.

We couldn't arrest anybody. You just called it in from Y 14 to callsign 4, they would contact the local police headquarters, which at the time was Serb police, who would then come down and shake their finger at the man, take him away and then let him go if the man was another Serb. If he was a Croat, you didn't call Serb police for a Croat, you'd call a Croat cop. If you stopped somebody here, they were all Serb outside the UNPA, and Croatian on the inside. Serbs would come in and pick up their own people, and leave but they never, ever, once entered the UNPA, unless they were escorted, for reasons of seeing their house or family. Croatians had family inside the UNPA and they needed escorts to get through Serb territory, to get to the Croatian territory. I never escorted anybody in, as that was callsign 4's job. If I remember correctly, it only happened once since we were at Y 17 that somebody wanted to come in and see their house that was blown up.

At Lipik we were basically in an old Serbian defensive position, WC 6, which was busier than WC 5. When you were standing at the WC, behind it there were Serb houses, and you could tell which ones were Croatian because they were all blown up. It was a huge defensive position. Mines, they had them all taped off. But we never found any mass graves, or anything like that. We just saw blown-up houses.

TAKING FIRE

I was shot at. It was nighttime on May 24th and me and my two friends were doing our thing. One guy was out there with the pair of binoculars, one guy was making coffee and I was sitting there writing vehicle numbers and licence plates down when all of a sudden I heard a "Pop! Pop!" sound, not a big bang, and dirt started flying up everywhere. The guy fired eight shots and that was that, we were down, turned out the light, and grabbed the radio. The platoon warrant and guys were doing a patrol up in that area, and as they were returning they heard the firing, and I said, "He's up there inside the woods in the defensive position but I don't know exactly where" and he just kept going. So I got on the radio to Y 17, back to our platoon callsign, and started giving them the spiel, and by that time the boys were saying, "Can we open up? Do you want to fire?" And I said, "No you can't fire. Our platoon warrant and too many guys are up there now. We were all hugged up against the sandbags, waiting for them, and there was a guy with a C-9 standing there looking around, but the lights were out and the generator was off, so the only thing we needed was a paraflare anyway. That was the first time anybody in our particular platoon had been shot at since we started there, but I don't know about the other companies. After that, it was every now and again somebody would get shot at. I don't think it was accidental, it was done on purpose but I don't think they were trying to hit anybody, I think they were trying to wake us up, annoy us, hassle us a little bit, and try to see if they could get us to move faster or whatever.

OPERATION BACK STOP

I was on that and we were on defensive operations. If we got hit here and they started rolling stuff trying to get through us, we moved back to this position and this is where we would hold, and we would hold off the Croatian and the Serbian hordes. What we didn't understand was why we were digging these defensives and then letting the Croatians or Serbs, pace them off. They had fixes on them, with mortars trained on them, and if they wanted to they could have destroyed them if we got in them. We didn't understand. The only thing that made sense was it was just all for practice.

SLEEPY HOLLOW

We called Pakrac "Sleepy Hollow" because there was nothing to do there, not a fuckin' thing. We did the same thing as before, WC 1 was the start of the UNPA in our area, so it was the busiest WC and we had to stop every vehicle. I mean, you'd have a line of traffic from here to Timbuktu, it was unreal. You didn't have to pull everybody out of their vehicle every time, you could just do a fast search, pop their hood, their trunk or whatever, and look under the seats and stuff. If you wanted to, you could get everybody out of the car. There were always different combinations that you could do with the rigs; there were tons of them all the time and you had to check them, because they were big enough to hide anything in and you'd get them to tip their cabs but we never found anything at WC 1. Nothing. Then there were WC 2 and 3. We were supposed to be there for two more months, but what happened was I went on leave and while I was on leave, they went down to Sector South.

ALLIES

We worked with Jordanians, Argentineans, and Nepalese but there was no comparison with us. We were more disciplined, more professional, and more enforcing of the UN code of ethics, morals and all that good stuff. The NIGERBAT, or the KENBAT had their weapons and stuff taken away from them by the Serbs and Croats and they were told, "You will not carry weapons, and you will give us diesel" and the KENBAT did it! The Kenyans gave the Serbs and Croats all their kit. There were a couple of Kenyan soldiers killed because they were mugged, but they gave their money and got killed anyway.

RE-DEPLOYMENT TO SECTOR SOUTH

Some of us were on leave and when we came back, our units had moved. They told us at Camp Polom, " Where we used to be, forget it! If you're from C and D Companies, it's not where you used to be it's where you are now. You guys have all moved. A and B Companies, get back on your deuces and go back to where you used to be. C and D Companies, you guys, C Coy on that deuce, and D on that deuce and have a nice tour, gentlemen!" They drove us back to callsign 4, where the guys from D Coy were going to be on Rear Party, and that meant that we had the rest of the packing up to do and then we were going to go down and that was what we did for four days. We stayed there and we cleaned up C Company's mess that they left behind and they left a big mess. They just threw stuff out of their buildings and garbage and just left it there! Anyway, we cleaned up as much as we could, and then we did a road move, which took a few hours. It was done during the day, as you could not go through the Serbian checkpoints at night.

I was first in a bus, then from a bus to co-driver for a big 5-ton POL truck [carrying fuel] and it was nice scenery except for some burnt buildings. As we were driving along we'd see camouflaged anti-tank guns and other Serbian weapons, until we reached this one Croatian checkpoint with a Polish contingent for the UN. Anyway, they held us up there for a good six hours, because, you could see the mines that they pulled out onto the road at night when nobody was allowed to go through, and they finally removed the mines and let us through. We drove down the road for another half an hour, and when we stopped at the next spot there were two T-72 tanks pointing their guns down the road. We pulled into this spot where we stopped for fifteen or twenty minutes, and then we consolidated before we moved down the road again. When we finally showed up at the French area, I grabbed my kit, and got off, "Where's my platoon?" "Uh oh, they're across the Krajinas." "Where the hell are they?" "They're down at the School." "Oh, thanks," and I heard shelling in the distance.

We wound up in a French area. They were a bunch of conscripts. They were just transport. They were logistics. We didn't work directly with them; we just kind of saw them. They did give us wine and water. We used to have cookouts with them. It was close to Gracac though. I stayed there for two days. When I showed up it was at night and I took all my kit off and slept underneath the trees. The next morning we got up, had breakfast, and after lunch we were supposed to get on the deuce and go down and join the guys from D Company, but it never happened as we were watching the important pontoon bridge, Maslenica Bridge, in the town of Maslenica.

DECOYS

Our leaders said that they would send two platoons down, and we'd do a three-day rotation, so that there was always a platoon up there in the bivvy site, and that's logical, so we did that, and for the first day that we got down there [to a field], well the first day I went down there with them, it was hotter than Hades and the heat was just unbearable! We went down and they had us set up hootches in the shade and get in them, stay in the shade, have some water, smoke and joke or whatever. One guy was on guard on the gun, and he would just sit there. I remember I said that I'd take over for the next shift, as it would give me some time to look around, so when I went down to the gun, and I was amazed and I thought, "Holy jumping! We're on a Serb mock artillery position." They had fake guns set up, that they had taken old cardboard tubes and made fake trails, fake barrels, fake everything and there were eight or nine of these 'guns.' They set up the position to fool the Croats, I guess. Now, that was fine, as we were only there for one night and everything was cool, but I woke up with a great big spider on my arm and luckily I wasn't bitten.

The next day, the Serbs moved in, put a gun position right behind us and started shelling away. The reason why they did this was so that whoever was on the other end couldn't fire back, because we were UN and as far as they were concerned, killing UN was not allowed! We did a deal which was basically, "You guys get out of here," and they said the same thing to us, because in a short time, they were going to start whaling away but nothing happened, and nothing came of it. They stopped firing eventually. That went on for a couple of days. Then, we did our watch up on the Maslenica Bridge, came back down, and the next day we switched over back to the top. I'd only been there three days and we were supposed to be there for six and we moved back up top, so I thought that was a great thing. I'd been lucky enough to be on leave and they only put me there for three days. So we moved back up to the French area, and we were there for three days and we watched movies, did gun shifts, sat atop a track keeping an eye out before we moved back down.

SECTOR SOUTH: THE SHELLING CONTINUES

We eventually went back down across the Krajinas. Now the second time we did that, we were there for an hour and a half, the boys were in the well swimming and stuff, and then the whole company pulled out, because the Serb commanders and the OC discussed that it would be best for the UN troops to leave because the Croatians were going to start returning fire and it would be best if we left. They said, "You've got five minutes to move." We bugged off to the French contingent. We packed up everything, grabbed everything and went, as it was going to start really soon. Just as we consolidated on the road, with all the vehicles lined up, when they started just as we started pulling away. Ka wump! Ka wump! Ka wump! They started dropping and we got out of there just in time. For about a week it was pretty easygoing, yeah, we did some humping, up the great big hill that was there.

We went back across the hill to a place called the school. It was in August, I think, my timing could be way off and it is just a blur to me now. We went back across the Krajinas and we went to the school. What the scoop was, we would stay there until we would get shelled, and it happened every time you went down there. As soon as they started shelling you'd have to get back in your vehicles and leave, because you couldn't stay there, as there was no bunker there at the time.

What was it like to be shelled? It was very scary. They said that they wanted to stay down at the school, as it was a good vantage point, and a good place to start from as any in Sector South. We went to a great big pit with red sand, so we were all down there digging and I'm telling you we filled sandbags! We filled and filled and filled. It was too hot during the day and you'd get shelled so we did it at night. We'd start at about 0200 and go to 0800 or 0900, they'd start shelling again. Tanks would pull up and they'd start pounding away at one another, and then rounds would start coming in. So, we'd stop what we were doing, grab the shovels and the ghetto blaster, duck into the track and leave to our crash harbour. We were at our first crash harbour digging dirt, and then we went to our second crash harbour, which was where the HQ was set up, in a house, and that was where one platoon stayed, while another was down in Karijn Plaza right there on the beach, and the third platoon was elsewhere. We were there and then we'd go dig and did this for about a week. We had this bunker that was set up so that you could have put two or three tracks in. They wanted to build a bunker on top of the hill, so we were humping sandbags up the hill one kilometre up and one kilometre back. It was rocky, raining, and it was night.

As soon as daylight came, we couldn't dig anymore because the moment they saw us they'd start shelling again. It was during the day, a couple of rounds landed too close to the bunker and they ripped the whole side right out of it, so we weren't going to stay in something like that because it wasn't reliable enough. I'm not too clear as to the reason why we pulled out of there, but probably because it was too dangerous, would be my guess. We moved again and we went into Gracac, into the Medak Pocket.

THE MEDAK POCKET

There had just been a battle there. As the convoy moved closer and closer to the town, I'm not sure who was in the town to tell the Croatians that the UN was coming but when they found out they went through the town and raped everybody, they killed everybody and their animals.

Animals, people, you name it. They raped women, did awful things with their skin, and cut body parts off that you wouldn't think able to be taken off.

The closer we got to where we were going you could smell it. It wasn't the dead bodies that they had just killed; it was the bodies that were there from before and the animals that were dead for a long time, burning or whatever. Our job was to take over the defensive position so that when we moved in the Croat soldiers would get out and C Company was to take over the Serb position. As we were driving down, we deployed all three platoons. As we were driving through you could see the Serb soldiers with their binoculars, all watching, and the artillery, mortars and tanks standing by. The Croatians stopped the convoy, and they tried to pull "I'm the biggest and the strongest." They had a SAGGER [anti-armour missile] or some type of ATGM pointed at us and the OC said, "Take that TOW and point it at that tank!" Vrewwww! The TOW system operaters were like, "Go ahead! Make my day!" A few words were exchanged and then they let us go through.

We drove through a lot of woods, which was a big Croatian defensive position and there were a lot of field areas where they were dug in and they had their OP set up with stakes and plastic, stuff like that. They were burning their bunkers and it wasn't an amateur production. These guys had been at war for some time, so they knew how to build bunkers, and they used concrete slabs, not sandbags. They'd dig a hole, put concrete slabs down, put slab on for a roof, put sand over it and grow grass. That was a bunker for them. To me that was a lot better than using sandbags! The trench system was pretty basic, backhoe straight across and they had their bunker set up. Whatever they could use.

We saw some BTRs, BMPs, T-72s, T-64s, and T-62s. There were old T-54 chassis, turret and gun with a new IR system on it. Some said the Serb army was better equipped, some said the Croatian army was better equipped, I would say that they both looked pretty good and they looked like they were about to bang heads.

The Croatians had taken over this town, and it looked like the Serbs were consolidating, to go in and take back what was rightfully theirs. That's what it looked like from my point of view, from what I had seen. I didn't really know what was going on, I'm not that high up on the food chain, but to me it looked like they were getting ready to have at each other, and this was going to be the tie-breaker. When we pulled in the Croats threw up their hands and gave us the thumbs up, as they were glad to leave. I'm pretty sure it was the same on C Company's side with the Serbs, so maybe some of the Serbs didn't want to taste blood, I don't know but some of the Croatians did, some didn't. Some were really upset that we were pulling in because they really wanted to have a battle and you could hear gunfire as you drove up. They did a listening halt once and you could hear it after we had all our tracks stopped and it sounded like a massacre instead of a battle. You just know, especially after you picked up bodies and burnt animals, when you walk up to an animal and it doesn't stink yet that they just shot it and walked away.

As far as the town went, it wasn't a very large town. There were a lot of houses in one certain area with a few houses spaced sporadically around and it was like a farming community. We pulled in to one defensive position and we stayed there. In the farm house right next to us, there was a big field with a defensive position set up. Some parts were not dug very well, as they just used a backhoe. We followed it up and there were ammo boxes everywhere, which they filled with sand and used them as sandbags. Phone line, landline, and casings everywhere, and I also found live ammo, AK bullets, grenade propellant blanks, and grenades. I could smell the sickening odour of bodies rotting as well.

Dense woods surrounded us, there was one in front of the trench we took over. It was a large mound of dirt we thought might be a mass grave. It was a long field surrounded by woods. We were pretty sure that the defensive position that we were on was a mass grave as well. They started digging up bodies right there and then they stopped suddenly when they realized that the bodies were civilians. The one that they cut the leg off by accident was only a poor lowly farmer. They immediately brought in the white UN backhoe and they dug until they finally found all the bodies.

We were there for the rest of the tour, which was almost a month and the smell lingered forever. It's probably still there. Nobody freaked out. Actually, a friend of mine in the section thought he saw a flashlight roaming around and we said that we weren't going to wake up the section commander yet so we'd go and check it out. So we waited and watched, until finally the next team came on to take over our spot. We said, "You stay here on the gun while we go investigate," so we went over and checked out the area and it was stuff still burning from two weeks ago when we first got there. They set everything on fire, man. Everything was on fire and it burned and burned, I mean, even three weeks after we were there, there was still smoke coming out of buildings and stuff.

When we first got there we had to make sure that the area was sanitary to live in. I mean, you can't live in a place with guts and stuff lying all over so we went out and picked up guts. I don't think there was any human guts there, just animal guts as far as I know. I didn't notice any uniforms myself but I'm pretty sure it was just animal guts, as it was a farm. We picked up all the animal guts and it was rotting badly, so we doused it in naphtha and gas and burnt it all. The smell was just unreal, even after the smell of the rotting guts and then burning it and you didn't know which was worse! Then we had to bring Serb bodies in from the hills that had been executed for HQ to examine. One guy's face was totally ripped right off. I think there were seven bodies initially, but they were still finding them days after. I offered my services but they wouldn't let me go. They were still finding bodies well after we had gotten settled in, I mean they found a woman in a swamp, they found a woman in her home with her genitals cut off, a young lady and her daughter burnt to death; they had raped them, threw them in a barn and set it on fire. They found the mass graves of animals, lots of animals...

There was nothing you could do to prepare yourself for this. Nobody there was affected by it, really, as I haven't heard any of us committing suicide yet but I've heard of guys losing their appetite, not being able to sleep well, and getting nauseated by the smell every day. The smell was enough to knock a horse dead, especially with all the human bodies, I mean, that particular spot's going to smell because of the bodies under and above the ground for a long time. In the morning the fog would roll in and remove the smell but then the sun would come out, it would get hot and it would be there all over again.

One of the members from another company told me that his section commander came down to our area and felt sorry for us because we were living in such poor conditions and when he came back he smelt like that death, as he brought the smell back with him.

DEBRIEFING

We left the Medak Pocket and went back up toward Gracac, where we spent our last week there doing some defusing, and debriefing. We had our smoker [a party]; we cleaned our tracks, turned in our ammo, and our mags, all stuff that had to be turned in. We wore our flak vests and helmets on the bus to go to Zagreb, got the handshake, thanks for coming out. We did medals parade at an area near the school, where we were setting up a spot for A Company, I think, and

These M-113 crews from 2 PPCLI are clearly relieved after the completion of the Medak Pocket operation. Intervening to halt ethnic cleansing operations took a physical and psychological oll, but standing up to blatant brutality when the rest of the international community remained paralyzed was something Canadians should be proud of. (photo courtesy 2 PPCLI/LCol Shane Brennan)

Princess Patricia gave me my medal. Anyway, we got the handshake, speech, good reservists, and a pat on the back, and God love you and then we found out who was on Main 1, Main 2, and Advance Party. So we went to bed and got up in the morning to get on the bus to Zagreb, where we boarded the plane home. We made a quick stop in France before we arrived in Winnipeg. We stayed for three days, cleared out our rooms, got our papers squared away, turned in BFAs, slings and mags and then we got our barrack boxes, which were sent on ahead of us. After that we partied it up, had a shower the next day, got on the plane and went home.

We had a debrief where they discussed things like, marriage and stuff but nobody at the debriefing I was at was married. They were discussing stuff about wives and kids while a bunch of us were just sitting there looking at each other. "Are you married?" "I'm not!" "Why do this?" They had a defusing while we were over there up at C Company's area. They sent in a padre from Ottawa to debrief us and discuss things that we didn't like and stuff we liked and did we feel remorse or anything like that. They went overboard. Nobody felt like they were going to go home and cut their mother's heart out or anything. As far as I could see, everybody was all right, fine. Everybody had a good sense of humour, black humour, because it is the best humour in these situations ... For example, the guys racing down the mountain with dead bodies were having contests, having a good laugh while they were doing it, trying to keep their sanity and it was the only way they were going to do it. I know right now if anybody had seen that on TV, they'd curse the army, and try to have us all committed into a nunnery here or whatever.

To unwind over there we got two beers per day, perhaps, if they felt like giving it to us and we had wine left over from the French. Every now and again we'd sit in the track, if nobody could see us, and have a few sips of that, or beer if we could get it or a bag of paprika chips. The guys within the section would talk about this stuff? Oh yeah, we joked around about it, typical TV-type humour. We didn't discuss it deeply into the psyche or anything but we looked around a little bit, had some fun with it and carried on.

MEDIA COVERAGE

I'd rather there would be no media coverage of what's going on over there. The press tried to come in once when we were in Sector West. They were going the wrong way, leaving the UNPA going into Serb territory with Croatian plates on the car, so we had to stop and inform them that with this car you'd best go back the other way and find another way in or out. If you don't you're likely to get hurt. They were like, "Why? How come?" "Because your plates are Croatian and they're Serbs where you're going," so he went back.

EQUIPMENT AND TRAINING IN RETROSPECT

Our APCs didn't have any problems but there was one section that had one that almost went off the road in the Krajinas because the drive sprocket broke on them. We would have rather had Bisons, I tell you, as it would have been ideal over there because we spent more time on roads than off. We spent 98% of our time on roads with the tracks so we would have rather had Bisons or Grizzlys or whatever. I don't think I had any problems depending on them, but they're old. In terms of modifications, some guys, like12 Platoon, had the turrets for the C-9s on the tracks, the ones with the .50 cal on them, but we never had them.

In terms of training, we should have had a lot less section attacks but a lot more defensives, and more FIBUA. We had dug a backstop and we were training for offensive when we were going to be in a defensive role. They say defensive is an easier thing to get into, you dig a hole, get in it, send out patrols, and set up mines.

PERSONAL THOUGHTS

The most exhilarating thing for me? There were certain times when we had to go, like in Lipik, and they found some stuff in a house that the Serbs got all in an uproar about because we were going to take it away from them and they didn't want us to. So they had a large armed mob there and we had our company there with their helmets, flack jackets and rifles and we were ready to lock horns and when the Sergeant Major said "Lock and load!" we locked and loaded and were ready to fight. There were many times, like when we were bringing bodies off the hill or filling bags or just a whole bunch of different times when I felt like a soldier.

Coming home was a big change, but nonetheless you adapted and overcame. I knew I was back in Canada when I had a toilet that flushed and the first thing I did was get into civvy clothes, rather than the Queen's Green. When I got home, for a while there, I was looking for my rifle and boots when I'd wake up. That was just normal stuff for anybody in the habit, but I don't recall any nightmares. I gave my girlfriend four trenches one night! "Here are four trenches!" I don't know! I don't remember any nightmares or anything, but she might have misunderstood what I said, as I was talking in my sleep. She said I talked in my sleep for the longest time but I don't remember any bad dreams and I don't recall any cold sweat wake-ups or freaking out. I just picked up a habit; I'd get up really early in the morning.

I'd do it again. There is a mission for the UN but maybe they should wait awhile to let the Yugoslavians bring themselves out before they go back in. I'm just a nobody, know what I mean? Myself? I never really paid much attention to anything there, as I was just there. It's kind of crappy to say that, I wasn't there for humanitarian reasons, I mean, a lot of guys were there for the money or for their stamps or whatever but I was there because I wanted to get out of Canada for a while, go on a tour, and see what it was like, to see if it was going to be what I expected. It was what I expected, hard work, and hurry up and wait.

CHAPTER FOURTEEN

CORPORAL ADAM SMITH

Rifleman, 2nd Bn Princess Patricia's
Canadian Light Infantry Battalion Group
Sector West and Sector South, Croatia, 1993

INTO ZAGREB AND DARUVAR

I came home for five days, for embarkation leave, and then I went back and I left on the 7th of April, one of the last to leave. We came into Zagreb and a number of guys started some rumours, "Oh I see bombed out buildings" and stuff like that, which wasn't true. Zagreb was barely touched when we got there and was standing, strong as it ever was. The first thing that we noticed when we started to land was that there were two fighter jets at the airport, sort of in the trees a bit, and that was kind of interesting. The guys took pictures. I think they were MiGs but I'm not sure. Then we hopped on buses and drove to where our position would be in Sector West. It was just outside Daruvar, which wasn't too far away, about one and a half to two hours away.

There were quite a few people around, and the scenery changed, as we got closer to our position. Finally we reached Camp Polom, and as we pulled in, the buildings started to have bullet holes in them, roofs missing, and flat buildings. Then we got on MLs to drive us out to our position, and just looking out the back of the ML, we saw many flattened buildings.

SECTOR WEST

Our area was in good shape and we had AQUA trailers. 3 PPCLI was there before us, and they had everything already set up, showers etc., so it was pretty good. Before I went over I expected to get off the plane, throw on our helmets and start running! I thought it would be like Bosnia, like you saw in the news, with bombing and stuff like that and it wasn't. I was quite surprised. It was like the war was pretty much over as far as we could see. It was relaxed but there was still tension there, because we were new and didn't know what to expect.

3 PPCLI's Rear Party left when we got there but we didn't have a chance to talk to them. Some guys stayed back for a second tour and they said it was a little different than when they were there before, more firefights and stuff like that between the Serbs and the Croatians.

That night, actually, I was in the bathroom when somebody threw open the door and said, "Is anybody in here?" I said "Yeah." He said, "Well get out here and get your shit on." A round just went through Stamp's window. Stamp was a 3rd Battalion guy who stayed back for another tour, and I sort of thought to myself, "Christ, this is the first day and we're already coming under fire," and I could just imagine being under fire and we had six months to go! I just went with my section commander who said, "Get over here!" and he told us, "I want you over here, you over there." He put me behind the ML, watching the front gate with two other guys. But everybody was out in positions, on vehicles and stuff looking through NVGs, the whole bit, and a NODLER was up on the roof. What had happened was Stamp, he had an accidental discharge and shot his own window out, but when somebody asked, he didn't want to get into trouble and so he said that a round came in so everybody was pretty pissed. After that, nothing really happened except that we started filling sandbags, making bunkers, firing walls, and fortifying the area.

SECTOR WEST: CHECKPOINTS

We initially located in a camp called callsign 4, which was our Company HQ and the reserve platoon, which was us, was located there. Then there were two other platoon positions, Y 17 and Y 14. One section was security for our position, another section did patrols and the last section did GDs, [General Duties], which was anything from washing dishes, filling sandbags, or fortifying, which is what we started doing. We hastily made a wall that was 30 feet long and 7 feet high with firing ports and then small bunkers, more walls, and stuff. Barbed wire was already up when we got there and we didn't have to do anything about that.

The next week we started doing patrols. We also did mobile checkpoints, where you just pulled up the carrier, blocked the road, stopped all vehicles and searched them. We did foot patrols during the day. The carrier would stop and three or four guys would get out, the carrier would go 5 kilometres down the road while we would just walk along the road, through the town and keep an eye out. We were watching for anybody carrying weapons. In Sector West, only the police were allowed to carry any kind of weapons and they were only allowed to carry pistols. The only way they were allowed to carry pistols was if they had their police ID on them and if they didn't have their police ID, we took their pistols and filled out a form. If you didn't have it on you, that pistol was mine so we'd take it, and lock it up in the back of the track, and they'd either come and get it or they weren't really police. A lot of them came back and said, "This is my ID," and we'd give it back. The thing is, what really made us mad was that nobody in our platoon really ever got to seize anything from anybody that they hadn't gotten back. It was always police that didn't have any ID.

Eventually we did get something. We stopped a car at a checkpoint and ordered everybody out. Anyway, these guys got out and this thing fell to the ground. Nobody took notice of it, they heard it but they thought it was some piece of garbage. They searched those guys and they had pistols on them and they weren't police, because by this time you sort of knew most of the police. We, said, "Do you have ID?" "No, No, No" so we said, "Okay fine, we're taking the pistols" but as one of our guys was searching the passenger, he noticed what had fallen down. He picked it up, looked at it and he said, "Holy Shit!" Our section commander said, "What is it?" It was a silencer for a pistol but the thing was, the pistols that they had with them didn't fit it so somewhere, this guy had something else, but it wasn't on the vehicle and it wasn't on them. Our section was the first one out of the platoon to make a seizure and everybody was pretty mad at us because we were the first ones.

We had one carrier, and an Iltis at first. We had an Iltis parked on one side of the road, and another on the other side, angled toward each other, so that if a car came up, it would have to make an 'S' to get through. Of course, you'd stop it between the two, search it and let them go or whatever. The Iltis was also used in case somebody saw us and tried to turn around and take off. The tracks are just too slow and too old, and the Iltis isn't much better.

On those things, we don't arrest, we just write down the licence plate number, name and type of car, so that if he ever stops later they can get him, like, they used to print out these sheets to take with you on checkpoint, so that if this car was on the list, you made sure that you checked it thoroughly because it had already been stopped.

The track drivers were behind the .50s just in case something strange happened and they also wrote down the information. There was one guy covering, one guy searching and then there was the section commander and the 2IC, in case anything happened. There were two searchers, since you searched two cars at the same time, one car coming from one way and another coming from the other and traffic was heavy. Sometimes we had lineups of cars. The thing was there was a gas shortage too, so every once and awhile when they got their ration of gas, everybody, for some reason, would get in their car and start driving. Sometimes there was a lot of traffic, and other times there was nothing.

We were involved in chases sometimes. One time we were beside an old factory and it just happened that at this point it was in the second month before we started to rotate within our company. It all rotated so that everybody had a break but they wanted us to use two tracks now, because they were starting to get scared that something would happen, and there was a lot of talk that the Croatians were getting mad at us for stopping them all the time, so we were using two tracks. We were right beside this factory and it just happened that beside the road at the junction into the factory, there was almost like a storm drain but it was covered with a grate and some of the bars were missing. There was only a gap of about a foot and a half wide so this guy came barrelling around the corner, they all drive like idiots, saw us, just slammed on the brakes and tried to turn around. Of course, with tracks, there was no way we were going to catch him. When he tried to turn around he hit where the grate was missing and he got his tires stuck, and the section commander said, "You guys, stop that car and make sure they don't go anywhere!" so the guys ran up and they started searching it, because they were mad that he was trying to run our checkpoint, and this guy had grenades in his trunk, AK-47 ammo, and he had an AK-47.

NOOSES IN THE WOODS

We were told to clear a wood for mine clearance but what in fact we were supposed to be looking for was mounds in the dirt, like unmarked graves. Our section commander and the guy that was close to him found a large mound of dirt and there were pieces of clothing scattered here and there, like little kids' shoes and stuff like that, so they marked it. Then he turned around, I think he was going to the bathroom or something, he just happened to look up in the tree and there was a noose still hanging from the tree. Then they started to look around, like, what the hell was this all about? There was a stump that was stained, which we assumed was blood, and there was another stained tree with bullet holes in it, which we figured that they threw somebody up against and shot them, threw them in a hole, covered them up and carried on. There was a road and there were houses lining the road but nobody lived there, everything was empty, and everything was gone. We were wondering where the hell did these people go? Well, we later found out that was where the people were. They had just been killed and thrown in the hole. This was a Croatian area, so those people were Croatian or they could be either, because everybody lived together.

JOHNNY ONE-FINGER AND THE RCMP KID

We used to give stuff to the kids in Sector West. They lived in the hills, 10 kilometres away, and you could just see their house through the binoculars. They used to walk down to see us and we'd talk to them, and teach them English. There were two girls and a boy, brother and sisters and they'd come down after their parents had picked a whole bunch of cherries, plums and stuff for us or made us turnovers, so we'd give them milk, bread, or money just to help them out as much as we could. I remember a track driver in my section, gave the little boy an RCMP patch that he brought back off leave, just for him so the kid was proud of it and he wore it. He came back down two days later without it and a big bruise on his head. The Serb police had beaten him up because he wore the RCMP patch with a Canadian flag on it and they hated anybody who talked to us.

We used to have this guy on his bicycle everyday that had a deformed hand, where his two fingers were grown together or something, and it looked like a big toe was on the end of it. We called him "Johnny One-Finger." He could speak English; I guess 3rd Battalion had talked to him all the time and he used to sell us all kinds of stuff, anything he could get his hands on to sell us to make some money for himself, like belts, and I bought one. We'd stop and ask how he was doing, "Any work today Johnny?" "Yes, I work all fucking day!" and we'd laugh because a Serb speaking English is one thing but when he swears in English it's funny! He used to carry four belts done up and he'd walk behind the WC, take them off, give them to us and say, "Tomorrow I'll pick up the money," and then he'd bike away. The police were always watching us to make sure that nobody would talk to us; they used to chase away the kids now and again saying, "Get away from those people!"

SURPRISE MOVE TO SECTOR SOUTH

I was near Lipik until I went on leave, my seventeen-day leave on the 29th of July. We moved part way through June and we weren't there a full two months but the plan was to move while I was on leave, so I was pretty happy about that. I went and visited my parents in France and my girlfriend came over to visit me, and then I went back on the 14th, as my leave was over on the 15th. I took the train back to Vienna to pick up the bus and drive back down. When I got to the train station in Vienna, I met up with everybody else who had the same leave date. I was talking to another guy in my Company and he said, "You know we moved, eh?" Of course it was time to rotate through, and we were supposed to go to Y 14, so I said, "Oh yeah, they planned on it." He said, "No, no, we've moved." I said, "What do you mean we moved?" He said, "We moved down south." I said " Like, down south where?" They were talking before that we might have to move down to Sarajevo in case we had to help whoever it was down there, I think it was the Van Doos, to help them out to escort convoys, and nobody really liked that idea because along with that was the rumour that we'd be there longer than six months. So, I was like, "Where down south?" and he said, "I don't know, I just heard over the radio that 2nd Battalion will move down south." I was like, "Oh Shit!"

We got to Camp Polom on the bus, and we sat there for four days until they organized a bus to ship all the guys on leave down to where the battalion was, so we got our kit, because they filled sea containers with everybody's non-essential stuff and all the guys' kit who were on leave, our webbing, flak jackets, etc. What I'd done was what everybody had been doing before when they went on leave, you'd take all your laundry and throw it into the laundry system, so that when you got back, everything was clean and you knew where everything was. When I got to Camp Polom my laundry was not in the sea container and nobody knew where my stuff was! All four sets of my combats were in there, all my socks, etc. What the hell was I going to do? They said to go down to the [regimental quartermaster] and it would be there. Well, our [company quartermaster] had come up the day before we got there and took all our laundry down, so all my stuff was down south and I was sitting in Camp Polom with my shorts and a T-shirt on with my New York baseball cap and my sneakers. So I had to sign out combats and stuff like that. Finally we got to move down south.

On the bus ride down, you sort of slept, listened to your Walkman but we noticed that we kept stopping at checkpoints as we moved further and further south. The checkpoints became more and more fortified. At first it was just a checkpoint with a barrier, a couple of Croatians or a couple of Serbs, and we noticed, "Hey, they've got AK-47s!" which in Sector West weren't allowed, and then as we went on it was, "Look, they have mines here!" They'd just push the mines out of the way and the bus would go through. As we moved even further along, there was anti-aircraft [artillery], tanks, the whole bit. I was starting to think, "Where the fuck are we going?" We'd been used to nothing happening but we finally got down there, and met up with the rest.

SECTOR SOUTH: WAR ZONE

We were just inland from Zadar, which is right on the coast, close to a town called Obrovac. It was about 50 kilometres from the coast and about a little less than that from Bosnia on the other side so we finally got into the routine down there. There was one platoon and it was pretty much the same thing at first, one platoon was in the rear, sort of R and R, and every four days, we'd rotate through. There was a platoon in the rear, and then you drove through Obrovac onto this hill. We called it "The School" because there was an old bombed-out school there, where there was a platoon sort of in depth there; next a platoon forward and we had to man an OP on the top of a hill to just watch and mark down artillery fire, mortar fire, MG fire, anything we could see. So we started doing that for four days, then we'd rotate. The only big difference at this point between Sector West and Sector South was the artillery. They were still bombing the shit out of each other here and there was nothing, no control whatsoever. In the other places everything was by the book, and nobody carried anything. In this place, we saw guys carrying machine guns, etc., and tanks would roll by, but all we could do was sit and watch.

At that point we were observing the Serbian side. The Serbians had pulled up along the Maslenica Bridge, which had a lot of coverage; it was a big bridge and an important crossing point. Before the war it was a resort place, and people had cottages but now the hillsides were black from fire. Some places had people, and some were great wide areas that were flat. The

In addition to existing stockpiles, both sides in the Croatian war relied on improvised weapons systems like this Krajinan Serb rocket launcher photographed in Sector South by Canadian troops. (photo courtesy of 2 PPCLI/LCol Shane Brennan)

school was standing, well, most of it was standing, the buildings around it, some were standing, and all were missing roofs, all were burned out. All the walls were brick and we slept underneath the stairs. All we were doing was sitting there and watching artillery fire back and forth, marking down where it landed, and where it came from.

You could see tanks moving in the distance, and then every once in awhile a couple of wheeled carriers would go by. Obrovac was a leave centre for the Serbs, where guys would come off the line. Everybody in the place, except for the women, wore camouflage, so you'd drive through the town and they were friendly enough, some of them would wave, while others would scowl, and there were hundreds of them. Obrovac was in a gorge with straight rock faces on either side. It was a beautiful little town on the river. The reason they picked it, we found out later, was because it was almost impossible to get artillery to fall on it and they tried and tried but nothing would fall in. You'd get some that would hit the side and rocks would fall down into the river but never in the town, so we sat back and watched artillery fall. I guess the thing that impressed me the most was the MRL, multiple rocket launcher system, and you'd just hear "Thupthupthupthup", wait, and hear "Wump wump wump wump" in a straight line. Wow!

I found enough of my kit so that I could get by, and I found my sleeping bag because they kept that in the track. I was on shift talking to the boys, telling them what my leave was like, and then that night I was on OP, which was two hours on two hours off, and there were four guys total. Of course I had never seen these guys as they had already been there a couple of weeks and all this was usual for them but I just sort of sat there with the NVGs on, looking around, and I saw artillery going off and landing, machine-gun fire, etc.

The Serbs had an artillery position about 500 metres behind us, and I had already been warned that at 0800 this stuff started to go off, so I was like, "Okay." At 0800, K-BOOM! and they only fired a few times because they didn't want counter-battery fire. I was like, "Holy Shit!" you know, because it was quite loud, and the boys were all laughing, calling me "cherry" and all this stuff because they had been there two whole weeks and I just got there. Eventually it all just became day-to-day stuff.

SECTOR SOUTH II: THE SHELLING CONTINUES

When we were at the school, we'd move back when our platoon moved into the rear for four days off, and I remember 11 Platoon was directly at the school and 10 Platoon was in depth, and we had been there for so long, we were ordered to start filling sandbags, as they decided to build a bunker, so we'd have somewhere to run if artillery ever fell on us. So twenty-four hours a day for three days we filled sandbags, constantly rotating people, twelve hours on, got to a pit and start filling. You'd go back to sleep, or whatever, and the next guys came in filling sandbags, all night with no lights because if we had lights on, we'd get fired on. The people that were at the school were 11 Platoon and 10 Platoon – no, I guess, this was the time where 11 Platoon was fixed and they were staying right at the school. We had moved to the other side of Obrovac to an old farmhouse, that we started to clean up, and 10 Platoon was just down the road from us. They were building a bunker as we filled sandbags and we never saw the bunker until later. They made a count of how many sandbags it took and this was the biggest bunker that I had ever seen. Just huge, the walls were five feet deep and, luckily enough, we built it. I think the count was either five or seven days that the guys at the school were shelled directly.

We weren't exactly sure, but we assumed that both sides shelled the school. Some of it would be like Boom! going off and Boom! it would land and weren't sure who was firing at us. So our company commander decided, to hell with it, we'd stay there, keep soldiering, as he put it, but when the CO of the battalion found out, he pulled them back. He went over the company commander's head and said, "You get those fucking guys out of there before somebody dies!" It was just stupid. He was trying to be mister cowboy and keep his guys there. The CO pulled everybody back, including us, way out of the way back towards where we were in the rear the first time and there we sat for almost a month.

We sat there because the CO thought it was too dangerous to go forward until it died down and it was about a month before we were able to finally move. That was just the beginning of September, about half a month after we were there, so when we finally got to move, they had finally gone ahead and said this is where 12 Platoon will be, this is where 11 Platoon is going to be, and so on.

We got lucky. We moved right onto the coast near this backwater, into a tiny town, and they told us nothing had happened in over a year. It wasn't very far from the school, so right away we didn't believe them. Those houses that we moved into were untouched, and a lot of guys got beds, instead of air mattresses, camp cots, or chairs. A lot of the building had been looted and the good stuff was gone, but beds were still there and stuff. Most of the guys had beds at first and then as we put up wire and we started to make more bunkers, then they sort of said, let's go into this house next door and get some more guys some beds. So mostly everybody had beds but a few people didn't because they couldn't find one.

SECTOR SOUTH: A NEW ROUTINE

Then we got another routine going. We built an OP and our job was to watch the Maslenica Bridge that was now destroyed and replaced with a pontoon bridge instead. All we had to do, for some unknown reason, was to count how many cars going east, and how many cars going west, but just normal, everyday vehicles. This was through binoculars to see them, eh? And we also had to take shellreps down, watch where the artillery fell and all that.

The Serbs and the Croatians had a routine themselves. In the morning they'd fire until about 1100 or so and then it got too hot, so they all went inside to drink slipovich, which is this homemade brandy. It's disgusting stuff! About 1600-1700 when it started to cool down a bit, they'd come back out and fire some more, then they would go in and eat, so there was another big gap and then they'd start firing when it got dark and fire all night. Just bomb the hell out of each other.

About our second day we got small-arms fire, which they fired into the dead ground in front of the OP, only 10 rounds or so and that scared us a bit, as it was only 50 metres in front of us and we called that in. Of course, our platoon commander didn't believe us. "Nobody would fire at us. We're UN!" I guess he was hard in the head, and he didn't learn much. Anyway, he came out, looked around, and said that if it happened again to call it in and he'd come out and see if we were lying or not. About our second-last day, it was the usual thing, artillery fire, and we tried to see if we could see the splash, which we did sometimes, but our second day, a tank battle started and the Serbian tank was about a klick in front of us hidden inside some buildings, like it had driven through it or it was in bushes and trees. Then we saw the muzzle flash from a Croatian tank, which was across a little inlet and you couldn't actually see the tank itself but you could see the muzzle flashes as it fired back. So they were going back and forth and back and forth and then the Croatian tank overshot the Serbian one and we saw the muzzle flash and then you could hear the round coming in towards the Serb tank, it sort of whistled a bit, but this one flashed and there was no sound. Where the hell did it go? All of sudden we heard this SWOOSH! right over our heads and it just kept going. We were like, "Holy Fuck!" So we got on the radio and just as I started to talk, we heard it explode and I said, "Did that land near you guys?" All I heard on the other end was, "Oh yeah!" It overshot them by 200 metres, and it was just luck that it didn't hit anything. They were wondering where the hell it came from. It was neat.

DESCENT INTO HELL: THE MEDAK POCKET

About a week later, we were told that we were going to move again, which of course everybody just laughed at. By this time we had moved around so much that nobody cared, they couldn't fuck us any more because we had 2 PPCLI written on our asshole. They just laughed and said, "Sure!" They then said that we were going to Medak. Everybody was like, "Okayy, where's that?" Nobody knew where the hell that was, so we moved and we were told we were taking over from the Croatians, right out of their trenches, and we had seen defensive positions and stuff in Sector West, so it was like, yeah, okay. As we pulled in, finally, because we couldn't get through the lines at first, the Croatians didn't want us in, and we didn't know why, but we realized later that it was because their sweep team hadn't finished picking up all the mess.

The whole company moved plus the TOW launchers. We had TOW just in case. Then there were medics and stuff like that. It was a good distance. Of course carriers don't move very quickly, and it was a four-hour drive. The checkpoint slowed us down even more, at least an hour. It was so frustrating, as we were right there. As we moved between the lines, we had gone through the Serbian checkpoint with no problem, they just said, go ahead, because they wanted us to get there so that the Croatians would stop bombing and shelling them. As we moved between the lines, we noticed that there were vehicles that went out on the low ground, anti-aircraft, stuff like that, carriers, large calibre machine guns, and they was impressive. Of course I had run out of film and I was pissed off. Then we were stopped.

So finally we got through this checkpoint, and we moved on. As we were pulling in along this dirt road I started noticing on the side roads there were Croatian carriers, tanks, arty, hasty arty positions, and guys with mortars, and I was like, "Holy Shit!" As we moved further and further into their position, buildings were still being burned, and they were still blowing up their bunkers so we couldn't use them. Then we started noticing dead animals, and the smell was just disgusting. Those guys, I guess, were bored or something, so they just started levelling everything, and any animal that moved, they shot. As we were moving through, I was thinking like, "This is it." I didn't think that I was actually going to make it out. Those Croat guys were still in their positions and we were just waiting for the Serbs to start attacking, or them to start attacking the Serbs. I was thinking, "We're fucked!"

You know, this is what I anticipated when I left Winnipeg but it had been so diluted that when the tour went on I forgot and didn't expect it. So, anyway, we pulled in and it took the dead animals and stuff to bring it all home, a black horse was nudging a horse that was already dead, and I just sort of looked and shook my head. It was one of those things that was so sad. Our CSM went out with an apple and the horse came right over to him. It was so weird because it was so trusting, here in the middle of a battlefield, and the Croats they had just shot its friend, so anyway, they named him Lucky because he was the only animal alive that we had found so far. We took over, when most of the Croatian carriers were leaving, moving back further, and then it took three days for all the Croatians to get out. We found out later that they had over a company sitting up over the hills above us.

We set up just along this trail. There were little villages around us but I believe we had already gone through Medak. There was no sign to say that this was Medak, but I believe that was what it was. It was burnt out, some buildings which where still standing had been taken over by Croatians. It was pretty much flat, fields and stuff like that, and it was all mined.

We pulled our carriers into the bushes and tried to hide them, like you can hide a white carrier! We started to dig trenches, in case the old ones that were there were on somebody's pre-plotted artillery map or mined. Our leadership decided to send people from every platoon together up along this trail into the hills to tell the company that was up there to leave. As they went up this trail, which was insanely steep, they started meeting people on the way and they were like patting them on the back. They said, "No, no, no, you can't step off! Boom!" They had mined everything and nobody knew exactly where, as they don't mark them down right. Within three days, everybody came down. As the planned shift of our guys came off the hill, we had new guys go up. As the new guys were going up, they started noticing things in the woods, and at first they didn't realize but it later turned out that there were dead bodies, Serbs. The Croatians had used them as pack mules, loaded them up with kit, marched them at gunpoint up to the top of the hill and told them to put down all the stuff, so the Serbs dropped everything, and then the Croats just shot them and rolled them down the hill.

I don't know what the count was, it was close to ten right along the trail, more elsewhere, guys just shot twice in the chest. We had taken the bodies and put them in body bags, and brought them off the hill, loaded them onto an ML, and then taken them back to where the UN hospital was where they did autopsies on them to see exactly how they were killed. One guy that they hauled off was missing almost his entire head and they said he was shot almost fifty times at point blank range in the head. Those guys were just shooting them just for something to do after they used them, shot them a couple times until they were dead and shot them more times for fun. Then we started finding civilians, one old woman they called the "Little Old Lady from Pasadena," and we had to name them so we would all know which ones they were, so anyway, she was missing. She was shot twice in the chest, four times in the back, and either one of her legs or arms, and her vagina had been cut open. She'd been beaten and everything, and the boys were just like, how could you possibly do that to someone? She was 70 years old. Then they found a mother and her daughter in a chicken coop, we'd assumed they had been raped, beaten and then from their waists down they had been burnt.

I was driving the track ambulance with the medics. They didn't have a track and driver, so I lucked out but I wasn't allowed to go anywhere in case something happened somewhere else. So I just sat back and watched. Our guys had to pass us because we were the furthest north of the hill and so they had to walk past us to drop the bodies off. The smell, I'll never forget it.

We were there until almost the middle of October, just a month. It didn't get any better. We went around with gasoline and burnt all the dead animals to cut down on disease, and then our guys started finding mounds of freshly turned dirt, so they thought there is nobody around here, so it must be mass graves. The leadership called in a backhoe from the camp 50 kilometres away from us so it came out and started digging it up and found dead cows. Of course for some reason they buried dead cows, but nobody could understand, until somebody thought, what if they killed a lot of people, buried them, threw some dead cows on top and buried the dead cows, people would dig up the dead cows and think, just dead cows are buried here. So, the backhoe scooped the old, disgusting, smelly, dead cows out and that's all we found, no dead bodies. Nobody could really explain it. Every morning whenever we got up, there was the same smell. The weather would push all the air down and the smell would all stay there and as the day grew on, and heated up, it would be less of a smell but the wind would blow a certain way and you could smell it, dead animals a klick away in the woods somewhere, whatever it was. The smell was still in our combats even after they had been washed.

We were there for three weeks before anybody could even have a shower and because we had just got up and moved, everybody's stuff was already dirty. So for three weeks we had no bathroom facilities, it was just a shovel in the woods. The Croatians that were there weren't that sanitary, they just sort of went in the woods, went to the bathroom, and just left it right there. So there was that smell, dead bodies, dirt, everybody was just so dirty, nobody cared anymore, and it was just the hell of it. I developed a rash before we moved so I had a no-shaving chit. I was lucky. We didn't know when we would get water; we could shave every other day, so personal hygiene was up to you.

Surprisingly, morale wasn't too bad. The guys just didn't care anymore they just laughed and joked, and pretended they weren't there, and it was only so long before we got to go home, and that was all they thought about, all they talked about, only twenty more days, whatever.

MEDAK: THE FRENCH ENGINEERS

The thing that I remember the most was around the 15th of September, probably later, the medics and I slept beside the track ambulance so that we didn't have anything to put away. If we got a call we could just get in and drive, and everybody was told, sleep in your combats with your boots on, rifle and everything in case something happened, just get up and run. So, we got this call about 0200, about two French engineers, one had come back, crawled into his CP with his legs blown apart. We said, "Holy shit, what happened? What happened?" and he said, "We hit a mine." Who? You and who? He said, "Dree," which was the other guy's name, and we asked, "Where was he?" and he just sort of waved his hand and passed out, because he had lost so much blood. So they called us in, to come patch this guy up, as they were only an engineer platoon and they had no medics. The box ambulance went, patched this guy up and ran him into the hospital, and we were sent out with the track to look for the other guy. They didn't know where he was, but they had a basic idea he was on the road, so we went with our OC and our CSM, who were driving in their Iltis, and a TOW missile launcher – for the night vision capability – and we began searching.

We were driving through this field, because they thought that he was on the other side, the CSM and the OC were sitting beside me saying things like go slow, stop here we're going to shut it off, yell and see if we can hear him, and shoot paraflares. As we were driving through this field, the OC was talking to his French counterpart, who was with us, who said, "Be careful of this track because this place is a minefield!" So I was like, "Oh Christ!" It was starting to rain, of course, it's 0300, I just woke up and now I had to look out for mines.

Well, the headlights were on so I could see the track, and it was just like a farmer's track, but it was narrow enough that I had to be careful so I didn't drive off it, so we drove up along the track, as those other French carriers were looking in different places and the TOW was behind us, searching with its thermal sight, when we pulled up to where these old houses used to be, and where we had to stop, there was a barricade with a string across, with a sign that said "Mines!" So I was like, "Oh great!"

They all got off and left me by myself, and the TOW had stopped about 500 metres behind me, searching, because it was all wood. They walked across the barrier and up the track. As I sat there with a flashlight looking around, I knew I wouldn't be able to find him, but I was looking anyway, all of a sudden – because we were going back towards the Croatians again – I didn't realize how close we were – but obviously we were too close and they opened up on us. They opened up on the carrier because it was still running and the headlights were on. Those rounds came close enough but didn't hit the track and you could hear them go by so I dropped inside, got on the radio, and told them that we had come under fire. They said, "Where are you?" I looked at the map, and where we were was not on the map; the map was small, and we were where it was cut off just like somebody had taken a pair of scissors and cut it off the map, so I was like, "Well, I don't know where we are." Luckily enough the OC, the CSM and the medic came running back, as they had come under fire. They came back to make sure nothing had happened, got in, and relayed everything that had happened. We pulled back and by this point they said, well, he's not here, but what they did was send the TOW on a side track to search, because if he were still alive he'd be throwing off heat. We went back to the [French] engineer's place and the OC said, "Go back to sleep and we'll wake you up if anything happens."

We finally fell fall asleep and twenty minutes later, the TOW came on the radio saying they found him so we all got back in, drove back out to where the TOW was, which wasn't very far from where we were driving on the side track. The only reason they found him was because they shut everything down and they could hear him screaming. By now it was about 0500 so we started off with a pioneer that we picked up, the OC, the CSM, the medic and myself driving on this trail through the minefield. The pioneer went ahead of everybody, looking for tripwires and saying, "Here's an anti-tank mine," and he'd mark it, and mark the trail as he went. We came across tripwires, so everybody backed up and lay down. The pioneer searched the mine for the tripwire because the Serbs and the Croatians take a bouncing betty mine, put one on one end of the mine, take the tripwire, and put one on the other end. Then what they would do was take the tripwires from more mines and tie it to that tripwire and do them in series, so that if you tripped one, the whole place went up and nobody was coming out.

So he searched it, and there were just the two, one on each end. He came back to the trail, we all lay down and he cut it. Nothing, luckily. He pulled back the wires and kept on going, came across another one, which had one more trip wire coming off it, so the same thing, we all backed up far enough away so that if they do blow, he was the only one to get it. He cut it and we waited: nothing. He pulled the wires back and we kept going. We got half way through the field when the engineers called us to come back, so the OC, the CSM and the pioneer turned around and went back. The engineers came out with mine detectors, stuff like that, so we finally got to the guy and the guy's platoon commander came out so that he could talk to him and relay to us where he was, and translate. We screamed to him saying, "Where are you? Where are you?" as we were getting closer and closer to the wood line, and he said, "I'm in a clearing," so we were thinking, okay, he's somewhere between here and the woods. We got to the wood, and there was nothing. We could hear him in the woods, as there were thin woods on the other side and another field, so we thought that maybe he was on the other side in the other field.

The engineers were walking through, and he was screaming, "Hurry up! Hurry up! I can't feel my legs!" The engineers were moving forward and they told him to scream again so we could hear and get a bead on him, and he was screaming and screaming and then he stopped to get his breath. It was kind of funny, but it was kind of spooky also when he stopped. The French translator said, "You want me to ask him to scream again?" and the second engineer, not the guy who was on the point, said, "Yeah, you'd better," then the guy up front said, "No forget it." "Why?" "I just stepped on him." He was right in the middle of the wood.

What had happened, was that those two guys were about 2.5 kilometres from their CP, they had no flak jackets, no radio, no rifles, no nothing. Now we were told, and it was an everyday thing, you don't go anywhere without your flak jacket. If you went out very far, you'd take at least your webbing, helmet, rifle and a radio. They were in the middle of the woods, and the only thing that we could think of was that they were either out here to do drugs or they were queer. Anyway, they had left their CP at 1800 the night before, walked along this trail, found three mines, which they just disarmed and kept going until they finally hit this one. The guy in the back, who was lying there when we found him, was holed from his waist down, except for his nuts; he just got lucky. The medic cut off his underwear, looked and made sure, turned to the translator, and said, "Tell him he's a very lucky man." The guy actually laughed and then he started crying again because he was in so much pain. The only reason he was alive was because it was so cold and rainy, that he had gone into hypothermia and stopped bleeding. He had two holes in his ribs, two in his arms, and one in his eye. Steve Akins, the medic from 1 Field Ambulance, was doing a pupil check, and he did one and it changed, did the other and it never moved, did it again and it didn't move. He changed the angle of his penlight and he just caught the piece of shrapnel. His iris was perfectly round except for one side that came out a bit; there was no entry wound or anything, it was just right there but he'll never see again. So we patched him up and while we did so the engineers cleared a route out. We picked him up on a backboard and loaded him on to the box ambulance to come back because it was faster than the track and they took off to the hospital and from what I understand, he went from there, took as much shrapnel out of him as they could, then he went to Zagreb where they operated on him again and then they flew him to Paris. That was the last we ever heard of him.

Oh yeah, It was one of those things where I came back, sat by myself and sort of thanked God, because just recently those guys from 1 PPCLI that went over were driving along a road with one carrier, a jeep, and another jeep and the last jeep hit a mine. Everybody just drove over it and Bang! It didn't matter if you were first or last, so I was sitting by myself, thanking God that it was over. It was quite a night.

STRESS DEBRIEFING CAMP

Then one week before we came home we moved back into a camp the battalion set up so that we could clean all our stuff and our weapons, did ammo verification, and then got the tracks ready for the handover. People were getting ready to go on Advance Party to go home. I was in main body so we cleaned the tracks inside and out, made sure there was no rust, which was on everything, and everybody's weapons were rusty. We weren't allowed to have mud on our kit, because we weren't supposed to bring it back, and we had one week of relaxed stuff where we did stress debriefings, and padres came in from Ottawa to make sure none of us were crazy.

They said that one out of ten had combat stress. Everybody was around each other for so long that if they changed during that period, it was a gradual change, so nobody really noticed it. So if you were screwed up by the end of the tour, to everyone else you were normal, but nobody really knew. You know, you really couldn't look at a guy and say, "Hey, that guy's fucked up," but the padres would come and say, "What was your most stressful moment? What sights affected you the most? What do you remember the most?" and questions like that. We'd tell them and get it all out, which is what it mostly was. We did that within our own section when something would happen. Afterwards everybody would come over, we were allowed two beer per man per night, when we had it, so we'd all get together, have a beer, have a smoke, joke about it, so that everybody would relax, so it wasn't too bad. They just questioned us and told us what to expect when we got home.

We were so far out of whack while we were overseas, our six months just stood still, and the rest of the world just kept turning, because it was the same thing every day. All we got for news was really old Winnipeg Press, a month old or whatever, and the Stars and Stripes from Europe. Basically we knew what was happening for the most part in the States but not for Canada. We had CNN in Sector West, as we had a small satellite dish, so we picked up all the English channels, and we had CNN from London. Wednesday nights it was The Simpsons, from 1930 to 2000, and everything just stopped except for the guys on shift. When we were in Sector West, there was one guy, the "Boy in the Box," we called him, who was just supposed to rove around the perimeter and make sure nobody got crazy. We had MTV until someone would fall and pull on the satellite cord and move the dish and that was it – we had to call in the guys from Camp Polom to fix it.

THOUGHTS ON MEDIA COVERAGE

The media always has a good guy and a bad guy, and the bad guy does this and the bad guy does that, and the good guy doesn't do anything. When you go over there you find out very quickly that none of the sides are better than the other. One guy does this, and the other guy does something else that's just as bad. The reason that my expectations were so high, before I went over, was because all we saw was news from Sarajevo and Bosnia, where the war is still to this day. If you were over there now, you would not go a night without artillery fire and machine gun fire but you don't hear it on the news. They only report the big stuff like the

Canadian UNPROFOR operations were conducted under intense media scrutiny. The international media was a two-edged sword: it could work for the UN forces by providing a "conscience" to limit belligerent action but it could also be manipulated by the belligerents for their purposes as well. (CF photo)

market square that got shelled. It was only the graphic stuff that caught people's eyes and they did it every day! You don't see anything from Croatia unless something happens to a peacekeeper. The press coverage is just inadequate. They say the Serbs do everything; well it might be like that in Bosnia, but I'm sure that the Croatians are no better.

LEAVING FOR HOME

We flew Air Canada on the way back, which was the best flight you could imagine after the tour. It was a Canadian 747 with the Maple Leaf on the tail; everybody was sitting there going "Oh Yes!" When the Van Doos got on the bus and pulled into the airport, everybody was just laughing at them,"Ha, Ha, suckers! Better you than me!" When we went into Winnipeg, the advance party was still there. A lot of the guys came home and they would have $10,000 in the bank and what were you going to do with it? Just start blowing it but we couldn't get our barrack boxes for two days and we came off the plane and they said, "Welcome, here are the keys to your rooms. See you tomorrow morning at 0900." The boys were like, "All right! Let's go get hammered!" A lot of these guys had been a long time without getting drunk. I had been drunk once while on leave and that was out of six months, so we were ready for a bender.

Everybody was waiting to go on a great big bender and there was $10,000 in your bank account and nobody was going to stop you except for the fact that you can't get to the barrack boxes and you had no clothes. Luckily the advance party was still there, so they'd lend you some clothes that they'd bought, and a lot of the guys had rented cars for the time that they were there. I had money, and I wanted a car so they drove to the mall to buy clothes, and we were changed, out at the clubs and tanked by the time 2200 rolled around. We finally got our barrack boxes two days later, and in the time I was in Winnipeg, which was about four or five days, I think I spent close to $2000 on clothes and booze. Then you went home and it was strange. When we were in Winnipeg, I was getting a drive to the mall and I was looking around, you know, it's like we never left. Somebody turned around and said, "That's exactly what I thought." When I got back home, it was all small things. I came back Thanksgiving Day, and my parents came over from France for a visit to see me at home. Everybody was there, and we had this big Thanksgiving supper and I was eating a lot, as I lost so much weight over there, and towards the end I was only eating once a day, but before I went overseas I was such a pig. I'm sort of quiet, you know, but I looked up from the table and I just blurted out, "Hey, salt and pepper! We never had it over there." Everybody laughed and I said, "What?" Everybody thought it was pretty funny but I didn't: it was salt and pepper and also I didn't have to go outside and dig a hole to shit!

A lot of us lost a lot of weight over there, and even my mother asked if I was sick.

MEMORIES

I had a few dreams on leave and a few when I came back but nothing bad. For some reason I remember seeing a giant black guy who had four arms but two of them were cut off. I don't know what the hell that had to do with anything but I never had a dream like that before! I had a dream of watching the carrier go off the road as artillery came in, and I remember that dream but I had never seen that when I was over there. I woke up screaming in France, talking in my sleep saying, "Holy fuck, did you see that?" It was interesting, the guys who came back, we'd call each other now and again to keep up with each other and ask, "How are you doing? Having any weird dreams?" and stuff like that. It was kind of strange but we wanted to make sure everything was all right with each other. The only problem when I came home was that I wouldn't park between two parked cars. I remember the padre at the unit, who came and asked me if I was adjusting all right and I told him about this. He said, "I can't help you with that." It's the only problem I have. It was strange seeing all your friends again.

I still remember the horse. When I saw that horse nudging the other one I felt like shit then. I felt sad but more like pity, and how could those people do this to each other? I appreciate what we have here now more than ever. Like, people say, "I hate living in Canada", and I think, "What the hell do you have to complain about? You live in a house that has plumbing, lights, and heat, and you have all your windows." Most people over there had windows out, holes where tanks had blown through the walls, and they just threw something over it and kept living. You'd see the UNHCR trucks come in and the people just start running, grabbing a box, and bolting. People lined up for gasoline, for bread, carried soup to other houses, and the whole place was just so sad. How you could live like that I don't know.

I don't feel that we accomplished much there in Sector West. At Medak, where we actually separated people to stop what was going on, it was more of an accomplishment. When we moved down south originally to the bridge, it was just a waste of time, because we just sat back and watched them blow each other away.

I would go back but not right away, maybe in a year or so.

CHAPTER FIFTEEN

CORPORAL DAVID MARGOLIN[1]

C-9 Gunner, 2nd Bn Princess Patricia's
Canadian Light Infantry Battalion Group
Sector West and Sector South, Croatia, 1993

SECTOR WEST: UNPROFOR FORCES AND BELLIGERENTS

We talked to the Kenyans, and played rugby with the British, Argentineans, and the Jordanians. The Jordanians were funny. They're not well trained at all. They're a conscript army anyway, and they picked any old Joe off the street, gave him a weapon and sent him off somewhere. They didn't even know how to put a battery on a 77 set [manpack radio]. I showed them how to do it.

We had a lot of respect from the locals and got along with them. I remember when we were in Sector North all the locals liked the Canadians a lot. Maybe not in Daruvar or places like that, you'd get dirty looks. Sometimes we'd talk with them and go over to their houses. I remember at the end of a patrol we went to a guy's house, his name was Giovanni. We'd go there for Raki, sausage, and homemade bread. He made his own. There was a domestic dispute once, which was something for the civilian police and we went over to help out.

These people were really poor and we gave them food. One lady, whose husband was killed, had two daughters and a baby boy. They really appreciated it. Then there was the old lady who brought the boys coffee at 0430 on the dot every morning. This really sticks out in my mind, I remember one night, it was really wicked weather, thunder and lightning, and I was thinking we're not going to get our coffee tonight. You could hardly see across the road. I swear to God, 0430 on the dot, it stopped raining, out she came with the coffee and we drank it. She went back in and it started raining again! Holy Cow! She must be something special for the guy upstairs to stop the rain for her to bring us coffee. She was a really nice old lady.

---

1. All of the Canadian personal names in this interview are pseudonyms.

We were doing this OP on top of the hill and there was this Catholic Church that was destroyed, the tombs were smashed in and there were these caskets inside all cracked open and you could see all these skeletons, particularly one of this guy who died in 1960. He had a red sash on and was dressed up. His bones were all over the place. It was pretty bad they had to do this to somebody's church. The worst for me was at an OP in Lipik and we were on the Serb side looking down on the Croatian side and a Serb came up to the house and he just wanted to look down. He was telling us about this glass factory down there where he used to work and showed us where his house was. He told us his wife and little girl were off in Sector North in a refugee camp and he hadn't heard from them since the beginning of the war. That was the saddest thing. She was Croatian and he was Serbian. The Croatians harassed her and she managed to get to the refugee camp. This guy was looking down at his home, or what used to be his home, and he would probably never go back again. Things go pretty deep.

SECTOR SOUTH: THE MEDAK POCKET OPERATION

We were in Sector South at Camp Kananaskis; all the troopies called it "Camp Cannabis" cause that's where the Head Shed is. They weren't smoking dope; it was just some of the decisions they made. Some were ridiculous and stupid things that made no sense at all. The company commander took us on a run one time to another camp, up this mountain, for no reason at all, and each soldier brought a rifle and a magazine and that was it. Anything could have happened. We were wide open on the side of this mountain with the Serbs and Croatians everywhere and neither side was too happy that they were down there, so I felt that it was foolish. We felt at risk because of PT! We could have run around the camp, there were enough roads there. When we first got there things were pretty quiet. Then the Croatians started their offensive and it started getting pretty hectic around camp. The Croatians were firing into it. We replaced the French who was there before.

We took over the OP on top of the mountain from the French. There was a field at the bottom of the mountain in the valley and one night a bunch of Croatians went in there and massacred 30 Serbians, like they just killed them and the French sat up there, watched the whole thing and they didn't do anything or say anything about it. So that's why the Serbs were really pissed off at the French. They actually didn't trust us at first when we got there but after awhile they started to trust the Canadians.

The French troops didn't want to be there. They were all draftees. That's the difference, eh? It was the same thing with the Regular Force and us. All the Militia, pretty much, wanted to be there more than the Regular Force because they were made to go over there but we all volunteered and knew that after six months was up we could go home. The regulars, the way they looked at it, another year and a half they'd be over doing the same thing again. So their morale wasn't as high as ours.

We were in this OP. We were supposed to be watching for troop movements down the road. There was a Serbian farmhouse there that we were supposed to watch. Every now and then you'd hear machine-gun fire in the distance but it wasn't anything major. Then one night it really started up. There was a big thunderstorm that night with lightning and the Croatians were all around us. We were up there that night and it was a wicked thunderstorm, and from the reports I heard the next day, we got in our O Group, the Croatians levelled three villages that night with artillery fire. Artillery was going over the top of our heads and you'd hear it whistling over. That was the first time I started getting a bit nervous, being around there, I thought, "Holy Cow!" I'm just waiting for the one to drop short and land right in the middle of the OP.

The shells, lighting and thunder were a really awesome show! And you knew the difference between the shells and the lightning, because the lightning flashed across the sky and with the shells, you could see the orange burst off the ground reflecting off the clouds. This was a couple of kilometres away from us. They were really getting pounded and it was demoralizing just to be up there listening to it. They were getting ripped apart. So anyway, I came off shift and went to sleep keeping one eye open that night just in case something happened. The day after that we came back off the hill. We were back down in Camp Kananaskis and that whole day there were explosions. Some were close to camp. The Serbs had a gun emplacement right outside our gate, 800 metres away. You couldn't see it as it was camouflaged and they had that going for a bit, so we started doing guard duty at the gate.

The Croatians pounded the crap out of the Serbs and stuff like that. In the town of Medak itself, it was 7 or 9 Platoon, that got pounded for twenty-four hours straight with mortars and artillery. Those guys were pretty demoralized. We had a couple of casualties. One guy got shrapnel in his hand and another two were driving to Medak and one shell landed in front of their vehicle. They got glass in their faces, and the driver got shrapnel in his leg. So those were the only three casualties. We were extremely lucky. Actually, they were the ones that got the Serbs to accept us because one night two drunken Serbs were shooting at them and they fired back at the Serbs. That put it in the Serbs' heads that our guys were for real. They turned tail and ran and we were pretty well-respected by the Serbs after that.

So anyway, after that, six days after we came off the mountain, we got bugged out into Medak, actually past Medak into the village of Citluk. That was the last village the Croatians had to take before they could actually get into Medak proper and kill everyone. That was the biggest thing. A lot of people lived in Medak. So anyway, we rolled up into Citluk, just our platoon, and we had TOW missile launchers as overwatch, that were back behind us in the town. The orders came down that night. We got everything ready to go and the next morning we rolled out into Citluk. We got down there and the platoon commander got us all sorted out, put us in our places, and we started digging our trenches. We were there three hours before we got attacked. Maybe not even that long.

The OC was going to come down and check it out to see what was going on. He didn't believe us at first. They wanted someone up on the road to guide the OC in when he got there and I got the lucky job. I was up there, maybe fifteen minutes, and all hell just broke loose. I was up there with no cover, no nothing, standing out in the middle of the road and the road was a primary target. That was when they started the attack on Citluk. They started shelling us; I was up there saying, "Oh Jesus! This is it! I ain't going home!" I remember seeing the 2IC across the street and bullets are firing everywhere and he's like, "They're just shooting over our heads!" And then it started getting really close, skipping off his feet.

He was next to a tree and the bark started hitting him in the face and I had the same problem. There was this wood across the road and a field pretty far away from us, and the section commander said that's where we'd put the guys to sleep. So we started taking sandbags over there, up over the hill and across the road, right out in the open. I was right on the hill with a sandbag over my shoulder, waiting for the boys to hurry up, and someone said, "We'd better get down there, they're shooting at us." I said "No way, we're UN. They wouldn't shoot at us!" Then I heard this VEE! VEE! Holy Jumpins! The guys are right – I'd better get down there!

Anyway, I was up on the road, I'm yelling at Malcom, "Get down! Get Down!" and something passed by me really close and an explosion knocked me over. I was on the ground and disoriented, not knowing what the hell was happening. "Holy Shit!" I crawled down into this big hole and they all thought I was dead.

I was yelling something wicked. I thought I'd got shot. I said, "Well, this is it, I'm making the 50-yard dash and I'm going to do it in under three seconds!" I never ran so fast in my life! I played football, and I never moved so fast in my life. I picked up my C-9, put my helmet on my head and just ran! The best thing I saw in my life was Barney and Langois, as they were getting ready in the hole to come out and get me. So I ran down and dropped everything. I remember seeing Malcom and Trebere, the C-9 gunner, in the back sitting in behind the carrier. Trebere's eyes were as big as saucers and he's like, "Holy fuck, boys! Start this carrier up, we got to get the hell out of here!" Malcom's trying to calm him down and then Barney took over and got us shaken out, like, proper fire positions and stuff like that. So, that was the end of that. That lasted maybe fifteen minutes or so. They hit us fast and hard but they didn't come into the position at all. They were just softening us up. I remember lying up against the berm; I was beside Barney, and these huge tracers were flying overhead, like "Holy fuck! What the hell was that?" Barney's like, "That's a 20mm!" "Holy Sweet Jesus!" They were chewing that village right up.

The Serbs were all drunk and firing their guns in the air, screaming "Yahoo! Yahoo!" After the first firefight they came over to a mortar position they had along the road beside a store. Anyway, they came over, brought a bottle of Raki and gave us a shot – baptism of fire, that sort of thing. So they were really appreciative of us. One of the guys was talking to a Serb who said, "You Canadian guys are very, very brave but very dirty!" We were a mess. We didn't give a shit, though.

We were scared to shoot. Like, I was kind of nervous to get up there and shoot because they could see the big UN helmet there and they were trying to kill us. It gave them something to aim at and we stood out. We weren't too far away from them. There was a hedgerow in front of us, 50 metre across the field and in another attack, we actually saw them in there downrange. So that was the first attack. The engineers were there too. We wanted the engineers to stay with us, as they had a couple of extra guys and they had a .50 and two C-9s, so we could have used their guns. But they said, "No way, Jose!" and they peeled out of there as soon as they were done. They were gone.

Another thing that was funny, like, all the times we had rations to eat, this time they brought out the hayboxes right onto the front lines. We were all lined up with our plates and mortars were falling all over the place! That was good, having a hot meal. So we got back to our position after we ate, and at dusk they started again. You could see the tracers really good this time because it was half light, half dark. There was a high feature out there. They came right at us. First they fired too far right, and then they re-adjusted and they were going right over our section's position again, landing a bit far behind, overshooting us. This was a 20mm and mortars. We just kept our heads down and we didn't see them again that time.

We were scared shitless but we were too tough to admit it. One of our guys was scared in the first attack and he admitted to it. At the time we thought he was a big chickenshit but now I think he was pretty brave just to admit that he was scared. It takes a lot of guts to say, "Yeah, I'm scared shitless." We were scared shitless too. We were kind of shocked. Don't they know who we are? We were just sitting there thinking it was crazy. Before dark the Serbians said that anyone moves after dark, gets shot, because they don't know who you are. They don't even move after dark. The sergeant then had four of us move back to a school at a crossroads and sit there for the night and we took two-hour shifts each. The main reason he did this was because he didn't know how long we were going to be stuck there. We were the ones selected to rest so that we'd be awake the next day. So what happened was, you'd have a shift of two hours each by yourself, and then you'd be sleeping. It was windy that night and the doors inside the school were banging and there were guys in the basement coughing, and we wondered who they were. They were Serbians resting too. We didn't trust them either. They could have sneaked up and done something. The entrance to the schoolhouse faced the front lines and I remember once I wanted to go take a leak. And holy frig, I went out there with my red lens [on the flashlight] and I don't know if they saw it but all these rounds started coming in the front door! Man!

It was kind of stupid, they had a desk and a chair right next to the door next to the classroom and all the other boys were sleeping right underneath the window and it was my turn to go on shift. I was there for a good five minutes and they were sitting at the table with the radio and the night vision goggles and then all hell broke loose again. I hit the floor pretty quick and I crawled over to the window. It felt like there were rounds coming in the window and towards me. I saw a lot of tracers reflecting off the window, off the walls and stuff. I made a few leopard crawls over and grabbed the stuff, and pulled it over to my sleeping bag.

That was the third attack and that's the one we actually started firing back. We saw a weapons signature in the hedge in front of us. I saw the whole hedge in front of us, 50 yards away, and you could hear the bullets winging through there. All you could see were weapon signatures lighting up muzzle flashes. I said, "McAlastair, this is it! We're going to get these bastards!" I put one burst right into the middle of the hedge, like, right where the weapons signatures were and I don't know if I hit anything for sure. Then there were two more at the end of the hedge of the row and I said, "I've got these guys!" So I opened up with a really long burst and McAlastair said, "Yeah you got 'em dead in the water." McAlastair was pretty sure I got them as he had the night vision goggles on. He was a pretty sharp guy. He could really pick out the weapon flashes and stuff. I could see it too with the naked eye. So I got a bead on them, and got them. Even the medics made their contribution too, as they had the old C-5, and they opened up with that. Then the Serbs started using their mortars and stuff. That was the biggest rush, that I could get back at these guys, the Croatians shelling us, trying to kill us. I shot at three men, one in the hedge itself, and then two at the end of the hedge. The sergeant had the C-6. He was deadly accurate with the C-6; he could hit the flea on a dog's ass at a pretty good range. He and Clarke were on the C-6 and they did a number on the Croats too. They were really good at that. The Croatians tried to hit us again. We put a stop to that right away; we put a lot of rounds downrange. So they gave up that one. Then my shift was off. They tried to keep our heads down but we turned the tables on them and gave it back. I assumed I hit the two, and McAlastair said 100% certain I hit the two on the edge of the hedgerow. The one in the middle I'm not too sure about, but there were two or three other guys in the hedgerow too. We went over the next day and checked for bodies. There were guts everywhere.

Not too much happened on the night shift. Then morning came and we got attacked again. It was raining a bit. So I heard people yelling, guns going off, and I was asleep and I thought, "Holy Shit! We're getting attacked again!" Everyone was going up there. I hopped out of the carrier, grabbed the first weapon I saw, which was Malcom's, and I got up on the berm and just as I got up, I told McAlastair "Grab the C-9 and come with me!" We got up on the end of the berm, and two rounds went by my ears, I could hear them, Veeow! Veeow! I double-tapped dash down crawl, sight picture and fired. I saw two standing at a kind of hole in the hedge, and I said, "Watch my tracer!" I sent two tracers downrange and then Kamp, Langois and Pry started hawking off rounds and we opened up with the .50s.

We got word that the Serbs were using their mortars. We had military observers back in Medak and they told us to tell the Serbs to stop using their mortars. I remember my platoon commander came over the radio and said, "If you want them to stop using the mortars, you come over here and tell them to stop using them. I'm not walking over there in the dark and telling them to stop." He got his point across. They didn't bother us the rest of the night.

The next attack, we just poured fire right into the hedge, as many rounds as we could and I remember the berms were slippery and muddy. It was a wall of bullets. I forget who it was on the .50 but we opened up with it. Every weapon we had available to us, like, gun-wise, we didn't use mortars or grenades but I would have liked to. This exchange lasted fifteen minutes maybe. A half-hour after that, I guess the Croatians wanted to sign a ceasefire and so for the rest of that day we got a shell every now and then. I remember the Warrant was walking across the street, and Barney told him to keep his head down or move faster. He said, "I don't have time for petty snipers." He was a real hard-nose guy but excellent. He liked to keep the morale up, and got a lot of stuff for the platoon. We never returned any more fire but they did mortar us again to see if they could get a last kill in.

In reacting to all this, I found it was the strangest thing. I don't know, I found that I was functioning like a machine almost in certain situations, certain actions. That's what I did. I didn't really think about it until afterwards. It's hard to say whether it was training or preservation that made you do things. In terms of teamwork, I mean, those guys were doing something to make sure I got back down into the friggin' hole. Everybody was spread out pretty good, and weren't all crowded up. When my partner said, "Follow my tracer" and we all knew where he was shooting, so we all shot there.

We had an ear test before we went over and there was nothing wrong with our ears and after, like at the end of the tour, they did another medical and I have a hard time picking out stuff from background noise. My girlfriend noticed it. They say I should get a hearing aid. It's the gunfire and the explosions.

As you got to the outskirts to Medak, there were a lot of Serbs in positions and on top of the hills they had anti-aircraft guns. Then when we got into Medak proper, there were soldiers everywhere running around all over the place. Every now and then an ambulance zoomed by. The HQ itself, the UN HQ, was pretty beat up. When you left Medak, then you got to go to a checkpoint. Our movements scared the Serbs and you could see that they didn't think that we would stay there that long. I think they thought they were going to get shelled and then they thought we would probably peel out of there and not protect the people. When we were there two Serbs got waxed and one was killed by a 20mm. He was mincemeat. Another guy was shot with small arms.

The rest of the battalion rolled through us to establish the buffer zone and they had the unlucky duty of cleaning up the villages that the Croatians had taken. There were a lot of mutilated bodies. The only thing left alive were the chickens; it was obviously too much effort to run after a chicken to kill it. Lots of dead cows though. We drove through there but it was basically after the clean-up and it still stank. Jesus, it reeked. We lived with that stench for the rest of the tour.

Everyone was really tired. We were tasked to man the gate of the road that was going into the buffer zone. Another section got to do patrols, foot patrols; they called it "hunting Croatians". They found, on one of their patrols, a little site where they found body parts, ID tags, needles, and helmets. That's where they patched up the Croatians we shot up, I guess. We established the buffer zone and then the next day there was a whole bunch of reporters, like military photographers, and we got word that the Croatian TV said that we killed 23 Croatians. They were showing the bodies on the TV.

The fighting gradually died out, and it was pretty much quiet. They were scared, each side, they'd have to come through us and they both knew what we were like. We wouldn't put up with that. We were proud. There was no way in hell anybody could say anything else about it.

PERSONAL ASSESSMENTS

We were kind of surprised that the whole operation came through and worked. You're not only physically tired but you're mentally drained. Then you start thinking, "Holy shit! I just shot someone up." At the time that it was going on, I didn't start thinking about it until a couple of days later. It was just an eerie feeling. You knew you had to do it cause if you didn't, he'd kill you or one of your buddies. So you got a guilty feeling. I do dream about it. It's not as bad as it was but you still think about it. It wasn't until I was back off my tour when it really started bothering me, and then it died down. Sometimes I wake up and I'm not sure where I really am.

I don't think there were too many Canadian reporters over there at all. Anyone that interviewed us was American. It seems like Canada doesn't really care. That's my impression. We weren't sure if the Canadian public was behind us. It's hard to say. All this stuff about Medak never came back to Canada. I think Canadians don't want to hear about it, the blood-and-guts stuff. They just want to see us feeding babies and helping old women and stuff like that. It's not like Cyprus. I don't think it's going to calm down there for a while yet. Up north we weren't doing anything. Once we got down south, that's when we started doing the job. We started putting our lives on the line for equal rights for everyone. That's what my motivation was: nobody deserves to be wiped off the face of the earth just because they're Serb or Black or White or Chinese or anything. Especially when we saved those people's lives, though I think that we got there too late. There were a couple of towns where all the people were tortured and all these remains were everywhere. I don't regret that we were there. We were basically doing nothing the week before. We just came a little too late. I think more UN forces should be there; we should send everybody over there and get it over with. I can't see dragging it on for ten years. If they keep doing what they're doing right now, they're going to wind up in a frigging quagmire and I think Canada is partly responsible for it too. The boys are hamstrung by a lot of stupid rules and there are going to be a lot more guys who are going to get killed.

Take, for example, the rules of engagement. We cannot fire unless you see who is firing at you. Those rules went right out the window once we went into Medak. We just said, "Fuck this!" and we gave them everything we got. You felt bad because you know you killed people. I don't know the numbers. But you feel bad because you took someone's life or you had a part in it but then again, you see all the people that they massacred. If you didn't kill them, they might have done more. I think that's the worst thing about war is that dilemma. If they're going to friggin' sit down and decide, well, this is what we're going to do; we're going to roll over them. I wouldn't question it. It was the same thing in World War II, going over to Europe from the Depression, with the Nazis and death camps. It's pretty well the same thing over there now except it's just not as large. It's still going on and it's wrong.

Let's get it over with quick.

Part III

Chances for Peace: Operation KHARON and the 12e Régiment Blindé du Canada in Central Bosnia, 1994

CHAPTER SIXTEEN

LIEUTENANT-COLONEL DAVID MOORE

Commanding Officer,
12e Régiment Blindé du Canada Regimental Group
Visoko, Bosnia 1994

I received a surreptitious phone call on the 11th of July, 1993 while I was at home in St. Hubert. I had taken over command of the regiment but I hadn't moved my family from St. Hubert yet. I had gone back to St. Hubert in preparation for the move and I was in the kitchen making strawberry jam with my wife and I was cutting the ends off the berries when the phone rang and it was one of my buddies. He called me up and said the secretary would disavow any knowledge of this conversation, but he told me that I would be taking the regiment into Bosnia, and that the details were being worked out. What the 'adults' wanted to know was, could it be done? Because the regiment had already participated with A Squadron serving with 2 RCR and D Squadron was currently in Bosnia with the Van Doos, the army staff didn't know if we had enough personnel power to do it. Off the cuff I said, "Yes, I think so, but we need about 20, 25% reserve reinforcement" and that was the way it happened. On the 5th of August at Gagetown, about 1600 hours, we got the warning order to go to Bosnia. That gave us sixty days to prepare, which was significantly less than any other unit had.

I had a Regimental Group. I didn't call it a Battle Group. That's a philosophical question; I don't call them battle groups because we're not there to conduct war and I think there's a message there. Whatever you want to call it, a battalion, that's fine, but I don't think you should call it a battle group because it sends a bad message to the belligerent factions. You're not there to fight. You walk around with blue helmets with vehicles painted white. We were there to support the operations of the UNHCR, that was what our mandate was and our mission was primarily to do convoy escort. I had been assured at the time by the UN chain of command, when I was conducting reconnaissance, that our mission in Srebrenica would be terminated by the time we arrived in-theatre but that was not the case. The battle group that preceded us exceeded by 250 people my regimental group but we retained the same taskings. To put that in the context, that was seven platoons fewer people.

The UN only paid for so many people so I thought the organization was pretty lean. Contrary to popular belief, there are some people in the 'food chain' who believed that we accepted tasks beyond our capability to perform and we didn't accept any new tasks. The only thing we did was carry on with the same tasks of the previous unit. Our headquarters wouldn't let us drop any of those tasks but we didn't take any additional ones. We just tried to maintain the same tasks with 250 people less, which was a significant problem.

The mission statement that you received through the command food chain, and the one that you actually had to accomplish were not the same. I remember as I was trying to tell my superiors back in Canada, people were saying, "This is not what we agreed to. This is not what you're supposed to be doing." Well, okay, but I'm here now and I'm under command and this is what this guy is telling me to do. We were supposed to be the primary convoy escort element for Bosnia-Herzegovina Command. The problem was that we were still in Srebrenica.

By the time we had arrived in theatre in late October the last member of the 2nd Battalion, Van Doos, was to have left Srebrenica. It wasn't until the second week of March 1994 that the last of my troops finally made it to Srebrenica. What happened was the static infantry elements that I would normally have had back in the camp, were 180 kilometres away i.e., I had an infantry company group in Srebrenica, which was four platoons, plus engineers, plus medical, and I had taken a slice of everything and sent it to the enclave: 160 people out of 780 were in Srebrenica. Because of the backing of the Drin hospitals, all of the traffic-control points, camp guard and things of that nature, I had to ground, on a rotating basis, one of my armoured reconnaissance squadrons to be camp security. That is what people couldn't understand. The collective wisdom was that we must have been taking tasks beyond our capability but I didn't accept one new task until the infantry company came back to Visoko and then we increased our scope slightly. We were in crisis management, and we were doing individual personnel taskings. We weren't tasking sub-units or sub-sub units, or sub-sub-sub units we were tasking people by name to do things. Plugging holes in the dam, from November, December, January, and February to the middle of March, until we got that company group back from Srebrenica. So we went there with a mandate to do convoy escort but our establishment was reduced by 250 people, which was the agreement. I'm not faulting anyone; I'm just saying that's what the agreement was. My superiors and the Canadian government assumed that that was what the situation would be but what happened was that there wasn't enough will, I believe, within the United Nations, to see that occur, and to bring that agreement to fruition. It just basically got delayed and delayed and delayed. The Serbs were allowed to delay, and it wasn't high on the agenda when General Rose came in and General Briquement left. General Rose's policy was to be more robust, to be more aggressive, and he was getting on with things like the Sarajevo exclusion zone.

The only UNPROFOR II unit that had a situation where it was spread out all over the place was CANBAT 2; we were the only one. The only organization that had a piece of it separated by x number of miles of territory patrolled by people, who at their whim, could decide that convoys didn't pass. We were constantly in crisis management trying to keep them supplied with food. They didn't eat fresh rations, they ate hard rations those people, for four and a half months.

We had a chance to get in a few sacks of potatoes now and then but on a number of occasions just getting in pop and chocolate bars, trying to keep their canteen stocked up was a significant problem. Trying to get them out for R and R was impossible, they didn't have any R and R, and we couldn't do it. We couldn't run an R and R program for them. We could run UN leave, but we couldn't run an R and R program, because we couldn't guarantee that they wouldn't spend three of the six days of their R and R sitting at a checkpoint, at Zvornik or some other godforsaken place.

My AOR sat within Muslim-held territory in which there was a pocket called the Kiseljak Pocket that was controlled by the Croats and touched a confrontation line which was shared with the Serbs. When we got in there it was open warfare between the Muslims and the Croats. The Serbs were allowing the Croats to get fuel, food, ammunition, whatever was required, by crossing the confrontation line, about 3 to 4 kilometres long, that they controlled but the Croats had to pay duty. You know, if they came up with five trucks of fuel, they had to drop one off, and food, they had to drop one off. It was a black market operation and they had fairly cordial relations with the Croats in the Kiseljak Pocket. I remember once when I was trying to get out of Sarajevo, I was blocked at a checkpoint and I saw the mayor of Kiseljak, a Croat, come up with his car, the gate would open, and he'd carry on to Sarajevo, or wherever he was going *[see Figure 14]*.

They had a very comfortable relationship. There was open warfare all along the confrontation line with the vast majority of the combat concentrated down in the northwest corner of the Kiseljak Pocket towards the Fojnica area, down to Bacovici, along the southern part here, with the Muslims pushing out of the Tarcin-Pazaric area down there, which was almost a pocket and it had almost been cut off for a long time. At one point UNPROFOR was air dropping food into them because they were cut off so, you had most of the combat occurring down there, and there was a little bit up here in the Kakanj area, and Krustcica towards Vitez, in this area. The other portion of the combat was along the area between Visoko and Kiseljak and the high ground. There was the regular stonking here between Visoko and Ilijas, by mortars, and rockets. I used to sit in my room at night and write in my diary or write letters to my wife, and I'd sit with the room blacked out and watch the tracers streaming out from the hills from the Serb side back to the Muslim side, and vice versa. So, all three factions were fighting and it was a hairy place to be. Coming from Canada, you trained for it, you were prepared, and you discussed how you were going to deal with stress and things like that, but it was still quite a shock. I think the biggest shock was when you arrived in Sarajevo. We came in through Sarajevo, and you stepped out of the aircraft, and saw the destruction in 3-D. Television couldn't do it justice, as the peripheral vision wasn't there. You started out on the road and they were shooting at you, and guys having anti-tank missiles fired them at you, and people threw hand grenades in your OPs. It was a pretty strange environment to be in. I remember leaving Visoko and arriving in Kiseljak with three flat tires.

In our AOR we were doing convoy escort. We escorted over 135 humanitarian aid convoys when we were there, delivering 8,000 tons of food but those were UNHCR tasks. We probably would have done more than that, if we didn't have to keep one squadron down for four and a half months. A [Squadron] would go on to the vehicles for a month, and B would do guard and then B would go on to the Cougars. We had a squadron of Cougars that just sat there tarped. Remember, I had that company group in Srebrenica until the middle of March. So we probably could have done more and UNPROFOR was screaming that they wanted us to do more escort. There was another aspect – for Months 2, 3, and 5 at any given moment you had 25% of your personnel who were on R and R or on UN leave. So take another 25% off the slice and you're pretty thin. We were pretty thin there for a while and I don't think that was well understood.

In terms of command relationships, I originally was reporting directly to a three-star UN general, who was Bosnia-Herzegovina Command. You had NORBAT, CANBAT 2, BRITBAT, and SPABAT and that was General Briquement's command. It was like that for three months. Finally, when General Rose took over, we changed. We knew that it was coming, and we were divided into Sector North-East and Sector South-West. When I was there I had Brigadier John Reith, who was also a Brit, and he commanded from the sector headquarters in Gornji Vakuf. This didn't affect

Figure 14: UNPROFOR II: Operational Situation in Bosnia-Hercegovina, 1994

the guys in Srebrenica, because they were under my command but I had to run things. For example, when I had to resupply them I would either go straight north up through Vares and up into Tuzla, through the 10 Mech Company facilities in the Tuzla air field and then move across Sarachi, go over to Zvornik, and then down into the Srebrenica enclave. At a later date we negotiated with the Serbs to go straight through Sarajevo.

That's the way it was and we had to live with it. The point had to be made, and I made it with all of my superiors and I have no qualms in making it again, is that for some strange reason there was a feeling out there that we or I or whoever, accepted tasks that were beyond our capability. We never accepted anything that we didn't already have and we couldn't get rid of any tasks. Our headquarters would not let us get rid of anything. At one point in time, we were so strapped for infantry that I had a Danish platoon under my command from the NORBAT commander, Colonel Ulf Henrikson, who helped us. I had a Danish platoon that was helping us in the Bakovici and Drin hospitals because I didn't have enough infantry. You helped each other out. I gave 8,000 rations to the 10 Mech Company in Vares because they couldn't be resupplied and they were NORBAT. I also helped escort NORBAT convoys up to their headquarters. It was for future considerations. You helped each other and you could come back and say, "Hey I helped out last week, I need a platoon for a month" and they'd give you a platoon for a month and that strapped them, because they had to pull that platoon somewhere out of their matrix so that doubled somebody else up. You're all there, on the same ground, same weather, and same belligerent factions. They didn't discriminate between Swedes and Canadians, and everybody was a target. You're there and you had to help each other out.

My relations with UNHCR were good. The guy that was there was Larry Hollinsworth, the Chief of Station. Larry liked whiskey so I used to bring Larry a 40-ouncer of CC once every couple of weeks, and Larry and I would sit down, have a little drink, shoot the shit, and talk about this and that. I think we gained a few hints. I talked to him one night, and he mentioned David Moore's theory of concentric circles. We were trying to get these aid convoys in and they were running aid convoys at one point in time, and it was haphazard. They would take an aid convoy from Zenica, from the warehouse, run it through Muslim-held territory down to the Croats, without dropping

Many CANBAT II tasks involved the armed escort of humanitarian aid convoys throughout northern Bosnia. The Cougar training vehicles used by 12 RBC, adapted to serve as armoured cars, were seriously outgunned by belligerent forces who were equipped with a variety of main battle tanks and man-portable guided anti-tank weapons. (CF photo)

anything off with the Muslims first so the Muslims would block the convoy. Nobody could understand why the Muslims were blocking the convoy. I said, "You should grease everybody's tracks around Zenica and then you keep increasing your circles as you're going out so everybody gets fed. You have to be going to everybody at once. You had to have a convoy going to the Muslims, to the Croats and to the Serbs. Something had to happen simultaneously, impartiality. You were not helping one, you were helping all because those people were dying, they were starving, and they were freezing. You can talk, as you may like, telling them you are impartial, but you have to show them, and convince them that you are impartial. So I talked about the concentric circles. I said, "You have to keep going out gradually Larry," and so he started doing it and the convoys started to move. There was less of what they used to call "spontaneous" demonstrations, where they used to have the bricks and the wood and all that paraphernalia stacked up on the side of the roads just in case they needed it to throw at the trucks.

Examples. The spontaneous demonstrations, in Kakanj, where we had to go down and break up a demonstration, were all politically planned. They decided that somebody wanted to make a statement so they grabbed women and children and went down and blocked the road. You were not going to run over those women and children and you were stuck. They started chucking rocks at you. Chucking the rocks was okay, but then they started endangering the drivers of the vehicles. That was when they crossed the line and that was when you had to be ready to shoot in the air or start to move. The goods were irrelevant. I once saw, between Vitez and Gornji Vakuf, five trucks get stripped in about forty seconds. It was like a school of piranhas, and I'd never seen anything like that in my life. The guys that were there had never seen anything like it, they backed off, and got the drivers out, that's what counted. Get them out of the vehicles; back them away and just let the mob have at it. The mob just stripped the vehicles, gutted them, and tore the canvas off. Those were 100-pound sacks of flour, and people humped two of them on their shoulders. Seriously, it was easily done in a minute. They just swarmed, and then they were gone. There were broken bags of flour, and stuff strewn all over the roads and then everybody got back in and we drove off. People came back and picked what was left off the road and you would come back and couldn't see a sign that anything had happened so that was the type of situation you were dealing with, those spontaneous demonstrations. Their intelligence was good and they knew when the convoys were coming. They had the phone lines functioning in certain areas and they had radios and they knew what was going on.

I dealt with all three warring factions on a regular basis. The Muslims and the Croats were within the confines of my AOR. The Serbs were across the confrontation line, but we had to deal with them in order to get the road open through Visoko to Sarajevo, which was called Route FINCH. One of General Briquement's biggest priorities was to get that road open because that was part of the operation lifeline and I had to negotiate with the Serbs. If we wanted to get into Sarajevo we had to cross Muslim and Serb controlled territory so you had to deal with the Serbs for things of that nature. We tried to find some mechanism to open some dialogue with them. I took a tombstone, a marble tombstone, to the first meeting that I had with the Serbs. The mayor of Ilijas, Serb-held now, and one of the Muslim businessmen in Visoko, Muslim-held territory, now stared at each other across the confrontation line, stonking each other with artillery, rockets, tank fire and things of that nature, and each had an interest in the tombstone. The fathers of those two guys fought as partisans with Tito and they were old buddies. Visoko was the industrial area, Breza was the energy source and Ilijas was the working class area. It was almost like a bedroom district and it was a little economic triangle.

The mayor of Ilijas, his brother had died of natural causes in 1992 and a tombstone had been ordered from the tombstone works in Visoko. No big hurry, and then the war erupted. I think it was in April when the initial clashes started, so they weren't making any more deliveries and this tombstone sat in the quarry in Visoko. I was trying to get some way to get a dialogue open. The Serbs didn't want to talk too much with me at that time but I won't go into the reasons for that. It had to do with previous administrations and things of that nature so I was trying to think, how could I get a foot in the door just to get in, sit down and get a look at this guy across the table and see what he was like. Then one day one of my LOs came up and told me that he may have found a lever. In Bosnia, your organization advances five LOs forward. Those guys preceded everything you did. Every time you had a meeting, they went across and they organized the timings and agenda. They are the pointy end of the arrow. We were in support of the United Nations Commissioner for Humanitarian Relief, UNHCR. We weren't there to do battle; we were there to protect ourselves and to protect people who were put under our care.

The LO came back and he said, "I think I might have a way to get in." He informed me that the Serb field hospital in Ilijas was running out of blood. Okay, I've got 700 people, plus we kept our own blood supply. We kept it for a certain period of time and when it was expired we destroyed it. However, it was still good, and you could still keep it for a while so I showed up with an igloo-type container with 30 units of blood in the back of my vehicle and I also had a truck on which the mayor's brother's tombstone was loaded. I pulled up to the checkpoint and they asked me what was in the truck. I told them it was Commander Delic's brother's tombstone and they knew exactly what I was talking about. I then told them I had 30 units of blood and you should have seen their faces light up. We arrived at the meeting point, the major got out of his vehicle, came up to me; and I introduced myself. While I was going through the pleasantries the tombstone was swinging over the side of the truck and it was lowered onto the ground in its wooden crate. I said, "I believe you've been having difficulty getting this for the last two years and by the way, I hear your hospital's out of blood." Those are the types of things you do. There were no weapons, no fuel, just good-will.

You must develop a negotiation technique. You had to identify who the players were. There are psychotics; you must identify who the psychotics are and what their agenda is, and who the good people are. There are a lot of good people over there that are sick and tired of the conflict, they just want to get it over with but they're being held at bay by extremists. An example is the Kiseljak Pocket. For a very long period of time the Kiseljak Pocket had two extremist groups, the Matrice (Serbs), the Apostoli (Croats), and the Muslims had their Black Swans. Those guys were veritable nut cases. For each side, those are their elite troops but for the other guy they were the terrorists, the nut cases. I viewed them as psychotics. They had their special purpose troops that they use for special tasks.

I dealt with the corps commander, the 1st BiH Corps commander, General Vahid Karavelic, and I dealt with the local brigade commanders. I dealt with the Chief of Staff for the 1st BIH corps. You could see in his eyes he was glad to see me when I showed up. We'd have coffee and we never bullshitted each other. Whenever he told me not to go down a road, I knew not to send anybody down that road because something was going to happen and I would inform headquarters that I thought something was going to occur in that area and we tried to keep an eye on it. I think he was genuinely trying to save lives. There was a civil war going on, and they wouldn't let you interfere with their war. If you did it was, "Sorry, you're in the wrong area," and that was it. I developed a pretty good relationship with this guy. On the Croat side I dealt with the operational group commander in the Kiseljak Pocket. Initially, I had some difficulty with him, because I thought he was a bit of a psychotic and it wasn't until I understood the problems that he was dealing with, which were the Matrice and the Apostoli, that I understood him. Eventually I found out from the last unit commander, who is a friend of mine, who told me that this guy, Brigadier Tole, had eradicated the problem.

Each group had a pattern, a way of operating. It was like the ritualistic consumption of plum brandy by the Serbs before the meeting, two hours of eating and drinking before you negotiate. You had to understand and adjust to each pattern, where they were coming from, and their religious quirks. You couldn't have meetings at such and such a time because they would be praying. You had to understand a little bit of their background. The Muslims felt they were persecuted. The Croats, the Ustashe during the Second World War, were trying to lose the stigma of their Nazi alignment. I tried to understand them, to sit down and talk to them. They would give you the normal political speech three or four times over. The Serbs called the Muslims the Turks. The Serbian derogatory term for a Muslim is a Turk. That's what I used to find interesting, when we were discussing the employment of the UNPROFOR Turk battalion in central Bosnia, I hoped that none of their boundaries touch on Serbian controlled areas, because I think fireworks would fly. That's my own opinion on that. I was asked for my opinion, where should those guys go, and I said that you want to make sure that they're not on the boundary that touches anywhere with the Serbs, because the Serbs will go bananas. A lot of people hadn't taken the time to go and sit down with the Serbs and understand them. A Muslim is a Turk and everybody is lumped together. You had to understand their pattern. If not, the whole thing went to hell on you very quickly.

As a bit of a background, I had 16 of my soldiers who were taken hostage in mid April of '94. They were held for about a week. During that same time we were engaged in an operation that was a follow-on to the Washington Peace Accord, which was signed in February of '94, whereby the Croat-Muslim Federation was conceived. There would be a cessation of hostilities, etc. Part and parcel of that accord was the separation of their forces along confrontation lines so that we could reduce the tension and start getting on with the political pacts, the economic co-operation, and military co-operation. They were going to create a joint headquarters, and there was going to be co-operation with their forces. Recently we'd seen in Bihac where Muslim forces received fire support from Croatian artillery. There was a joint headquarters in Sarajevo right now, and there were Croatian officers who were there doing planning with the Muslim officers. We were told during that hostage-taking to implement the Washington Accord and the vehicle for that would be the separation or disengagement of the Croatian and Muslim forces around the Kiseljak Pocket, the Croatians being on the inside of the pocket and the Muslims holding them at bay. Approximately 80 kilometres of trench-line bunkers, with many thousands of soldiers facing each other, some places at less than 10 metres. I'd been in the bunkers, walked the line, and they were facing each other at spitting distance, or grenade-throwing distance almost. That was quite a significant operation to plan, it was a significant operation to conduct, and it didn't see very much light of day back in Canada because it was snowballed by the hostage-taking, which was much more sensational. The hostage-taking in itself was just another political statement, the term was, and "It was the same dance, just a different tune." That's all it was, and was one of the vehicles the Serbs used whenever they felt threatened. They will continue to do so and they recently have done so with the RCD's 55 Canadian troops, same Observation Posts that we had, doing the same mission, and when they felt threatened they snapped them up. As long as we continue to have people operating in a Serb-controlled territory, there will always be a threat of that.

The Kiseljak Pocket operation was a different operation to plan, different terrain, very mountainous terrain, a lot of motivation was required, and a lot of bile was generated. People had been killing each other for mere metres, and they pushed these lines out. Friends had died and they didn't want to see this territory given up. We had to negotiate this. The military leadership on both sides was totally distrustful of each other, to the point where we were haggling over a word, which was a Croatian word, or Muslim word. Same word, it was just how the intonation was on the word that determined whether it was Croat or Muslim and things of that nature. I mean really bone-aching, balls-aching negotiation. At the same time we were being distracted by the hostage situation, but we still managed to accomplish a lot, that didn't make the light of day. I spoke recently with a friend of mine who is a Civil Affairs Officer in ex-Yugoslavia and of all the things that were accomplished in Sector South; it has stood the test of time. There have been improvements on it, but that is the sort of the cornerstone document and we, our unit at that time during April '94, were responsible for that. We were given the task, we planned it, we negotiated it, and we executed it, and it stands today. There is peace in the Kiseljak Pocket. There are regular buses running, that never occurred before, people don't die on the confrontation line anymore, mines have been lifted, and roadblocks are gone.

This was a significant peacekeeping type of achievement but it really didn't make the light of day because it was snowballed under by the sensationalism surrounding the hostage-taking situation. Everyone knew that it would come to an end sooner or later, once the Serbs felt that they had flexed their muscles enough and showed NATO how tough they were. The Canadians were about 16 of 400 detainees, and here we go again. Recently, it's happened again. When we executed the disengagement operation to separate the Muslims and the Croats, everybody was involved, the entire battle group. I think it has been an injustice to the people who served with me over there that 16 people should dominate the agenda like that.

READING FROM MY DIARY HERE:

"**This is the 5th of April 1994.** The Croats are visibly paranoid in Kiseljak. There is no reason to wipe away what progress has been made to date through paranoia. Remember, we're here to assist and implement accord, as agreed to by them. (I'm making reference to the Washington Accord which had been agreed to, signed in Washington, had been ratified, and now we were in the process of implementing that accord. Our mission was to get the Muslims and the Croats, the Croats being inside the Kiseljak pocket, and the Muslims surrounding it, to back away from each other along 80 kilometres of confrontation line). At 0900 I left for Bosnia-

Herzegovina Command and the Joint Commission executive committee meeting to discuss the mapping of the Kiseljak Pocket buffer zone. There were four senior BiH representatives (Muslims) and four senior HVO (Croat) representatives present. The senior Joint Commission observer chaired the meeting. The meeting was another example of the HVO's unco-operative attitude towards the entire endeavour. To begin with, newly promoted Brigadier-General Tole, who after being designated by General Reith at the last joint commission policy committee meeting as the HVO "toad of the week" and who had replaced Mario Bredera, started by saying, "What do we say when asked about what progress the HVO has made in delineating the withdrawal lines around Kiseljak?" He turned to another Croat officer and said, "What do we say?" because my translator translated for me exactly what was going on. So they weren't there to co-operate. When asked where his map was, Tole said, "CANBAT 2 and Sector South-West Headquarters had it." (Not!) After sixty minutes of going around in circles, Tole agreed to go and get his map and return with it at 1230. In the meantime the BiH reps and we sat around and discussed all kinds of banal issues. When I asked them why they hadn't pinched the Kiseljak Pocket east of checkpoint Sierra 1 (that's the Serbian checkpoint down on the southeast side where you come across the Serb line into the Kiseljak Pocket), they replied that Serb artillery and their lack of ammunition prevented the operation. All the BiH reps, especially Zlatan, agreed that a phased withdrawal by sector was the best way to disengage the troops around the pocket. The two BiH brigade areas north and south of the Visoko-Kiseljak road had seen very little fighting and the level of animosity in those areas was extremely low. (They hadn't fought too much, so they didn't hate each other to the same degree that others in other areas did.) I suggested that we get the HVO to agree to pull back in those two areas first in order to build on success. The BiH rep stated that the Bakovici-Fojnica area and the Lug-Nodbari area, where very intense fighting had occurred, were probably the two sectors to be disengaged last, after some confidence had been established through the successful withdrawal in other areas. (After they had seen the momentum start to roll, they would be compelled to move. If we tried to move them early on in the negotiation, they would resist and that's exactly what happened.) At 1250 Brigadier Tole returned with his map upon which the proposed HVO withdrawal line was drawn. The BiH had agreed several weeks ago to withdraw up to 2 kilometres in most areas but the HVO map was a farce. When transposed onto the master map, the line was the same as the existing confrontation line, with several minor concessions. After two and a half hours of again going around in circles it was decided that no one on either side had the authority to approve or disapprove the proposed buffer zone. Therefore, another meeting of the 'adults' would have to occur tomorrow morning at 0900 hours. I recommended to Zlatan that he bring the deputy commander of 1st BiH Corps and Abdulla Ahmic, the chief of staff, and he agreed. I drove Zlatan back to Visoko, dropped him off at his apartment and then returned to the camp.

"**On the 6th of April of '94**, after morning prayers [meaning the daily Orders Group], I whisked off to Kiseljak in order to begin another round of head-butting with Brigadier-General Tole. I am not too optimistic about the outcome; however, we'll just keep banging away at them until they give a little. I was astonished at what awaited me at the Joint Commission executive committee meeting in Kiseljak. The Croats, who had refused to budge on any issue yesterday, were now totally co-operative. Brigadier-General Tole had a map on which a plus or minus one-kilometre-wide withdrawal line was drawn, and a series of nine proposed OP locations. What the hell had happened? As "Floyd" (a Joint Commission Observer – read: British SAS) transposed the Croat proposal onto the master map, the acting Joint Commission Observer took me out into the hall to discuss the unexpected change in attitude. He said that subsequent to yesterday's meeting the HVO political advisor had been invited by him to go to the Officer's Club (which is a cafe across the street from the main HVO barracks in Kiseljak) for a drink. Upon arrival at the cafe, they were joined by Colonel Andric and Brigadier-General Vrbanac, the latter being the 3rd In Charge of the HVO army. The two officers tore a strip off Tole and told him to get with the program or else. The browbeating lasted thirty minutes and Tole was a babbling fool afterwards. After the lines were drawn on the master map, we then discussed the requirement for security forces within the buffer zone. As directed by General Roso, who commands the Croatian HVO army and General Delic who commands the Muslim army, each side had the right to leave up to 30 men per brigade AOR in the buffer zone. With the Muslims this was a relatively simple thing to work out, as 1st BiH Corps was composed of eight or nine brigades around the Kiseljak Pocket. However, the HVO had a brigade of 8,000 to 9,000 troops within the pocket organized into battalion AORs. To simplify matters, the Kiseljak brigade was renamed an "Operational Group" with subservient brigades. The bottom-line agreement was for up to 300 men to remain within the buffer zone in 3-to-4-man locations. This is reasonable because the circumference of the pocket is plus or minus 80 klicks. The HVO and BiH put their platoon AORs on the map and then I placed the rough location of the nine proposed CANBAT 2s OPs within the buffer zone. Thereafter I signed the map. The BiH took the map back to Visoko for Commander 1st BiH Corps to sign and were to return at 1500 hours for the HVO to then sign. In the interim period Tole invited the acting GCO and myself to have lunch with him at the Officers Club. It was a relatively pleasant affair; however, some of the statements made during lunch gave me food for thought. Tole said the reason that the HVO Croat politicians had signed the accord was that the U.S. had used the big stick on them but the Croats doubted whether the Federation would succeed. The Bosnian Croats didn't trust the Muslims as far as they could throw them and they said that they were protecting the West's interests in squashing the expansion of Muslim fundamentalism further to the west. What was the problem? Couldn't the West understand? At the end Tole called the map a piece of fiction.

The ECMM report (that's European Commission Community Monitors, these are the people dressed in white) had some very interesting statements. Dario Kordic (he's a very influential guy from the Vitez Pocket, a Croat), said, "The Kiseljak pocket would prove a very hard nut for UNPROFOR to crack during the negotiations. Ivica Rajic (he was involved with the Apostoli and the Matrice and he was known as Victor Andric in other incarnations) was still firmly in control with his band of extremists. It appeared that the HVO was unable or unwilling to reel him in or get rid of him. That augurs poorly for what we want to accomplish in the area. The report also stated that General Mladic, the Supreme Serb Commander, was falling from grace because of his recent failures in the Maglaj Pocket to the north. On CNN this evening the first detailed reports about the fighting east of Gorazde came in. It appears several villages had been overrun and plus or minus 3,000 are fleeing west returning into the pocket. Unconfirmed reports put the Serbs on the eastern outskirts of Gorazde itself. Nevertheless Karadic and Mladic asked General Rose to come immediately to Sarajevo to discuss a comprehensive ceasefire in all flashpoint areas. The Serbs like to negotiate while they fight.

"**7 April**. During lunch, "Floyd" (the British SAS officer) appeared with his replacement team and was all smiles. The signed disengagement agreement had been sent to Gornji Vakuf at Sector

South-West Headquarters last evening. He met with Tole and company and Zlatan and company this morning. They had begun discussions concerning the detailed procedures governing the disengagement of troops. They had decided to withdraw from two brigade sectors per day beginning with the area north of the Visoko-Kiseljak road and move counter-clockwise around the pocket. Floyd had told them to start developing the logistic support plans for the separation of forces, i.e., transport accommodation routes, recognition signals, and things of that nature. The aim is to convince them not to pull disengaged troops back to another confrontation line but to garrison these troops as quick reaction forces used to relieve elements of the security patrols stationed temporarily in the buffer zone. We have scheduled a meeting for 1300 hours tomorrow in Kiseljak. Some very interesting information has popped out of the Kiseljak Pocket. Firstly, Branco Stanic, the HVO Commander in the Otigosce area just east of Bakovici, has been quoted as saying that he will never occupy a trench with the BiH army and if forced to, he will "kill the Turks from behind." He cited the loss of plus or minus 400 of his comrades, adding further that if there were any co-operation between the HVO and the BiH he would leave the HVO. Personally, I received this news with great joy. He should be locked up and the key should be thrown away. Meetings between UNPROFOR and the local military authorities in the Kiseljak pocket confirmed that the extremist elements still retain considerable power, notwithstanding all the goodwill window dressing that is occurring. The HVO still runs Kiseljak and the outlying areas. Furthermore, Ivica Rajic a.k.a Victor Andric, is still subtly in charge of all of the activities within the pocket. The same Colonel Andric with the acting GCO had a meeting with Tole and Vrbanac the other day. Apparently Mate Boban (the Croatian nationalist leader) took over and sanctioned the name change and this is the reason no one within the organization is allowed to see the alleged war criminal. Two gangs, the Apostoli and the Matrice, are currently active in the pocket and they are hard-core extremists. It is believed that the situation in Kiseljak should improve as General Rose has decreed that all extremist groups be redeployed to Usara in the south. After supper I met with Floyd and his replacement team (commanded by "George") with the soon-to-be approved map of the Kiseljak buffer zone and proposed location of our OPs. We discussed the angle of attack for my meeting tomorrow with Tole and Zlatan. Floyd presented a very sound disengagement plan including all the nickel-and-dime details that must be worked out before we can get on with it. I asked the acting operations officer to take the proposed plan of attack and prepare crib notes for tomorrow's meeting.

"**8 April.** At morning prayers I explained to everyone the methodology that will apply to the disengagement of the forces facing each other around the Kiseljak pocket. I established the order of priority for establishing the OP line, telling the A Company commander to get out on the ground and confirm the location of the OPs with the local commanders, i.e., Muslim and Croat. I also discussed with the acting OC A Squadron the problem of the heavy weapons still located within the area of the Sarajevo Exclusion Zone. After lunch I went to Kiseljak for another meeting of the Joint Commission executive committee. Tole and an aide and Zlatan and another BiH Corps officer were present, as was George and his team. The aim of the meeting was to discuss the nuts and bolts of the upcoming separation of forces. All agreed that we'd go counter-clockwise around the Kiseljak Pocket. Numerous other points were discussed and it was decided to tie down the loose ends at the first CANBAT 2 Joint Commission subcommittee meeting tomorrow at our camp. Brigadier Tole got slightly hot under the collar when I raised the issue of mines and used the example of people being killed and maimed in Cambodia. He didn't like being compared to Cambodians. So what. One of

George's boys said he'd received information from a BiH source to the effect that Andric a.k.a Ivica Rajic had apparently gone to the Kresevo area in order to discuss the ceasefire/peace accord with members of extremist elements in the area. The word is that Rajic will attempt to infiltrate into Serb-held territory before he can be brought to justice for atrocities, amongst them the Stupni Do massacre last October 1993.

"**9 April 1994.** At 0915 hours the first meeting of the CANBAT 2 Joint Commission subcommittee was held. The executive committee members and a slice of the civilian-military representatives were present from each of the two sides. I was very glad to see that Brigadier Tole had decided to come. Luc and I (that's Luc Duschesne, who was my Civilian Affairs Officer) co-chaired the meeting that had a very extensive agenda. After a brief introduction, Major Beaudry, my Deputy Commanding Officer, provided a resume of the discussions at the Joint Commission policy committee meeting yesterday in Gornji Vakuf, chaired by British Brigadier Reith. Things are progressing well, however there are several problems with the mapping of the buffer zone in the areas of Konic and Dastansko (north out of our area, which is of no significance to us). The Joint Commission policy committee certified the interim procedures for freedom of movement and checkpoint control. Subsequently, the two police chiefs sat privately to discuss the nickel-and-dime aspects of the freedom of movement accord. All in all, the Joint Commission policy committee was very happy with the progress towards the beginning of the withdrawal of forces on the 13th of April. The local Visoko TV and radio press were invited to film the introductory process, then they left while substantive discussion occurred. (I brought in the media to use that as leverage on these guys. You know, there's peace coming, you've got to put pressure on these guys for peace.) I led the discussions related to the ceasefire and withdrawal of forces. Essentially, we staffed all of the discussion points we dealt with yesterday. I'm beginning to feel more confident that we actually may be able to pull this off! I then passed the word over to Luc who dealt with the freedom of movement, infrastructure repair, joint convoys, and commercial activities. Reference bus lines, I said we should try to make bus movement less restrictive than the Visoko-Sarajevo bus agreement that we have with the Serbs. All agreed. The transportation commissions of Kiseljak-Visoko will work out the details. I'd said we'd provide security initially, however once it becomes commonplace we will stop. The discussion to re-establish PTT (the telephone company) between Visoko and Kiseljak dragged on. In the end I suggested that the repairs to the Vis-Kis line wait until a later date, as the Serbs control much of the Vis-Kis road from their positions on the high ground to the east and can interdict at any time. I can't protect the workers until we get an agreement from the Serbs to allow the repairs to occur. The BiH representative suggested an alternate repair line. There is a water pumphouse on the confrontation line near Brestokov (it's on the confrontation line between the Muslims and the Croats) that provides water in some areas of the Kiseljak Pocket. It was turned off by the BiH at the outset of the fighting. I asked the BiH to turn the bloody thing back on. An HVO civilian representative said he was worried that the BiH may have poisoned the water. I looked at him for several seconds and told him that if he liked, I'd drink the first glass of water. During the meeting I was informed that a BiH policeman had been struck down by one of our vehicles during a civilian employee run into Visoko. The policeman had been given first aid on the spot by one of our MAs [our medics] and had suffered life-threatening injuries. He had been evacuated to our Field Surgical Team due to the extent of his injuries. The MPs were dispatched to the site. (We're sitting in the meeting and all of a sudden, boom, this guy turned out to be the brother of the local brigade commander who subsequently threatened us with death because if his brother died, one of our soldiers would die. This is the type of garbage that's going on over there.) At the conclusion of the meeting we invited everyone to have lunch while Luc, Mersed Sainovic, Mayor Josip Boro from Kiseljak and I did an interview with each radio and TV station. (To put the pressure on them, we stand up and say "Yes, look, we're making progress." To put the torque on the politicians to make it happen.)

When they're standing in front of the tube and you're standing there and you're saying "Oh yes, they're doing quite well, they're co-operating ..." I began by providing a resume of military activities which are related in the ceasefire, Luc followed with a synopsis of the issues related to the freedom of movement, infrastructure repair, joint humanitarian and convoy movement co-operation and commercial revitalization, and Mersed Sainovic, the Muslim political representative, and Mayor Boro, the mayor of Kiseljak, locked things up with their own impressions of the meeting. Afterwards I went down to the hospital to see how the injured policeman was doing.

"**10th of April.** Nothing associated with the disengagement.

"**11th of April.** I phoned chief of staff Sector South-West Headquarters, Colonel Perez Navarro (he was a Spaniard). We talked about various things. One of the things we talked about was he said that our plan to withdraw systematically by sector over a period of two or three days around the Kiseljak Pocket was not supported by Brigadier Reith. I explained to him that at the three meetings I had attended with the acting JCO, Brigadier Tole and Zlatan, everyone, including Floyd and his JCO boys, agreed that the best and most secure manner to accomplish the disengagement was to do it methodically over a period of several days. He said no, it would be done in one day. Eighty kilometres. I said, "Fine sir, I'll get right to it." Click. Everyone in Sector South-West seems to have forgotten that the Croats and Muslims decided to reach an agreement, a peace accord. Brigadier Reith has said on numerous occasions that we're here to assist you in implementing their accord. The HVO and the BiH want to implement it over several days beginning on the 13th of April. What's the problem? In the end I told Colonel Navarro I'd advise the HVO BiH reps that that's the way it is, the 'adults' in Gornji Vakuf say to do it all on the 13th of April, so that's it. At the meeting between the HVO and the BiH reps at 930 I told them of my discussion with Colonel Navarro and the modification to the concept. The BiH immediately agreed to disengage in one day. However, the HVO needed to return to Kiseljak to get approval from their military hierarchy. We agreed in principle to disengage half the line in the morning from 0900 to 1200, and the other half in the afternoon from 1400 to 1700 hours. We will reconvene at 1700 hours today to review the order, to make any final corrections and sign it. Afterwards I went to my room to wrap up three pipes that I'd bought for Martine (my wife) and the kids. The ops officer brought to me the revised draft operations order for the disengagement of the Muslim and Croats around the Kiseljak pocket. After making some minor corrections, I told Bob to clean it up and to immediately fax it to Sector Southwest for their final approval. At 1700 hours, Zlatan and Brigadier Tole arrived to hash out the final details of the disengagement agreement. The principal bone of contention was the removal of mines, anti-personnel and Claymore type mines from the confrontation line and within the buffer zone. Tole hadn't received the minutes of the 8 April '94 Joint Commission policy committee meeting, so he wasn't ready to sign our agreement. I went to the ops centre while everyone had supper and phoned Sector Southwest. I spoke to the military aide to Brigadier Reith telling him to fax the page regarding the agreement on mines from the minutes, because I was so close to cracking the nut. Back in the meeting with Zlatan and Tole I finally got the Joint Commission policy committee April '94 meeting minutes, one page, which dealt with the removal of mines. Tole finally agreed. At 2100 hours we signed the joint order and had a small toast to the occasion. An historic moment! We had a joint document written in English and Serbo-Croat with three signature blocks, the Croatian Commander, a CANBAT 2 Commander, and the Muslim Commander. This is a first.

"**12 April '94**. During morning prayers, I informed everyone that the joint operations order for the disengagement had been signed last night. I told them that notwithstanding Brigadier Reith's desire to accomplish the operation in one day, the most important aspect was the security of our own personnel. I didn't want anybody blowing off a leg or a foot because he was trying to attain some hypothetical unattainable timing. I said the key to success was today's detailed foot and vehicle reconnaissance of the various BiH and HVO sectors. The conference tonight served to tie up the loose ends. At lunch I spoke to George who had just returned from the first series of recces on the ground. Both he and "Dave" had noted that the BiH defensive positions were virtually deserted with only two or three men along an entire sector of a given battalion frontage. They also noted that the HVO, particularly in Branko Stanic's AOR, were totally unaware of what was about to occur. When shown a copy of the joint order they were completely surprised. While the first portion of the line will be relatively easy to disengage, the second portion, which is located in very rugged, mountainous terrain with thick pine forest will be more problematic. We will see tomorrow, I guess.

"**13 April**. The appointed day! I'm feeling very tired and impatient this morning. Hope the Croats and the Muslims have their shit together today. Went to 1st BiH Headquarters to pick up Zlatan. The BiH looked somewhat confused. Their LOs didn't arrive on time and Zlatan appeared very apprehensive. We'll see whether the orders were passed out or not. At 0900 we picked up Brigadier Tole in Kiseljak and proceeded to the Kulikes feature, which is on the southeastern portion of the Kiseljak Pocket (the northern side of the southeastern corner, adjacent to the Serb confrontation line) to view the first area in which the withdrawal is to occur. There were only 4 to 5 men in that Croatian position. To the north, smoke could be seen rising from the BiH bunkers, and to the east plus or minus 700 metres the Serbs could be seen milling about. This area is the one which both the Croats and the Serbs are very nervous about. No one knows what the Serbs will do as the defences thin out. Both want to retain plus or minus 10 extra soldiers along these specific areas of the confrontation line. The Croats had obviously begun to thin out yesterday. Tole had a good grip on the process. Suddenly over the radio came the message I'd been dreading. One of the BiH brigade commanders was refusing to withdraw. I spoke to Zlatan who was furious. He said he would go to the area of Bilalovac and the high ground to the east and kick the asses of the brigade commanders. Tole and the Croats said if the BiH don't move neither would they. The whole process ground to a halt! Ceasefires were reported north-northwest and southeast of Bukovici. The fighting began. For five minutes the situation remained tense. When Zlatan left I contacted my headquarters in Visoko and told them to inform

Reith that the operation would not be completed today. Brigadier Tole suggested we go and have a coffee at the HVO Officer's Club while Zlatan did his thing. Excellent idea. After plus or minus one hour, Zlatan returned saying that the disengagement was progressing on the BiH side of the line. Tole radioed his local commanders to confirm movement around Kalikovac. Suddenly I received a message saying the brigade commander in Bilalovac still refused to move his troops because he saw no HVO movement to the rear. The HVO in the meantime were waiting for the BiH to move. A stalemate had set in. I took Tole and Zlatan and went to see the 24-year-old brigade commander. He was a dynamic, well-spoken and intelligent young man who simply couldn't do it when the time came. After forty-five minutes of coaxing and stroking, he agreed to withdraw. The problem was, of course, that the HVO had gotten wind of the delay so they decided not to move either. The whole process had ground to a halt again. I told headquarters to inform Reith that we wouldn't be able to confirm whether the entire 75 or 80-kilometre length of the confrontation line had been disengaged. We'd need another day. We went back to the HVO Officer's club and decided on a plan for tomorrow. I told headquarters to organize as many teams as possible for tomorrow. I told Zlatan to get on the phone and kick ass, especially with the commander of 232 Brigade and the 9th Mountain Infantry Brigade north of Tarcin. Tole, Zlatan and I will do the second portion of the line tomorrow, starting at 0900 hours. The toughest nut to crack will be Branko Stanic and his band of psychotics in the area of Bakovici. Upon return to Visoko I phoned Brigadier Reith and apprised him of the situation and the problem encountered. He wasn't particularly happy but I said we should be able to confirm that the entire line has been disengaged by tomorrow night. I told the ops staff to pull people from everywhere in order to get the mission accomplished tomorrow. The problem is the rugged mountainous terrain. We will do our best."

On 14 April '94, the second in command and the ops officer came in the room to tell me that they had received a garbled UNMO report from our UNMO team in Ilijas that the two observation posts on the Serb side of the confrontation line at OP QUEBEC and OP ROMEO had been "detained." I noted in my diary: "Here we go again." So at the same time when we're trying to disengage the confrontation line, we've got our guys held hostage. High profile? The separation of the Croat and Muslim forces never saw the light of day because the hostage-taking was much more sensational than separating the Croats and the Muslims. Six days later, I came out of the hostage-taking fog. I was totally consumed by it. I don't want to go into the specifics right now, but you can imagine why I was totally consumed, it was coast-to-coast news in Canada. At that point in time that's when I let the sub-unit commander who was in charge of the operation really sort of take over and get on with it, because I didn't have any horsepower to go on. That was Major Meloche. So he was the guy that actually went out, he had to get down to the nickel-and-dime detail morning prayers. "The picture painted around the Kiseljak Pocket looked very good with an infinitesimal amount of ceasefire violations yesterday and yesterday evening. However, the rogue mortar operating in the Plocari/Nadbari/Lug area is still causing us some grief."

At 10:15 21st of April, Brigadier Reith arrived for a short visit. He addressed the personnel in the camp who were available. He thanked the soldiers for their fine work that they had accomplished over the past six months; he cited the great progress we'd made to date around the Kiseljak Pocket area and the role they played in making it happen. Afterwards we retired to my office for a discussion. I gave him a comprehensive sitrep on the disengagement of forces around the pocket and outlined several problem areas like marking barrier minefields, the removal of anti-personnel mines within the buffer zone, the contention over the Kresevo-Tarcin road, and the rehabitation of the buffer zone by civilians. Reith told me to raise the issue of public mine awareness at every opportunity.

We left the camp and went to visit OP KILO BRAVO, which is located slightly southwest of Plocari. On the way there we passed through downtown Visoko, Checkpoint 2 and the Vis-Kis road into Kiseljak itself. It was an unreal sight in contemporary Bosnian terms. Both town centres were bustling with people, shops were open, and small children with school bags on their backs waved wildly at us. At Checkpoint 2, there was a lineup of cars on either side with people hugging and embracing those they had not seen in one or two years, and women laden down with shopping bags returning from Kiseljak buying goods. This sight convinced me that we had made an impact; we had made a significant difference here. The dead and wounded have not been in vain.

CHAPTER SEVENTEEN

MAJOR LOUIS MELOCHE

Squadron Commander,
12e Régiment Blindé du Canada Regimental Group
Visoko, Bosnia 1994

I took over command of the squadron in July 1993 and I deployed my squadron to Yugoslavia. I had to convert it from Leopard tanks to Cougars to get to Yugoslavia. I commanded my squadron in Yugoslavia from October 1993 to May 1994. I followed the geo-political problem when it started and I was fortunate to command a squadron in an operational theatre.

OPERATION KHARON: THE KISELJAK POCKET DISENGAGEMENT

How we got the disengagement done took almost two months of preparation on the ground and negotiation. General Roso, who was the HVO or Bosnian Croat commander, and General Delic, who was the BiH or Muslim commander, didn't talk to each other and that was one of the big problems. It all started in December 1993 when General Briquement decided to have a high-level meeting between these two gentlemen. The meeting happened on 16 December 1993 in Camp Visoko (the Canadian camp). I was involved in the security for these gentlemen and their delegation there. That was one of the first times that those guys started to talk together.

A good result came out of it. After that, they held a Joint Commission meeting in Gornji Vakuf, so all the big boys were talking to each other at a very high level. We are talking higher than Corps level, that is, at Army level. After that, this led down when those big guys said, "Yes, we want a peace plan, yes we want to do it," but it had to come down through the belligerents' chain of command all the way to the bottom. We, as part of the UN, had the responsibility to implement the desires of those gentlemen and how it happens on the ground is not always the way that the higher levels want. You had very different commanders in between before you got down to the soldiers in the trenches, who hold the rifles. He had been shot at, his mother had been raped, and all that. To tell him to put down that weapon, well, you had to take it very slowly. The same sort of thing happens in the Canadian Army. You go to the section commander, to platoon, to company, etc.

Most of my work was done at corps and brigade level in this operation and all the negotiations that I did were at that level. Once they had those big agreements at the JCO's meeting, we took it to a local meeting. Those meetings had the high guys from the Muslims and the high guys from the Croats meet. The Croats were easy, as there was only one man, which meant one pocket, and one guy in control of the whole pocket. Originally, the guy controlling that was Mario Bredera who was a hard man to deal with. You never could perceive his emotions, and I called him the "Iceman." It was hard to sense how he felt whenever you were suggesting something to him and you never could get any reaction, not even an eye reaction. I liked to get a reaction to see if the man was alive or if the guy understood what I meant, because when you worked through translators, you wanted to make sure that the buzzwords that you used were translated properly. For example, I learned a lot of the language down there to make sure that my translator was really saying the real buzzwords if I was in disagreement with him, wanted to argue with him, or I wanted to tell him to "fuck off." If it didn't make any sense I would go and pound my fist on the table (sometimes you had to do that) and if the translator had never used the word 'Jabano', I knew she didn't translate my words properly, as 'Jabano,' meant this [an upraised middle finger]. I would say, "You tell him 'Jabano'," to make sure he knew that I was mad and I was not happy with him.

So, for the Croats, one guy was basically in charge, Bredera originally, and then it reverted to Tole. When the War Crimes Commission finally started to work, Bredera suddenly disappeared. Was he thinking he was a suspect or something like that? We don't know. He just disappeared. I saw Bredera on many occasions after that in the Kiseljak Pocket, walking around in uniform, but he never returned to the table; Tole took over for him.

On the Muslim side, the situation was a bit different because you had three corps around the Kiseljak Pocket on the Muslim side and the Muslim HQ in Visoko controlled two of them. We also had various brigades around and the ones to the south around Tarcin were controlled by the Muslim command in Sarajevo. So, you had to deal with those two guys, one in Visoko, and one in Sarajevo. You had several liaison officers coming to those meetings and that was how we went from Gornji Vakuf to the locals.

Now, how did we implement the disengagement on the ground? We had the meetings in Visoko, where Colonel Moore was presiding, and I was at those meetings also. We formulated a peace plan that the Croats and the Muslims finally agreed to in early February 1994 at the political level. It had to develop so that the word got down to the brigades and it took a bit of time. The implementation of this started for us with CANBAT 2 in early March 1994. So how do we get this going? First of all, we had to know exactly who was who in the pocket, and who was where in and around the pocket. Before that, we had to get clearances from the belligerents for our freedom of movement everywhere we went. Right now we were only going where they wanted us to go, and on the roads that they wanted us to use. But in order to implement the peace plan, this was not acceptable. In Gornji Vakuf, they agreed that we could use specific roads that were controlled by the UN, and these became UN roads.

In my sector, there were two roads, the road from Visoko to Kiseljak, where we put a checkpoint that was right in the middle of the confrontation line between the Muslims and the

Croats, and the other road was the road from Kiseljak to Busovaca and the UN checkpoint was near Bilalovac, also in the middle. Those were the two roads that were agreed on in the global peace plan for central Bosnia, and they were in my AOR. I controlled those roads and UN movement was controlled by me. There were still belligerent checkpoints but the aim was to gradually remove them and it took a lot of work. But you don't tell those guys, who have been at war for many months, suddenly the next morning, "Okay guys, your leaders have agreed to a peace plan, let's do it!" They will not let go of their weapons like that and it doesn't work that way. You had to use confidence-building measures and they had to trust your capability to repulse the other side if it tried to come through or if the other side didn't follow the peace plan. They had been through so many peace plans before that they didn't trust this one. They thought that this one was just another peace plan. So right away the UN commander for the sector started behind, way behind.

The first thing I had to do was to organize some confidence-building measures. How do I do that? What I did was to go around to see every corps commander and I got a blanket clearance, with my name on it, that I had freedom of movement everywhere in my AOR. I could use any road, or any track in my AOR and that created a problem because of the mines. There were communications problems for the commanders to communicate with their troops that there was a guy moving around and that you had to give him complete freedom of movement without stripping his vehicle all the time. That took a lot of time, but with that piece of paper I was able to go anywhere. So from there, once I had those blanket clearances from the corps commanders, I went around to meet every brigade commander, shake their hand, tell them who I was, why I was there and what my aim was, and to check out what their aims were.

Did they want the peace or not? I had specific people who told me clearly, "Yes, we want the peace. We will give you 100% co-operation and it's not a problem." There were other people who specifically told me "No, I will resist you any way I can because this is just another peace plan and it won't work. Plus, I was a bum before the war, now I'm a warlord, and I am a somebody now and I don't want the war to stop. I have interest in this, I am making money, and I am a somebody." Some people told me that specifically, right to my face! I could give you the names: Latko, Ivo Kulis, and Dramac. Those were three battalion commanders that did not want the peace to start. After that, one of things we had to do was to see who was who in the zoo. The only way to get that information was to go on the ground and walk around. We walked the confrontation line on the Croat side, and the confrontation line on the Muslim side in order to make a map and that map would be my start point for the disengagement of the forces, Operation KHARON. I had to know who was who, where the trenches were, where the weapons were located, and all that. The peace plan also restricted weapons, and those greater than .50 cal had to be removed from the lines so we were looking for weapons at the same time. Once I had met all the brigade commanders, I asked for blanket clearances for my patrols. Everybody knew me, everybody was happy with the plan I offered them, and I wanted it implemented gradually, building confidence, and getting the ceasefire violations down before we started doing anything. I needed everybody's co-operation to do that so, I had my people patrol everywhere. That way I was able to spot weapons and have them removed to the weapons collection point, everything that was not 'legal' or not agreed to in Gornji Vakuf, i.e. .50 cal machine guns and up. Each side was allowed to have an active site in the southeast pointing at the Serbs because once there was no threat between the Croats and the Muslims, and then there was a threat from the

Serbs. I had to monitor that and we had to check the elevation every time they fired a round to spot which way it went. The active site was allowed to continue doing its thing against the Serbs, even though they really didn't fire any rounds from the active site. We'd have been in a very funny position if they had fired and the people that were there on the ground knew there would be counter-bombardment on them from the Serbs.

So I went around, I shook everybody's hand, made a map, and my patrols were going everywhere. So what do I do with this map? At the same time I asked the belligerents to make me maps of their lines but I didn't want the Muslims to have the Croat positions, and I didn't want the Croats to have the Muslim's trace. Once I had all this data, I had one beautiful map. I had the Muslims trace compared to the Croat trace, and there were discrepancies. Each side was trying to gain a bit of ground so that if the peace plan didn't work, they would occupy more advantageous ground than before. We used GPS and our map was very, very precise but it took time and we had to go out on the ground to do it properly. It was the only way to do it. Once I had a Muslim trace that I was happy with, and what I mean by this was that the trace that they were giving me was the same as the one that I had plotted on the ground. Once I had those together, we took everybody in to the local JCO meeting and said, "Okay gents, I got a Muslim trace here, and I got a Croat trace here and this is the start point for the disengagement. How do we go? Do you want the Muslims to see your trace, and do you want to see the Muslim trace?" The belligerents agreed to that so that they would be able to say, "No, no, no, he's not there. He's there. I own this piece of ground and they don't." I was the umpire in this process because I had walked the ground and once they all agreed to that, we did a final map, and they both signed the map. That was the map! Nobody could move from those positions forward or backwards and that was THE map *[see Figures 15 and 16]*.

Now it was time to negotiate the withdrawal. How did they pull back? The rule of thumb was a couple of klicks to withdraw, one klick on each side to create a buffer zone of two klicks. At some places this didn't work, like where there was a big mountain on the edge, and if you went back you were down three mountains and people didn't want to do that because they had too much tough ground to regain after that. So we went with a local rule that I approved, it was line of sight one kilometre and so, you would apply the logic. Where do you determine the middle line? I went back at them and told them, "You give me the proposed line of withdrawal" and they proposed to me where they would withdraw. It was coming from them, not us and as you can see, everything I did so far was to use them to achieve the disengagement. Really, I was just a tool to implement the peace plan. I did not invent the peace plan, I did not impose anything, I just took everything from them and that was the key to success. Every peace plan that you try to impose by force, I don't think will work, but if you go like this, it will work.

Now, it's easy to say that like that, it's the general briefing of the situation, but how did it work on the ground when you had a hard-headed guy in this location, who lost his family, and where half of the village was gone? You had a village like Drin where they hadn't seen any UNHCR or they hadn't had any humanitarian aid since the beginning of the war, or you had a little village where you had Muslims kept in a village by the Croats and once in a while extremists would come and rape the women and beat the men. That is why I had to go round systematically, sector by sector. In the original plan, confidence-building was the key to success and to limit the number of ceasefire violations. I can remember one incident near Bakovici and Fojnica that involved the two hospitals were in our AOR. We knew the sector fairly well because we had gone many times to the hospitals, resupplying them when we were shot at on Route SALMON, the

241

road from Fojnica, and we had to keep our heads down in our turrets around there. We'd hear a BING! on the Cougar once in a while. Sometimes we'd get a burst of .50 cal over our heads, just making sure that we knew they were there and vice versa.

So how did you get the ceasefire violations reduced? Well, when you had a hard- headed guy commanding the Croat sector of Otigosce named Ivo Kulic, the guy who had stolen a .50 cal from us at one of the hospitals, well you knew that this guy was an asshole and you finally convinced this guy to work with you for the peace plan because you were threatening him with putting his name in the Special Envelope. The Special Envelope was simple. Whoever was not giving me 100% co-operation, I would put his name in an envelope and write down why he was in there and I would give this to Colonel Moore when he went to Gornji Vakuf for his meeting with General Rose. He would give the envelopes out, one to the Muslim representative and one to the Croat. Either the envelope was empty or full but they didn't know that at the time, as it was the same size of envelope and it embarrassed whoever was not co-operating. You can rest assured that shit accelerates as it falls and they knew that so when I had to use this trick, I said, "Hey, listen. You don't want to work with me, fine. Your name is going to go in the envelope" and they knew what the fucking envelope was. Believe me, co-operation improved!

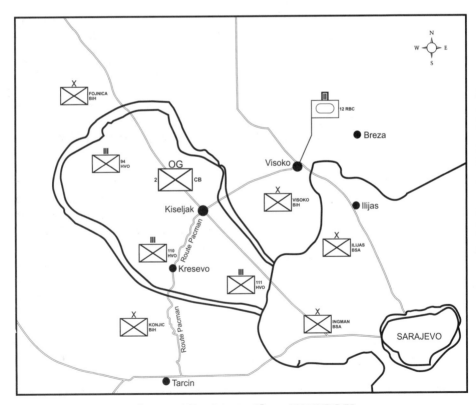

Figure 15: Operation KHARON:
The Kiseljak Pocket Prior to Disengagement, 1994

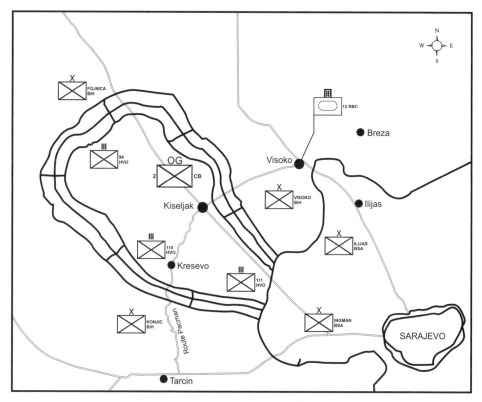

Figure 16: Operation KHARON:
The Kiseljak Pocket After Disengagement, 1994

Ivo Kulic in Otigosce had a high level of ceasefire violations in his area and I had to monitor that. The Muslim commander told me he was getting shot at so I put Canadian OPs all around the pocket as part of the confidence-building measure and I had to negotiate the locations of every OP with the commanders on the ground. Some wanted the UN OP on their side; others did not, since it could sometimes attract fire and that took a long time.

I knew this confrontation line by heart. I did it by air, by vehicle, and by walking. The disengagement started early March on the ground and we were able to do Op KHARON on the second week of April. The groundwork that led to the separation of the forces took about five weeks of intense work. I had people out in OPs, and I was out at 0600 and returning at 0800 after negotiating all day long with those people.

I had a Canadian OP near Grodiski Kovo where I knew that rounds came from the Croat side, because my OP reported it every morning. If there were only two or three rounds, I would not bother with it, because that was chickenshit. They could be cleaning their weapons, shooting dogs, or whatever but when you got over a hundred rounds, I would get a bit pissed off and I went around and talked with those guys. "Listen, last night, your guys fired over a hundred rounds. You told me yesterday that ceasefire violations would stop in your sector. You gave me your guarantee for that and I would like to see your commander now." He said, "I am the commander." I said "No you are not. Obviously you are not in command here if you gave your guarantee and the shooting has not stopped. You are not controlling your soldiers. So who is your boss?" The guy did not like that when I told him that and I remember his face. I got a reaction from this particular iceman, as his face went red and I was happy with that. I knew I had touched a soft spot in his ego. The next night, the ceasefire violations were nil from that side in that sector. Yeah, I had to use all kind of things.

The guy in Fojnica, the Muslim brigade commander there, was a gentleman and he was an old JNA soldier. He knew what tactics were, what strategy meant, knew how to do a defensive plan, and he knew how to fight. He was a soldier by trade, where in other positions, people were soldiers because they were in command, because they had no brain and big arms or they were the local guy who had a lot of money. This guy knew exactly what he was doing and he was a gentleman to talk with. You could talk soldier-to-soldier and get a soldier's answer from him. Once the map marking was done, we had to do the actual disengagement then we had to negotiate the return of the civilians. The civilians that were living in that valley, for example, or in Bakovici, their houses were in the middle of the buffer zone. They wanted to go back home and didn't want to be refugees. We had to negotiate that. Then it was a question of the males. The males from 16 to 60 are potential soldiers, so they would allow the kids and the ladies, but they wouldn't let the males go. There was also a large mine threat. Where were all the mines?

We blew up an APC on a mine trying to get an OP set up and this happened near the Serb's line. We tried to get an OP in on 29 March and I will remember that day. The Muslims assured me that there were no more mines on that trail. I had an engineer sergeant with me, and I told him to double-check. I had walked that trail about four times. Before you set up an OP, you had to recce it and this location was a hot spot given its proximity to the Croat and Serb lines. The Serbs were there and the Croats were afraid that because of the peace plan, the Serbs would take advantage of the situation. I had to put an OP here to keep the Muslims and Croats confident that the UN could monitor Serb movements. We found two mines, and then the APC moved forward with me in front with the Muslims. If they wanted to walk in front of the APC with me, it meant that they believed that there were no more mines. They were not that crazy. BOOM! We blew an APC. The driver was a bit shaken up but everything was okay. The Serbs thought we were firing at them, so they started to fire at us, the Muslims started firing back and then the Croats started up.

Once the withdrawal of the forces happened around the Kiseljak Pocket, we developed Confidence Platoons. Both sides were allowed groups of 30 to 40 soldiers in each sector. I divided the sectors into sub-sectors that corresponded to those battalion frontages. They were allowed to have 30 soldiers wherever they wanted and they had to tell me where they were. I told both sides where the other platoons were so for example, if we took a sector, there were 40 Croats here and 40 Muslims there. If you took another sector, we had 30 and 30. How did you control the numbers? It was easy because I had guys going around doing verification and they never knew where I was going to check next.

I had guys going around and counting soldiers. How did you know if there are 30 soldiers and not 40? We made ID cards for the sectors. It was one card, one soldier, and one weapon. What about turnover? Well, the other soldier arrived without his weapon, took the card and weapon, and the other went back so there were no more than 30 armed people at any point and time in that sector in the buffer zone. Once the buffer zone was created, they all agreed but these guys knew each other. For example, what separated the Muslims from the Croat was a mountain that overwatched a lot of territory, and it was one of the first points we wanted an OP on. I was on the Croat side and I wanted to go on the Muslim side. I went across, instead of going around. I went to the forward Croat position where the separation was 12 feet between the trenches! They all knew each other and they were playing cards with each other and drinking coffee together! There was no fighting and no ceasefire violations here. They were there in principle and because they were told to be there. I said, "Okay, I want to go there" and he said, "No problem, you can come." The Croat took me for about four feet. "Those are my mines, and there are no mines from here." The Muslim came out, did his four feet, and said, "Well, in between, I don't know." That must be why the physical fitness standard in the Canadian Army includes broad jump!

You can see on the map that the lines were close and people could see and talk with each other. Some of the checkpoints were really funny. The Croats had one on the road from Gromiljak to Fojnica, on Route SALMON. The fighting had gone back and forth through this sector near Bakovici and they were firing at us on the road. At the Croat checkpoint and the Muslim checkpoint, the guys there lived together in one house. One was 70 years old and his brother was about 75 and they never gave us problems. That was the reality of the war there. It was really local people fighting, and they only brought in outside units for specific operations. When the fighting was happening around Bakovici, the Muslims reinforced near the end of November 1993. Their reinforcements moved around central Bosnia wherever the fighting was and you could see the movement of troops. I remember getting caught there at Fojnica Bridge, in December before the peace plan, and suddenly 400 soldiers surrounded me. They were moving somewhere else and you knew exactly, by being on the ground every day, talking to people, finding out what was going on and what was the projected plan for the next couple of days. For example, if you entered Kiseljak and everybody was in the streets, you knew it was a quiet day. If the next day you went down and there was not even a cat running around in the streets, then you knew you had to keep your bloody head down.

I also ran into Muslim extremists a few times when I was in Visoko. When I had to go and deal with the locations of the camp they were in, I was at the time responsible for the main camp's security, and we rotated squadron responsibilities. They didn't talk Serbo-Croat, those guys. The ones that I saw spoke a limited English, but my translator could not talk to them in Serbo-Croat, as they did not understand it. They were from Lebanon, I think. I saw Serb extremists when we did another operation and those guys were sent to kill me at one point. Relationships were somewhat limited when a guy came up to you and said, "My aim in life is to kill you because you did such and such an operation." You didn't have a tendency to stick around long. You let him go and you went also so whenever we met extremists, you could see that they were dressed differently, they did not mix with the normal soldiers, and they did not receive orders from the local commanders but they were receiving orders from somewhere else. The local commander could not control them. I remember around Bukovice, there were extremist Croats facing extremist Muslims. I talked to the local commander in Bukovice and I told him to control these guys when we wanted to reduce the violations of the ceasefire agreement. He said, "I cannot control them. They are there, they are on my ground, but they have their own orders."

There were two patrols, one Croat and one Muslim that met one night and had a firefight, so we had to go and pick up the bodies and see who shot whom. The Croats were saying that

The driving distance from CANLOGBAT in Primosten on the Adriatic coast through Mostar to CANBAT II in the interior of Bosnia was not great by Canadian standards, but shelling, sniping, rugged terrain and infrastructure collapse caused innumerable delays for UN convoys. (CF photo)

the Muslims shot them and vice versa. It was obvious that there was a patrol trying to snoop in and they bumped each other and that was why the confidence-building measures were the key to the success of the operation and that took over five weeks to do.

The other issue was the road from Kresevo to Tarcin, Route PACMAN. That road was opened before we got there by another Canadian contingent and Canadians repaired and monitored the road. Then the belligerents took it from us and we couldn't use it anymore. That was one of the roads going down to Mostar and Split and we got that road re-opened with the peace plan. It took a lot of time, as there was a lot of emotion involved, a lot of fighting in there and nobody wanted to give it up. The only way to take it back was to open the road for UN forces only, no civilians, and no belligerent forces. The only vehicles authorized in there were UN, unlike the other roads feeding into Visoko.

We did organize civilians to meet on Sundays and we had the belligerents agree to a list of people who could go back and forth across the buffer zone. I put Muslim police and Croat police at the UN checkpoints and they were part of the inspection process but they were unarmed. They could see the UN was doing its job and I put them there as part of confidence-building, so they could see what we were all about and we were behaving correctly. Thus, we could have freedom of movement for UN vehicles; the gate went up, and no questions were asked, nothing. When belligerents wanted to go through, both sides' police had to agree and they had lists that they agreed on. This guy sold things in Visoko and he lived in Kiseljak, so the local authorities had a number that they had to agree with so that we could issue permanent passes. The checkpoint was open from such an hour to such an hour, so they couldn't go in the middle of the night. The police were there for the opening hours. We had people there twenty-four and seven, mind you. The numbers that were agreed on in Gornji Vakuf for the freedom of movement of civilians were not enough and I had to make a decision. The belligerents that I was trying to implement the peace plan with, believed in me as the UN commander, so they had to trust me. I could not continually turn around and say, "Gornji Vakuf said this." I had to make local decisions. One of the decisions was that on Sundays, people could meet at the checkpoint and I got people to agree to that at the local Joint Commission meeting. There were a lot of family reunions happening at the checkpoints on Sundays but we still searched people, just in case.

Nobody could go back or in or out because the local police monitored what was going on. We just took their ID cards at the checkpoint, they went into UN territory, which was in the middle, talked, picked up their papers, and went back home. The first Sunday about ten people showed up and the second Sunday, about a hundred people showed up and then the word got around that this was working! The Sunday after that, we had fifteen hundred people. This was all necessary to get the military to believe in the peace plan. The civilians, the basis of the military locally, had to believe in this and that was one measure we used. The civilians had a lot of influence on the soldiers, because they gave them food and housing.

The other thing I did was to go around to the villages and talk with the local mayors and police as much as the military. They knew they could reach me at any point and time and all they had to do was show up at a checkpoint and ask for me. Within twenty-four hours, I would go there, or one of my representatives. I always sent my LO first, so I wasn't bouncing around for low-level things that could be solved otherwise. The people knew that whenever they needed us, they could talk to us. The problem was, what happened after we'd been there six months and a new rotation came in? Luckily, the guy that replaced me was a very good friend of mine so I took him around. It took us a few days and nights to go around and shake every hand that had authority, talk to them, and go over specific detail so that nothing was forgotten.

THE ROTILJ CONCENTRATION CAMP

In the Kiseljak Pocket, on the Croat side, they removed the Muslims from the Pocket. Removal was done in many different ways by burning their houses, taking them prisoner, killing them, or telling them to move and they ended up as refugees somewhere else. Some of them did not want to leave, so they regrouped them in Rotilj, a little village of about fifty houses surrounded by a plateau. The village was down in a little valley and it was well hidden. The access to Rotilj was very difficult and was very controlled by the Croats. The Croats took all the Muslims they could from the Pocket, and parked them in Rotilj so you ended up having fifty houses with 40 to 50 persons per house living there, 2000 to 2500 people, two to three families per 12-by-12-foot space including sleeping quarters, and no furniture. They also had no doctor. When the peace plan started, I went there to get the Croats to go there with some assistance but they were afraid that I would discover things there and they knew that the War Crimes Commission was coming, so they were afraid. I went there with a Canadian doctor. They had older people that were suffering from all kinds of things that simple medications would take care of and you had people who were used as slave labour to dig trenches, young people that were beaten, ladies that were raped, all of that. I went with a UNHCR representative but we had no mandate to help those people directly, so what I did was I brought the tools in that could help them. There were Croat spies in the village, so you had to watch who you talked to. Some people were talking to me and suddenly they stopped, and they would not talk any more. I asked, "What's going on?" The translator explained to me after that this lady was passing through, she was spying for the Croats and they didn't want to talk in front of her. They knew that if they talked too much, the extremists would come that night and beat them.

In that village, I was able, through the UNHCR, to organize a switch from Rotilj to Kakanj where there were civilian Croats held like the Muslims in Rotilj. We did an exchange with the Sarajevo refugee commission and it took two times for the exchange to work because "Snake Eyes," the mayor of Kakanj, had mixed up the papers the first time so that the Croats were pissed off and they didn't want to let the Muslims go. That is why confidence-building is very touchy. Everything you did, said, or tried to implement had to be well thought out. When I went to meetings with the brigade commanders, I had notes on what I wanted to achieve and everything had to be pre-planned.

THE PROBLEM OF MOKRINE

Mokrine was far from Sarajevo; there was a Serb line there, and a Muslim here. There was a battalion controlled by the Tarcin Brigade (Muslim) and Tarcin was controlled by Sarajevo, so the communication between the brigade and the corps HQ was not happening. You could see that this brigade was forgotten by their corps HQ and nobody took care of them so the civilians and the soldiers here were almost abandoned. Whenever we showed up for the peace plan, even though we had the blanket paper from Sarajevo in order to go and talk to this guy in Mokrine, but he didn't want anything to do with me and there was a lot of fighting between there and Kresevo. Those people had been irritated a lot and they hadn't seen any UN aid in two years. They hadn't seen Médecins Sans Frontiéres in two years and they had a lot of sick people. I got UNHCR involved within ten days after one of my patrols escorted an aid convoy to this village. I made sure first of all that UNHCR went and assessed that there was a problem there, and yes we would send aid and all that but we were not at liberty to make that assessment. We could just sound the alarm and ask them to check. I made sure that the next day the convoy escort was beefed up so that it could make it in and it did. The next day, by co-incidence, I went to Mokrine to say, "Hi! How are you? Remember me?" and from then on I never had a problem with co-operation in that sector because the people knew me and now supported the peace plan. I never had a problem with them after that and I could get anything from them. They offered to let me stay there; they offered me a house, two wives, anything.

My aim was not really to give them aid, as that was not my mandate, it was UNHCR mandate. My aim was to get the military situation sorted out so that we could disengage those forces but I could not do that as they were too irritated and didn't believe in the peace plan. So what method did I have to use? Well, I saw that the people were walking around barefooted, that the kids were not dressed properly and it was bloody cold. I saw that there were no fat people in the village and if there were no fat people, there was a good chance that people were not being fed properly. I saw that 90% of the people didn't have any teeth in their mouths and they were not getting the proper vitamins. Those were all factors. How do you go about achieving the aim? My aim was to get the military situation sorted out in order to disengage the people. You couldn't say, "Yeah, in Gornji Vakuf they agreed to this" and expect it to be implemented. The local commander in Mokrine would not have agreed to anything unless we had helped get aid.

We had to be on the ground. If the military way didn't work, you had to find another solution. You were a soldier, you were given a mission by your commanders, and you just went with that.

THE IMPORTANCE OF OPERATION KHARON

There was not a lot of doctrine for UN missions. It was a bit of peacekeeping and a bit of peacemaking, because we had to force a couple of issues. It was a disengagement mission. But the role of Canada in central Bosnia was to assist humanitarian action and this was a humanitarian action and it was part of the mandate. I called it disengagement in the execution paragraph of the orders I gave. What I thought personally was that Op KHARON was like a trial. They tried that type of operation around the Vitez Pocket and it did not work out as well. Op KHARON was something that was implemented slowly and people in Gornji Vakuf were pushing us in order to accelerate the process. I said to the CO, "Let me go, I know what I am doing, and I need time." Confidence-building was the key to success of this thing. That is the reason it is still in place today as we speak in January 1995. To really answer your question, I think it had an effect as a model, how it was done, how it could be done, and the result. People are amazed that it worked. It was only by using common sense, being involved and being on the ground.

PERSONAL ASSESSMENT

It was a reasonably rewarding mission. What I did down there was for the people down there and I did the mission as a soldier. I did not bring any flashback home, like a lot of people did. I feel that the mission that I did, the job I did with my soldiers down there, we did something and we accomplished something. When we started there at the end of October, the war was raging and we were fighting our way through with convoys. Every time we went out we were shot at, had stones or snowballs thrown at us, and we were part of the problem. We were never safe. To give you an example, when I arrived there my soldiers and I went around in my Cougar with our helmets and frag vests on. To indicate to the locals that I believed in the peace plan, I started to drive around in my jeep without frag vests, and without helmets. I went around the lines dressed like that but I was the only one allowed to do that in my squadron. They had to believe me, and that I believed in their peace plan but I admit sometimes my shorts were a bit brown! That happened. What we did down there, arriving in central Bosnia with the war raging, leaving there with a peace plan up and working, being able to travel around in a jeep and being able to go around and people were waving at you instead of people throwing rocks, not being shot at, or having the CFVs [that is, the ceasefire violations] reduced to zero and all that, I think we did something down there!

The leaders that I had at every level were superb and my soldiers were the greatest! I could not have done this alone; I could not have done it without them. Discipline was a big thing with me and there was no other way. I was very, very strict on them and there was no grey; it was either black or white and there was no ambiguity. Whenever they had orders that they didn't understand, they were not allowed to interpret. Interpretation was zero. Tolerance was zero for interpretation. They got specific direction and that was the way it was. They were great. They did what they were asked and more, they got involved and they believed in that peace plan. We wanted to leave on a high note, which we did.

CHAPTER EIGHTEEN

CAPTAIN JACQUES CABANA

Squadron 2IC,
12e Régiment Blindé du Canada Regimental Group
Visoko, Bosnia 1994

OPERATION KHARON: THE KISELJAK POCKET DISENGAGEMENT

I was the 2IC of B Squadron, 12 RBC in Operation CAVALIER Roto 2, and during the period in question I was acting OC for B squadron, while Major Meloche, the OC, was out on UN leave. I was acting OC for three weeks and just at the beginning of that period was when the disengagement of the Kiseljak Pocket event happened. Now, to give a little bit of background on the operation, it had been at the high level planning for three or four weeks, as I understood it. There would be disengagements throughout Bosnia between the Muslims and the Croats, notably the Vitez Pocket, the Kiseljak Pocket, and a few other areas where the Muslims and Croats were engaged. They had unified their political system, called the "Bosniacs" now, and parallel to that they were unifying their military organizations. This had been tried before, unsuccessfully, a year and a half or two years before that when they had unified and split up again. This had been going on for about three weeks to a month. I was aware of this. We had started and the first thing that we had done in our sector was establishing weapon collection points. We had established two weapon collection points, one in the Croat sector (Kiseljak) and one in the Muslim sector (between Tarcin and Kresevo). The aim here was for the belligerent forces to bring their weapons above .50 cal machine gun, mortars, artillery, tanks, everything. They actually gave us two or three token items, just so that we wouldn't be able to say that the UN hadn't been given anything. The Muslims had given a couple of artillery pieces with ammunition stamped with Wehrmacht markings from 1943! This stuff was in crates with the old swastika and eagle crest on them. Obviously, it was none of their major equipment items!

When we established the two weapons collection points, we also established two UN checkpoints. Now, before we did that, the belligerent forces controlled all the roads. We wanted to take the two major roads in and out of this pocket and put them under UN control. Normally you had a confrontation line, with a Croat and a Muslim checkpoint at either end. We wanted to establish UN checkpoints between these two spots, so in the initial phase, there would be a Muslim checkpoint, no man's land, UN checkpoint, no man's land, and Croat checkpoint. The aim was to initially get the belligerents to accept the UN checkpoint and then once we had established ours, then bring LOs [Liaison Officers] from the belligerent checkpoints to see what we were doing, and then eliminate their checkpoints. They would realize that there was no point in having their own if we were controlling things and that's exactly how it happened. One was along the road leading from Visoko to Kiseljak; the second one was on the road to Vitez. It happened exactly that way.

The Muslims were initially very co-operative; it took the Croats a bit longer. Eventually after some kicking in the rear end, the Croats co-operated and they took down their checkpoints on either side. By the time that we finished, we were manning both checkpoints and traffic was going through with no obstacles whatsoever. We turned the checkpoints over to the MALBAT [the Malaysian Battalion] because the famous MALBAT Company, that was near Visoko, had just arrived in January 1994. They put the company under our command because they lacked something to do. We established the checkpoints and everything was going fine. We did this for economy of effort, as they certainly didn't work the same way we did and didn't control their troops the same way we did. The MALBATs were suspected, highly, of dealing on the black market. At a later stage, when they had been on the checkpoints for a couple of weeks, I visited two different Muslim battalion commanders with the sectors that were overlapping the checkpoint area. They were complaining that the MALBAT guys were taking over the black market in the area since they controlled the checkpoints. It was investigated but never proven. There were certainly complaints from the belligerents.

As far as we were concerned, we wanted to map out the Kiseljak Pocket. What we wanted to do first was to be able to know exactly what the Pocket looked like. We started flying over the Pocket. I personally went a couple of times in helicopters, about half a day's worth each time, flying over the trench lines. The first thing we discovered, to great surprise, was the fact that the trench lines were continuous the whole way around on both sides, except for the southern part which was more hilly and wooded. It was almost continuous. Major Meloche had started that, and I anticipated that I would be taking over. We wanted to map the lines with the different units on it. So one of the tasks Major Meloche was doing every day was visiting different sectors on both sides to establish who was there and meet them first-hand.

When Major Meloche left, he left on a Saturday. At that moment he had flown many times over the trench lines, had almost all the officers and senior NCOs going over it once. We had started spotting a few heavy weapons. We saw a couple of T-34s [very old Russian tanks] down in the Muslim side of the house, southeast near Tarcin. We had reported some artillery pieces through the liaison system. These were taken out of the area. We knew at this time about 75% of who was on the ground, what belligerent units were where, and what their lines of responsibility were but there was still a lot of work to do. We also had met about 75% of the local commanders on the ground. So, basically we went from a situation where the regiment had been escorting convoys through to a situation where we had been asked to gather heavy weapons, talk to the people, and get a dialogue going. Eventually we were to implement the peace plan.

Sunday was a normal day for me, normal squadron operations. At 1900 hours, I was called up by the operations officer's office. I put my stuff on, walked across the way, and then I am told that the famous peace plan, which was supposed to come down to us eventually, has now come down! The general officers commanding the Croat forces and the generals commanding the Muslim forces in BiH have sat down and signed a peace accord that says that as soon as possible all the pockets, including Kiseljak, will be disengaged. In general terms what they wanted to do was have everybody pull back one kilometre. There was an exclusion zone one kilometre back from the trench lines on either side, and there would be, depending on the sector. But in ours, the Kiseljak Pocket, it was put up along the trench lines, split up into ten different regions. Within each region, each side was allowed to keep thirty men, which was called a "confidence" or "insurance" platoon. These guys were allowed to have their personal weapons, plus they were allowed to have five "controllers," who were allowed pistols only, and these controllers were senior officers, like LOs. It was to be enforced by ID cards. We had to physically make these cards for each sector. Eventually, when we would patrol the sectors, we could line everybody up, and everybody should have a card with a number on it. If not they were in violation. The controller cards were there in case a senior officer visited and he would not be considered part of the thirty limit.

There is always a catch. The catch-22 with that one was on the night that I was briefed, the operation was to commence at 0600 the next morning. This was not expected. We knew it was coming, and to be perfectly honest, we had discussed this. Earlier, Major Meloche and I were in front of the map and he said, "I'm going to be gone for two to three weeks. It's not going to happen in that period, we know that. But just for the heck of it, how would you do it if it happens when I am gone with the few forces that we have?" We had a squadron with an effective strength of 85 people, with 10% on leave, leaving seventy to seventy-two people. I had three recce troops of Cougars and that's it. Three times 21 with 10% gone. We were running five Cougars per troop and 15 times 3 equal 45 people.

I remember looking at the problem and saying that I would anchor the operation from the Kis-Vis checkpoint and swing around counter-clockwise. He told me that this didn't make sense. Just like staff college in Kingston: everybody has a different opinion. He had a completely different scenario, so we just left it at that.

Two days later I was talking to the ops officer, who was briefing me, knowing that the next morning we've got to do it. The orders came from above, from the senior UN HQ in Gornji Vakuf. The way they had planned it, they wanted to do it like my plan, anchored from the Kiseljak-Visoko checkpoint and swinging it around counter-clockwise. When I was given the warning order, the first thing I said was that I could not do it. I didn't have the personnel, I didn't have the time to plan it, and we had to recce the thing first. There were a million good reasons not to do it right away. I was told that Brigadier Reith wanted us to start the next morning to show our goodwill. We had to hit the iron while it was still hot. All the cards were in place, both sides were willing, and it was widely believed that if we waited too long, people would change their minds. So we got it started right away.

I got about a hundred extra people for the operation, which brought my total forces available up to 170 people and they came from all sorts of areas in the unit. Initially, the plan was to divide the pocket confrontation line into ten sectors, that's twenty sectors, ten per belligerent, so I needed twenty teams. We agreed that each sector would have three or four people. They would start at one end of the sector and just walk along the trench lines up to the end of that sector, each sector being 10 kilometres long. As my UN people with the flag and blue beret were walking, the troops on either side would leave the trenches, sort of a bulldozer effect.

As we 'bulldoze' in, everything leaves and they go back one kilometre. It was supposed to be done in synch on either side of the pocket so the Croats could see the Muslims in the trenches opposite leaving and they could also see the UN guys advance at the same rate. Like on a parade ground!

We started to figure out who would be on the teams. Obviously you couldn't put a trooper or a corporal in there, and we also needed a translator for each of these teams. Translators were hard to come by so I got almost all of the translators in the UN Sector. I got all the Canadian forward air controllers, the LOs, and even the British exchange officer came along. We mustered everybody, including junior officers. We made twenty teams with a lieutenant, a sergeant or warrant officer, a master corporal with a radio and we had to have vehicles for each team. Some areas were almost inaccessible. In certain areas, the belligerent forces could not see from one trench line to the other.

I started jotting notes in my Field Message Pad, but it wasn't fit for the task. I really didn't know what I was getting into when I walked over to the ops office. I didn't have my junior general kit [map case] or anything. I grabbed the nearest blank piece of paper, folded it into four and started taking notes on one side and writing the orders on the other.

We gathered all of these teams together, just trying to figure out who was on what team. I called an orders group for 2200 that night. By that time I had put the trace on my map, and I was trying to decide what to call the operation, which is an interesting story. It didn't have a name but it came so fast to me. My actual last name is Charon de Cabana and I'm a very big history and genealogy buff. That's my pastime. I remember looking into my name. Cabana is a surname my ancestor picked up when he came to Canada in 1699 and it was the name of his company commander. He spelt Charon with only one 'r'. I wondered where Charon came from and I found two possible origins for the word. One is the trade. Charon is a cartwright, someone who repairs carts for horses. A 'charon' or 'kharon' is a demon from the Greek mythology. Operation KHARON. In Greek mythology, there was the River Styx. When you died, you had to cross it to get to hell and Kharon was the ferryman. George Petrolikas, a Greek Canadian in our organization, understood it and I knew I was doing something important. I had to put a signature on this. I don't want it to be Op CABANA, because who would accept that? So I thought that the River Styx could be the buffer zone that we want to create between the Croats and the Muslims. The Kharon demon could be we UN guys, patrolling this buffer zone. For lack of a better name, I'll call it Op KHARON. I never explained it to anybody; they probably thought it would be too corny. I was in a hurry to give the orders. I thought it was cute and I didn't really have time to explain to anybody what it was. After the first day when we sent the sitrep [situation report] to the Sector South West HQ, we sent it Op KHARON sitrep and they adopted it too.

I called my Battle Captain. He came up and sat down, I'd already sorted out the number of translators, trucks, and radios. We checked to see if we missed any small details, like mine tape. We were concerned about that. I convinced the Ops O that on the first day we were going to do a recce. We only had ten teams. It was a two-phase operation. Phase 1 was to recce the sector with the teams. My concern here was that the Muslim forces had a real problem with the passage of information and that was the biggest problem with the operation. The belligerents' company and platoon commanders on the ground won't have been told about this. When we show up, they'll just tell us to bug off, and that they don't want to participate. Phase 1, then, was to recce the first five sectors. Phase 2, we'd do the disengagement. So we did the first five of the ten sectors. Day 3 would be a recce of the last five, and Day 4 was the disengagement of the last five.

It is obvious to this 12 RBC armoured soldier, equipped with his C-8 carbine, frag vest, and 76mm gun that duty with CANBAT II in Bosnia was hardly "peacekeeping." (CF photo)

So I gave orders. There were practically no notes with everything coming off the top of my head. I was giving live orders for a live operation. I was sending a hundred guys into hostile sectors with mines and stuff and I wanted to make sure that nobody got shot or stepped on a mine for no good reason. We had never done this before; this was a new type of operation for us in our regiment. We had just been escorting convoys in Bosnia and doing a little bit of liaison work and we didn't do anything on the ground outside of the roads.

There were ten sectors. The belligerent forces had agreed to go back a kilometre and leave 30 men in each sector. Our side of the deal was to establish a UN OP in the buffer zone at each of the ten sectors. They were saying, and it was perfectly logical, "We agree to get out of there, but I mean, what insurance do we have that once we leave the other side's not going to take our trenches? We want the UN to establish OPs." My job wasn't to establish them right away; but it was to do the disengagement. We had to have recovery vehicles in case they got bogged down, and we had to have ambulances in case somebody stepped on a mine. Communications was a problem. We have thirty-year-old radios that aren't that reliable given the terrain and everybody had to eat too.

I was mostly concerned about mines. A week before we had a carrier run over an anti-tank mine and almost killed the guys inside. Fortunately, it was an engineer carrier and there was so much stuff in it, that it absorbed the shrapnel. The driver had anticipated the problem so he had opened the cargo hatch on top and opened the ramp a little bit, thinking that if he rolled over an anti-tank mine, at least the concussion was going to go out, and not tear everybody to bits. They blew a big hole in the carrier. A few days before that, a Cougar hit an anti-personnel mine, which just rattled the side of the Cougar, but it was something to watch for. The Directing Staff for this exercise for me was a mine.

The next morning at 0600, everybody set off. Everybody was lined up at the main gate and they took off for what was supposed to be the recce of the first five sectors. It turned out that our logical plan never came off. The belligerents in the first sector had been briefed, they knew about it, were happy to see us, and started to leave. They had already removed their weapons and crated them up. The first calls I got on the air that morning was that these guys were leaving their trenches. I got on the air and told everybody Phase 1 was finished so we can't do the recce because they are already moving. We're already in Phase 2. So we started it and things were relatively uneventful.

In one of the sectors, I guess 5 or 6, there was an artillery captain, "Bullethead" we used to call him, who ran into a Muslim battalion commander that hadn't the slightest idea what was going on. They just saw these UN guys come up. Since the disengagement was happening so well everywhere else, we were a bit complacent. We had to go through the Muslim chain of command to get this guy out. I talked to the Muslim LOs on this, and it took a couple of hours. The funny thing that happened, though, since these guys were not moving, the Croats started to come back. They got pissed off and went back into the trenches and it created a domino effect. Eventually this had repercussions on the two end sectors.

But Op KHARON almost went down the drain. What has to be said also is that these troops were taken out of there because they were needed elsewhere to fight. So it was not just a goodwill thing. The Croats and Muslims had their own motives as well. I remember talking to the company commanders and they were telling me, "We're leaving but we're not going home. We're going somewhere else to fight." So it was economy of effort for them. Still, it was very close to Sarajevo, and it was very twitchy.

There was a sector that touched the Croat lines. There was a point where you had Croat and Serb lines. The Serbs never wanted to co-operate, and they never wanted to be part of this plan but we were still able to make it happen.

So on the first day there was a lot of confusion; some guys didn't know about it, but most did, but the guys who didn't screwed it up. Eventually what happened was at the end of it, we got 80% of the disengagement done. Because of the slow start on one of the Muslim sides, the Croats came back, and I had 80% done from one checkpoint to the other one. So Day 2, we went again, I deployed a squadron HQ near Bakovici on a high point on the confrontation line so that we could have constant communications. The Battle Captain deployed there with Cougar patrols as protection and he stayed there forty-eight hours. We just had an APC; there were no 577s [M-113 Command Post vehicles]. We had a 5/4-ton truck and an APC. That was it. I deployed the SSM's [the Squadron Sergeant Major's] APC as the Squadron HQ, which was quite dangerous actually, as the point they deployed on had seen very, very heavy fighting. He stayed there and assured communications for the second half of the operation.

The second day, the exact same situation happened. It was going well for part of it. Day 3 I did the last 20%. Day 4: the first day that this thing is over and done with, I kept the ten teams, but I down-scaled the ranks, so sergeants could be in charge of them. I put patrols into the sectors. I told the belligerent forces that every sector would be patrolled once for the first few days. On the first day, of course, I'd read in the papers that every peace plan ever devised in Bosnia fell to pieces after a couple of hours or days, so it was very important to get this to continue. The first hours were going to be crucial and lo and behold, the first morning of Day 4, there were communications problems.

Remember that the Croats were isolated in a pocket with interior lines of communications. The Muslims, because they are on the outside of the belt, are spread out a lot more and they've got to go through their Corps HQ in Visoko. If they want to talk to the people on the southern tip near Tarcin, they have to go all the way around to Visoko. There are no telephone lines because the Croats have cut them. The Muslims don't have good radio communications and they can't go around through Sarajevo because that's Serb territory. So I remember the

Muslim battalion commander in this sector telling me that he hadn't had any orders from his Corps HQ for weeks. The Muslim corps commander had briefed me on this, so I went and saw these guys myself. I was anticipating that these guys were going to tell us the same thing further down the lines and that the disengagement would stop. The problem was solved. The Muslim units further down had no problem.

These other guys were isolated, in terms of communications. At 1000 I got word from my patrol over there, that the Muslim battalion has reported that the Croats have gone back into their positions on the other side. By 1400, if the situation was not solved, that the Muslim battalion's brigade, the HQ in Tarcin, will re-deploy the whole brigade back into the trenches. He gave us an ultimatum.

So I looked at my watch, it was 1000, and we had four hours left. So I got on the phone and talked to the Croat LO, Colonel Lucic. He was in contact by cellular phone with all of his units down to platoon level. He could talk to everybody. So he told me that he's talked to his people, and that they have not gone back into their trenches. He said that the lights that the Muslims saw during the night were the insurance platoon, so that was okay. It turns out that this Muslim brigade commander did not really understand the 30-man thing and he overreacted. Finally, by negotiation, I got him to postpone the ultimatum until 1600. I went to brief our CO, but he wasn't available, so I briefed the DCO. In a nutshell the DCO told me that it was my problem, and to sort it out. It was noon, and everybody was going off to lunch, and I said, "Gee whiz, I guess I'm not going to have lunch today." So I hopped in my jeep and arranged a meeting with the senior Croat LO, the senior Muslim LO, and the senior UNMO. I had the Muslim brigade commander in Tarcin briefed, and then he postponed the re-deployment. I arranged a meeting for 1400 in Croat territory, so I had a patrol get the Muslim LO, Colonel Zlatan, and the Croat LO, Colonel Lucic. I got these guys together and we looked at the map. Finally the Croat colonel said, "Well, I'll get our general." So he brought the general around, Brigadier Tole. He came in and I showed my map. I put it on the top of my jeep, and I said, "This is the situation blah blah blah," and Tole said, "Yeah, okay." He picked up a cellular phone, beep, beep, beep, beep, called the guy and said to the Muslim LO, "I can guarantee you that there is no longer anybody in that sector." Colonel Zlatan was satisfied with what he got. I said, "Now we have to inform your brigade commander in Tarcin. Can you get out your cellular phone or whatever?" Zlatan said, "I don't even have radio comms or line comms with them." "Well, " I said, "we'll ride up in my jeep and we'll go down there and speak to them." I told Brigadier Tole, "When I come back from there, I will just confirm with you that everything is fine." By this time the ultimatum had been postponed again to 1900. Tole told me, "If at 2000 the Muslims have gone back in the trenches, I'll bring back my whole corps into the whole Pocket." I told him I'll be back before 2000 and confirm.

So I got in my jeep and went as fast as possible to Tarcin. It turned out that this guy had never been briefed on the plan, had no idea what the different elements were and no idea about what the guarantees were. He was really happy when he was briefed. It turned out that that day was the anniversary, second or third, of the war, and there was a big party outside firing AK-47s in the air and everybody was drunk. They offered me cakes and liquor and all sorts of stuff. They were really happy.

There was a Muslim minibus beside my jeep and my driver said, "Look at the tires on the minibus." They were the same as the tires on my Iltis; they had been ripped off from an Iltis. We could see the Bombardier label, "Made in Canada" on the tire. There were two Hip helicopters right in front of the Muslim HQ. You know that they are not allowed to fly anything in the air, but they had two big transport helicopters there.

So I went back and saw Brigadier Tole, and told him everything was solved. That was a major event. I had to get the head people into it. There were little problems later on but I anticipated problems in other areas and for the following week I went to see everybody on the ground. We started to establish UN OPs in the buffer zone. We handed out the little cards and everything seemed to be fine. When we were establishing OPs in Fojnica, I went to see the Muslim brigade commander, and he told me about ceasefire violations in one of his sectors. Somebody was patrolling into his sectors. I told him that I was surprised. I hadn't had any reports before. He saw that I didn't believe him and he said, "If you don't believe me, I'll kill ten of them. I'll line them up on the sidewalk in front of the schoolhouse across the street. I'll kill ten of them just for you, Captain Cabana, and I'll line their bodies up on the sidewalk and you can come and see them tomorrow, then you'll believe me!" This guy was not very happy. That was the tone I was dealing with. Two days later, he shot one. It was a Croat guy and the Croats admitted doing it. Just little things like that.

The peace plan held. There were enormous problems establishing the OPs because they could never agree as to where they would put them. So we put them where we wanted them and had them live with it afterwards.

The last thing I want to say. Two days after this happened, everybody's attitude changed on both sides and now I was starting to arrange meetings between commanders. This was helpful in avoiding the collapse of the peace plan. It is always at the platoon and company level where people start firing again.

THE SIGNIFICANCE OF OPERATION KHARON

The overall significance of Op KHARON as far as I am concerned, and I will have to relate to an event that happened later on, was that this was an area where we had troops shot at and injured, we had vehicles destroyed, there were UN personnel killed in that area and fighting between the belligerents was happening when we went there. We got into that sector, there was a war going on and the UN convoys were held up for hours and days. We could not get to the hospitals in Bakovici and Drin. Op KHARON proved that it was possible to stop fighting, to get the two sides talking at eye level, to get them to agree on a peace plan, and to implement that peace plan. We did this within 25 klicks of Sarajevo. The thing is, five days after Op KHARON started, the UN controlled the main roads, there were no more belligerent checkpoints to stop us, and the forces had left the whole trench system, which was 80 kilometres long. Only a few months before, it was an area with lots of fighting. So I think Op KHARON proved that these peace initiatives are possible.

STAND OFF, BOSNIAN-STYLE

Two or three days after this, I got a call from the British chief engineer from Sector Sarajevo HQ. He told me that in the Lepinici Valley, there was a hydroelectric line supplying electricity to the whole area in north Sarajevo that gave electricity to 150,000 people. It, apparently, was in my Squadron's AOR. I was given a tasking order from the regiment to do an infrastructure tasking. This major gathered Croat and Muslim hydro engineers, civilians from both sides, he put together a team that were going to repair these gigantic electrical lines that had been cut. The big wires were just dangling on the ground. So I was given the tasking to protect these guys. We did the recce on the first day, and the areas where these people were going to work was a huge minefield. I drove by a Serb artillery observation post, right in the buffer zone between the Croats and the Muslims. I went back at night and told the Brit major, I've spoke to my regiment and its too dangerous. We have to clear the place first. To protect the hydro guys, I had to bring carriers and Cougars in to protect them and use winches to lift the hydro wires back. The Brit major said, "Listen, I know its in your AOR, and I've been ordered to go through you guys, but this is going to bring electricity back to 150,000 people. If you are not willing to protect me, I'll do it anyway. I'm going tomorrow morning."

I told him he must have been kidding. I said, "Listen, if you are going to go anyways, fuck it, I'll go too." So I went to the operations and told them we'd do it anyways. I had already given orders for this tasking. We would take five Cougars plus an engineer section. So the Cougars would protect us with their 76mm guns, and a Canadian engineer section went to see what was going on, plus an APC with a winch to get the lines up. I did the recce the day before and I talked to both sides. I told them what was going to happen, and I decided to do it until the engineer sergeant told me it was suicidal to do it.

The belligerents agreed to de-mine the area using their resources for one day. But the engineer sergeant told me, "Sir, they did the same thing in another spot and we blew up a carrier. What guarantee do we have that it's actually going to be done? We have to do it ourselves." I explained all these problems to the regimental 2IC and we agreed that we would wait until the area was de-mined. I then told him they were going to do the operation anyway whether we went or not and if they got shot at or blown up on a mine, all we would read in the papers was, "We were supposed to be protected by CANBAT 2 who didn't show up."

So we went the next day. Lieutenant Sean DeCaluwe was the Troop Leader. It was pouring rain, the Croat and Muslim hydro guys met for the first time in three years; they used to work together before the war in Sarajevo. They had a couple of sips of coffee and they start working on these pylons. The five Cougars were positioned on the roads facing the Croats, Muslims, and especially the Serb artillery observation post up on a big hill, the one we called "Ostrich." I had UNMOs with me, and an UNMO team with the Serbs, so we had reliable communications. The thing's going on and when the time comes to bring the winch in, I asked the engineer sergeant, "Is this path de-mined?" He said, "I was there with them and I wouldn't have done anything differently. I haven't prodded every inch of it, and there might be something there." So now I had to make the decision. Do I send the carrier into the minefield? So we opened the cargo hatch and the rear hatch, everybody's out of the carrier, and the driver wore his frag vest and helmet, with frag vests on the floor around him. He'd be backing into the minefield, track link by track link, "click, click, click." I was right with him. If he blows, I'm going to blow with him. Either we did this or the repair didn't happen. I thought this was a worthwhile task. I had the civilian foreman beside me telling me when to stop. The poor driver had sweat pouring down his face, even though it was pouring rain and he was looking at me with terrified eyes. I had asked him if he wanted to do it and he said yeah. It was an EME vehicle, not an engineering vehicle. So it was going back and I remembered the civilian guy told me it was okay to stop. I yelled, "Stop!" and I've never seen an M-113 stop so fast.

Then the UNMOs called me. "The Serbs on the mountain in the OP have just decided that if we are not out of there by 1500, they are going to shell us with artillery!" I looked at my watch and it was 1400! I said, "They can't be serious! I have this operation confirmed! The deal was that we fix it." "No, now it's 1500." I talked to the foreman. He told me the whole operation would take until tomorrow afternoon. So I had Sean come up. I briefed him on the situation and gave him another set of orders. I said, "The situation is what I just told you, mission is to sit beside me with a manpack radio talking to the Cougar troop. The minute one round lands, you are going to open fire on the Serbs. I want you to position your five Cougars so they can fire on that hill and I want you to laze [use a laser rangefinder] and I want you to load." Sean looked at me, "Is this a joke?" "No." So he walked back to his troop and gave orders.

I talked to the foreman and asked him what he wanted to do. He said, "There is no way we're going to stop now." The day before I had talked about this problem with the British major and he said, "Don't worry about it, Jacques, because the first rounds that are going to land are not going to land where you are, because chances are they will not land directly on your position. The Serbs asked me where we were going to work and I gave them a six-digit grid [map reference], which was a kilometre off to the west. Human nature being what it is, he'll probably fire the first round off at the grid I gave you. Then they'll see that they fucked up and you have a minute to react."

I briefed Sean on this. "The first round will not hit us, but you'd better hit that fucking OP with a first round." I asked him to load four HESH [explosive rounds] and one Smoke. If we miss, they'll at least see a smoke puff and see we've fired at them. So 1500 started ticking around, it was ten minutes to three, and I talked to the UNMOs who were talking on their cellular walkie-talkies. I told them to tell the Serbs that we have no intention of leaving and you can remind them again that I have five Cougars that will open fire on them. I went to the UNMO and told him to brief the Serbs that the Cougars were repositioning. As we were talking they were repositioning and lazing the OP. So the UNMO told this to the Serbs and the Serbs said they were still going to open fire at 1500. So five minutes before the deadline, I asked for confirmation and the Serbs still said they were going to do it. I put my helmet and gloves on. I looked at my watch and Sean was sitting beside me with the manpack ready to give the order. Two minutes before 1500, we got a call from the UNMOs that the Serbs had decided, "Well, we thought about it. You guys can stay till tomorrow at 1500."

That was nice of them.

CHAPTER NINETEEN

LIEUTENANT STEPHANE GAGNON

Troop Leader,
12e Régiment Blindé du Canada Regimental Group
Visoko, Bosnia 1994

VISOKO, BOSNIA: TASKS

The first time I heard about the deployment was in October 1992. There were rumours but it was not known which squadron was going. Originally it was decided that the recce squadron would go, and it would be formed from volunteers, but most of the volunteers were from our regiment. So I volunteered and I was selected to be part of B Squadron.

In May, we took a military flight from Quebec City straight to Split, in Croatia, and then from there we took a bus. Then we transferred into deuces. We put our flak jackets on from there, with helmets and things. We had our weapons and ammo at this time and we had to lock and load at this point. We went up to Visoko in deuces and Visoko was the main base for us.

We had escort tasks, recce tasks, and our main job was to escort convoys. We had a bit of job escorting UN and European Community relief convoys. We were to make sure belligerent forces did not engage them. The Cougars had the full war load of ammunition, basic loads of 76mm main gun ammunition – High Explosive Squash Head (HESH), Cannister (like a big shotgun round) and Smoke. At the beginning we had only two boxes of GP machine-gun ammunition. We also had smoke grenades with the dischargers, but we didn't put them on unless we had to. We also had personal ammo. The crewmen had pistols and C-8 carbines.

Our first task was patrols. We were there on the 7th at night, about 2300 hours at night. The next morning we were already getting into Cougars, beginning the transfer of tasks. I was doing tasks with another lieutenant so he could show me what the situation was. So the next morning we were doing the job right away. It was patrols – we had to do patrols between Visoko and Kiseljac. That was a MSR, a Main Supply Route, between BH Command (HQ for the UN – UNPROFOR) in Gornji Vakuf and it was a main route between them and Visoko.

This MSR wasn't exactly an autobahn; it was just a small road, very full of curves and things, and lots of sheep on the road. It was very narrow and was the only road we could use to get to Kiseljak safely. There was an autobahn there but we were not able to use it because we had to go through Serb territory. The Serbs didn't want us in their territory, so we had to go through Muslim territory up to Croatian territory and then we did the patrols there and came back. We had a little base there in Kiseljak, which was an infantry company, the Van Doos Company and it was a combat support company. It had mortars, TOWs, and all kinds of nice stuff.

We had to make sure this road stayed clear. We had to do what we call "overwatch". It was kind of an OP. We had to watch the Bosnian Serbs and, if they were firing at us on the main road, we were there to respond. We'd put a patrol of two vehicles up on "overwatch" and move the other two patrols up and down the road; one patrol down the road, and then back. We were static on the side of the road, maintaining observation and keeping our 76 millimeters aimed at them. We weren't using any night vision at all, because most of the tasking was done during the day. It was only at the end of the tour that they began to do night patrols from about 10 to midnight, which was unusual. In UNPROFOR SOPs you can't do anything at night, but most of the time we were coming back from convoy, and things like that, at four o'clock in the morning.

A typical day on the MSR as a Troop Leader in the recce organization revolved around the planning. Most of the things we had to plan were which recce patrol (which pair of vehicles from the seven-vehicle troop: each troop has three patrols) would do the patrols. You have to decide which patrols are going to go there, what time, and do a schedule. As Troop Leader you are active in your troop, you don't stay at the base and just plan the stuff. You go because most of the time you had at least one troop on UN leave at one time. After the first month up to the last month you always have one troop on leave – either on 72-hour leave or on R and R. So that means you have to participate in the patrols and the overwatch, not just hang about the base.

Traffic on this road was mostly Muslim – most of it was city people. There were a few military people moving on this road because there were a few military camps around and there was a training area for the Muslims. There were a lot of mountains around, so the Bosnian Serbs could see the main road; and they had weapons aimed at it. The closest Serb bunker was at 1,350 metres so it was quite close and they could engage anything with a .50 calibre machine gun. Most of the time that's what they did, just erratic fire to scare the UNMOs when they came through in Land Rovers. It was not safe to go in Land Rovers so sometimes we escorted them, or just did the "overwatch" and making sure that if they were fired upon, we would fire back to cover them.

Our rules of engagement with the Cougars were to respond if you were fired upon. If it was determined if it was aggressive and effective fire, that is, it was hitting you, you could respond with the same force that he was using. So if he fired .50-calibre fire, you could too. If it was very aggressive fire, like your Cougars are being hit and bullets are going through your vehicles, your only choice was to fire the main gun, then you fired the main gun. But it was only as a very last resort. I never had to do this, though I loaded a lot of times in some situations. I loaded cannister in the chamber, but if we were taking pot shots on the checkpoint, our people didn't want us to go any farther.

CHECKPOINTS: ON THE ROAD TO BUSOVACA

We were going on one of these roads between Busovaca and Kiseljak, which was a UN-controlled route going to Visoko, because the usual route from Visoko to Zenica was blocked and we had to go around. So when we took this road the Muslims didn't expect us, so we went through a Croat checkpoint and we had to stop there for a few minutes. The Muslims saw us and once we were at their checkpoint they stopped us because they thought we were dealing weapons or doing something with the Croats. They put mines right in the middle of the road, just after a curve so we couldn't see the mines and as soon as we reached the mines, they all jumped in front of the vehicles with RPGs [rocket launchers] and things like that. Then they got into their trenches. We had to stop, and we couldn't go any further.

I was kind of scared because it was the first time it had happened. I didn't know if they were just faking or doing it for real. They had real mines and real RPGs. They were very aggressive and everybody was running around the place so you could see that they were preparing to fight. They were cocking their weapons and aiming at us with the RPGs. My vehicle was the second from the front and then I had the fuel tank trucks, what they called 45-foot fuel tanks, behind me. So I couldn't go back. I couldn't do anything. I was stuck there. I was on a curve, the road was very narrow, and it was like being in no man's land, between the Croats and Muslims. I got scared a bit, and I talked with a sergeant that was in the convoy, and I tried to talk to the Croat, but he didn't speak English or French. I could hear that he was speaking German. So I asked if anybody in the convoy could speak German and there was a guy that spoke a bit. So after two to three hours, we finally spoke and arranged things. He wanted to inspect our vehicles to make sure we hadn't dealt in weapons or ammunition or anything like that. We arranged something for them to inspect our vehicles and then to carry on. I called the OC and he didn't want to let them in our vehicles or anything like that so I asked for an interpreter but he didn't come right away, and we had to wait.

We were all very nervous. I put a cannister round in the main gun, loaded the GPMG, loaded the 9mm, and loaded everything, and every weapon on the vehicle was loaded. The driver was

UNPROFOR's voi sacree *was Route PACMAN, a road cut through the hills and forests west of Kiseljak. Without it, aid could not have been delivered to the besieged Muslim and Croatian communities north of Sarajevo. CANBAT II was responsible for route security which included Checkpoint Charlie at the summit of the mountain. (Author's Collection)*

hatch down; the gunner was ready to fire. It was the first time and we were a bit scared as everybody was aiming at us. Just after about an hour or so, we talked with the guy there and we made the chief of their group come to us and talk. Once we began talking we didn't put our weapons down, they put their weapons down a bit, but they weren't moving from their positions; but at least the tension got down a bit. Then the Canadian liaison officer came and a second pair of Cougars was standing by to come and help us in case anything went wrong.

After that the liaison officer got together with the interpreter and we talked with the guys there and everything got arranged, and we got through without any problems, but we had to give them our vehicle's registration numbers. Everything was okay after a few hours but it was pretty tense for a while.

This happened to us a number of times: not just Croatians but Muslims too. They'd point their RPGs at us, as that's what they would use to scare us. We knew that with the Cougar that a RPG would get through the armour quite easily. When it was just small arms and things at the roadblocks, I just got down there and talked with the belligerent guys and say that it was our mission blah blah blah, what we were doing there, and there was no need to get angry about it.

THE CONCENTRATION CAMP

Sometimes they didn't like us moving around in certain places, because there was a concentration camp or things like that. They didn't want us to go there but sometimes we had to go recce those places. We were going there anyway but once we got there, they'd just get all around us with RPGs. They had masks on their faces so we couldn't take pictures of them. We were at one place that was about 8 kilometres from Kiseljak. It was a small village with Muslim people in there but it was in a Croat pocket, surrounded by Croats. In the small village there were civilian Muslims living there but the Croats put all the Muslims in the same place, and they were harassing them by going there at night, burning the hay for the cows, taking their cows, and they took their wood for the stoves and things like that. We had heard rumours about this going on and that the Croats were beating them so we had to find this out. So we were told to go and recce and talk with the local people to see what was happening there. So an interpreter and I went there, and as soon as we arrived there were about a hundred Croats all around us with RPGs, masks and things, live grenades, and everything. We got stuck there for a few hours. This was really tense too, because they were making threats at us about killing us.

I got down on the ground and talked with the guys there and I was scared. We didn't have the means to do anything there about the situation with the civilians. We finally got out of there safely without any injuries. A few threats and they almost shot the interpreter who was with me. So I had to deal with this, and take the decision. They wanted to keep him as prisoner and to let us go. That was the deal that was made. I said, "No, that's not acceptable." So I had to talk to the interpreter because he was scared, shaking, and out of his mind. I had to calm him down and once it was done I had to deal with a lot of things. The command in Visoko, I don't think, were aware of what was happening on the ground, exactly.

In this situation I asked for a liaison officer, and I told the Croat guys, "Listen, I got an interpreter and liaison officer talking with your boss now. They are making arrangements for us to come out, because you're not supposed to do that to us. It was arranged and we were supposed to come here. You were supposed to be aware." But, we didn't have any liaison officer. I had to make gestures and hand signs, telling him that something was going on to deal us out of there, but it wasn't really true. The command wasn't sending any liaison officer. They said at HQ, that he was already dealing with something else and we don't have any more. They should always have one on standby to help in a situation like that but we didn't have all the support we wanted. I had to deal with this group and finally get out. We got out by talking, and we had to let them inspect all the vehicles. They stripped all of our vehicles, like bare-naked vehicles and took everything out of the vehicles. They checked under the motor, all the rounds and everything. They took all the rounds out. We had M-72s and hand grenades, and stuff like that, and they took everything out. They wanted to keep the weapons. So I had to deal and talk with the guy. He threatened to kill me with a grenade if I didn't get out of there and let them take the stuff. I said, "No fucking way! It's not going to happen." But we were more aggressive. It wasn't the first time and we were getting used to the threats and coercion. We weren't real scared this time. What was scary was thinking that if they wanted to fight we were in a hole and we couldn't get out of there by fighting.

We had three Cougars, that's it. No ground support and no air support. There were a few NATO planes there but we had no Forward Air Controller. We asked for it but we couldn't have it. We asked for lots of support but nothing was coming out of that so we had to go with the means we had, which wasn't much, just talking. It lasted about two to two and a half hours; but we finally got out of there. Once he wanted to kill my interpreter, and then once the thing was all over I told my interpreter to get back to the vehicle. I said to go away, and he went. By the time we were coming back to the base, we saw the liaison officer coming toward us, two and a half to three hours after we requested him. But we did what we were asked to do anyway.

ESCORT OPERATIONS

We also did convoy escort. We had to escort our own supply convoys from Croatia, on the coast, inland to Visoko. We would get up at four o'clock, start rolling at five, and go to Ploce where we would pick up the convoy and it was a good six-hour drive. It's not that far but there are a lot of mountains and hills, narrow roads and dirt roads. It was quite something to go there, going at five in the morning and getting there at eleven or noon. We had lunch, [the pre-cooked packages called] IMPs, and then we were waiting for the convoy. The convoy was supposed to be there about one o'clock or two o'clock, depending. All the time there were a few filters that were breaking so we had to replace them. There were flat tires that were to be changed and things like that. So they always came late to this RV [the rendezvous] and once they got there we had to escort them back to Visoko, because they were a full convoy with rations, fuel, ammo, and stuff like that. These convoys consisted of Canadian MLs, lots of 10-ton trucks, 45-foot fuel tanks and things like that. So we took them, and usually there were about 5 Cougars escorting them, or 3 Cougars, depending upon how many people and how big the convoy was. Now to get them through the mountains, back to Visoko, it takes at least eight to nine hours to get them back, because of the flat tires, filters, etc. Usually we'd get back around midnight, and sometimes at three o'clock in the morning. One time it was twenty-eight hours on the same operation, from point A to point B.

The route was clear most of the time but there were Croat and Muslim checkpoints. Every time you were crossing no man's land there was a Croat checkpoint and a Muslim checkpoint. It was all Croat and Muslim territory. There wasn't any Serb territory in that area. We had to go through all the checkpoints. If they were blocking us, we had to deal with them to get the convoy through.

If we were attacked, we had to get them through the attack, safely, and then fight if we had to fight, and go if we had to go. But, the method of the time was to protect the convoy and to make sure there was no stealing of the stuff by the locals. We had to make sure there were no engagements.

We were, however, engaged on the road most of the time. All sides were shooting .50 cal at us, three or four feet above our heads, just to scare us. As long as the bullets didn't hit any of the vehicles we didn't engage or stop. The Cougars stopped, and the convoy just kept going by, and we just traversed the turret and aimed the gun at them. Lots of the time when we were going through some cities, the Croats and Muslims were fighting and the bullets were flying all over the place. Sometimes they were not firing directly at you, they were fighting against each other. They were frustrated, and sometimes they fired at us.

But we were in the middle of a war there, so you had to make sure the convoy stayed out of this, sometimes by using secondary roads, or something like this. Most of the time we stayed all the way on the same road. We had little shelters on the way, like a British camp there, at Mostar. If we couldn't make it in one day, or if the Muslims were blocking the road because they didn't want us to pass, because they were fighting, then we had to stay in a place and we tried to stay in a UN camp. It wasn't always available and sometimes we had to sleep in the middle of nowhere, with bullets flying all over the place. We had to make sure the convoy was not hit, to make sure there were no snipers firing at us. That was our main task in the convoy.

Tactically, if I had five Cougars, I'd put two up front, one in the middle, and two at the back. The front Cougar was a junior call sign, with me right after. So, if we were stopped at a checkpoint I could get out and I was right in front to deal our way through. I was in the first one if we were being shot at. Like there's one up front of me who can fire while I am taking position, making my decision and my plan. Usually I would put one in the middle and one at the end or two at the end depending on how many vehicles I had – sometimes it depended on the mechanics if we had an up vehicle, but most of the time – five vehicles, two up front, two at the rear and one in the middle to make sure there was protection everywhere in the convoy. Finding the strategic vehicle that needed the most protection, the Cougar would go with this vehicle.

I was in charge of the security of the convoy. But once I took over the convoy I'd go to the convoy commander and say, "Okay, I am in charge of security so everything that is going to go on the air will be me and will be for security means, and I am to make decisions. If I tell the convoy to carry on then you carry on and we do our thing." I was in charge of the convoy. Most of the time it was a sergeant that was convoy commander but sometimes if it were a captain or a major in charge of the convoy and you're in charge of security and in charge of the convoy, then rank can be a problem. Like, they were making decisions such as "We'll go there instead, because we're being engaged here, and we're going to go there." I'd say, "No, Sir, that's not the orders I have. We have to go there, there, there, and do this because we're going to get shot at. That's not the way it's going to work, Sir." There was no place for disputes there.

We had problems with mines. Most of the time there were mines on every checkpoint. Every time they didn't want us to cross a checkpoint, they just put mines all over the place. Sometimes we had to go and take them up, and pull them off the road ourselves. While doing this we were engaged by snipers, who didn't want us to cross. That was touchy. Most of the time they didn't booby-trap the mines, but we didn't know if they were booby-trapped or not. We were just taking a chance by pulling it aside. Sometimes they put logs on the road, and mines under or around it. That was their main means of stopping us, or firing just in front of us.

Most of the time, we didn't have engineers with us. If we were going on recces, like places we had never been before, they would send a recce engineer sergeant, to recce mines or booby traps, and have them check bridges to see if they were damaged and if we could go on them. There's a good thing. We were a recce squadron and were qualified to do bridges, to do route recces and stuff like that. We could evaluate basic booby traps, etc. We had specialists, like Sergeant "The Beast" Labonte, who had been with the Assault Troop, who were qualified in mine warfare.

We also went to escort a convoy going to Srebrenica. We had one infantry company at the beginning of the tour that was there in the pocket, protecting the Muslims. Not quite protecting but making a presence there. The Bosnian Serbs didn't attack or harass the Muslims at this time. There was a no man's land between the Muslims and Serbs, and we had to take the convoy from Visoko to a place called Tuzla. We had to go just a little bit further than Tuzla. I don't remember the name of the place there, and we had to get them through the no man's land because there was fighting between them, and we had to get the convoy through. From there we couldn't go in Serb territory, because they didn't want the Cougars there. So from there the Serbs escorted the Canadian resupply convoy. It wasn't UNHCR.

We had to go up to no man's land, get them on to Serb territory. At the first Serb checkpoint we had to stop, let the convoy go through and come back to Tuzla. So we slept there for one or two nights waiting for the convoy to get back. If they weren't there we had to wait another day, and if they weren't there after that we had to call them on HF [radio]. There was a British camp there in Tuzla so we could go there. Tuzla is a small city. We didn't get into the main city but stayed outside Tuzla. We were sleeping on an airstrip, an old combat airstrip, like a plane bunker. It was mined all around the tarmac, so we had to stay on the tarmac. We couldn't go on the side because of the mines, as the British hadn't cleared it yet. They had just put up a big piece of mine tape around the mined areas and they said to stay on the tarmac, as it was the safest place. We were sleeping there, parking the Cougars on the tarmac, and putting the tents between the Cougars, or sometimes we were sleeping in the shelter there, because we were engaged a few times by artillery. The Serbs would shell the airfield, and we were sleeping there, so sometimes it was quite touchy. Rounds were falling a hundred metres away from us, which was pretty close.

People react to this quite fast. They reacted well. At the first round they all wondered what the hell is that. There was a little plane flying around, and what the Serbs wanted to do was shoot this plane down. It was a Muslim plane trying to land. Unfortunately, we were just under this plane, and so they tried to take the plane out with artillery, which was almost impossible. We were just under it and were receiving the rounds and everybody got in the vehicles in about thirty seconds or so, threw everything on the floor, and everyone got in the vehicles. I don't know how they did it so fast. Shrapnel and dirt was flying around and Boom! You could hear the shrapnel go whizzing by. "That's a real one now, let's go!" We had already decided to crash out of our harbour to make sure everybody was safe and we moved down to another position to wait there. Later we came back to the old position when things calmed down.

We did hear about the Danish tank company, the one with the Leopards. They got there after I came back from Tuzla and went to Tuzla to retake the airport. They engaged belligerent bunkers and killed 11 of them.

We did some work with the British. Sometimes we had to escort wounded Croatians from the Croatian pocket in Vitez to the Croatian pocket in Kiseljak and we had to get through this Muslim pocket. We had to take the Danish ambulances to get the Croatian wounded to Kiseljak where there were helicopters waiting to take them to Croatia to fix them up, which was pretty frequent. Sometimes we worked with the Brits in Vitez because there was a Brit main camp there. Sometimes they would send vehicles with us, one or two Warriors. They're quite aggressive because they had armour on it that was quite thick and nothing was going to get through it. They stepped on mines with it and it was just like running over a rock and they were not scared. They had good vehicles, so they went for it and engaged the belligerents. They didn't even have to be engaged for them to take this action. If there was an engagement near them they fired right away and they didn't allow anybody to take advantage of them.

We went to the Sarajevo Airport lots of times while doing convoy escort. They began in the middle of the tour to take us out of Bosnia by Sarajevo to go on R and R, so we had to escort our people, our deuces full of people, to Sarajevo to the airport, or sometimes we had to go there and get the UNHCR convoy and take it where it was going. One time I had to escort 7 fuel trucks to the airport. They were going to the airport to fuel the planes or something like that. We tried four or five times to get them through to the airport and the Serbs shot up the airport each time. We were going there almost once a week.

PERSONAL OBSERVATIONS

The funniest thing I saw was a cow jump a ravine. The cows and sheep go on the side of the road. The person who was watching just had them freely on the road. Sometimes we were going quite fast in the vehicles in order to get to our destination on time. One time this cow jumped right in front of our vehicles. We hit the brake so the cow got more scared than us and she just jumped the cliff but she got back up on her feet. She had dropped about 250 metres, which was a good drop.

The happiest thing there was to see the children when you gave them food or things like that. That was the thing you remembered because they had nothing. Sometimes it was cold and rainy, and they weren't dressed properly. Sometimes it was really hot and they had nothing to put on or to eat. Some of them were really skinny and looked really sick. That was one of the things that wasn't fun to see, but when we gave them something or some comfort, or some food, we felt good inside. A lot of our guys did this. Most of the time we would get a few fresh rations such as oranges, apples and things like that. Sometimes we would be going through villages and would have to stop for a pee and all the kids would gather around and we would give them little candies or an apple or some little item. It was quite a good feeling to help. They said don't give food to kids and don't do this and that, but sometimes you do it anyway.

My people were excellent, excellent people and highly motivated. They wanted to get this job done, and they did it very properly and very well. They were professionals. I was very impressed with the guys I had there like my gunner Corporal Rene LaRie. He was an excellent guy, and very experienced. He could, if I went down, or something happened, would have been able to take control of the troop, or at least say something to the Troop Warrant. He could have taken over my Cougar right away as crew commander. He made very good decisions, was always ready, and the Cougar was always in top shape. He was an excellent guy. Most of the guys were like that. When you went there you kind of matured. They think more deeply when they take a decision or see something happen and they react right away with the right decision or the right thing to do and they don't hang around. They are really professional soldiers.

In terms of the belligerents, I wondered what they thought about Canada. I heard some funny things, some very funny things. I was stuck in this little village where I had a gun at my head. A Croatian came to me and spoke English. He said, "Hey, you Canadians. You should resolve your problem with Quebec and Canada before coming here trying to resolve ours." I started to laugh, and said "What do you want me to say?" So I said, "My mission is to do this and this, and blah, blah, blah." It was funny to hear things like that. These were Croatian people. He came to me, had a mask and a gun, like Oka. "Yes," he said, "you should try to resolve your problems of Quebec before coming here." I told my people afterwards and they were quite surprised. Most of the time we were well regarded, because some of the people were waving at us and telling us good things about Canada. "We would like to go to your country" and stuff like that. Some people had the Canadian flag and were waving it at us. Most of the time they were giving us a good time and sometimes it got us out of hard situations.

For example, in this village we went through we were taking a recce and the guy said, "We are keeping you detained because you're dealing weapons with the Muslims." And I said, "No, we are not dealing any weapons or any ammunition." He said, "Yes UNPROFOR is doing things, and they want us to die and blah, blah, blah. " I said, "We're UNPROFOR, but we're Canadian. As Canadians we don't do these things. Have you ever heard of a Canadian trying to smuggle weapons, ammunition, food or anything to one of the factions there?" He said, "That makes me think about the situation" and he let me go through. It worked most of the time. Sometimes they looked very aggressive. I would say, "Hey, listen we're Canadian, Canadian." I would show them the flag, and "Oh, okay," and the tension would go down a bit. Sometimes the belligerents were very stressed and they wanted to fight but we showed them the flag and they relaxed. The Brits, as I said, were aggressive, a lot more aggressive, and they hated the Brits. So, if they come at us and pointed a gun at us, I would say, "Hey, Canadian!" and they put the guns down but if it was a British flag, the fellow would have shot me.

BACK TO CANADA

It was hard. It was really hard. You were used to a war situation where you saw all kinds of stuff like death, and firing – real war that is not like a movie or anything. Then you came back here and then you were aggressive, because you've got all this aggression and frustration accumulated for six months and you weren't able to do anything about it there. It would be like the same situation here of being in a bar and having to wait to receive the first punch to reply. In Bosnia, it was with bullets. So it was frustrating. You accumulated the frustration and came back here aggressive. You're nervous and always searching for your weapon. It took me a good two weeks to adapt to the peaceful place we have here. Every big noise you heard you'd crouch down, you're more aggressive and you don't talk, like I wouldn't talk to my wife that much. You know, it is quite something. It takes time to resolve it and it took me a good two weeks.

We had two conferences on stress counselling before coming here and one since coming back here. The only thing about those is that we were doing a kind of group therapy so everybody was to talk to get the frustration out, to tell what frustrated him, what he could have done better, or what he had done, what his experience was there, and let out all the emotions and things. That was mainly the thing going on in the stress meetings and it was useful sometimes. Some people accumulate frustration and never let it out. If they didn't have this counselling they might let it out on their wives or their kids. Some people don't deal with it well. I think that it could be more personalized, one-on-one. I know it is longer, and costs more, but I think it would avoid most of the problems when we come back.

I just had sleeping problems and nightmares. I had that for about two weeks, and then it stopped. I dreamed. It was about the situation I mentioned when they wanted to kill the interpreter. I dreamed I was in a situation like that and they killed the interpreter and we had to get in a fight. Nightmares about situations that happened, not nightmares that are just dreams, or something that you remember are worse than what really happened. Or, they could be about something that could have happened, you talked about it and forgot about it and carried on with task after task. You forget it, and once you come back here it is peaceful and you have time to think about it. So it comes back during the day, you put it aside and it comes back at night. Poof! You have a dream, and wake up in the middle of the night, and whooeee! It takes about two weeks.

I was happy about what we had done, but it wasn't what I expected. I expected a more peaceful mission to get food to people and things like that. Most of the time we were escorting our own convoys, and escorting our own people who were working for us over there. I'd done ten, maybe eleven UNHCR convoys, and maybe fifteen or more, in six months. That's not a lot, but I'm proud of it. At least I brought food to some people. We could have done more than what we did and we could have done more convoys. There were convoys going places without any escorts. They were stopped and sometimes attacked, or were stolen. There weren't enough guys on the ground to do everything.

We could have done something else like the guys in Srebrenica did a real good job. They had to protect the Muslim pocket. It was an excellent job there but so few guys did that. I didn't have the chance to do this. I just did convoys and escorted them there, but as I said we worked for us. I would have liked to have worked for UNHCR or done something for the people, or something like that. I liked my experience a lot and I would go there, I would go back.

CHAPTER TWENTY

LIEUTENANT ROD DOUCET
Troop Leader,
12e Régiment Blindé du Canada Regimental Group
Visoko, Bosnia 1994

I'm originally from Nova Scotia, from a small town in the southwest called Clare. I joined the army in 1989, and went to Royal Roads Military College for four years. I arrived at the regiment in May of 1993 and in October we deployed to Yugoslavia.

I first heard about the Yugoslavia operation the day we were deploying our annual exercise in Gagetown. I think that we had just received a warning order for a regimental tactical group, 12 RBC being the tactical group going. So, the morning of our deployment to Gagetown they assembled the whole regiment and told us that we would be deploying to Yugoslavia and that our training in Gagetown would be cut to about a week and a half. We would be coming back to Valcartier and starting our training. I was anxious at first. Just being fresh out of the Armoured School and having heard the war stories from other people, it was a kind of anxiety mixed with excitement. A kind of "don't know what is going to happen," "kind of neat" experience. Actually, I was really looking forward to it. For me it was finally a chance to prove what I knew. An application of what I'd been taught.

We did the standard refreshers on C-7, C-8, C-9s, Cougar gun camp, first aid, and a lot of lectures on mine awareness. We had historical background and intelligence reports then towards the end we got into the real meat of the training and went out and practised convoy escort, patrols, a little bit of OPs, but mostly it was convoy escorts. Our training prepared us very well. We had already sent two squadrons before that, so the knowledge was there on the basis of what they taught and we had a fair amount of experienced people.

We flew into Zagreb and then flew from Zagreb into Sarajevo. That was a bit scary. Actually I was a bit scared getting to Zagreb because I didn't know how far the fighting was around us but I was told not to worry about Zagreb because it is in Croatia and it was pretty safe. We were told we would be taking a Russian plane to Sarajevo. That was scary in itself! We piled in there and flew down to Sarajevo and got out at the airport. It was quick, and we were told to get out as fast as we could. They gave us our frag vests and helmets. Then they loaded us on the back of trucks, waited until everyone was all loaded up and then they moved us out to Visoko. We were half expecting and wondering when the first round was going to come down. Everybody was nervous and excited because of just being in a new zone. You could tell some guys were really nervous, as they would be chain smoking and such. For me it was a very weird experience. Seeing what Sarajevo looked like was my first taste of what a battle zone looked like. I had never seen that in my life and for me it was a real eye-opener seeing how much of the town got beat to shit, and all that. I had seen the coverage on TV but they were only pictures. On TV you don't have the smell and you don't have the visual image three feet from you, life size. When all these senses played into account with me that's when I got the full grasp, and the full realization hit me. It's a weird smell. It was a smell of cold, burning coal smoke. I find that's an old smell. It's hard to describe. It's a peculiar smell. Maybe concrete, oldness, decay, drab, and dirtiness. I think it was one of the first things I noticed. We wound up in Visoko. How large a town is Visoko? It's hard to tell. What could I compare it to in Canada? I could only compare it to a medium-sized town such as Yarmouth, Nova Scotia, back home.

There were actually a lot of people walking around. Especially, when we got to Kiseljak we started to see a lot of people on the street walking around and by the time we got to Visoko it was getting a bit dark, but there were still some people walking around.

In terms of our base there, I don't think that we had a name for it, just Camp Visoko. What we had were names for the buildings. We kind of termed the building we were staying in the Megaplex. Basically it was a big, three-level concrete building. Where the administration was we called the Crystal Palace, because they had all the comforts. There was a bit of rivalry between the two. Some of us called ourselves CANBAT 2 and the other side were CANBAT 3 and it caused a few fights on certain occasions. There was friendly rivalry and also unfriendly sometimes. It depended upon how much the other guys got tired of it.

I had a recce troop of seven Cougars. It was my first taste of reconnaissance. Now they teach reconnaissance in armoured Phase 4, whereas before they didn't. It was formerly a separate course. Our Cougars were getting old but they were ideal for the job we were doing, because, number one, they're wheeled vehicles, and they go fast. Concerning our job there, it was basically staying on the roads and for fast mobility they were good. What I like to criticize about the Cougar is our armament system. Our sights are archaic and the gun outdated. I don't think that it is necessary to have a 76mm mounted on that thing when what would have really done a good job was a 30mm. The ideal vehicle that I found down there was the British Warriors. They are very agile, very fast, tracked vehicles. They have a good armament; a 30mm Rarden automatic cannon and they had the composite armour right on the side. When they were facing somewhere they were facing broadside. And they had a really good gun on them. To me that was the ideal vehicle down there.

Some modifications were made to the Cougars in Yugoslavia that are being adopted in Canada now. One is the Pitman arm on the steering. I think that another modification was putting a cover on the area where the rounds are stored so that if the Cougar flipped over the rounds wouldn't come out. That's the only two mods that I can see that we have made. The rest was fairly standard. Our machine gun was the old C-5. Personally, I wouldn't trust that weapon if my life depended on it. We had it here and trained with it on the range but it's a fairly old weapon.

FIRST MISSION

The first taste of going out was in doing the changeover. When we got there we had to do a changeover with the other troop leaders. So, they brought us out and I was my partner's gunner. He was teaching me what the routes were, what roads to take, what not to do, and what the safe areas were. That was my first taste of going out. Seeing a bit of the countryside and seeing a bit of the people was a pretty awe-inspiring experience going out for the first couple of times. Meeting the warring factions was pretty interesting and it was mostly Bosnian Croats at the time. I remember doing a run to Vares. I was doing a run up there with my partner and I think that Vares still belonged to the Croats back then and that it was in imminent takeover by the Muslims. A lot of stuff had been brewing, and there was a checkpoint before getting to Vares, which was heavily guarded. The people there were heavily armed and they had the old Claymore mines set up on the side of the houses. It was a hairpin turn and when you came in with your Cougar the Claymore mines were set about head level and they had a couple of mines on the road. I think that it was a fairly important area.

What I noticed there was the tension. You could see it but you could also smell how thick it was. For me it was, "Holy Shit, what is this?" I think that after a little bit of haggling the belligerent guy let us through and we came back through later on. That night my partner had to go out again, and that was the night there was a big push by the Muslims. He had to go back to that same checkpoint. There were tracers going off all around, as there was an exchange between the checkpoint and the mountains. I guess the belligerent was shot in the leg and they picked him up and put him in the Cougar. He was bleeding all over the place so they brought him to the closest doctor. I don't know if he lived or not. He was pretty pale. That was, I think, my first real taste of the action down there.

It was hard to take in reality. When you grew up in Canada you were fairly secure, and you didn't have to watch where you're walking. You just walked on the grass and on pavement and you don't have to worry about getting shot, depending on which neighbourhood in Canada but you led a fairly secure life here. In Yugoslavia it was a totally different experience. You had to watch where you walked because it was littered with mines, and you couldn't take a piss at the side of the road. You couldn't do this, and you couldn't do that. If a bullet was going to fly towards you, you heard a crack. You didn't know what it was but you took cover anyway. It was a whole different ballgame.

I found it different from all those movies. In the movies people are shooting. You look at things, then there is a firefight and you see everything. You see the bullets and tracers. They shoot at you here and you're just looking around and wondering where in hell it came from. You CAN NOT see it, and you don't know where it comes from and it's very scary. You hear that bullet whistle by and it might have missed you by an inch, you don't know. Part of the problem is target acquisition.

I think that I had the best troop. They really were a great bunch of guys and really stuck together. They were really a tight-knit group, especially after we had a tragedy in the troop that really brought the guys together even more. We had a Cougar flip over a bridge and it killed two of the crew. It was at the end of November and they were two really good guys. A lot of guys were really good friends; they were close before, but I think that this brought them closer. They saw the importance of helping each other out. In addition to this, the leadership I had in my troop was next to none. A good bunch of guys.

CONVOY ESCORT

Things were still pretty tense when we got there. Basically, what would happen is that every night at a certain time we would have an O Group. The Battle Captain would be the one responsible for giving out the taskings. We called them taskings, not missions, as they were really routine tasks. He had a board and would say, "1 Troop, tomorrow you have to supply two Cougars to go here to do this. These two people, you have to go here to meet this certain person, go to this area and then come back." Then what we would do is look to see whom we had available and we would task according to detail, according to what we have. Normally a patrol going out was two Cougars, if it was a small convoy. The longer the convoy, or the greater the importance of the convoy, the larger the number of Cougars we sent out. It was a Patrol Leader going out with his junior call sign, most of the time.

One fairly routine task we had was patrol of Visoko-Kiseljak. We basically sent out two Cougars on our patrol, three times a day, patrolling up to Kiseljak to BH Command, staying there for a bit, turning around and coming back. Their task was to keep that road open. It was a fairly important route for us because that's where all the UNHCR convoys went through each day. They would come in from Zenica and come down to Visoko. Since BH Command was in Kiseljak it was important that we kept that open.

I think that the Croats were the ones that were causing a fair bit of shit. They had a checkpoint just before coming into Kiseljak, and sometimes, depending upon their mood, they were sometime bastards about it. They had blown a crater into the road with some mines there. We had asked them to move it. They said they would but they never did. It was a continual squabble with them. Basically, the Muslim checkpoint was easy to go through. They would just wave us through. But every time we came right before Kiseljak was the big thing. They had all the mines laid out, and it was a big point with them. They had to do the vehicle checks and ask a million questions. We weren't letting them inside the Cougars; we were just opening the door for them to see. A big thing for them was to look inside the Cougar. They thought it was kind of neat. Sometimes they just wanted to piss us off, to show us that they had control, and not us. They wanted to see if there were any Muslim refugees in there, doing some contraband, or stuff. Basically, if we were loaded with cigarettes or booze – it never happened to us but it happened to UNHCR people – they seized the stuff for themselves. It was getting to be a pain in the ass. I had to get off the Cougar all the time, put on the frag vest and helmet, get down, open the door for the guy, close it, and continue down the road.

They tried intimidation with me once. I was bringing a dignitary from Kiseljak, a Canadian colonel, who had visited Visoko, and I was bringing him back to BH Command that night. It was nighttime, and the locals had set up this rule that after a certain hour you couldn't go through their checkpoints any more but we went anyway. I was stopped at the checkpoint where I got off and I asked the guy to pass, that we were bringing someone back to BH Command, and we would just go through and come back, in five minutes. They said, "No!" I called on the radio and told HQ they wouldn't let us go through. They said to continue negotiating. So I tried. He was this young guy, about eighteen years old, and he was the kingpin at the checkpoint at the time, and thought he was pretty big. They had the barricade down, and we just stayed there with lights on. The young guy came out again and put them two mines in front of each vehicle. He went inside his cabin and came out with an RPG-17. His buddy, in the little cabin, shut off the spotlight, took out his RPG-17 and aimed it at us. I didn't know how serious they were.

I was thinking, "Jeeze, I've got to get the fuck out of here. I've got to back up, and get the fuck out of here." What was worse was my junior call sign was right in front of me, so the belligerent was aiming right at his vehicle, and the other guy was aiming right at mine. My other call sign was sort of panicking. He was calling back to the base, saying, "Come on, make a decision, tell us to get out of here." I was trying to get him to calm down. I called back and said calmly, "I don't think that they want us to go through. They have one RPG-17 aiming at us and they have four mines in front of our vehicles. I don't think that it would be wise to go through." So, they said, "Back off, turn around and come back." So we backed off, turned around and went back. It was a fairly tense situation – time to change the shorts. It was a very close call. I think that they were pumped, really pumped. Again, you don't know to what level they are joking, are playing with you, or how much intimidation they will actually use before we actually crack. I think that they knew they could get away with it. They were also unpredictable. It was a well-known fact that after four o'clock it's their custom to start drinking. After four o'clock it would start to get dangerous, because you'd find these guys intoxicated on the checkpoints and it was not a time to mess around.

On some occasions I had good relations with the belligerents on the checkpoints. We'd strike up conversations and talk about how things are going. You'd talk about home and family and how it must be rough out here today, and kind of cold. Christmas is coming, what are you going to do for Christmas? Stuff like that. Actually we had a really good rapport with some Serbs when we were doing an OP. We were doing an OP because they were complaining that some Muslim snipers were shooting at them all day. So, we sat up there, right next to a Serb bunker. They were just as curious as the Croats and they would come up and look inside our vehicles. We'd do mobile OPs with the Cougars. One guy would watch and be on radio. So, these Serb guys would come up and they'd bring coffee up to us, and some cake. They were just as curious about us as we were about them and some of them were really friendly.

Interpreters were the only way we could communicate. It was hard to find the soldier who could speak a little bit of English. Some did, but most didn't. Sometimes we didn't have the interpreters, so it was just like a lot of hand signals. Actually we got the finger from the kids, but I think the older people influenced the kids. There were a lot of kids throwing rocks, giving us the finger, and stuff like that. A lot of kids on the street asked for candy, and food.

One time the adrenalin was really pumping and I was scared shitless but it was a kind of high. Okay, this was exhilarating in the meaning that I was pumped. I escorted this French general to Vares, where he had a meeting to set up. It was just a junior callsign and I – a two-Cougar patrol, and we had two little jeeps. We went up on top of a mountain where he had troops, and a lookout point. Right next to it was a Croat pocket. They were still fighting with the Muslims so we said that we'd bring him up there. We went the route, and halfway up the route you heard the whistles, like a whistling – SSSSSSSSSSSS and then this loud vibration just knocked me in the back of the head. Boom!!!! My junior callsign was in front of me and he looked at me with this look on his face. I yelled, "Stay Down!" So, we're still going up, and all shit started to break loose. By the time we got up on top of the mountain, there were mortar rounds coming all around us, within 100-150 metres of where we were. I could see snipers in the houses. We were stopped once. I looked over and there was this guy who was shooting from his house, and he looked at me, and I looked at him and gestured – where's it coming from? He looked at me and indicated that he didn't know. He was just shooting anywhere. It was a big disaster up there. I guess the French guys were pulling out the same time we got up there. So we got them all organized, put them in one big convoy, and said we were getting out of there. I think that it was the Muslims up there that had brought up their little vans and were loading bodies up on their vans. I was looking at them and said to myself, "What carnage." I kept saying to myself, "I've got to get down this hill, I got to get down this hill" as the shells were coming closer and closer and closer. We finally got down there and it was such a relief that we made it.

THE PSYCHIATRIC HOSPITALS

The summer before my regiment went down we found the hospitals, at Drin and Fojnica. I think it was the Van Doos that found them and when they got in they found that the staff had totally abandoned it, and left all the kids in there. So they cleaned it out and CANBAT 2 had to start sending a section down there to maintain and protect it. When we got there, my troop was the first one to send a section out there and we were basically the hospital defence. I went down to visit once and it was not a pretty sight. The kids in there had a lot of physical disabilities and deformities, as well as mental disabilities. It was mainly a hospital for children and orphans. The conditions were just deplorable that these kids had to endure – the smell was really bad, really rank. Many of these kids had bedsores, dirty open sores, from being in bed too long. We had just started the process of cleaning it back up but there were a lot of things they were missing like adequate heat, light, and fuel. A lot of the runs we did down there were to supply fuel to keep the hospital running.

There was another hospital that was a couple of kilometres down the road where the old people were. We sent people down there too. They would do a shuttle down there to keep an eye on things. It wasn't until the second rotation went through that all the shit hit the fan. That's when the Muslims and the Croats were starting to skirmish in that area and things got very tense because the fighting got to within 300 metres of the hospital.

Our people in the hospitals did a really good job. A lot of them were really brave. They had come to the point where they couldn't bring the staff in because there was too much danger. One side threatened that if they saw any staff there they would kill them. The shelling got really started in the town and they had shot at the hospitals. We actually sent down a large protection force, some Cougars, to defend the hospitals if we had to.

Caught between Croatian and Muslim forces fighting over the Kiseljak Pocket, the remote Drin and Bacovici Psychiatric Hospitals contained medical staff, orphans, and patients who were subjected to abuse by the belligerents. Despite many assertions to the contrary, CANBAT II, led by 12 RBC, was successful in securing, protecting, and feeding the occupants. (CF photo)

It was a good thing that it didn't come to a firefight between us and the other factions. The town had been taken over by the Croats and then it kind of settled down.

The guys that were there did a lot to improve the conditions there. For what the people had, we improved their living conditions. As Canadians we're very resourceful, and I think that's because we're very comfort minded. We live for comfort, so we'll do anything to keep things comfortable and we're really resourceful in that way. The guys were ingenious in what they did. They helped greatly – changing diapers and a lot of other selfless acts. There were some really deformed people, most people back here would just look at and throw up, and be very disgusted. We went in there and gave them some affection, hugged them, and gave them friendship. That's one of the taskings I am most proud of. It's a dirty tasking but it's a rewarding one.

PATROLLING

Route recces, towards the end when it looked as if peace was kind of settling down and they were opening up more of the roads to us, were easier and we were getting more freedom of movement in some areas. Relations were getting better so we were getting more freedom to move around, and hoped to patrol some roads that we, the UN, had never gone through before. We went to villages that had never seen UN people before and they were really surprised. They reacted like kids in front of a toy store. They were gawking, looking, and very curious. They are very curious people. Big crowds would mass around and they would look everywhere. I don't think they knew where Canada was. A few of them knew and they'd say, "Canaski" or something like that. I think that was their term for Canada. Some towns had taken a real beating, and some of them were deserted because they had been cleansed. It was really eerie. You'd go by a house that was half destroyed and you'd see a doll outside, or you'd see a shoe and you'd always wonder who the owners were. These are things that went through your mind. You always wanted to know the history of the place, or the history of the people here, where they were now, or what they were doing.

UN LEAVE AND BACK TO BOSNIA

I had my UN leave at approximately one third of the tour, and I came back to Canada. It was the middle of winter, so I took my girlfriend to Mexico. I needed the warmth, the peace and quiet, and I needed to be far away from the distraction and the noise. I came back to Canada, visited some relatives, my family, and then I had to go back. I had only two weeks off. When I went back to the unit, it was hard to accept the reality of being back there after having so much fun back here. Then I had to get used to it again. For about a week I was kind of depressed, not wanting to be there, missing people back here again, and wanting to go home again. After that you'd get back into the groove of things. So you kept on going.

CONVOY TO SREBRENICA

We were trying so hard to get the Van Doos out of Srebrenica. We were lacking manpower to guard the camp, so we had to keep a squadron back and we had to rotate through with the other ones. So eventually we got stuck with camp guard and yes it was boring, and yes it was tedious, and shitty hours because it's shift work, but it was something we had to do. Eventually we got to go to Srebrenica. First of all it was a long road trip. It was about thirteen hours and we went through Vares, through Tuzla, and from Tuzla we came down to Srebrenica. We couldn't go across Bosnia. There were lots of shorter ways, but the way the roads were set up and the checkpoints, you couldn't go through here, and you couldn't go through here, and you had to have permission from their HQ. So you really had to set up appointments two days in advance, as a lot of clearances were needed but we basically got there. Srebrenica, for me, was very desolate as a town. I was there when it was overcast and cloudy, and it just emphasized the desolation and the desertedness of the place. We were resupplying our own people and doing a changeover. We met up with three-hour delays at checkpoints and it was very late by the time we got there.

Our guys in Srebrenica liked it there. They were far away from the mother nest so they had a bit of autonomy, which is always good. It was their little sector to control. The guys were well. They didn't have a kitchen like we had so they ate rations there for six months. IMPs for six months, and the showers – well, they didn't really have good bathrooms they had makeshift bathrooms. The living conditions could have been better, but they were a fairly happy bunch of guys. They had TV, they had a VCR, they had the movies, and they had their own little mess. Even though it was a pretty large town, to have a company group in there, they felt that they were accomplishing a lot. I didn't get to tour the whole town, but apparently they had OPs set up that covered the whole area. They basically did a rotation from the main camp.

MORAL SUPPORT, ALLIED UN CONTINGENTS, BELLIGERENT RELATIONS

I found, actually, that I received good support from home. At Christmas time every soldier was delivered a gym bag full of gifts. It was set up down here, all over the country, and they had mass funds to send all these packages down to the soldiers. We got letters from people, mainly schools, congratulating us and telling us how proud they were. As far as support went I was really glad to see the support we got from Canada. Usually the Canadian people are very anti-military, very, very anti-military. But the support was an eye-opener for me and maybe I am wrong and maybe a lot of people do care about us. A lot of the guys that were up there wrote back and they kind of kept pen pals. I didn't. I was just too busy. I wrote one letter back. I took a letter from this girl and read it and I said I'd write this girl back. So I wrote back and said thank you for the support, we really needed it, it was refreshing to see, and was a big morale booster for us. It was a big morale booster when you saw all this support, because, we're off on our own, a little Canadian contingent far away from home. That's what we needed was support. In terms of the media coverage, some was good, and some wasn't so good. I know that a lot of journalists were out there looking for sensationalism and that's what they got. They gave us a bad name. We have a good reputation in-theatre and of all the contingents there I think that we were the most respected.

From the three factions that were there, this is what people were saying: "Canadians are nice. Oh, you're from Canada." They would be really friendly.

A lot of the other UN contingents loved coming to our camp, as we had the best facilities. I toured a lot of the camps around and we had the best food, the best living conditions, and the best atmosphere. I visited the Swedes in Tuzla, the Swedes in Vares, the French in Sarajevo, and the Brits in Vitez.

Other countries like Malaysia, Egypt, and Jordan, had terrible sanitary hygiene and were kind of ignored by our people. The Malaysians were watching a bridge for us and they had just come in. The guys were very friendly, but they were disgusting. They would call us to come pump their shit house all the time, and they would wait until it was flooded. They have no concept of hygiene, or sanitation. I would never eat or sleep at their camp or anything like that. They offered me coffee and I would refuse politely because I told them I was in a hurry. These are stories that filtered out from some other people – they said don't ever eat or use anything of theirs.

In terms of the Brits, the Brits are Brits. They had a bit of a snotty attitude. They had the good equipment so they could afford to be. They are aggressive people. And these are the guys that didn't take shit. Someone shot at them and they'd make sure that they replied. They had that attached to them all throughout the tour. The Brits are hard and the French are known to be hard too. They had problems dealing with the belligerents because of the tensions that they have created. We don't create the same kind of tension because we tried to avoid any exchange unless it was absolutely necessary. An exchange of fire I mean. We'd negotiate to the death, whereas they wouldn't. I don't want to generalize or I don't want to say that this is for certain, but that was my impression. The Swedes were the same way. The Swedes had a take-no-shit attitude. The Nordic Battalion got their Leopard tanks in. Once they got those in and anybody shot at them, it was like a couple of rounds of HESH going downrange at a bunker. They got in a huge standoff once with, I think, the Serb extremists, the Chetniks and this made the news too.

I bumped into these guys once on an operation we did. These guys are hard to describe. They wear a black hat. They usually have a beard and they are very fanatical. You see it in their eyes. I think that some of them are mercenaries. This Swede guy was telling me that during that standoff there was a Chetnik there and he talked very American. So, you never know who is there. These guys drive around and have these nice little white trucks, with human skulls on the hood, as ornaments. They're basically uncontrollable and the Serbs will admit that to us. My friend, who was also our Troop Leader, ran into one during an operation who was pointing his gun at everyone. My friend was kind of getting nervous, so he asked, "If this guy continues, do I have permission to pop him in the head?" because it was getting pretty tense. I guess the Serbs said that we would be doing them a favour because they are really uncontrollable. I heard that his name was Vlasko. Everybody had their psychotics over there.

We're a good peacekeeping force. I think that we are made for that. We're very effective at negotiating and trying to work out peaceful solutions in situations. That's the attitude we had down there.

BACK IN CANADA

I think that I kissed the ground when I walked off the plane. It was a totally new outlook. People don't know what they have until they don't have it any more. They go to a place like that. People take a lot of things for granted. I know that I did but I am aware of it now. It was hard trying to get back into the mentality of civilian life down here, mainly because I'd walked through a mall. I was very, very bitter because I'd look at people and think that they had no concept of what they had, and how lucky they were. They had no idea what I'd been through, and what I did. They were just going about their merry little lives, shopping and laughing, having all these luxuries and comfort. It gave me some difficulty and I was bitter for awhile. I was somewhat resentful. I felt superior, in a certain way, to other people who hadn't gone. That feeling you get. I thought, "I'd been almost killed, I'd been shot at, and you're just a plug." It went away after awhile. I realized that it was my job. I had a job to do and it wasn't anybody else's job. I had to take it; I had to deal with it and it just kind of flushed itself out of my system.

In terms of my guys, I didn't have to counsel anybody regarding any stress problems. There was a debrief with the Padre. We had some really good briefings about how to settle back into the family. They took that into account this time and there were some really helpful hints. I was just a bit nervous walking around when I got back. We were so used to watching where we were going. The adjustment period was really small for me and I found that I adjusted very quickly. It was one of those experiences that I am really glad I had and it was a positive experience in my life. The situation that was there, I don't wish it on anybody, but it's kind of nice to have it, and I don't regret having it. I'll never, never have a regret going. I don't think that I want to go again, because once was enough for me, but I can look back and say I've done this, it was rewarding, and it was enriching. I have seen this part of life and I think that I feel more complete now.

CHAPTER TWENTY-ONE

LIEUTENANT JASON STEEVES

Liaison Officer,
12e Régiment Blindé du Canada Regimental Group
Sarajevo, Bosnia, 1994

LIAISON OFFICER: SARAJEVO

I had a lot of freedom because my job was very flexible and no doctrine to it whatsoever. There is nothing we do here in the Canadian Army, written in a book, that tells you how to be an LO. You can see Brigade LOs written down somewhere but it's not the same game, it's completely different. I had a driver, with an Iltis, and because I was in Sarajevo, I had a sergeant who took care of operations as well. We had three people there all the time. I speak English, French, and by the end, some Serbo-Croat.

First of all I wasn't supposed to go to Sarajevo. Someone else was supposed to be there. When we showed up the first night, the senior LO had a discussion with the LO in-theatre and they decided to change around people and they shifted priorities, which is why I got sent down to Sarajevo. They just said, "You are going to Sarajevo tomorrow morning so get your bags packed." I didn't have much to pack. Someone came and picked me up in an Iltis, the sergeant who was there before. "Welcome Sir, it will take us a half hour to get down there." I met the LO who was already there, did a tour of the city and he took off the next day. The handover was about 30 minutes long – basically "This is where you go if you don't want to get shot, and this is where you are supposed to be," and that was it.

I was commanded and controlled by CANBAT 2 in Visoko, but the French in Sarajevo supported me. We were in what was called the PTT building, which was the old telecommunications office building that the UN took over and the French have it right now. When I was in Sarajevo, there was an Egyptian battalion, Ukrainian battalion, and two French battalions. The French had the nucleus of the HQ for that sector, but there were some British officers, some Ukrainians, there were some Canadian officers working there and Egyptians. I was the LO with CANBAT 2 since we were so close. Most of my time was spent in Sarajevo but I went to Visoko once a week and that was it. On the weekends I went up to get an ops briefing from the duty officer and to give an operations briefing to the operations officer. He'd call me into his office, and he'd say "Jason, what's going on?" I'd tell him what the French battalion was doing, this is what the other battalions are doing, and this is what the belligerent battalions are doing in the area, it was fairly dull but every once and a while it was interesting and important. Most of all, it was important for him to know what was going on with the Serbs because the Serbs that we dealt with were in Ilijas but their corps commander was just outside Sarajevo in a place called Bukovice and it was with me that he had the contact. For liaison work, convoys, clearances, or grievances, it was all done through Sarajevo and that was why the operations officer wanted to know what was going on with the Serbs in that area. It was all inter-related.

SARAJEVO: THE MILITARY SITUATION

It's fairly simple to describe. It's a horseshoe around Sarajevo. You have a mountain called Mount Ingman here, which is held by the Muslims, and Zdinci, that's the Muslim-held area on the other side, and the only thing that separates the two is the airport. Their two areas were not connected, but there was a tunnel that existed under the runway. At the airport there was a French battalion, and Lukavica was where the Bosnian Serbs Corps HQ was located. They called it Sarajevo Romanjia Corps, the corps surrounding the city. Stacked north of Sarajevo, in Vogosca, there were three brigades and there were five brigades surrounding the city with three stacked on top of it. So you had Rajlovac Brigade, north of Sarajevo, Vogosca Brigade north of that brigade, then the northernmost was Ilijas Brigade and Ilijas Brigade was the one CANBAT 2 dealt with during the hostage-taking at the bridge.

They are not brigades, as we know them, they are about the size of two companies or a battalion to battalion-plus strength. They were mostly pure infantry. I knew the brigade commander at Rejlovac, personally. He was actually an engineering officer who commanded an infantry brigade. He was only a captain at the time, but because of the problems of positions, he was put in charge.

Common accommodation for Canadian soldiers serving with UNPROFOR generally included the modification of damaged or destroyed houses into white sandbagged bunkers not only for protective purposes but also to provide a visible UN presence in the area. (CF photo)

They actually did have armoured brigades, but not as we know them. They are mostly ad hoc organizations. Vogosca Brigade, up in the mountains north of Sarajevo, sat in trenches and that was their job. They all had BMPs, BTRs, the Otter M-60 vehicles (like a BMP) and they had a lot of those as troop transports. They also had a few tanks in the southern part of Sarajevo and they had T-55s shooting down into the city from the old Olympic bobsled track. There was a lodge up there on the mountain. That was on CNN and that was where the UN took away a few of the tanks; the Bosnian Serbs used to park tanks there, at least three of them.

When we were there during my tour the Muslims did a fairly large clean-up of the city. There used to be a Croatian brigade in the city, because Sarajevo was very cosmopolitan before the war and in fact all three ethnic groups occupied the city. There was a large group of Croatians who stayed in the city after the war started and they became a brigade. They were loyal to the Muslim cause, but they were also Croatians. What they did was they divided up into a big rectangle in one area of the city. They were, in effect, Muslims but they were called the Croatian Brigade. In Sarajevo, it was hard to tell what you were, as most of the time you had mixed parents.

In terms of the nature of the conflict in and around Sarajevo, it was strange. For a while, the Serbians were shooting fish in a fishbowl. Even where [UNPROFOR] BH Command was, in the Kosovo Valley near the old stadium and the arena. It was right in the valley, and if you looked south from this valley, you'd see a large mountain where the Olympic sites were, and they had positions right down that valley where they could shoot anything that moved because they had a .50 cal sniper rifle shooting right at BH Command. A Canadian, Brad Smith, was the G2 [the Intelligence Officer] there, and he got a .50 cal round in the doorway. He was working, turned the light on, and the round came in the doorway. A .50 cal sniper rifle!

SNIPERS IN SARAJEVO

Sniping isn't what we know it as. We hear of sniping all the time from the journalists, right? Sniping could actually be some drunken soldier with an AK-47 and the media was going to report it as sniping because someone got shot with a bullet. That was sniping to them; it was a bullet, and someone was dead. There are real snipers. I remember one time the Muslims set up kind of a sniper hunting team. They went out and did counter-sniping activities. The police in Sarajevo had a building that was a sniper OP. I was there one day with the UNMOs and they pointed out exactly where the positions were, the known snipers on the Serb side. What the Serbs did, this is classical sniping, is they would bore a hole in one wall, an outside wall, go back through that room on the inside, go past another wall into another room, and bore another hole through it so they are completely protected. They were given an arc of responsibility and in one building, that sniper could have three arcs set up for that one room.

This is pretty sophisticated activity. They've had several years to prepare these positions, and it was not like they just walked up to the building and put a few sandbags down. They actually bored holes in the walls and had arcs set up. They had maps with the positions on it with the other arcs of the other snipers. Sarajevo had long tramways running through the city east and west, and a couple of the cars were still there that were used as sniper screens. They also used old sea containers set up like Lego blocks with pathways in between, so you had two blocks set up with a path of about three feet wide so that people could walk along the side, and they had one stacked on top of it to act as a fence to stop the shooting from the south coming down into the city. Most people, called it "Sniper Alley," and the locals would walk three blocks up where buildings protected them and where the streets were perpendicular to the sniper positions. One sniper shot at 800 metres to a 1000 metres range, and they figured he watched a person walk as they entered behind the screen, timed the person as they walked for however long it took them to walk by pacing, and he shot the person through the three-foot gap in the two sea containers. Not only did he shoot that person, but when someone came by to look, that guy got shot too. They were very good. The Bosnians got one of the Serb snipers. She was the Romanian Olympic shooting champion back in the 1980s, and she was working with the Serbs. The counter-snipe team found her, and killed her.

The rumour was that the Serbs had a platoon-sized sniper unit, which was apparently controlled by one guy called Dragan. Nobody knew his last name or anything about him. Dragan is a very common first name for Serbs, sort of like Bob in Canada, and he was the guy who controlled the snipers. The 30 or so snipers got pay incentives for every person they killed. They used AKs, or whatever they had and sometimes 7.62 Russian Dragunov sniper rifles. The more people you killed, the more money you got. Those were all rumours that we got off the UNMOs. We heard a male Bosnian is worth a certain amount, a female is worth more, a pregnant female is worth even more since she is bearing a child that will serve in the army but we couldn't always get confirmation on that sort of stuff.

LIAISON OFFICER IN SARAJEVO: ALLIES

My opinions on what was going on changed throughout the tour. When I first got there, "Christ, Sarajevo, great! Excellent! I'm 21 years old and I'm going to get killed!" Then after a while it became fun and it was a really interesting tour. Six months working with the French and British, and every day was a new experience, as we had something new every day.

The French had a different attitude. Their concept of operations was completely different from Canadian, British, and American concepts of operations. They had a completely different way of dealing with things, and a different men-officer relationship. My French counterpart was a major, a Commandant, which was hard to get used to, as I was only a second lieutenant and he was the liaison officer I dealt with the most. That didn't matter once we got to know each other and we developed a certain rapport.

An anecdote: I remember trying to go down and buy some wool socks at the French QM store. That was all I wanted and I hated going down there because the French soldiers gave me a hard time because I spoke Quebecois French. It was different, really different. I walked in there and said "Est-que je peut a mois a deaux pair de bon delais?" ("Can I have two pairs of wool socks?") and he looked at me and said, "Excuse me Sir, what did you say?" I repeated it. "Sorry, I don't understand." They went and got me a case of coke. No, I said, "the things you put underneath your feet and in your shoes." "Au, chaussettes Monseiur!" I used the word "baut" which is a Quebecois word, and it didn't make sense to them in French. As soon as he heard between the feet and the shoes, he understood. "Fuck, just get me the socks." When he came back he turned to his friend and said, "He speaks French but I don't understand what he is saying." That was what their attitude was. They laughed at me because I was speaking French and they knew I was speaking French, but they couldn't understand it! But it wasn't always that bad. It was just certain expressions that vary in Quebecois that they didn't get. They loved working with us and they called the French Canadians their "little cousins." They called me a "false cousin" because I was English and spoke French. "Bonjour mon petit faux cousine." It wasn't an insult, they were just joking and I became friendly with most of them.

We went to morning prayers with the general. Everyone shook hands with everyone and then when the general walked in, we went to the inside of the horseshoe table and shook hands with everybody. It took five minutes to do this. The French were really polite about this and they closed off the kitchen Sunday nights in the mess. Then the officers would go upstairs and drink wine by candlelight and have French bread and it was in excess of $200 per serving. When they came over, they brought a portion of their wine cellars from their home stations and it was like having a mess dinner in the field. When I first got there, the policy changed after the UN heard about it. You could get a bottle of wine at lunch and at dinner per person! You just go up and grabbed a bottle of wine, as it was rationed but you could have white or red. There was more wine in the FREBATs than water and we could have a bottle of wine or a glass of water, which was quite something in an operational zone. The French, of course, controlled the airport and they got the job done but I couldn't understand how they worked. I just took the end result and didn't worry about it and worked with it so that was what I ended up doing. They have a different concept of organization. They understood it but I probably never will!

The Brits brought a company down when there was a big influx in Sarajevo. When the UN circled Sarajevo with a ring of steel, they took most of the heavy guns out. The Brits brought an infantry company down with Warriors and after a while, the Brits stayed there. We opened up a route called FINCH because the route we originally took was round about. When the Brits and the Canadians opened it up north of Sarajevo, there was an agreement that Sector Sarajevo had struck with the Serbs, and it was in the actual peace plan that we had to have free traffic between Visoko and Sarajevo. Then there was the civilian bus that was supposed to run in between Sarajevo and Visoko. It would take Muslims from Sarajevo to Visoko and bring people back to Sarajevo. A list of names was given to the Serbs twenty-four to forty-eight hours ahead so that the bus could move between the control points. The Brits would escort it up with the Warriors, and they would turn around and come back empty, then the Canadians would turn it around and escort it with Cougars. That's how I wound up doing a lot of work with the British, trying to organize the time tables, call-signs, frequencies and whether or nor we'd have a place to eat for the night when our Cougars came down. They'd have to stay in Sarajevo.

They were great fellows to work with, using a different system as well. The only person who was called "Sir" in their unit was the CO. Majors were called by their first names. It was hard to get used to that "Call me Bill" even if you were a captain. The British soldiers had a different mentality as well. They were very strict, and very proud of what they did. Smart saluting, focused people, no jerking around, and get the job done.

Then there were the Russians who were completely different. Most of the battalions, when you went into their camps through the gates, they'd welcome you, you'd get saluted, shown around on a tour of the camp, and see the vehicles. The first time we went to a Russian camp, it was on the Serb side, which was different. We were on the side of a hill that was very exposed to Muslim sniper fire. I remember I would not go through that area. You just did not. When I first went through there, I was amazed because they had cords running across the buildings in the streets that were exposed, with blankets hanging from them as sniper screens and there were sniper screens everywhere. The buildings were all shot up. When I first went there, I presented myself at the gate. They only had one gate and buildings and barbed wire surrounded everything. It was amazing what they had done. They were in the old police training school, which was given to them by the Serbs. I was told to wait outside the gate until I got an escort.

I could not get inside the camp! We were eventually ushered into the HQ building into a small room, about 5 feet by 9 feet, with a couch and a coffee table. An interpreter came in and sat with us, a Russian Serbo-Croat interpreter and I had to use my interpreter to translate from Serbo Croat to English! They talked Russian; she talked Serbo-Croat to my interpreter, who relayed it in English to me. I know they spoke English but they didn't speak it to me. You can figure that these are all Russian majors; to get that far in Russia they should have been bilingual. All business was conducted in that room and I never saw the operations centre, never saw the operations room, and never saw anything outside of that room.

There was an armed guard at the door that would snap to attention and salute us when we walked up. I remember being at a medals parade and they did a firepower demonstration and they did karate as well. It was a Russian Special Forces unit that was there and they were all blackbelts. They started beating themselves with pieces of wood, and breaking bottles over their heads. I remember one big fellow came out of the crowd, who was part of the show, took his shirt off and they start breaking two-by-fours over his back. He was just huge. People were saying, "They must have cut the boards half way through first." No they didn't, because one of the boards would break and they would smash it over his leg over and over. They hit him about five times with the board and it wouldn't break. They just gave up. He picked it up, smacked it over his head and broke it. They were airborne and that guy was crazy. Then he lay on broken glass and they broke bricks with sledgehammers on top of him. The idea was that the glass wasn't supposed to penetrate the back, a mind over matter kind of thing. They didn't quite get the hang of it and he was bleeding profusely. They took a big board and scraped the glass off his back and he was just laughing.

That display was designed to impress everybody. We got to look at their weapons, their night sights, and the new BTR-80 but I didn't get a chance to drive it. The only UN people that were there were the French general, the French senior officers, and myself. I got invited because we were doing business with the Russians; we did some operations with the Russians at the time. It was a really interesting experience. They said they liked Canadians and they thought we were very friendly.

Most of the friends I made were with UNMOs, two Brits and two New Zealanders. There was also a Canadian, Captain Don Haisell, from the RCR in Petawawa and he was the ops officer for Sector Sarajevo. He was controlling Kenyan lieutenant-colonels, and people like that. It gives you an idea of how highly Canadians are respected.

I also worked with the Joint Commission Observers, the JCOs. When I worked with them they were looking for weapons. I took them north to Breza in a French helicopter where we picked up a Muslim LO from the brigade we were going to go see, and flew over gun positions with those guys. They wanted us to drop them off in the Muslim area, 30 or 50 klicks from anywhere, and they said, "We'll yomp it back." Come on, now. They worked in teams of four, with an officer and three NCOs and each team had a SATCOM with them. I remember the JCOs; the one I worked with was "Brian" in Gornji Vakuf, for a while and the operations room was cordoned off with black curtains in a certain area. We'd get a lot of information, like when Gorazde was happening, we got a lot of information from the JCOs before it would come down through the chain of command, because they had men on the ground. They did recce all the time, and worked with our armoured squadrons. The JCOs worked directly for General Rose. We asked, "Who's your boss?" and they said "General Rose." They didn't wear rank insignia because they didn't want anyone to see them and they wore UN berets and had long hair. They were in Sarajevo for a while. I saw "Brian" in Sarajevo and I later saw him in Gornji Vakuf.

LIAISON OFFICER IN SARAJEVO: THE BOSNIAN SERBS

My job: The technical job description would be, I got clearances. Any traffic traversing the lines of confrontation had to have clearances on the Serb side and I would go everyday to their corps headquarters with a list of vehicles that would be traversing with the vehicle registration numbers, UN licence plates, and what would be in the vehicles in a detailed fashion. "We're transporting food. We're transporting this, that and the other thing." It was a big job when we had Srebrenica because we started in January to use a route south of Sarajevo, instead of the long way around through Tuzla, so I would guide them to Pale, across the mountains. Pale was the Bosnian Serb government HQ and their army HQ. They had a UNMO team there, led by a heck of a good Irish guy, Paddy. I remember getting stuck one night when we ended up having a split convoy escort. We had two Cougars coming back from Sarajevo, and I would pick them up in Pale, because to get to Pale from SIERRA 1 (Srebrenica), through Serb territory, there were a lot of turns and tricky things, and a lot of interior Serb checkpoints. We had problems with them at times, because we had the 76mm gun and they didn't want anything over .50 cal traversing through. When we brought M-113s through, they didn't want tracked vehicles traversing through so we brought an UNMO team to escort them through and they negotiated when our vehicles got stuck. It was now 1900 hours by the time we got them and we were told not to move. I talked with Paddy and there was a Brit working there with him, Roger, who was bilingual Serbo-Croat-English, and he came with us. We found a house and this old lady put us up for the night. We paid $10 each I think, they fed us breakfast and we stayed there.

At Srebrenica, the convoys needed clearances at army level, not corps and sometimes at government level and Paddy handled all that. He had a machine called a CAPSAT, which is basically a laptop computer terminal with a parabolic antenna. It sends a signal up to a satellite and it bounces down. "Paddy, this is the convoy, we're coming through." He would take that off his CAPSAT machine, print it up and fax it, because he had a fax line with the Serb HQ in Pale. They could communicate by phone, but clearances and official functions were all done by fax, so if the Serbs wanted to close things down, they would tell us only one fax machine was working and there would be no clearances but they wouldn't allow him to come up to their HQ. He tried a few times to hand transport clearances but it was mostly done by fax. If they didn't want convoys to get through, we'd hear, "Our fax machine doesn't work." I have no idea what their motives were. No clue.

I did have face-to-face dealings with the Serbs all the time in other areas. Major Indic, the Sarajevo Romanjia Corps senior liaison officer, was in charge of the liaison cell, political and military. An ex-JNA intelligence officer, a major in the ex-JNA, he was a very smart and shrewd man. He was the nemesis of many LOs in Sarajevo as he was a very mean, cynical man and a hard man to deal with, but if you were not talking about business, he was an easy man to get along with. I met him on average three or four times a week. I'd walk in, "Hey, how's it going?" and we were on a first-name basis. We would get into screaming matches a few times. He found it very hard at first, dealing with a Canadian second lieutenant, because he was dealing with generals, colonels, and majors, and this little Canadian second lieutenant showed up! He knew my rank and he didn't have to ask because he knew all about me but, after he realized that the only way of dealing with the Canadians was through me, things got better. I was insecure at first but, of course, anybody would be insecure even a captain, or a senior captain, political or military, would be walking into a Sarajevo Corps HQ to meet the senior LO, would be insecure and I think I had a beer that night. The learning curve was very sharp and it never stopped. I had to be on my toes with this guy or I would have been put on the persona-non-grata list for a while.

I wanted to go meet the brigade commander at Vogosca, because we were interested in opening a route up north though there and we wanted to put a patrol through. I went to talk to the brigade commander instead of dealing with Corps, because dealing with Corps was a long process, as nothing got done and Corps wouldn't let us do it. So I went to talk to the brigade commander, I made an appointment through a Canadian UNMO that I knew there, and he got me the appointment with the brigade commander without going through Corps. At that time they were trying to cut down on the brigade-level negotiations, and they wanted all of it done through Corps. So I went through the first checkpoint, after I left the city, and they asked, "Where are you going?" "I have a meeting at 1000 hours in Vogosca with the brigade commander." They said, "Well, he's not there." Well, that's funny, I just set it up this morning." "He's not there. The meeting's cancelled." "Well, okay, I've got to go to Visoko anyways, so you might as well let me through." I could get to Visoko on that road, through Ilijas. He said "Okay." There was one guy, I knew in passing, at the checkpoint. I didn't know him well, but he'd given me a drink once in a while, a fairly amiable old man, working with the police militia. On the way I drove past Vogosca and I stopped and saw the UNMO I knew, the Canadian. I said, "Listen, funny thing at the checkpoint. They just told me the brigade commander wasn't in." He thought that was odd. He picked up his phone and called the brigade commander. "He's in, and he's waiting for you." So I went to my meeting and we talked. It wasn't really a business meeting, it was an introductory meeting, I'm the Canadian LO, and stuff. I had a good meeting, and he wished me luck. I went up to Visoko and I had to write an Officer Professional Development Programme (Opie Dopie) exam the next day, so I was going to stay the night and study with the boys.

That night Mike, the Canadian UNMO in Vogosca, called me and he said, "Jeez, you're in shit." He drove all the way down to Sarajevo to get onto the satellite phone. "You're in big trouble. Don't drive back through Rajlovac to Sarajevo because they'll kill you." What do you mean? "You've been put on the Rajlovac Brigade persona-non-grata target list." It was too bad, because the guy I knew there, Radic, I met many times at social occasions and he even took me out for pizza once. "He's now put me on persona non grata? What's wrong?" "I don't know, I haven't figured it out yet, but go back the long way." Then I got a call from the LO in Sarajevo with the French. "You've been put on the persona-non-grata list for the corps as well and they don't want to see you!" "Well, I've got to get to Sarajevo." So I drove through the checkpoint in Sarajevo, called Indic, the LO at Corps, and he said, "Don't call here Jason, I don't want to see your face! Send your sergeant." What the hell is going on? "Let it boil over a couple of days." Anyway, a day later Mike came back. "You're in shit because you lied at the checkpoint." "What do you mean, I lied at the checkpoint?" He said, "You lied, therefore you are persona non grata." Come on, now! They figured I lied because I went to Vogosca anyway and they were pissed off because I had a meeting and they didn't approve it. They lied to me and told me the Vogosca brigade commander wasn't there. After a while I went to Indic and talked to him. I knew the interpreter in Vogosca fairly well and he got in touch with Radic; he's the guy who was pissed off at me (the guy who'd bought me the pizza) and Radic only had information from Indic, the Corps LO and he got false information. When Radic heard my story face-to-face, he apologized for what happened.

I failed my Opie Dopie.

On the whole, they loved working with the Canadians, and they were professional. They respected that. We knew what we were doing, even if it was an area that we were new in but we would do our best and we would be organized. It wouldn't be a jug-fuck and no swinging from one side to the other. They knew where we stood and we weren't arrogant, we weren't French and we weren't Brits.

VLASKO, A.K.A. "SKULL"[1]

I remember the first time I met him. It was my first day on the job. I was in Sarajevo at the time, when I got a call at the airport on the phone. There was an incident in Vogosca and Vogosca is in Serb territory on Route FINCH. They told me to take care of it but we didn't have the interpreter. I drove out there in my Iltis, and they'd had a Serb APC parked there that had shot at the front Cougar and hit it. I came screaming up and I told the driver to slow down. The Serbs were pointed the other way and we didn't want to scare them. The convoy was coming in from Visoko. Sure enough, as we came around, the gun traversed over the back deck and started shooting at us. We were going to stop right here! I put my foot outside the door and all the guns came up and pointed at us. I was not moving till the UNMOs came and got me. We talked and worked it all out. The Serbs started inspecting the convoy and there was no problem, and we let them have at it.

All of a sudden this black jeep thing rolled screaming up and it had a human skull with a black toque on it and a Chetnik symbol painted on the front and then this guy got out. I guess he had just been shot in the leg, because he had this piece of wood tied to his leg as a splint and he was limping around. He had a gun on each hip, one at his ankle, and one under each arm. He was carrying a rifle, had a knife strapped to his thigh, and he had twigs in his beard and stuff. He didn't speak, he kind of grunted. I went and presented myself. "Don't touch him Jason!" the UNMO yelled out. "Don't touch him!" "Why?" "He'll kill you." "Aw, come on!" I went up and tried to shake his hand and he just looked, grunted at me and started poking around the convoy. What the hell? He climbed up on back of one of the deuces, so I grabbed his arm and pulled him down. Then the UNMO said, "Oh, oh!" He looked at me and I swear he was going to go for his gun or something like that but there was a little twinkle in his eyes. And all of a sudden a panel van went driving over the overpass, the door slid open, and a TV camera from Serb TV poked out and they started filming Vlasko. He looked up at this, and his arm was twitching, right? He said, "Ahhhhhrrr!" rounded up all of his boys, got back in his jeep, and they buggered off at the high port. They turned a siren on and chased the van. That was the last I saw of him. I saw a picture of him in *Time*, Vlasko the Chetnik.

Vlasko was the guy who chased the Dutch UNMO through the city of Vogosca. I was in the UNMO operations office at the time talking with the Canadian contingent, when all of a sudden

---

1. A UN intelligence report described Vlasko thus: "Vlasko The Chetnik is reportedly the leader of a paramilitary platoon of irregulars who wear black uniforms with skull and crossbones on the back and drive black cars with similar markings. On 7 Nov 93, Vlasko and his unit were aiding HVO defenders in Dastansko Village and allegedly forced Muslim villagers to prepare defences or they would blow up the local mosque. On that day a NORBAT II soldier, forced to fire a warning shot, hit a steel bar and a splinter slightly injured Vlasko on the lip. After temporarily taking three NORBAT troops as hostages, he demanded a signed statement saying he had been wounded by UNPROFOR. The local UNPROFOR commanders gave him a note in English saying 'This man is an asshole and should be shot on sight.' Vlasko dutifully accepted the note and released the hostages."

we heard this call over the Motorola: "Huh! Huh! Huh! Come and get me! I'm being chased on foot!" We were never on foot, always in a vehicle. Vlasko chased him out of his vehicle and was chasing him through the streets at gunpoint! Anyway, he lost him and went back to the house. The major tried to sort things out. Then there was another call on the Motorola. " Vlasko's sitting right beside me now and he's apologizing. What do I do?" "Well, accept his apology and get a drink!" He was a terrorist and apparently he rolled barrels of dynamite down the hills at Sarajevo.[1]

LIFE IN SARAJEVO

I remember New Year's. I had dinner and we started partying in the Men's Mess at the PTT building in Sarajevo and everyone was having a good time when two tank rounds came in. The Serbs shot them. BOOM! BOOM! The music went off and everything stopped. The lights were kind of dim, until the generators kicked back in. The French colonel in control of the building came in, "Okay, party is over. Get mobile." But we kept on partying. Orthodox New Year's was also fun too but they were behind a bit on the old calendar. What they did was take all the tracer rounds out of the links, linked them all together, so they had a belt of tracer, put it in the machine guns and fired into the sky. There were tracer rounds everywhere that night! Artillery illumination rounds were going off, and it was an unbelievable sight as everybody joined in and the next morning they were all hung over. Another memorable thing was the children in the Kosovo Hospital, and once a week I'd go there with candies that my mom sent over from a bulk candy store in Canada. I'd go out and give them candy on Saturdays. I just love kids and I feel it's a terrible thing that they're getting hurt over there. I remember the Christmas I went over, I knew an American, Matt, who is now teaching in Colorado Springs at the military college there, who was the intelligence officer in Italy over in Ancona and he would come to Sarajevo to pick up information. We'd end up meeting and we became fairly good friends. I gave Matt $150 and he went and bought toys, dinky cars, and stuffed animals and brought this stuff to me, which I gave away at the hospital. You should have seen the looks on their faces!

THE MARKET MASSACRE

That was the same day that the market massacre took place. Kosovo Hospital was two blocks away from the marketplace. We heard the explosion, then we heard screaming, and people were coming to the hospital with their arms mangled. I knew roughly where the explosion was, so we took the jeep down. There were two Brits with us and they stayed there at the hospital and Matt came with me in the jeep. Matt and I grabbed all the field dressings that we had with us in the jeep, grabbed all the disinfectant that we could, and ran into the market, and there were people screaming and walking around. It wasn't a pretty experience. We started giving first aid to people but the crowd was incredibly hostile towards us. Very hostile! Matt and I were the first people on the spot and a French engineering captain came in right afterwards. I remember getting hit in the back of the head with a fist or a stick and I was knocked down onto the ground while I was trying to transport wounded people to a car and then to a hospital! They were hostile towards us because the UN was supposed to be protecting Sarajevo. Matt doesn't remember a thing about that incident as he blocked it all out. I remember he put a field dressing on a man whose shoulder was blown off but he doesn't remember doing that. Not a thing.

I came back from the market, washed the blood off my uniform, and I had to give my statement to the operations officer in Sector Sarajevo about what happened. Apparently they'd already seen my jeep on CNN. I remember the journalists. They came running down the street and one of the guys I knew, Jim, was over there on the left-hand side being trailed by about twenty journalists. "Where did it go off Jason?" "It went off over there." I pointed in another direction and they all scampered off in that direction. I was laughing. There were a million journalists running around when we were trying to pick up dead people! "Go get them, boys!" Five minutes later they come back and said, "Asshole!"

The media are everywhere in Sarajevo. There was everyone from Christiane Amanpour, who has a posh-posh type of style, to people like Jim, who was living off rice for months and he lost 30 pounds when he was there. They didn't have any money. He was a photojournalist but he wasn't selling any pictures.

The coverage was glorified and theatrical in some aspects. For example, someone wrote an article about me in my hometown newspaper and the caption was, "Hope for Sarajevo children is a home-town boy from B.C." or "Young man shot at 15 times bringing food to hungry Muslims" or something. I mean, come on, right? They're not lying, but they make it look good so people will read it.

I got whisked up to Visoko to do a stress debriefing. I didn't want to do that but it is a useful procedure, in general. It is very useful. I have a Bachelor degree in psychology, and at the time I didn't feel I needed it but everyone says that, right?

LIFE IN SARAJEVO

It was very moving once you got there. I remember taking my interpreter out, Iliyana, who was from Sarajevo and she took me to the old Law Building, the Museum, and the old Town Hall, which became the Sarajevo City Library. Very cosmopolitan in its design, it incorporated things from all three ethnic groups. The huge stained glass roof was completely knocked out and there was a two or three-foot corner still left. That building was the town hall when Archduke Ferdinand was in power. Just down the street was Footstep Bridge where he was killed. It was kind of moving to sit there, look at it all, and see where he came afterwards, after the first attempt. Other interesting places where the restaurants. That was fun. What we would consider a diner, they would consider a four-star restaurant, and we would be eating rice with some hamburger, and maybe some frozen vegetables with some gravy but the service was impeccable! Absolutely impeccable! There was another restaurant in a basement, stone walls, red floor, and candlelight and the proprietor would play the violin. The meal was very meagre, as all the food was smuggled in basically. That's what restaurants were like there. There was one place that made an amazing puffed pizza, a dome pizza. UNHCR finances or partially finances a beer factory, a brewery, because they had a pure water source a couple of hundred feet below the surface. So they partially financed them to pump water up and the beer was made with anything they could get their hands on. Sometimes it was wheat, sometimes it was rice or barley and the colour was different in every bottle. It was called Pivot. It was good beer and it was pasteurized so if you went to a restaurant, you drank beer.

There were little kiosks in town that were mirror images of the French PX. You could buy everything that was in the French PX even UN badges and stuff like that. People were walking around with Sector Sarajevo sweat suits! When I first saw that one, I thought "Holy Christ!" I saw a whole family of four people decked out in them, and they had the UN crest with Sector Sarajevo on it in dark blue. It was bizarre, symbolically. There was so much to talk about in Sarajevo and it was such an interesting place. I went to see the movie Basic Instinct that was subtitled in Serbo-Croat. The theatre was on the priority grid for electricity in Sector Sarajevo. It made sense for morale purposes and it only cost $3, which was all right. It was just down the street from BH Command and I went with Richard, another Canadian, and the guy who took over from Brad Smith. He came in as the G2 for the headquarters.

My replacement came on a Hercules flight. Instead of sending the Senior LO, they sent the Sarajevo LO and it didn't make any sense. I was scheduled to go back on the last flight but I had two weeks to wait. I didn't want to go to Visoko to sit around, as that was too boring. I asked to go to Gornji Vakuf, as I knew the LO up there and he didn't like it there so I said I'd go! I knew a lot of people there. When the Brits moved in they took a lot of their Sarajevo people and put them there so I went up there and it was amazing with lots of Brits and Spanish. Sector South-West was CANBAT 2, two BRITBATS, SPABAT and MALBAT. They had Malaysian officers there, too. Basically as an LO, I was a duty officer, and I visited Split, and did a bit of liaison work, what we traditionally know as an LO in doctrinal terms. That's what I did. Like in a brigade HQ. I was there when Gorazde happened. They sent a British company down there in Saxon APCs, the big square ugly things and we had to keep track of their progress. That was the most exciting thing that happened when I was there. There was a white Mercedes, with a machine gun running around robbing people and we'd get about two reports a day from people who were mugged. The thugs in the white Mercedes had cut a hole in the roof and mounted a machine gun! I saw it one day, and it was pretty funny.

PERSONAL ASSESSMENT

I would say it was the most significant event in my life in general and my career, to date. Easily. I have grown up a heck of a lot. I was over there as a 21-year-old second lieutenant and I saw a lot of things. My work wasn't integral to our battle group, and I was a nice-to-have LO; I wasn't a need-to-have LO. I don't want to give the impression that what I did in Sarajevo was very important to the Canadians in Visoko. It wasn't. It helped a lot, particularly with the clearances. My situation was completely different from what they were doing and I was very lucky. They must have had a lot of trust in me to send me down there by myself.

It was nice coming home and I went fishing. I basically came in, got my mess kit, and picked it up so I could go to the Graduation Ball at Royal Roads Military College two days later! I flew into Vancouver, spent the night there, and went to Victoria to the ball. It was fun. It was interesting, driving at normal speeds, and obeying laws again. In Sarajevo we drove at 120 kilometres an hour so we wouldn't get shot. As soon as I finished the ball I went fishing.

EPILOGUE

In the summer of 2001, I traveled once again to the Balkans on a research trip in preparation for a history of our operations in KFOR. I took some time to revisit those places in Bosnia and Croatia where the events of this book took place. I kept a diary of my impressions:

• I'm up at Primosten at what used to be CANLOGBAT. It has reverted back to a holiday campground, which is kind of eerie. You can still see some of the foundations and things that we put in here specifically for our work. But other than that all the bunkers are gone, all the Hescobastion is gone, all the sea containers are gone, the trees are flourishing and it's relatively peaceful. The road net between Split and here has been repaved and reconstructed. Tourism is definitely flourishing six years after the war. And there hasn't been a single sign of the Croatian military, and very little police presence during my entire trip up the coast. It's hard to believe that six years ago, this entire coastline was under threat and that ARSK Serb forces could have broken through at any point in time along the coast and cut this main coastal highway off. It's so tranquil now. Before I remember BM21 multiple rocket launchers and mobile reserves moving backwards and forwards. Now there's construction equipment and tourists, it's very strange. I'm reminded of Ken Bell's book *Not In Vain* where he did before and after pictures of the Canadian campaign in Europe in 1944. It's very similar in texture to that.

• I've passed Zadar and I'm approaching Benkovac, which is in the old Sector South area. I still see a lot of destroyed buildings, but again this is now way off the beaten path, it's no longer the front line between two groups of people fighting it out with the UN sandwiched in a two-klick wide buffer zone. I can clearly see the Velebit Mountains. Still leery about a mine threat in here even though I've seen no signs. I know there are a lot of mines in here, and I don't think they've cleared them all. I don't think the maps were that good. But it's really quiet, a lot of farming implements around here. You can bet that there are zero Serbs, that they're all gone.

• I'm in the greater Zemunik area and there are houses here that I clearly remember being occupied; they are all gutted, roofs down. There's not even a dog in sight now. This is a village of approximately fifty houses strung out along a lane and it's basically all destroyed. It must have been taken out by the Croats during Operation STORM in 1995 because this was a front line area. Oh, there's somebody actually working the field there, growing grapes. For the most part the houses in here are destroyed though there's a couple that have been reconstructed. Maybe two out of fifty. Some Croatian graffiti which translates to "we came, we saw, we kicked their ass, thank you." A lot of that around here. This is a bit different. This place I do remember as a thriving community. And it's dead, it's totally dead. I am headed down what used to be one of the patrol routes to see if we can find where the old platoon houses were. Again I am approaching one of the other villages here. I wish I had a 1:50 000 [map], I could remember exactly what it was called. It has the Velebit mountains in the background. It's totally dead too. There doesn't appear to be any reconstruction going on. The road's nearly overgrown. Now I definitely feel like I'm in the middle of one of Sergio Leone's westerns. Again all the buildings have everything taken out of them, they've been stripped. The roofs are all off. Again, more graffiti.

- This is very different from what I remember in a couple of ways. When I was here there was the Zone of Confrontation, which had a lot of destroyed houses in it and there were mines, booby traps and everything. But it was between the belligerents and there were communities on either side of the line that were thriving. This is one of the ones that had been thriving and it's been turned into a ghost town like the rest of them.

- I'm not sure if I'm going to proceed further down this route. It's a decayed road and I'm literally surrounded with destroyed buildings. I'm very concerned now about a mine threat. It's just incredible, there are destroyed buildings everywhere, as far as I can see in every direction. Again, this is very different from the last time I was here. This was, I recall, a thriving community with a lot of people in it. I also recall going through here sitting in the back of an M113 APC, with men from 1 RCR and I recall stopping and handing out candy to kids along here. This is a Serb area, or was a Serb area. God knows where those kids are now.

- I met a charming Croatian couple here. They were in their sixties, they are literally the only people living around here and I explained to them that I had been here in 1995 visiting with the Canadian troops and they knew exactly what I was talking about. I think this had been their home prior to the war when it was a mixed community, and they had been run out of it at the start of the conflict. When Croatian forces retook it in 1995 they basically reclaimed their house, but there are only one or two or maybe three other families within about a thousand meters of here that have done so. They explained that some of the routes and most of the area has been cleared of mines, but most of the mines are down by the old confrontation line. Mostly UXO around here and they showed me some UXO lying around. It gets piled up just like in France, disposed of maybe.

- I think what's bothering me right now, and this is going to be a bit callous, but it isn't necessarily the loss of human life in this area during Operation STORM, that's sort of a given. This area was overrun despite the fact that we had United Nations Protection Forces here. These forces were ultimately not capable, definitely not capable, of deterring the Croatian Forces with their overwhelming armour and mechanized capability. It's very clear our people were overrun in here. I saw a dismantled UN bunker. Although this isn't on the scale of Srebrenica and it probably was more of a military operation than an ethnic cleansing operation it still fits within the same band, within the same category.

- I'm headed on the main drag outside of Zemunik on the hard pack, headed towards Obrovac and there's still evidence of massive fighting in here. Mortar splash on the road that's barely patched. The Croatians have laid the foundation for what looks to be a four- lane highway through part of this. That should cover up the crime pretty well.

- Frankly I don't know how anybody can continue to live in here, in ones and twos. The couple I was talking with said, jokingly, that at least it was quiet now. I think there'd be a lot of ghosts. A lot of ghosts in here.

- I just found the OP that I stayed at the first night I was in Croatia. I was sick as a dog, had the flu or something. But basically it was a building that was converted into a bunker-like complex. It's all been stripped, although I found the remains of Hescobastion sort of at the base of it. Kind of an eerie feeling. Back then all the buildings around it were destroyed anyway. So, not much is changed there.

- A bit of a funny thing happening. I'm driving through this area, my mind is flipping back and forth to the time when I was here last. In a way, I can remember some of the buildings, when they were whole, and now that they're not, it's just sort of like, it's like this weird before/after movie. Objects too. Like, I remember this wreckage of a Peugeot sitting on top of a stone fence, for some reason—and I just drove past it. That hasn't changed.

• Row after row after row of ghost villages, it's almost unbelievable. It's not one or two, it's entire areas. Completely depopulated. Even now, even six years since the peacekeeping forces were removed by Operation STORM.

• It is strange to note that the operations in this area were incredibly vital for all sides, vital enough to spend lives over, for people to die over, and now it's a rural backwater, a long way from the shores and tourist industry of the Adriatic. If one pulls back the veil far enough, the veil of the Adriatic tourist complexes, you'll see this hideous corpse behind it.

• It's hard to come away from this without feeling that everything we worked for here was just thrown away because of some decision in New York. I remember watching the sort of proto-CIMIC activities that were being conducted by the Canadian Battalions as they rotated through here. Now that's all just trashed. Very difficult not to come away with a sense of failure. But who's failure is that? Who owns that failure, those failures? I refuse to believe it should be owned by the men of the battalions that were serving here. They did their damndest to keep the peace here and prevent a larger war. Nobody can take that away from them.

• And the Croatians, what did they achieve? They've acquired a vast rural area that has nobody in it. There's virtually no farming going on up here. Some people have returned to their pre-war homes but they seem to be in the minority. They got rid of a population they didn't want and prevented themselves from being destroyed by it. I look back at this and I don't think there is any hope in hell of ARSK Serbs and the Croatians living side- by-side in some multi ethnic society here. I just don't think it would have worked, too much bad blood.

• I am now headed up towards where the camp used to be and I'm approaching the point where the Serbs drew down on us, when they pulled the AKs out of the trunk and we ran through it in this mini-bus. We all had our body armour on and I had some adrenaline pumping that day, that's for sure.

• I'm just past Gracac and I'm up in the area just before the Medak pocket and I'm passing village after village that are empty shells. Burnt and with no roofs, the whole bit. There's mountains on either side. It's fairly wooded. Not quite what I expected, but then it never is. My primary concern of course is keeping a low profile in here. People around here know exactly what happened. And I understand that there have been problems with Canadian camera crews coming up into here and being unable to film. Hopefully the profile is low enough and that my car has Zagreb plates that nobody is going to give me the gears, but again, I'll keep the photography somewhat discreet. I have no clue what kind of security they retain up here. But this is basically a very Alberta-like valley, it reminds me of the foothills, sort of up near Cochrane. It's sort of a narrow valley, it can't be more than, oh, at the most ten clicks in width. I'll have to double-check that on a map, but again, lots of trees, one two-lane road. But again, building after building, stuck off in the trees, destroyed.

• There is some traffic however and there's the odd individual living around here, so far. Other than that there's a farm with those very noticeable cone-shaped haystacks or right next to it, a bunch of burned out buildings. Here is a whole series of other ones with no roofs.

• There is a brand new Catholic church with nobody around it and a destroyed Orthodox Serb church just down the road from it.

- The irony behind this is obvious in the sense that I've gone from one of the UN's worst defeats to one of our greater successes but since it was kept quiet because we actually killed people, almost nobody knows anything about it.
- Special Police unit just passed. Very interesting.
- Now the valley is widening out a bit. It's a bit more than ten clicks at this point, though there's still foothills to the left.
- It's pretty eerie seeing these town or village signs, like in Europe, where they have it at the start of this town and at the end you have the same name crossed out with a big red slash to tell you you are leaving. I've just been through one of these places and it has absolutely nobody living in it. So the red slash really highlights that point.
- After you get to Medak proper, the valley gets more populated. I passed a Croatian Army monument. Some armoured vehicle, obviously improvised, a memorial to a series of personnel who probably died in that region, or this region.
- I'm in a village where the buildings look a bit too new but there are some bullet marks there. This is to the right side of the road from Bilaj. Almost all the buildings here have been reconstructed, there are no more damaged buildings. Unlike the rest of the areas that I've driven through, although I've just stumbled across a Catholic churchyard and graveyard. That building is brand new. It's extremely difficult to tell where the massacres took place.
- My pre-Operation STORM map has names of towns which aren't even marked on the road anymore. And there's apparently no means to get at them in terms of side roads or laterals. I've come across a hamlet and it's exactly the same thing. Every building here is brand new in terms of new covering on it. There's no war damage around here whatsoever.
- It's a bit spooky knowing full well that somewhere around here there are five hundred to a thousand bodies buried, unmarked, totally forgotten. Probably the entire families, given the rural nature and the demographics here. It's almost obscene to see a marked graveyard.
- I think somebody's done the Orwell here, I'm having extreme difficulty finding the original Bilaj.
- I found an old road which is very, very overgrown that corresponds to the map that I have, which looks like it goes to Liki Citluk. Looks like nobody's been on this for a very long time however. And it does head over towards the base of the Velebit mountains. So I'm hopeful this might be the one I'm looking for.
- It's pretty spooky back here. Just saw Ustashi symbols spray painted everywhere There's at least seven or eight houses that have been taken out. I don't know if this is Citluk or not but it's something. I can't see Dave McKillop bringing his APCs in here, but on reflection it probably didn't look like this seven years ago either. It's like going down an overgrown green tunnel. Destroyed buildings, stuck in amongst the tall grass and the trees. It's as if the Romans had fought a battle here thousands of years ago.
- It appears my journey is at an end and there's a gate here that blocks off Citluk that's locked. As far as I can tell. There's several burnt out houses here, but I'm not sure how far in this goes. I'm going to take a look.
- I just met a local who seems to be squatting up here on some land by himself, an old gent, who, in our usual forms of communication tells me that Citluk no longer exists. It's totally gone. I had no reason to doubt him. Particularly in this environment.
- I just drove over a trip wire, which is down fortunately. I can't tell what it's hooked up to, or was hooked up to and I'm not about to start poking around the underside of the bush to figure

out exactly what it is. Another fucking close call in this place, not my first.

• I've reached the outskirts of what is now called Gospic, which consists of at least fifty buildings, fifty houses. The Croatian Cops are actually running some kind of trap, traffic stop trap thing here. And I asked him, "Wo ist Citluk?" Without prompting he said "Kaput!" I said "Ah, Operation Donner und Blitzen" sort of thing, and he's like, "Ja!" So it's not even on the map anymore.

• Back to civilization of a sort. Gospic itself has been revitalized. There's a lot of people living there but the northern outskirts and towards Medak is all one big ghost town, and that's not surprising. Especially the young people. I was speaking with a girl here who says nobody goes near the place, they don't want to. They told me it's haunted and that they're not supposed to go out there.

• There's no doubt that Medak remains a place trapped in time. I mean, just the feeling of being on a main highway with people on it, going towards a destination where there are other people, is an incredible contrast. It's very difficult to record feelings, gut feelings or intuition or whatever it is about a particular place, but Medak is for the dead.

• Bosnia is different, particularly in the former Canadian AORs.

• It is very interesting wandering around Ilijas which is now probably ninety to one hundred percent Muslim. The high school has been completely rebuilt. The OP that we occupied is no longer up on top. The facility that I was held in by the MUP has now been converted to a kindergarten. I was able to speak with the two of the people that run the school. It was explained to me that basically the Bosnian Armija had swept through Ilijas in the last days of the conflict and the Serb population had basically fled. It was rather weird. The most jarring thing about it was of course that the former interrogation centre/holding facility now had all sorts of cartoon characters in the windows and other things

• The thing that struck me about the trip from Visoko to Ilijas was how quick it was and the amount of activity and traffic on the road. I recall that road being totally dead. There was not a thing moving on it except for us. There were no people around in any of the hamlets alongside the road. It was a very, very strange experience and then of course the Minarets in the communities along the highway and in Ilijas itself were quite striking. Still a lot of war damage or ethnic cleansing damage evident. Whereas it took forever to get there from Visoko to Ilijas in 1995, we just zipped along this, basically an autobahn- like road and we were there in minutes. It's almost as if none of this happened or if it did happen it happened fifty years ago.

• We drove on up to the road to the former Papa and Mike checkpoints on the bridge, which of course are cleared. There's lots of traffic moving back and forth but all the buildings around the bridge, including some that I had visited on the previous trip are all thoroughly destroyed. The fighting that had gone on in the area had totally pulverized the small community near Papa and Mike. From there we headed up to Visoko proper and went to the camp. Camp Visoko is now occupied by the Greeks and the Portuguese SFOR forces. One of the notable things is that the Hescobastion and the concertina barbed wire that ringed the camp, which was new when I got there in 1995 is still there and still holding up. The barbed wire is all rusty of course. The layout of the camp is fairly similar although the functions of all the buildings are different. It wasn't hard to figure out exactly where everything had been. The old Crystal Palace building, the headquarters building, is the backwater of the base and the maintenance section which was in the basement floor of the Big Four building is now the main operation centre for the Portuguese.

- We moved on to Route Dove between Visoko and Kiseljak but I couldn't find the position where CANBAT 2 had the bunker with the Cougar parked next to it to deter Serb snipers. It's totally gone. Kiseljak of course is still a thriving community economically, with a brand new huge Catholic Church built up on the hill. We pressed on and headed north. We got directions to go up through the Drin and Bakovici Psychiatric Hospitals up near Fojnica and it really wasn't difficult. I was able to navigate there by memory alone. We got to Drin and went inside and had a conversation with the Director which I believe is the same man that was there in 1995 when I visited. He was obviously a very tired, though not a broken man, but very tired of having to maintain this institution. He informed me that the situation was reverting back to pre-UN days and that they were having severe problems of all types. I was taken up to one of the wards I had visited six years ago. I was looking specifically for some murals that our people had put up there which have now been painted over. The only English speaking person in the building I discovered was a Scottish psychiatric nurse from Edinburgh and she came out of the room and said, "Oh my God another English speaker." It was rather funny. And so we had a very animated conversation. Tragically it turned out she had been nursing a psychiatric patient in Edinburgh who had been one of the medical team, British Army Medical Team that had encountered the hospital prior to the arrival of CANBAT 2 and this individual had, in part, become a psychiatric case because of what he saw in Drin and she decided that she was going to come to this place and plans to work here for the next three years. I asked her, were there any remnants of Canada's contribution to the hospital? So we went downstairs and here's pictures of Captain Chris Lemay and Sergeant Stoneham from my March 1995 visit. It was quite astounding. They are all framed and put up on the wall. And next to it is a certificate presented to the hospital from CANBAT 2 saying that Canada would never forget Drin.
- It was getting late in the day, we wanted to press on to Bakovici. We saw that infamous graffiti that one of the journalists had taken a picture of back in 1995 that said "Welcome to Hell." Well it was still there which was rather intriguing. We retraced our steps down to the MSR throughout the Kiseljak pocket. Back down at Kiseljak my intent was to head up the former Route "Pacman," which I came in on in 1995. In 1995 the UN had improved an old logging road which essentially by-passed the Serb controlled areas around Sarajevo and this functioned as the main service route for humanitarian relief in Northern Bosnia and it took hours to move along it I recall. We, luckily, had a 4-wheel drive vehicle. The astounding part about it is, that such a critical artery has been totally neglected. There's very little maintenance on it and it's basically a washed out logging road. I could not even find the position of "Checkpoint Charlie," where the Dragoons had a significant control point set up. It's almost as if it didn't exist, there was not even a single sand bag there. It was totally deserted there. We worked our way down to Tarcin and back to Sarajevo.
- Does time heal all wounds? I hope it does.

- Sean M. Maloney
Bosnia and Croatia,
May - June 2001

GLOSSARY

2 IC	Second In Command
4 CER	4 Combat Engineer Regiment
4 CMBG	4 Canadian Mechanized Brigade Group
12 RBC	12e Régiment blindé du Canada
.50 cal	A Browning .50 caliber heavy machine gun
AAG	Arrival Assistance Group, part of the unit that prepares the unit to return from overseas
ACAV kit	Armoured Cavalry kit for the M-113 APC consisting of extra protection added to the vehicle
AK, AK-47, AKM	Kalashnikov assault rifle
AOR	Area of Responsibility
APC	Armoured Personnel Carrier
ARSK	Army of the Republic of Serb Krajinas
Badger	a tracked combat engineer vehicle used by the Canadian Army. It is based on a Leopard tank chassis
BAT	battalion. Generic term used to identify UNPROFOR units. For example, a Canadian battalion would be CANBAT, Nepalese battalion would be NEPBAT, a British medical unit would be Brit MEDBAT
BiH	Bosnia Hercegovina
Bison	an eight-wheeled armoured personnel carrier used by the Canadian Army
BMP	a Russian-designed mechanized infantry combat vehicle
bouncing betty	an anti-personnel mine that jumps out of the ground and explodes at groin level
BSA	Bosnian Serb Army
buddy-fuck	to deliberately backstab
C-6	Canadian 7.62 mm medium machine gun
C-7	Canadian 5.56 mm assault rifle
C-8	Canadian 5.56 mm carbine
C-9	Canadian 5.56 mm light machine gun
callsign	a numerical radio designator for a vehicle and its crew, eg, 32A is the second vehicle in the second platoon of C company from a battalion
Cannister	a main gun round used by the Cougar. It is essentially a large shotgun-like round for use against troops
CAPSAT	a type of satellite communications system
Caritas	a Catholic relief organization
carrier	an armoured personnel carrier, APC
casevac	casualty evacuation
CCUNPROFOR	Canadian Contingent, United Nations Protection Force
CDS	Canadian Chief of the Defence Staff
Chetnick	used as a derogatory term for the Serbs by their various antagonists, but also used to describe Bosnian Serb terror groups and sometimes their special operations forces
CO	Commanding Officer
Cougar	A turreted, six-wheeled armoured car used by the Canadian Army
CSM	Company Sergeant Major
CS Gas	non-lethal riot control agent
CSCE	Conference on Security and Cooperation in Europe
CUCV	5/4-ton truck
DAG	Departure Assistance Group, part of the unit that prepares the unit to deploy overseas. (Arrival Assistance Group is the opposite)
Deuce	two and a half ton truck, MLVW

ECMM	European Community Monitoring Mission
FIBUA	Fighting in Built Up Areas, city fighting
flinch, flinch factor	the degree of a panic response to an event. "The flinch factor was high at the start of this operation"
FST	Field Surgical Team
"G" positions	staff positions in headquarters: G-1 is personnel, G-2 is military information, G-3 is operations, G-4 is logistics, and G-5 is civil-military relations
GD	General Duties, garbage cleanup and the like
grip	the degree of personal control over a situation or oneself; can also be a verb, "These guys were gripped"
Grizzly	a six-wheeled armoured personnel carrier used by the Canadian Army
Harrier	a British vertical take off combat aircraft, usually operating from one of the British aircraft carriers in the Adriatic
headshed	headquarters, HQ
HQ	headquarters
helo	helicopter
HESH	High Explosive Squash Head. A main gun round used by the Cougar, HESH can be used against buildings, trenches and vehicles
HLVW	Heavy Logistics Vehicle Wheeled, an eight-ton truck, called an "HL"
ICRC	International Commission of the Red Cross. The Red Crescent is the Muslim equivalent
Iltis	a Canadian jeep-like vehicle
IMP	Individual Meal Packet, Canadian Army rations
ISCC	Infantry Section Commander's Course
IV	intravenous solution
JAG	Judge Advocate General, military lawyers
JCO	Joint Commission Observers, cover for British special operations forces in the Balkans
JNA	The former Yugoslav National Army
Land of Boz	Bosnia-Hercegovina
LdSH (RC)	Lord Strathcona's Horse (Royal Canadians)
Leopard	a main battle tank used by many NATO countries. The Danes had a squadron with UNPROFOR in Bosnia
LO	Liaison Officer
Log Wog	Canadian soldier's term of endearment for logistics personnel
M-113	a tracked Armoured Personnel Carrier used by the Canadian Army. This vehicle has many variants, including a fitters' version for repair, an engineer version for engineering tasks, as well as the standard APC version
M-577	the armoured command post version of an M-113
Mag	Magazine
medevac	medical evacuation
ML	an MLVW
MLVW	Medium Logistics Wheeled Vehicle, or "ML. A 2.5-ton truck
MRE	Meal, Ready to Eat, American army rations
MRL	multiple rocket launcher
MSF	Médicins sans frontiers, an NGO
MSR	Main Supply Route, Main Service Route, a road that is critical to movement
NATO	North Atlantic Treaty Organization
NCO	non-commissioned officer, Sergeants and Warrant Officers
niner	numerical radio callsign for the unit commander, the CO
NGOs	Non-Government organizations, eg., the International Commission of the Red Cross, Médicins sans frontiers
NODLR, NOGS, NVGs	night vision equipment

OC	Officer Commanding
O Group	Orders Group, when the commander gives his orders to his principle leaders
OJT	on the job training
OP	observation post, protected position of observation
opie dopie	Officers' Professional Development Program. A series of exams given to Canadian Army officers so that they can be promoted
op, ops	operation, operations
Ops O	Operations Officer
OT-64	an eight-wheeled Czech APC used by some UNPROFOR units
PAFFO	Public Affairs Officer
PPCLI	Princess Patricia's Canadian Light Infantry
PT	Physical Training
PUAFO	pack up and fuck off, pronounced "pwafo," to move out quickly, bug out
RCMP	Royal Canadian Mounted Police
RCD	Royal Canadian Dragoons
RCR	Royal Canadian Regiment
recce	reconnaissance
ROE	Rules of Engagement, when to shoot, when not to shoot
RPG	Rocket Propelled Grenade, a shoulder-launched unguided anti-tank weapon
RSM	Regimental Sergeant Major
RRB	Radio Re-Broadcast site, a position on the high ground to relay communications
RV	rendezvous
Sammy the Serb	a British term referring to the Bosnian Serbs
SAS	Special Air Service, British special forces
SATCOM	satellite communications system
sitrep	situation report
slag, slagged	to deride. "They really slagged him because he fucked up"
SSM	Squadron Sergeant Major
T-34/85, T-55, M-64	tanks used by the belligerents
TI	thermal imagery. A method of target acquisition which focuses on the heat given off by the target. The TOW Under Armour vehicle and the NODLER use this method
TOW	Tube-launched Optically-tracked, Wire-guided, anti-tank missile
trace	delineated area of responsibility or route sketched out on a map using chinagraph marker
TUA	TOW Under Armour. TOW missile launcher mounted on a M-113 APC
tubes	mortars. "The Tubes" refers to the mortar platoon within a Battle Group
Turks	Serbian derogatory term for the Bosnian Muslims
UMS	Unit Medical Section
UNCIVPOL	United Nations Civilian Police
UNHCR	United Nations High Commissioner on Refugees, the UN relief organization in Bosnia
UNMO	United Nations Military Observer
UNPAs	United Nations Protected Areas
UNPROFOR	United Nations Protection Force
Ustashi, Ustasha	derogatory term for Croatians dating back to the Second World War when Croatian nationalists fought alongside the Nazi SS
VAB	a wheeled French APC
Van Doos	The Royal 22nd Regiment
water buffalo	a water trailer
WEU	Western European Union
WO	Warrant Officer